DAMES

Dansk Center for Migration
og Etniske Studier

**EUROPEAN RESEARCH CENTRE
ON MIGRATION & ETHNIC RELATIONS**

MEASURING IMMIGRANT INTEGRATION

List of Figures

Contents

Published by
Ashgate Publishing Limited
Gower House
Croft Road
Aldershot
Hampshire GU11 3HR
England

Ashgate Publishing Company
131 Main Street
Burlington, VT 05401-5600 USA

Ashgate website: http://www.ashgate.com

British Library Cataloguing in Publication Data
Reinsch, Peter
      Measuring immigrant integration : diversity in a European
      city. - (Research in migration and ethnic relations series)
      1. Immigrants - Netherlands - Social conditions 2. Social
      integration - Netherlands
      I. Title
      305.8'009492

Library of Congress Control Number: 2001091689

ISBN 0 7546 1815 3

Printed and bound by Athenaeum Press, Ltd.,
Gateshead, Tyne & Wear.

Measuring Immigrant Integration

Diversity in a European city

PETER REINSCH
European Research Centre on Migration and Ethnic Relations,
Utrecht University, The Netherlands

Ashgate

Aldershot • Burlington USA • Singapore • Sydney

List of Tables

Acknowledgments

More than ten years ago, I developed the conscious ambition to write a book on the concept of immigrant integration, and on the processes to which it refers. This study is in many ways an exercise in personal perseverance. Yet it clearly could not have been completed without the help of countless others. Forgive me for only mentioning a significant few.

Han Entzinger occupies a crucial position. When Han first heard of my desire to carry out this study, he volunteered to arrange the necessary stipend. Where other advisors might have stipulated the research route to be followed, Han has always conveyed his confidence in my cognitive capacities. He did continually encourage me to simplify my thoughts and texts, largely to little avail. So then, with later drafts, Han marked the many excursions into prose and metaphor with which I veiled the enduring confusion. I thank him for his trust, and his criticisms.

Roelof Hortulanus offered not only his extensive expertise of Dutch urban issues. As a colleague and friend he has somehow always succeeded in supplying the support I sought, be it an empathetic ear or an intellectual sparring mate. If anyone shares credit for the conception of this study, then it is he. It was Roelof who for Utrecht University initiated the Haarlem project that serves as empirical focus in this book. Since the project's inception, he has monitored my activities with the enthusiasm of the researcher who - had he not been so consumed by his other initiatives - would have loved to do them himself. Undoubtedly the results would have been substantively different. Never however has he insisted upon his point of view; his intent has been always to cultivate and clarify mine. I thank Roelof for his myriad forms of encouragement.

Without Haarlem residents this study would have had no focus. Jouke Kromkamp and Mariëlle Spruyt are the two Haarlem civil servants who deserve particular mention here. It was Jouke who back in 1992 insisted that the proper way to revise local minority policies was to record, and respond to, the perspectives of local minorities. It was Mariëlle, and her colleagues at the municipal Bureau for Research and Statistics, who provided the necessary information and inroads, so that we could collect and convey residents' views. Both were invaluable during the project, and more than responsive to my continued inquiries, once the project officially ended. Few if any of the 600 residents interviewed are aware that their responses have been subjected to such extensive analysis. Which is all the more reason to thank them for the time and trust they have invested in our research initiatives.

Since I started this study four years ago - to make more sense of the survey data - many colleagues and friends have offered a critical eye or ear. Three in particular have given continued response: Mascha Kunst, Jan Erik Dubbelman and Pretty Liem. As my research partner during the Haarlem project, Mascha later volunteered her time and competence to tactfully decimate my dreams of producing this book in record time. Once my writings displayed a degree of coherence, it was Jan Erik, my longtime compeer on the misuse of racism and social statistics, who dissected the drafts. Throughout the process Pretty, as my office and Ajax companion, contributed unrelenting empathy and insight.

Comparable to my ethnic affinities, I find my academic affiliations forever diverse. I am continually attached to a dynamic pattern of overlapping entities. In the seven years that I have been associated with Utrecht University, I have reaped the benefits of my multiple identities. At various levels, I have been quite at home as a member of: ERCOMER, the 'City and State' as well as the 'Culture and Minorities' Project groups; the Capacity group for Economy and Policy; the Department of General Social Sciences, and the Netherlands School for Social and Economic Policy Research. I thank my friends and colleagues in all these organizations for their inspiration, and their support. On a more formal note, the completion of this study was expedited immeasurably by a research stipend from the Dutch Ministry of Public Health, Welfare and Sport.

I am blessed with lots of family who are less directly responsible for the contents of this book. My parents and siblings in the United States have always endorsed my academic endeavors while accepting my expatriate perspective. Anneke Snijders and her family essentially sponsored my first Dutch studies a quarter century ago. Thanks again. Finally there is Lea. As my partner the past 15 years she has monitored - if not provoked - every fluctuation in my well-being. You will not find her between the lines; she is more responsible for this book's spine.

When all is said and done, it was only I who wrote this one.

Peter Reinsch
Amsterdam, The Netherlands

1 Introducing the Issues

In this study the concept of integration is used to explore the various ways individual immigrants relate to more indigenous residents of a Dutch city. The individuals, with all the diversity and dynamics of their everyday lives, will be ranked upon a single numerical scale representing their degree of integration. Around this illusively simple instrument revolve two central concerns, namely:

- the attributes and activities that differentiate between those who are integrated and those who are not, and
- the presumptions made and the conditions created by social researchers to infuse such measurements with a degree of validity.

Why one should be concerned with such matters is the topic of this first chapter. The study's social relevance is first located within the context of ongoing policy debates that focus upon immigration as a European - and more specifically a Dutch - social issue. Then integration as an academic concept is introduced, as I note that the controversial role it has played in public debates reflects more theoretical ambiguities. Besides these broad and abstract concerns, I have more immediate and practical reasons to conduct this study; these are presented in the third section. The various research inquiries are subsequently introduced, offering an outline of topics treated in the forthcoming chapters. To close the chapter, some mitigating remarks are placed concerning my personal motives for conducting the study.

Immigration and Social Policy

Soon after the establishment of a European Common Market in the late 1950's, the demand for laborers among member states exceeded the supply. Besides drawing immigrants from (former) colonies in the southern hemisphere and Asia, so-called guest workers were recruited from various lands surrounding the Mediterranean (Castles and Kosack, 1973). The immigration surplus did not subside with the economic recessions of the subsequent decades. Instead, family reunification and refugee movements altered more the character than the magnitude of the flow (Castles, 1984). In the late 1980's, around eight million non-European nationals were residing in the 12 member states (EECom, 1990). By 1995 this number had risen to 12 million, approximately 3.2% of the community's population (Eurostat, 1998). The acknowledgment that immigration had evolved beyond a temporary and regional character compelled governments at various levels to develop and implement integration policies.

The policy practice of course is quite diversified (Hammar, 1985; Castles, 1995; Bryant, 1997; Vermeulen, 1997). Whereas policies in Germany were long characterized by differential treatment, legitimated by the notion that only those of German ancestry are genuine German nationals, in France the policies are based more upon objectives of cultural assimilation, as citizenship can in principle be acquired by all who embrace the national culture. Dutch policies have focused more upon objectives of multi-culturalism, i.e., immigrant groups were provided with services and facilities to cultivate their cultural heritage, and to expedite an eventual remigration. When the permanence, and marginalization, of immigrant groups became apparent (WRR, 1979), the national government - and most municipalities with a sizeable immigrant population - implemented policies aimed toward the provision of complementary educational and welfare facilities (Entzinger, 1984, 1985). The establishment of such services constituted an acknowledgment that immigrant and other minority groups have particular needs and rights to participate in society according to their own customs and convictions.

In the 1980's, the closure of many industries that had relied upon migrant labor led to a drastic increase in unemployment rates. Due in part to family reunifications, the percentage of foreign-born primary school children increased significantly. Accordingly, the focus of Dutch debates shifted away from issues of multi-culturalism and more toward sources of social deprivation. The Scientific Council for Government Policy reflected these developments where it proposed that multi-cultural policies be replaced by more intensive educational programs to improve the labor market position of young (second generation) immigrants, and by measures to encourage equal-opportunity employment (WRR, 1989; Entzinger, 1994).

With that report, the notion of integration was introduced into Dutch immigrant policy debates. By 1994, the national government had transformed its minority policy into an 'integration policy ethnic minorities,' based explicitly on the consideration that (Tweede Kamer, 1993/94:6):

> The term integration policy more properly expresses that the social integration of minority groups, and the persons affiliated with them, is a reciprocal

process of acceptation. To this end concessions must be made by those integrating as well as by the society in which they settle.

An important implication bound to this policy transition is that immigrants are viewed less as members of an (oppressed) group, and more as individuals with socially problematic attributes (cf. Reinsch, 1990; Miles, 1993). This is exemplified by the requisite courses in Dutch language and culture prescribed for newly arrived immigrants (van der Zwan and Entzinger, 1994; Tweede Kamer, 1997). The shift however has not been accompanied by a clear conception of social and policy objectives. There remains a wide range of viewpoints concerning the goals of immigrant integration (Fermin, 1997), the basic impediments to their realization (Engbersen and Gabriëls, 1995a), and the progress booked by individuals and groups within this process (Vermeulen and Penninx, 1994, 2000; Veenman 1994, 1999, Tesser et al., 1999).

Integration and Social Theory

As a concept, integration has done service in a wide range of scientific disciplines. It generally denotes a process in which a certain unity is realized. Such abstract denotations are ambiguous by definition. Does integration signify the process itself or the eventual culmination? Does the unity refer to agents of change or the forces they wield? With my particular concern for individual immigrants' relation to their urban environment, a brief excursion was taken through social science literature that highlights a concept of 'community integration.' It revealed that the concept commonly refers to initiatives to help the mentally disabled out of sanatoria and into public life. This research tradition, in a nutshell, shed light on some fundamental issues: community members are expected to be productive, self-reliant, and sociable (McColl et al., 1998). Besides this insight into basic types - or what will later be denoted as *end-goals* - of individuals' integration, the excursion illustrates several research obstacles surrounding the integration concept: the diversity of social phenomena denoted as integration easily leads to academic misunderstanding; the criteria used to measure it are encased in moral strictures of social desirability; and when the focus is too narrow particular research subjects might be inadvertently construed as mentally ill-equipped. In this study, a more comprehensive concept and focus is developed to contextualize rather than problematize the individual immigrant.

For the analysis of immigrant integration, Schermerhorn (1970) has provided in my view the most comprehensive theory to date. In his study, presented more as a *framework for theory*, he focuses upon integration processes at the (macro) level of nation-states. Within the framework he distinguishes between independent, intervening and dependent components, and thus suggests a specific causal sequence and hierarchy of relations. The three dependent components identified in the framework may be construed as central dimensions of integration processes and are roughly aligned with the types of *community integration* referred to above. In chapter two these components will be presented and drawn upon to develop a framework (i.e., a conceptual model) more attuned to my purposes.

Schermerhorn's framework is particularly comprehensive in its potential to represent a diversity of social processes, including processes of cultural diversification. Other theories pertinent to immigrant integration have been developed that are more explicit (i.e., refutable) in their causal reasoning. Gordon (1963) for instance postulated the sequence in which seven types of integration are enacted. One of his more important premises is that once immigrants have become locally productive, other types of integration will follow (1963:81). Characteristic for Gordon's theory is the ultimate range of effective unity: integration is realized in all variant types as immigrants literally dissolve into their new social environment. In the framework devised by Schermerhorn, such *assimilation* processes are conceived to be but one of four ideal-typical 'patterns' that characterize the relation between groups. Distinctions between *centripetal* and *centrifugal* trends play a crucial role. Trends that favor subordinate (e.g., immigrant) groups' participation in the (structural) institutions and conformity to the (cultural) standards of the dominant (e.g., indigenous) group are considered centripetal, while centrifugal trends increase the social and cultural distance between subordinate and dominant groups (1970:81). For Schermerhorn, characteristic for the integration process is not the *direction* of these trends, but the *agreement* between subordinate and dominant groups regarding their direction.[1] In other words, the integration concept pertains to situations in which immigrant and indigenous groups agree upon integration objectives, as opposed to situations in which immigrant and indigenous groups differ concerning the purpose of the process.

The four general patterns are presented in figure 1.1. The first two represent integration tendencies. Pattern A refers to processes in which both dominant and subordinate groups support centripetal trends. When both groups support centrifugal trends, a B pattern exemplified by 'cultural pluralism' or 'autonomy' applies. The other two patterns, 'forced segregation' and 'forced assimilation', are characterized by resistance and tend toward conflict instead of integration.

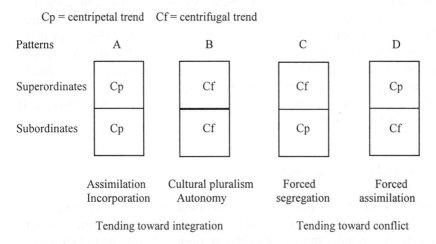

Cp = centripetal trend   Cf = centrifugal trend

Patterns	A	B	C	D
Superordinates	Cp	Cf	Cf	Cp
Subordinates	Cp	Cf	Cp	Cf
	Assimilation Incorporation	Cultural pluralism Autonomy	Forced segregation	Forced assimilation
	Tending toward integration		Tending toward conflict	

Figure 1.1 Congruent and incongruent orientations toward centripetal and centrifugal trends (Schermerhorn, 1970:83)

These conceptual distinctions provide a basis for this study, specifically a basis upon which processes of cultural diversification can be seen as 'integrative'. Integration is perceived as a process in which immigrants comply with the local activities and objectives of indigenous inhabitants. This implies that the activities and objectives of the indigenous inhabitants are just as pivotal - and as problematic - as those of immigrants. The process varies according to the nature of the activities and objectives shared. Whereas the integration concept in Dutch immigrant studies commonly refers to a more or less discrete range of social processes, distinct from assimilation and autonomy (Shadid, 1979:87ff; Entzinger, 1984:40; Risvanoglu-Bilgin et al., 1986:3; Mullard et al., 1990:58; Prins, 1996:27), the more general conceptual framework presented in the next chapter encompasses a more diversified and continuous range of social processes.

The adaptation of an abstract integration concept implies that its ambiguities will be retained. Besides the lack of agreement among scholars as to the distinction between types of integration, a central obstacle by the concept's utilization is the lack of concrete criteria for its identification and measurement. Under what conditions for instance does Schermerhorn's assimilation tendency disintegrate into one of forced assimilation? When is an immigrant culture or, more precisely, immigrants' cultural objectives incongruent with those of indigenous inhabitants? For decades this obstacle has been emphasized both by exponents (Landecker, 1955:27; Angell, 1968:386) as well as opponents (Miles, 1993:177) of the concept's use. Another point of confusion is the issue of context. I have already noted that Schermerhorn's study focused upon integration within the context of nation-states. Most comparative studies on immigrant integration (implicitly) focus upon this context (cf. OECD, 1998). The process of individuals' integration within urban environments generally refers to a more concise spatial setting, and has its own social and theoretical issues. These will now be briefly introduced.

Surveys and the Local Context

In the early 1990's the policy shifts on immigration had its consequences for Dutch local governments. Besides the dwindling availability of state funds for the separate services provided minority groups, the consequences of this shift were not entirely clear. Authorities in the city of Haarlem wanted to revise existing minority policies for the coming decade, and commissioned colleagues and me at Utrecht University to collect and convey the views of local residents. To this end, besides extensive discussions with representatives of various local organizations, and the analysis of policy and social trends, 600 survey interviews were held with adult Haarlem residents. The interviews covered a wide range of issues pertinent to local policy and everyday life in a 'multi-cultural' setting, soliciting from individuals their views, positions and experiences. While the sampling technique offered any adult resident the chance to be selected and interviewed, the survey was so stratified that detailed conclusions could be drawn for the larger immigrant 'minority' groups, namely the Turks, the Moroccans, and a combined group of Surinamese and Dutch Antilleans.

The diversity of perspectives and patterns of activity revealed in the study led to the formulation of three general policy frameworks, each complete with objectives and tasks per policy sector, and estimations of their popular support (Reinsch et al., 1995:187ff). The political - and normative - choice for one of the frameworks was left to local authorities (cf. Kunst et al., 1995). As for its theoretical relevance, the survey provided a unique opportunity to systematically compare the views and experiences of immigrant and indigenous urban residents

Upon its completion however, I was left puzzled by a series of problems. To begin with, the (impending) local policy shift from a focus upon 'minority' *groups* to one upon 'non-integrated' *individuals* raised the issue of target groups. Where minority programs could be designed and offered to individuals on the basis of their affiliation by birthright with a specific immigrant group (cf. van Amersfoort, 1974:37; Penninx, 1988:47), no criteria were readily available to locate the 'non-integrated' resident. Such residents will be denoted in this study with the descriptor *estranged*. This term alludes to antagonistic partner relationships that in my view best represent the condition of non-integrated individuals. Unless immigrants are perceived de facto (and stigmatized) as estranged, more refined policy criteria and adaptable monitoring instruments are necessary to designate those immigrants whose situation is at odds with local objectives.

But what are valid integration criteria for urban residents? When one acknowledges the widely divergent meanings attributed to the notion of immigrant integration - by scholars, public officials and the general public - then an adequate instrument would have to allow for a diversity of criteria. When variations in local circumstance are considered, the importance of this quality is immediately apparent. The range of problems, opportunities and local policy objectives confronting Dutch immigrants may differ markedly from those encountered in Bradford, Bremen or Besançon.[2] With the Haarlem study a conceptual model applicable at the local level had been developed, in which three distinct sets of policy objectives were delineated. The number and attributes of estranged residents according to the divergent objectives remained unclear, and consequently the extent in which divergent policies would target divergent groups.

If such a conceptual model was available, the question remains whether it could lead to valid empirical measurements? This issue may sound technical, but again it is informed by (policy) practice: should officials want to identify and locate the locally estranged without reverting to preconceived generalizations (such as 'minority groups' or 'the foreign born'), then instruments are needed that can compare the integration of any and all residents. For such purposes, structured interviews in which residents are randomly surveyed seem to present the most expedient and equitable measurement technique. This issue is also informed by the Haarlem survey: although it was not designed to measure the integration of individual respondents, it did contain numerous indicators often drawn upon in academic literature and policy debates. Upon completion I was lead to wonder how the data could be ordered and supplemented to identify and characterize estranged residents.

These various issues can be succinctly summarized. To monitor individuals' integration into their immediate social surroundings, a conceptual model is needed that:

- allows for divergent integration objectives;
- provides a framework to order and evaluate empirical observations; and
- elucidates concrete criteria to designate the locally integrated.

Research Issues and Design

The challenge presented by the issues above entails the development and operationalization of a conceptual framework in which normative elements (e.g., individual and group objectives) can be readily distinguished from theoretical ones (i.e., attributes that affect the realization of objectives). It should moreover offer the possibility to monitor individuals' integration within a local (urban) context. My intention is to develop a formal model of immigrant integration, and then use it to order and evaluate the Haarlem survey data. With these various activities, I seek an answer to the following question:

What can structured (survey) interviews among immigrant and indigenous residents of an urban locality reveal about their differences in integration?

To properly convey the nature of this challenge, and this study, I should clarify what is meant by a *formal* model (cf. Kaplan, 1964:258ff). Any model is a simplified representation of reality, and in the social sciences such representations are commonly constructed with concepts. Models become theories when the relations between their concepts provide not only a simplification of reality, but also an interpretation of how reality evolves. A formal model is a model *of* a theory, inasmuch as the relation between concepts in the model remain largely open to interpretation. By developing a formal model to order and analyze the Haarlem survey data, the model's *potential* to reveal theoretical and normative issues will be illustrated. The word potential not only alludes to the limitations and possibilities bound to the Haarlem survey; I am concerned with more general problems by the operationalization and measurement of concepts pertinent to immigrants' integration into European cities.

The study will consist of seven more chapters. In the following chapter the general conceptual model is presented. Using Schermerhorn's theoretical framework as a point of departure, a refocus is made from the level of nation-states and their interrelations to the level of urban residents and their interrelations. There, three primary dimensions of social process are perceived that delineate individuals' relation to their social environment:

people occupy social *positions*; in these positions cultural *orientations* shape their perspectives; and through social *behavior* (in their positions, with their perspectives) with other individuals they make and sustain (interethnic) contacts. For each of these dimensions a series of concepts is delineated to specify formal aspects of the relation. Further differentiation is provided by the parameter of *domains*: the environment can be subdivided into social and spatial sectors in which individuals exchange services and goods. Finally, within each dimension individuals are confronted with dilemmas whose resolutions shape and alter the nature of their relations. The resolution of these dilemmas can, in their combination over dimensions and in their recognition by entire groups, be construed as normative *objectives* or individual *end-goals*. Chapter two, in short, is structured around the conceptual issue:

What are the primary parameters that constitute the immigrant integration process?

In chapters three through six problems and possibilities are considered that are tied to the operationalization and measurement of the conceptual model. My departure point is the premise that, to implement and evaluate local integration policies, individual integration processes can be monitored via survey research techniques. By considering the specific components of the model, per dimension and per domain, the tenability of this premise is systematically examined.

Chapter three begins with observations concerning the context and practice of survey research among immigrants. Several issues characteristic of the survey activity are reviewed that affect the measurements made and therewith the conclusions that can be drawn. These reflections revolve around the inquiry:

What factors limit the adequacy of empirical observations derived (solely) from survey interviews with immigrant (and indigenous) individuals?

Some contexts and characteristics of the Haarlem survey are presented in the chapter. It culminates with the presentation of a *local integration index*. The index combines survey respondents' scores upon five measures deemed denotative for their degree of integration. This standard serves in the remaining chapters as a point of reference whenever the (statistical) significance of a given characteristic (i.e., position, orientation or behavior within a given domain) is evaluated for individuals' integration.

Three chapters are then devoted to operationalization and measurement issues pertinent to the three respective dimensions of immigrant integration: in chapter four components contained within the *positional* dimension are considered, in chapter five components within the *orientational* dimension, and chapter six the *behavioral* dimension. Each of these chapters is divided into sections corresponding with the six domains of integration. Within most sections, data from the Haarlem survey will be presented, to examine the significance of domain-specific attributes for individuals' degree of integration. The data will also serve to illustrate specific measurement issues, although to clarify the issues extensive references will be made to other research. The presentations in these three chapters revolve around the two inquiries:

What significance may be attributed to individuals' various positions, cultural orientations and interethnic contacts, as indicators of their integration within the local (Haarlem) context?

What methodological obstacles, pertinent to the operationalization of individuals' social positions, cultural orientations and personal contacts, render the (survey) measurement of immigrant integration particularly problematic?

In short, in chapter two I present a formal model of concepts pertinent to the observation and interpretation of individuals' integration. Then from chapter three through chapter six I order and evaluate the Haarlem data within this framework. My purpose on the one hand is to interpret the significance of the measures made, on the other hand to consider the possibilities for more adequate measurements.

The methodical examination of empirical data culminates in chapter seven. The systematic comparison of survey measurements reveals a variety of patterns worthy of more general theoretical interpretation. While illustrating the utility of the conceptual model, summary answers are presented for the central and the various sub-inquiries that have guided my investigations in the previous chapters.

A primary motive for this study concerns the possibility to conceptualize and perceive individuals' integration into localities characterized by - in Schermerhorn's terminology - cultural pluralism. This motive is associated with Dutch policy objectives, referred to in the first section above, in which the rights of minority groups are acknowledged to live according to their divergent customs and convictions. Moreover, it reflects my own convictions concerning the benefits of local diversification within the

European context of globalization. In the concluding chapter, this explicitly normative issue is reviewed. More specifically, I address the question how social research, and social policy, can contribute to the realization of European cities in which cultural diversity is retained as an objective of immigrant integration.

Personal Purpose and Pretense

In social science, as in public policy, integration may be valued as a means or as an end, either as a means of achieving a desired state of affairs, which may or may not be described as integration, or as a desired state of affairs for the attainment of which integration may or may not be the preferred method. At the same time, there is another dimension of complexity, namely, whether, in respect of either means or ends where such a distinction can be maintained, integration is sought as something that would be both wholly true and true of the whole (or either of these) or with some lesser, more qualified connotation. Therefore, it is often easier to be clear about what is deemed to be a lack of the desired degree or form of integration . . . rather than the desired state itself.

Furthermore . . . parties may differ as to either what substantively would be equally integrative for all, or, given that what it means for one party may not be the same for another, whether integration is desirable at all . . .

Another plane of variation further to all of those thus far mentioned has to do with what the integration in question is integration of. For instance, it may be of culture, society, polity, nation, economy, personality or space, with say, planning, policy, analysing, building, negotiating and other avenues of endeavour, together or separately. The approaches and indicators preferred vary too . . .

So the entire subject is a miasma, a minefield, which one would be well advised to be wary to enter. (Apthorpe, 1985:401)

I encountered this warning in 1994, at the beginning of the Haarlem project. It has been a source of inspiration and reproach ever since. For I vacillate in my critique of the concept's ideological ambiguities and my appreciation of its theoretical complexities. As lofty and vague as my goals might be, I am aware that with each presumption or clarification that this study conveys, a wave of criticism and confusion is possible. The reader is thus forewarned: as this study vacillates between attempts to clarify the integration concept, and attempts to comprehend urban reality, the forthcoming chapters will regularly reflect an entrapment in my own miasma. Nevertheless, such vulnerability is embraced, with the conviction that my experiences and reflections will be of value to all concerned with the relative deprivation, disaffection and solitude experienced by residents of European urban environments. Let me note a few more concrete qualifications.

To begin with I am quite devoted to a sociological perspective, i.e., the conviction that society is more than the sum of its individual participants and that individuals can only be understood within their social context. The nature of the analysis however - an extensive review of numerous integration indicators within a formal model, instead of a more intensive examination of the relation between several factors within a theoretical model - ultimately inhibits explanations along disciplinary veins. Successful integration will not and cannot be attributed here either to sociological, or to economical, psychological or biological determinants. With the presumed perspective, the opportunities to perceive immigrant integration processes from the vantage point of other disciplines will be insufficiently used.

Even the sociological knowledge wielded calls for a distinct degree of humility. The sheer quantity of relevant sociological literature that pertains to the various concepts considered in the coming chapters would require numerous lifetimes to consume. I can only attest to an awareness of the social science research literature on immigrant integration that in the past 20 years has enlivened academic debate in the Netherlands. Although in the coming chapters many excursions are taken over the border in search of solutions to measurement problems, I hope that many issues, which remain unresolved here, have been effectively unraveled by others elsewhere.

Finally, this study should help other social researchers systematize and ameliorate the analysis of immigrant integration processes in other cities. This is indeed my pretense. It may also be informative by the analysis of more general social integration processes, rural and urban. This however is not my pretense, as I will remain focused upon issues affecting the individual immigrant within an urban environment. The framework and measurements pertain to processes in one European city; their relevance for other cities remains to be seen.

This section could be construed as a premeditated *not guilty* plea; its purpose is more to prepare the reader for various irritations and disappointments. Immigration and local integration are processes so complex, that any pretense of virtuosity or objectivity deserves disdain. I hope that the considerations presented in the coming chapters ultimately cultivate more mutual understanding in academic and policy debates.

2 Framing the Conceptual Model

The immigrant arrives as an outsider, even when the arrival has been announced or anticipated. The individual's estranged situation can be perceived in many ways, with even more ways to conceive and evaluate his or her endeavors to become part of the new environment. It is essentially this process - inasmuch as it transpires to the satisfaction of all concerned - that I refer to with the concept of integration. However, to generalize beyond this one hypothetical newcomer, the integration concept is endowed with attributes that help to compare and evaluate the diversity of processes individuals undergo. In this chapter these attributes are presented, a network of concepts whose interrelations form the subject of endless theoretical debate.

My efforts to conceptualize the process in generalized terms revolve around the query:

What are the primary parameters that constitute the immigrant integration concept?

My purpose is to sketch the contours of a formal model that in the forthcoming chapters can be used and elaborated upon to order and interpret empirical data. Due to the subject matter this chapter will remain quite abstract, which doesn't lend itself for leisurely reading. To perceive the diversity of concepts and issues within a comprehensive framework warrants the effort. The remaining chapters however can be read and presumably understood without becoming first acquainted with the separate parameters' derivation and circumscription (an overview is presented in figure 2.1 at the chapter's end).

The first order of business is to acknowledge the focal points when perceiving hypothetical newcomers and their new environments. I have spoken in the previous chapter of immigrants, minorities and refugees, and these terms can be supplemented by others (e.g., ethnic groups, aliens, and the oppressed) used to designate an estranged category of individuals. To perceive their degree of integration - literally the progress realized in becoming part of the new environment - such categories are regarded within a given context. The basic parameters that define the perceived categories (actors) and context (environment) are delineated along two analytical lines. The first is the *perspective* from which the process is viewed, i.e., the social and spatial position from which the process is perceived, including the criteria used to appreciate it. I will concentrate upon the subjective point of view conveyed by immigrant residents in response to survey questions. These may not only diverge significantly from each other. They may also differ from the perspectives held for example by indigenous residents, local officials, and social scientists. In this study these alternative perspectives are not necessarily more objective, only more implicit. Dependent upon the perspective, various categories of actors are perceived and foreseen with problems and possibilities.

The second parameter is the *focus* with which the process is circumscribed. The primary focus in this study is a micro-level consideration of urban adults. A diversity of concepts is introduced that in the coming chapters serve to order their relations with each other. The integration processes that individuals experience are intrinsically related to processes between groups. They are imbued with social significance within this context. In this chapter first a more *macro*-level conceptual framework is presented that pertains to the relations between groups. Micro and macro foci are perceived within contexts, in this study primarily the social and spatial boundaries of a locality known as Haarlem. However, neighborhood, national and even global contexts will not be ignored.

Based upon the conceptual framework developed by Schermerhorn, a distinction is made between three primary types or *dimensions* of local integration: structural, cultural and interactive. These will be expounded upon sequentially in the second through fourth sections. For each dimension, central concepts will be introduced that denote processes in and between local groups. Complementary to these macro concepts, concepts pertinent to the integration of (immigrant) individuals are then derived. Particularly important are the central objectives and end-goals that denote the disparate options with which groups and individuals are confronted in their local activities.

Individuals - in their relations to their local environment - occupy a variety of positions, maintain a variety of orientations, and behave in a variety of manners. Social scientists, policymakers and local residents all use social and spatial distinctions to categorize the various aspects of everyday life. For instance, within a *domain* of work, distinctions can be made in individuals' job position, labor orientation, and professional contacts that affect their endeavors in other domains. Pertinent to processes of local integration, six domains are delineated in a fifth section.

While immigrant integration is a process, it presumably is a process in which at any empirical moment individuals' progress can be evaluated with end-goal criteria. To this end disparate criteria are considered in the sixth section for the designation of integrated individuals. Although the correspondence is empirically and theoretically problematic, the criteria reflect (a combination of) divergent objectives or *visions* of local integration. The distinctions in individual end-goals and local objectives embody the normative standards that differentiate the integrated from the estranged.

Having circumscribed levels, dimensions, domains and objectives of immigrant integration, by the end of this chapter the network of concepts will have taken the form of a neatly structured cube. In closing, the static character of the model will be considered. For even with finely tuned instruments capable of near continuous measurements, the social scientist can only estimate how the parameters of the models change with variations in perhaps the most central parameter - *time*.

Actors and Activity: Individuals and Locality

References to newcomers - and efforts to comprehend their local estrangement - necessitate presumptions as to the subjects and objects of research. In this section, the units of analysis within the model are circumscribed that denote various actors involved with the integration process. First I consider the hypothetical newcomer, and the diverse qualifications used in this study to differentiate him or her from other individuals. This implies a distinction between the newcomer's perspective, and my perspective as a social researcher. Then I consider matters of focus, noting that within the newcomer's environment, integration processes are conceived and interpreted at various levels. More concretely, I am lead to distinguish between individual, group and local integration. With these distinctions made, I defer to Schermerhorn's more general conceptual framework for a presentation of three basic issues.

Immigrants, Minorities, and Ethnic Categories

Without memory and history, we all arrive continually anew. We find ourselves surrounded by objects and others whose attributes and actions are in need of comprehension. If only to decide whether it's wise to remain in and become part of the surroundings. When I as social researcher consult newcomers to measure their progress in this process, I should avoid disparate assumptions that potentially distort my perspective. On the one hand, when focusing upon newcomers instead of the environment they focus upon, I try not to assume that the personal attributes perceived have any essential relation to the obstacles they perceive. In terms perhaps more concrete, it implies that newcomers - as subjects of research analysis - do not necessarily embody the obstacles that inhibit their integration. The perception of these obstacles is indirectly but ultimately the research objective. On the other hand, if a strict distinction between 'newcomers' and their 'environment' is maintained, the continuous and reciprocal relation between the research subject and object is ignored. In other words, I must presume that the perspective and actions of newcomers - and social researchers - do affect and are altered by the environment they perceive.

These methodological observations on the relation - and interaction - between the researcher, the newcomer as research subject, and integration as research object, will be elaborated upon in chapter three. To refrain from further references to hypothetical newcomers, three qualifications are introduced here that are used extensively in the forthcoming chapters to categorize the research subjects.

Immigrants and indigenes According to common English usage, an immigrant is someone who has moved into a country or region. In the forthcoming chapters the term will refer to individuals and groups of a non indigenous origin. Considering for instance the various multitudes who in the past millennium have entered the geo-political region known as the Netherlands (Lucassen and Penninx, 1997), a very large proportion of the Dutch population has immigrant origins. For the focus upon Haarlem, the term will refer only to first or second generation immigrants, i.e., those inhabitants who were born outside the Netherlands or who have at least one parent born elsewhere. According to this definition, which coincides with general Dutch policy and research formulations, approximately one-sixth of the near 16 million inhabitants of the Netherlands has an immigrant status.[1] To what extent these millions of recent arrivals consider themselves Dutch, or for that matter the extent in which indigenous Dutch[2] consider themselves immigrants (cf. Hall, 1991), is more an issue for study than a point of departure.

Minorities and majorities The term minority has played a central role in Dutch academic and policy observations on immigrants in the past two decades. In van Amersfoort's definition (1974:37), which was later adopted by the Dutch government, the term refers to a collectivity that occupies an objectively low social position and is limited in its potential to participate effectively in political decision-making processes. For van Amersfoort, a minority is continuous in its nature, in that it applies to more generations, and individuals' affinity with the group is given precedence above their other social categorizations. By the presentation of empirical observations, I will consistently compare the integration of individuals grouped within three *minority categories,* namely immigrants of *Moroccan, Turkish* and *Surinamese or Dutch Antillean* origin. These three categories contain the four largest target groups of Haarlem and Dutch minority policy. Two other categories will be consistently differentiated within the analysis: indigenous Dutch (i.e., those born in the Netherlands of Dutch-born parents), and 'Other' immigrants. One should not assume that these latter two categories represent a *majority,* as individuals are contained in both who according to policy distinctions are members of ethnic minority groups.

Ethnic groups and categories An ethnic *group* refers to those who have a 'real or putative common ancestry, memories of a shared historical past, and a cultural focus on one or more symbolic elements defined as the epitome of their peoplehood' (Schermerhorn, 1970:12). The shared memories and common cultural focus imply an awareness among the group members that they are allied with each other. Ethnicity is in this sense more than a qualification, like the foreign origins of an immigrant, that can be ascribed to individuals based on objective criteria. It also refers to a subjective affinity that emotionally binds the group members. The term ethnic *category* is less common in the literature. It is used here to refer to any one of the five collectivities (i.e., the four immigrant categories and the indigenous Dutch) compared in the forthcoming chapters. Besides their common geo-political region of origin, I do not presume that individuals within an ethnic category share any common cultural orientation. When references are made for instance about Turks, the qualification refers only to their (1st or 2nd generation) region of origin. Only when references are explicitly made in terms of *ethnic Turks,* (who can be differentiated e.g. from *ethnic* Kurds) am I referring to a qualification that individuals use to characterize themselves.

Individual, Group and Local Integration

Much of the theoretical observations on immigration, ethnicity and integration focus upon these processes within the context of nation-states. While the scope is seldom explicit, there are obvious reasons why nation-states commonly serve as context. The nation-state, at least in most European versions, is the spatial entity in which the jurisdiction regulating the relationships between individuals and groups is most extensively developed. It is the political entity whose power and provisions elicit allegiance from individual inhabitants. Ideally, at least among nationalists, it also represents the social entity that serves as a banner for the common heritage and objectives of its inhabitants.

The framework presented here pertains to a more immediate context, namely any densely populated geo-political entity, in which an individual can conceivably encounter any other inhabitant during everyday activities. This environment will be generally referred to as a *locality* although, dependent upon the issue and context, references will be made to the *city*, the *urban environment*, the *municipality*, and *Haarlem*. From a researcher's perspective, I am inclined to perceive the locality's boundaries in geo-political terms. The inhabitant's perspective suggests however that the boundaries be forever in flux. Dependent upon the specific locality, inhabitants have the possibility to seek work, attend cultural events, and meet with friends in neighboring localities. It is less feasible, when compared to the nation-state as context, to see the locality as an isolated entity, independent of national and global processes. The consequences of this limited context for the conceptualization of immigrant integration will become clear in the coming chapters. For a brief preview: I note a greater emphasis upon the everyday contacts with fellow inhabitants and upon the spatial characteristics of individuals' activities.

Having described the (soft) boundaries of the scope, I now adjust the focus. It can be altered to observe integration processes in variant detail. A general distinction is made here in three levels of analysis, and these correspond with three levels of integration. These are described in sequence, beginning with the level that attracts my primary interest.

Individual integration The focus that provides the greatest detail corresponds with a *micro* level of analysis. It is at this level that distinct individuals are perceived, active in establishing and maintaining relations with other individuals in the locality. In accordance with Schermerhorn's distinction (1970:14), the integrative nature of individuals' endeavors is interpreted as their active and coordinated compliance with the ongoing activities and objectives of other local residents.

Group integration When the focus is adjusted for observations at a *meso* level of analysis, the individual detail is gradually replaced by an accent upon groups of individuals. Not only are individuals seen to dissolve continually into and emerge from groups, the centripetal and centrifugal trends proceed more immediately and clearly along group lines. A distinction can be made between dominant groups that apparently set trends, and other groups that vary in their compliance to these trends. Taking the cue again from Schermerhorn, I note that each group is involved in a two-way process of compliance. Integration concerns on the one hand compliance with the activities and objectives of other groups, particularly the dominant ones. On the other hand, group integration is an ongoing process of realizing and retaining the affinity of individuals.

Local integration At a *macro* level of analysis, the focus upon the locality has lost the individual detail. Indeed, group activities fuse into more historical entities social scientists call institutions, while other groups simply dissipate. Even the dominant groups no longer appear the absolute trend setters. Their existence and activities could be construed as institutional reactions to developments that originate beyond the boundaries of the locality. The centripetal and centrifugal trends at this level are an interplay of groups and institutions. At one moment the entire institutional pattern appears obscure, and even the boundaries of the locality seem porous, but then group interactions gradually realign and define the institutional pattern. Local integration is this two-way process in which the activities of local groups, and the response to external pressures, reinforce local boundaries and objectives.

There are two basic observations that I derive from the continual dynamic within the locality and the continual shift in focus. The first is that no immediate and absolute correspondence exists between the patterns and trends observed at one level, and those at another. Individuals form and respond to group and local processes, participating in a seemingly continuous chain of reciprocal cause and effect. The processional chain never fuses in absolute centrism, nor are there simultaneous centrifugal trends at all three levels that mark the locality's absolute dissolution. This observation, admittedly obscure in its metaphor, reflects a sociological presumption concerning the relative autonomy of individuals and localities. It also reflects an ideological presumption that the process will never end. The second observation is a postulate that I intend to clarify (although it cannot be verified) in the forthcoming chapters. While the correspondence between individual and local integration is never absolute, the greater the local integration, the more trends (i.e., shared objectives) with which the individual must comply. A contrasting formulation provides perhaps greater clarity: where local integration is lacking, empirical criteria for individual integration are wanting.

The distinction in three levels of analysis is arbitrary. It is made here to suggest the limitations of any single, static focus. This limitation applies to the model presented in this chapter's remaining sections, and the empirical observations in the forthcoming chapters. Via a micro focus upon individuals, generalizations will be formulated concerning the relative integration of entire ethnic categories. However, the study will not elaborate upon conceptions, nor does it possess the focal potential to comprehend social processes, at higher levels of analysis.

Three Primary Dimensions by Immigrant Integration

With the description of three analytical levels, I have implied an ongoing dynamic between actors upon all these levels. Moreover, I have visualized the dynamic with Schermerhorn's notion of centripetal and centrifugal trends. To derive a more substantive conception of integration processes, the nature of these trends needs further differentiation. I distinguish three dimensions central to any dynamic between individuals or groups. In this sub-section I outline these dimensions, and associate them with distinctions made by Schermerhorn.

Imagine at a micro level how individuals vary in their *positions* relative to each other. When we liken the locality to a large marketplace, a newly arrived and socially dispossessed immigrant can be metaphorically perceived at the periphery, whereas indigenous residents are generally more centrally located and possess more social goods for market exchanges. I am referring to what Schermerhorn (at a macro level) termed 'the differential participation rates in institutional and associational life' (1970:16). Schermerhorn alludes here to social *structures* within societies, the various *positions* individuals and groups occupy within these structures, and their prospects for mobility, i.e., for changes in their position. A centripetal trend in positional terms would be characterized for instance by a more equal distribution of social goods among individual residents, who thus metaphorically share the strategic locations at the market center. A centrifugal trend would be contrarily exemplified by the evolution of a more diffuse marketplace, characterized by the dispersion of particular goods over various locations, and by a greater discrepancy between residents as to their opportunity to acquire goods. As for local objectives, the centripetal trend represents the pursuance of social *equality* while the centrifugal trend can be perceived as the pursuance of *civil liberty*. These distinctions will be elaborated upon in the next section.

The second dimension concerns individuals' cultural orientations. What significance does the newly arrived immigrant attribute to his or her local position? Does a more indigenous resident in a comparable market position express divergent needs and convictions, for instance concerning the value of a particular good? Schermerhorn formulated the issue as 'the extent of satisfaction or dissatisfaction . . . with the differential patterns of participation . . . together with accompanying ideologies and cultural values' (1970:16). In the forthcoming chapters, with the focus upon the Haarlem locality, orientational issues will indeed revolve around individuals' satisfaction with the local situation. However, as will be elaborated upon shortly, the individual and collective pursuit of satisfaction revolves around central cultural objectives of *unity* or *diversity*. As to marketplace trends, the issue is whether immigrants should - centripetally - conform to a local culture, or whether they are - centrifugally - expected to develop their own personalities.

The third dimension concerns the actual behavior individuals exhibit in their contacts with other locals. Imagine our immigrant has acquired a position near the center of the local marketplace, and has adapted a cultural orientation more conducive with this position. Does the immigrant behave differently when confronted with other immigrants? How do the more indigenous residents behave when confronted with an immigrant in their midst? A centripetal trend would involve an increasing contact between immigrants and indigenes upon the marketplace. When one or both collectivities opt more for so-called exclusive contacts within 'the group' a centrifugal trend may be perceived. Behavioral issues are intrinsically bound to those of position and orientation. The premise here is that the behavior of individuals and the interactions between groups cannot be simply clarified by differences in positions or orientations; the (lack of) interaction affects these other two dimensions of integration. Such issues are associated with the third dependent variable in Schermerhorn's framework: 'overt or covert behavior patterns . . . indicative of conflict and/or harmonious relations (and their) assessment in terms of continued integration' (1970:16).[3] In a fourth section, this *interactive* dimension of local integration will be considered further.

The issues bound to differences in structure and position, culture and orientation, or interaction and behavior are fundamental to the social sciences (cf. Thurlings, 1977).[4] Besides Schermerhorn, many other social theorists have underwritten their significance for the conceptualization of integration processes (cf. Landecker, 1955; Parsons, 1960; Peters, 1993; Engbersen and Gabriëls, 1995b). There is a great deal of discrepancy as to the boundaries between these abstract distinctions, particularly concerning those delineating the structural and cultural dimensions on the one hand and the interactive dimension on the one other. Many studies on Dutch immigrant integration only distinguish between structural and cultural dimensions (e.g., Campfens, 1979; Shadid, 1979; Entzinger, 1984; Risvanoglu et al., 1986; Veraart, 1996). My primary consideration by the adoption of a three dimensional conceptual model is that distinct theoretical, methodological and policy issues focus directly upon the measurement of individual behavior and group interactions.

In each of the coming three sections I will focus first on a macro level, introducing concepts central to processes of local integration. Then the focus will be altered to present concepts more pertinent to individual integration. Processes of group integration, inasmuch as they are perceived and conceived within the local context or are derived from observations of individuals, will be considered more implicitly in later chapters.

Structure and Position: Enclosure and Engagement

Social structures are figurative constructs that represent man's relation to nature and to fellow man. My purpose in this section is not to review local social structures; I introduce only those concepts deemed central to an analysis of local integration. They subsequently serve as a basis for the positional concepts pertinent to an analysis of individual integration.

Social structures function for the production and distribution of goods. There are an endless variety of goods that individuals and groups need or want. These can be material goods, such as food and lodging, medicine and money, or immaterial goods such as education and companionship, welfare and work. In this section several notions will be circumscribed: the idea of commodity markets and objects of exchange, the idea of vertical or horizontal barriers to market mobility, and the idea of market regulation and state intervention. These are then complemented by a more microscopic focus. Individuals may experience their lack of possessions as freedom or deprivation, their position within various markets as dependency or engagement, and their benefit from market regulations as increased opportunity or larceny. The conceptual basis that binds these issues is the tension between two structural objectives of local integration: the realization of *social equality*, and the minimization of (state) constraints to *civil liberties*. The contradictory character of these objectives can be succinctly formulated as a dilemma: local authorities must either condone continued inequality, or opt for the injustice of constraints.[5]

Commodity Markets and Conditions of Exchange

In order for individuals or groups to acquire a particular commodity, what goods or services must they provide in exchange? These can take the material form of capital. For instance the acquisition of housing, a material good, commonly involves the exchange of funds or other tangible goods in return. The distribution may also be tied to the exchange of immaterial goods. Access to schools, jobs and a wide range of leisure arrangements, may be conditional upon particular loyalties (e.g., to the state or professions) or upon the possession of specific rights (based on age, experience, local ties, etc.). Characteristic for the exchange process is the investment of time and energy. Education for instance, besides the price of tuition and the immaterial rights and duties bound to (generally youthful) age, typically involves years of sacrifice. Such sacrifice presumably applies for the fulfillment of any basic need (cf. Maslow, 1970; Adler, 1977): when groups lack capital and social rights, their primary means to alleviate their structural marginalization is the investment of time. This principle is the key to understanding the structural dilemma. An equal distribution of social rights and capital would negate endeavors (of the rich and righteous) in the past; alternatively the diminishment of inequality requires extra sacrifices (from the poor and immoral) in the future.

Of course, the distribution of any particular social good can be contingent upon the exchange of either capital, rights *or* time. Two other central notions, segmentation and regulation, help represent such variations.

Segmented and Pillarized Markets

Are there a variety of channels through which the good is exchanged? The number of markets existent for a given good is obviously dependent upon the conception of the good. One can perceive for instance a single labor market on which all kinds of labor are supplied, but within this market various labor segments are discernable. Distinctions in labor are made according to many criteria: e.g., educational level, economic sector, production activity, or professional status. And each of these criteria refers to factors that suggest an explanation for the marginalized labor market position of immigrants or other groups. They may suggest for instance that the supply of the particular labor good simply exceeds the demand.

I focus here on labor markets, but such distinctions can be made for any social good. By dissecting the market into more concrete market segments, the distinctions may indicate the differential access to one market *segment* for groups active upon another segment. I am referring here specifically to conceptions that address the limited upward mobility of immigrant groups. Such conceptions are found for instance in: theories on split or dual-labor markets (e.g., Bonacich, 1972; Niesing, 1993), theories of housing succession in which immigrant groups receive access to neighborhoods only when indigenous groups depart (e.g., Park and Burgess, 1976;

van Amersfoort, 1987), and theories that conceptualize ceilings to immigrant educational mobility (e.g., Ogbu, 1978).

Besides distinctions in a hierarchy of markets, parallel segments may exchange the same good but to divergent groups. Specifically relevant here are distinctions along ethnic lines, for instance, separate (or segregated) job markets that capitalize upon labor supplied by a particular ethnic category. Conceptions such as *ethnic capital* (Sowell, 1981a) or *immigrant enclaves* (Portes and Manning, 1986) refer to the potential or real existence of such markets. Within this context the concept of *pillarization* warrants attention: the organization of markets along parallel chains of exchange, each regulated by a group with distinct social objectives. The concept of pillarization is particularly relevant for a comprehension of Dutch social structures. In the first half of the 20th century, the distribution of goods and services was mediated along four distinct pillars to Protestants, Catholics, socialists and 'others' respectively (Lijphart, 1968; van der Horst, 1996). Separate social services were available within each pillar: housing cooperatives, schools, media, trade unions, and leisure arrangements. Due in part to secularist processes, the significance of pillarization in the Netherlands has waned since the 1960's. For issues of immigrant integration it remains relevant for at least two reasons:

- A variety of markets are still segmented according to pillarized distinctions, although market differences are no longer fundamental (inasmuch as market access is no longer determined by exclusionary processes).
- The idea of separate social institutions along ethnic lines may be considered morally suspect but it still serves in policy debates as an optional path for immigrant integration (cf. Tromp, 1992; Pettigrew, 1995).

Regulation and Intervention

Various mechanisms structure the way a market functions, and these mechanisms may be controlled by or geared toward the needs of a given group. The notion of social inequality refers to mechanisms that generate *prosperity* for certain groups, while precipitating relative *poverty* for others.

The notion of constraint provides a means to comprehend such processes. Constraint is namely ambiguous in its meaning, as it denotes mechanisms of repression or restriction that limit the activities of individuals or groups. It may refer then to mechanisms that limit the market access of marginalized groups and consequently generate unequal distributions. It may also refer to mechanisms explicitly designed to diminish inequality, for instance by compelling market providers to increase exchanges with marginalized groups. In this ambiguous sense constraint is neatly aligned with the notion of freedom, alluded to in objectives of *civil liberty*. In its ideological connotation, a 'freedom to' (e.g. 'act') generally suggests an absence of (market) restrictions and the subsequent differential access equated with inequality. Contrarily, a 'freedom from' (e.g. 'poverty') suggests the presence of (market) access, though more in a 'centripetal' than an 'equitable' sense. Within the formal model, these two forms of constraint are differentiated by the concepts of regulation and intervention.

The differential distribution of social goods on any market is the result of *regulation*: the rules and restrictions, natural processes and behavioral norms, principles and objectives that restrict and legitimate the interaction between market actors. Market regulations that affect the supply of labor for instance are related to: legal restrictions on minimum wage levels and the employment of children, demographic processes (such as wars and baby booms), cultural norms (e.g., concerning womens' role), entrepreneurial principles and profit motives. Rules, norms and objectives are in themselves cultural factors (that as components of the cultural dimension will be encountered in the next section); the focus here is upon their analytical potential to delineate (alterations in) market structures.

The notion of market regulation implies the existence of unregulated markets but, as the examples suggest, any individual's (lack of) market position or behavior can be traced to patterns of regulation.[6] The notion of unregulated or 'free' markets is commonly reserved, within liberal ideologies, for markets void of state intervention. National and local authorities have three basic channels to regulate market structures, associated with their respective market roles. They can supply a given commodity, demand the commodity, or provide the legislation and jurisdiction to alter the distribution of a commodity. Within all three roles, state authorities affect market access and acquisition. In short, there are myriad ways in which the state regulates market processes, and such regulations are not necessarily made to limit social inequality. The notion of *intervention* is then reserved in this study for references to those state activities implemented for the explicit purpose of improving the market access and prosperity of socially marginalized groups. This definition does not carry the presumption that the intervention actually alters the commodity's distribution to any significant extent. It simply associates the notion with the state's responsibility to promote social equality.

Macro concepts such as commodity exchange, market segmentation and regulation, represent (structural aspects of) integration as a process of *allocation*: the distribution of a social good to individuals and groups hinges upon their allotted position. Such conceptions are complemented - or countered - by micro concepts that reflect individuals' activities and *opportunities*. These latter conceptions characteristically represent (structural) integration as a process of *acquisition*: the possession of a social good hinges upon individuals' potential to secure market positions. The tension that envelopes the conceptual polarities of allocation and acquisition reflects theoretical and political issues central to Dutch debates on immigrant integration (cf. Rex, 1986:81; Penninx, 1988:54ff; Fermin, 1997:46ff).

Social Position and Prospects for Mobility

Having introduced basic concepts for the analysis of structural conditions pertinent to issues of local integration, I now turn to (the perspective of) the individual immigrant. In the previous paragraph a series of (micro) notions were mentioned that comprise a complement to more local focal points: opportunity, position, and possession.

The concept of *opportunity* refracts the notion of relative scarcity: the greater the scarcity of a given social good, the less opportunity a given individual has to possess that good. Opportunity refers to circumstances that optimize the probability of acquiring a certain social good but, like the notion of probability, it presumes an element of chance. Individuals may experience their opportunity as *prospects*: the estimated chance individuals perceive to acquire a given social good.

Opportunity varies with the availability of a social good, but it also varies with individual circumstance. More specifically, opportunity varies with *position*: the extent in which an individual (already) possesses a social good or the means of exchange to acquire it. In the market metaphor it is reflected by the location an individual has on a given market. Is the person in a position of *engagement*, where there are optimal prospects to meet and exchange with other individuals, or is the person *detached* from market activity? The qualities that determine such differences in position vary from one market to the next, and from one theory to the next.

For example, a central policy and theoretical concern is the importance of labor market position for immigrants' positions on other markets. Do those immigrants with paid work have more opportunity than those without? Presumably a job enhances individuals' opportunity to find adequate housing, have friends and feel good.[7] Acquiring a job however can be considered on its part dependent upon positions within markets for educational degrees and social skills.

This abstract characterization of positions, and their interrelations, easily leads to conceptual ambiguity. Bourdieu for instance has promoted the concepts of economic, cultural and social capital. Delineated succinctly here, economic capital refers to an individual's assets as to material goods, knowledge and skills; cultural capital refers to an individual's pattern of norms and values; and social capital to an individual's contacts and ties with (influential) others (Bourdieu, 1992; Roelandt, 1991). These three types of capital largely correspond with the three dimensions of individual integration delineated in the formal model. The comparison invokes several clarifying remarks.

Bourdieu's concept of economic capital corresponds with the notion expounded upon here of scarce social goods, the *possession* of which is a matter of competition between individuals. Success in accumulating possessions is expressed as a person's (relative) *wealth* or *deprivation*. The goods may be immaterial (such as knowledge or political favors), but they are perceivable inasmuch as they can be exchanged and also possessed. Moreover, they have a generally acknowledged value that can be expressed in material terms.

The idea that *cultural orientations* and *social behaviors* (Bourdieu's cultural and social capital respectively) also form objects of market competition is less tenable. An individual may aspire to adapt a particular cultural orientation, or to maintain specific contacts and ties. However, such personal characteristics are not possessed in the sense that they are acquired in exchange for other goods (except time). This is not to deny that an individual's status is rooted in cultural capital (i.e., a particular cultural orientation). A physician's position for instance on the job market is commonly attributed a high status, and the status is rooted in the specific cognitive and moral components considered characteristic for physicians' cultural orientations. However what remains marketable is the *objective* position, not the *subjective* orientation. Similarly, an individual's civic position may be rooted in his or her local contacts and ties (i.e., social capital). Favors for instance are exchanged on the basis of individuals' acknowledged position within a political network, but the network itself is not an exchangeable good. Like any abstract distinction, the three dimensions are theoretically and empirically intertwined.

Immigrant integration implies a dynamic. The integration of individual immigrants not only alludes to a subjective dynamic between social positions, cultural orientations and local behaviors. It also alludes to an objective dynamic between (a hierarchy of) social positions. This latter dynamic is embodied in the notion of *social mobility*: an alteration in an individual's social position. Whether this alteration can be perceived 'vertically,' i.e., as an improvement or decline in position, is in part a methodological issue considered in chapter four. It is above all a normative issue, dependent upon the perspective taken and the criteria used to evaluate the integration process. For an evaluation of individuals' social positions, these criteria are related to the structural dilemma concerning inequality and constraint.

Positional Detachment: Deprivation and Dependency

Two central concepts have been alluded to in the sub-sections above without explicit consideration, namely *marginalization* concerning a group's integration and *detachment* concerning individual integration. To conclude this section, these two concepts are brought in relation with the respective structural and positional dilemmas.

The concept of marginalization generally denotes a group's minimal participation in the central institutions of a society. Within the market metaphor used here to visualize local structures, it refers to a group's peripheral location upon local markets and consequently the limited access to social goods. Dichotomously opposed to marginalization is the concept of *enclosure*, which denotes the group's occupation of more pivotal market locations (cf. Schermerhorn, 1970:125ff). Whether enclosure is characteristic of a group's local integration, or contrarily of their local oppression, ultimately hinges upon the *legitimacy* and (centripetal or centrifugal) *direction* of local objectives. The group itself may opt for instance for a marginalized location rather than conform to the constraints of market regulations. Contrarily the group may aspire to more local exchange as a channel toward greater prosperity, only to encounter barriers to more enclosed market locations.

The concepts of enclosure and marginalization are complemented at a micro level by concepts of *engagement* and *detachment*. These denote the spectrum that represents individuals' secured opportunity to acquire local commodities. Referring again to the market metaphor, it contrasts the powerful image of the (engaged) *market broker* with the phlegmatic image of the idle individual. This latter person is not necessarily socially isolated, characterized by a minimum on local contacts, but his or her opportunities for local mobility are minimal. Turning again to the labor market for an illustration, the currently employed individual who scans the personal network in search of job opportunities may be considered more engaged than the newcomer whose search is limited to newspaper want-ads.

Allusions to the spectrum between engagement and detachment denotes in this study an individual's (combined) position on the various local markets.

From the perspective of the (hypothetical) immigrant, the distinction between engagement and detachment corresponds with the positional dilemma between dependency and deprivation. Liberated from the constraints bound to social engagements in the land of origin, the immigrant may hesitate to engage in local market trade. With perhaps little to offer except one's energy and time to labor, why relinquish this one commodity for the prospects of an education, job or home? Because as long as detachment is maintained, then one remains deprived of local goods and services. To attain these commodities, the immigrant must commit to exchanges, with their variant dependencies. There is of course a broad range of market exchanges and their corresponding dependencies. The focus in this study will be upon individuals' dependency on the state for the provision of necessary goods. Whether state dependency can be considered an 'upwardly mobile' form of engagement is again a normative issue. This positional dilemma between *dependency* and *deprivation* will be (re)considered in this chapter's penultimate section.

Culture and Orientation: Diversity and Conformity

The previous section focused upon the nebulous qualities of social structure. Regarding culture, the problem is not so much its imperceptibility but more centrally its ambiguity. Each word on this page is a manifestation of culture but it is never entirely certain which meaning a certain word may have for a given reader. This ambiguity forever limits the possibilities to clarify the notion of culture; in this section only those cultural concepts are briefly outlined that serve in this study by the measurement of immigrant integration.

I begin with a succinct review of the *culture* concept, tracing its theoretical evolution from a reified entity to an ambiguous symbol. This ambiguity leads to the notion of *cultural orientation*: individuals within a locality, competing within a given market for specific social goods, rely upon (a diversity of) culture to interpret their perceptions, and to instill their behavior and that of others with meaning. These orientations are not necessarily determinants for behavior, nor are they necessarily shared. I then return to the notion of *ethnicity*, touched upon in the first section, as a basis for cultural differences relevant to immigrant integration processes. Two parameters are presented, cohesion and toleration, whose interactions circumscribe the continued significance of ethnicity and other bases of cultural difference. Finally Schermerhorn's notion of *cultural congruence* is reviewed, and its micro level complement, *conformity*. A primary issue addressed in this section concerns cultural diversity and whether it can be understood as a cohesive and congruent (centrifugal) trend.

Cultural Patterns: Cognition, Morality and Expression

In everyday usage (cf. Allee, 1977:94; Sinclair, 1987:345), the notion of culture has four basic meanings pertinent to integration processes, each of which reflects particular theoretical perspectives. *Culture* may be construed as:

- society or civilization;
- the material and immaterial products of human endeavor;
- intellectual, artistic and behavioral refinement; and
- the ideas, customs and arts produced and shared by a specific group or society.

The concept used in this model corresponds most with the fourth variation. The idea of culture as synonymous with civilization dates back at least a century, to a time when social scientists were more concerned with unraveling the difference between man and other animals (cf. Gilmore, 1992:404 ff.). It was in this era that Edward Tylor's classic definition of culture was launched (1924:1):

> That complex whole which includes knowledge, belief, art, morals, law, custom, and any other capabilities and habits acquired by man as a member of society.

This conception is indeed so broad that it possesses little potential to differentiate between culture and other potentially human activities. Still it contains the limiting presumptions that such activities are 'acquired' and part of a single 'complex whole.' The second meaning, culture as man-made products, also dates from this era, and is more a complement than a serious alternative to Tylor's notion. Here culture is not human 'capabilities and habits,' but more exclusively the concrete manifestations of mankind's activities. Both these notions conceive culture as a commodity, a tangible entity or mental quality acquired and possessed. This reifying quality applies even more to the third everyday definition of culture as refinement. Here culture has become scarce, a quality that hierarchically divides the elite from the uncultured masses.

For my purposes, a concept of culture is needed that does not presume it to reflect a singular, desirable social entity, but instead a variety of customs and objectives that serve to regulate and appraise the distribution of social goods. With reference to Schermerhorn, a concept of culture is needed that captures 'the extent of satisfaction or dissatisfaction . . . with the differential patterns of participation' (1970:16). This means a concept sensitive to variations in individual states of consciousness, to how these individuals evaluate (market) activities, and to how such 'mental programs' (cf. Hofstede, 1980:14) may alter through time and circumstance. Kroeber and Parsons (1958:583), in delimiting culture from structure, provided a general definition adequate to these purposes:

> Transmitted and created content and patterns of values, ideas and other symbolic-meaningful systems as factors in the shaping of human behavior and the artifacts produced [by] behavior.

Culture can be perceived here as any dynamic pattern of symbols that is more than a fleeting fantasy, but is not entirely lucid nor determinant in its significance for human behavior. A central conceptual issue concerns the delineation and distinction between patterns of symbolic meaning. At least three distinctions are relevant for the conceptual model, namely *domains, components, and polarities*. These will be circumscribed sequentially:

- For each market in which social goods are exchanged, (divergent) cultures can be distinguished that signify and regulate transactions. Thus with respect to the job market recurring patterns may be identified, substantively distinct from the patterns bound to educational, housing, and welfare markets. Confusingly, markets may in themselves be considered the producers or distributors of culture, particularly those concerned with immaterial social goods (e.g., welfare services and local schools, cf. Rex, 1996:21). In a forthcoming section a distinction in six domains of immigrant integration is made that delineates the primary local markets.
- Within each domain, the cultural patterns consist of distinct, though conceptually interrelated, components. The possibilities are literally endless: distinctions between norms and values, between legal and informal traditions, facts and principles, immaterial ideas and material artefacts. Within the conceptual model a broad distinction between *cognitive, moral,* and *expressive* components of culture is made (cf. Peters, 1993). In the domain of labor for instance, a distinction can be

made between the technological knowledge needed for specific forms of production (cognitive), the principles that legitimate patterns of distribution and exploitation (moral), and the collective value and satisfaction associated with the finished products (expressive).

- *Cultural diversity* refers to a plurality of (partially) conflicting or *polar* symbolic systems of meaning within a given domain. Within the domain of labor for instance, two values have characterized individual beliefs since the advent of the Protestant ethic: one in which work is construed as a form of salvation, and another in which it is at best a necessary evil (Mok, 1990). Whether these are contradictory values reflecting the dilemmas contained within a single work ethic or, contrarily, are indicative of conflicting cultures, remains a matter of perspective, conception and conjecture. In short, it is an issue bound to the evolution of the culture concept. By presuming that a plurality of cultures may characterize a given domain, and that they are not necessarily related to cultures prevalent in other domains, a culture concept is used that is attuned to *diversity* and the dynamics of time, locality and marketplace (cf. Barth, 1969; Geertz, 1973; van den Berg and Reinsch, 1982; Vermeulen, 1992).

The concept of culture plays an often dubious role in debates on immigrant integration, in that perceived positional and behavioral differences are seen as - seemingly intrinsic - diversions and even deficiencies in immigrant cultures. Rather than presume that differences between immigrant and indigenous cultures are germane to the integration process, the distinctions made here serve instead to examine the possible significance of such differences. This is not to deny that cultural patterns can be perceived for instance among immigrant Turks that differ greatly from patterns observed among more indigenous residents. Whether these differences indeed coincide with the cultural polarities pertinent to local domains remains to be seen.

Cultural Orientation: Affinity and Imagery

At a micro level, complementary distinctions are conceivable around the notion of *cultural orientation*. Cultural orientation refers to the variant and relative significance attributable to specific cultures in forming individuals' identity (and guiding their thoughts and actions). Parallel to the culture concept, distinctions can be made in elements of individual cultural orientation pertinent to specific domains of exchange. The concept captures an adherence to a diversity of cultures within a domain, and the dynamics (i.e., *reorientation*) associated with cultural change. Within the domain of labor for instance, the concept of labor orientation refers to the pattern of knowledge, beliefs and affections that constitute individuals' ambition and capacity to seek, acquire and fulfill positions on the labor market.

Culture and cultural orientation are concepts designed to monitor and interpret processes within a variety of local domains. Their formal and abstract character however is prohibitive, since a great many polar cultures can be conceived that make up potential differences in individuals' orientations. When individuals are seen to be unique personalities, how can similarities fundamental to individual integration be recognized? Or, in Schermerhorn's terminology, how can centrifugal and centripetal trends be discerned? Schermerhorn himself focused upon 'the extent of satisfaction or dissatisfaction with . . . the differential patterns of participation' (1970:16), i.e., upon *expressive* differences. In the examination of the Haarlem data, I too will focus upon measures of satisfaction to identify orientational differences in individual integration. To examine more substantive theoretical issues concerned with the relation between cultural orientations and individual integration, I will focus particularly upon differences in ethnicity. The focus is arbitrary, since orientational differences in class, gender, or generation are also associated theoretically with cultures that transcend the boundaries of particular market domains. The degree in which ethnicity serves as a fundamental criterion that clarifies cultural differences between individuals is signified by the concept of ethnicization. More specifically, ethnicization refers to the local process in which the salience of ethnicity as orientational focal point increases in relation to other systems of meaning.

With ethnicity as focal point, two parameters will be derived and illustrated. Allow me to assume, for the next few paragraphs, that the cultural diversity within a locality can be consistently ordered along a single border. On the one side is an 'indigenous' culture, on the other an 'immigrant' culture. The elementary differences between these cultures can be observed in all market domains. A centripetal cultural trend would be a gradual fusion of these two cultures into one. A centrifugal trend would be, for instance, an evolution into three or more distinct cultures. The course of this process hinges upon two cultural parameters pertinent to (the two ethnically distinct) local groups. The first concerns the *cohesion* within each group, the second the *toleration* with respect to the *other* group.

Ethnic cohesion refers to the degree in which a group or category is culturally homogenous and perceives itself as a communal whole. A state of *cultural unity* is reflected for instance by common language, education and heritage (cognitive components), by shared beliefs and ideals (moral components), and by the observance of common cultural symbols and activities (expressive components). It is also reflected by a consistency across market domains. When for instance the immigrant culture with respect to the labor market is found ill-adapted to local processes, an immigrant faction or the entire group could adopt the indigenous labor culture. Across domains and their elementary components, the diversity of discernible factions suggests a lack of cohesion within the immigrant or indigenous group.

Ethnic cohesion pertains to processes of inclusion, i.e., a culture gradually encompasses more domains of local life or in its compatibility depreciates the group's susceptibility for other systems of meaning. The complementary concept of *toleration* pertains more to processes of exclusion. Toleration refers to the disposition toward the *other* (Saïd, 1978), throughout this study the *other* signifying members of other ethnic categories.[8] The perception of *other* groups or categories, concerning their cultural divergence from the own-group, can be considered, at least in theory, as a continuity ranging from highly similar to highly different (cf. Kleinpenning and Hagendoorn, 1991). The appraisal of this distance can also be seen as a continuity, ranging from a hostile aversion to an enthusiastic acceptance of the perceived cultural difference (cf. Hagendoorn, 1993; Walzer, 1993).

Corresponding concepts at micro level are provided by affinity and imagery. *Ethnic affinity*, as complement to cohesion, refers to the degree in which an individual perceives him or herself as member of an ethnic group, and gives priority to this membership above allegiances to other groups and categories. A minimal affinity may coincide with positive imagery for other ethnic categories, but this is not necessarily the case. Individuals may, in their ignorance of ethnic polarities, be oblivious to all distinctions along such lines (cf. Phinney, 1990:508). Contrarily, a conscious ethnic affinity may motivate individuals to consider cultural distinctions with other ethnic categories, and eventually lead to multipolar affinities. The individual counterpart to ethnicization is denoted by the concept of *ethnic orientation*. It refers here to the variant significance attributed to the immigrant (or indigenous) cultural origins in forming individuals' identity.

The hypothetical locality perceived in the previous paragraphs offers in its simplicity insight into the complexity of cultural processes. Already with only two cultures, individuals can vacillate greatly in their market orientations toward one culture or the other. In practice the boundaries between cultures, and their divergencies, are rarely clear. Considering the symbolic diversity and ambiguity of European urban life, the notion of immigrants 'choosing (only) between two cultures' (Eppink, 1981) seems naive. In chapter five the methodological issues associated with the perception and measurement of cultural orientations are elaborated upon. Specifically, the theoretical assumptions and activities will be outlined, necessary to discern whether an individual indeed is oriented more toward one culture than the other. To close this section, I turn now to the notion of conformity.

Cultural Incongruence and Disorientation

Imagine the bewilderment of a lone immigrant upon first arriving in an urban environment, confronted with new and weird perceptions. On the basis of experience and hearsay, only so much is self-evident. Quick to imitate, the immigrant notes that even the simplest of everyday actions elicits a wide variety of indigenous response. Either each situation differs imperceptibly from the previous one, or each indigene differs radically from the next. Or both. The immigrant, or any individual for that matter, can never be certain whether it's the prevailing culture that makes no sense, or that it's the person self who fails to fit.

I am of course overstating the case. Disorientation is rarely absolute. Via communication with (indigenous and immigrant) others we all gradually familiarize ourselves with the divergent ways to perceive and behave when surrounded by strangers. Moreover we continually reflect upon and revise our own moral culpability. With the case I emphasize the interpretative problems - for immigrants and social researchers - when confronted with cultural diversity. When (most European) localities are characterized by divergent cultures - that in themselves are permeated with disparities and archaic elements - how does one identify those cultural components crucial for individual and local integration? To this end I adapt Schermerhorn's notion of *(in)congruence* (1970:83). He used it to refer to the consensus between dominant and subordinate groups concerning the (centripetal or centrifugal) directions of intergroup process. Here it will refer specifically to the (lack of) consensus between indigenous and immigrant groups concerning local integration *objectives*.

The central cultural issue for instance pertains to objectives of *unity* or *diversity*. Do indigenous groups favor a fusion of cultures (i.e., unity), exemplified by the gradual reduction of cultural polarities within market domains? Or do they welcome (i.e., tolerate) more cultural polarities and therefore greater cultural diversification across local domains? When indigenous groups concur about these objectives, congruence is realized at (indigenous) group level; when immigrant groups consent to the same objective, congruence is realized at the local level. These conceptual distinctions are clearly little more than formal: instead of substantively identifying those cultural components crucial to local integration, the notion of congruence simply denotes that local groups concur concerning a given component's significance.

At the micro level of individual integration, the complement to cultural (in)congruence revolves around the notion of *(dis)orientation.* This notion reflects the tensions surrounding processes of group and local integration. Indigenous residents may for instance all underwrite objectives of cultural unity inasmuch as they expect immigrants to converse in the indigenous language. The individual immigrant who only speaks in his or her native tongue may conform to the language skills and objectives of entire immigrant categories. But the failure to speak the indigenous language is incongruent with local integration objectives. The limited language skills formally qualifies the individual immigrant as *disoriented,* but should the qualification be attributed to entire linguistic communities? The apparent paradoxes only increase where objectives of cultural diversity prevail: the individual conforms via nonconformity; the desire to conform denotes an individual's disorientation. The choice between objectives of cultural unity or diversity presents itself consequently as a dilemma: cultural *conformity* implies the denial of individual personality; the cultivation of personality fosters local *anomie.* The resolution to this dilemma is, I think, to focus not upon individuals' right to be different and their right to belong. The focus should be upon those cultural components that tax the limits of toleration. Toleration refers to the inherent right to disagree; cohesion refers to the social necessity to agree about something.

Interaction and Behavior: Exclusive and Inclusive Contacts

Theoretical and policy debates on Dutch immigrant integration commonly focus upon *structural* or *cultural* factors. Within this context, the (lack of) interactions between ethnic categories could be construed as the problem in need of clarification. In social research however interactions are largely overlooked as a distinct parameter of integration, either by associating them intrinsically with structural factors via the concept of *participation* (e.g., Veenman, 1994:9), or by using a culture concept that encompasses immigrants' interactions with the surrounding society (e.g., Vermeulen and Penninx, 1994:3). Here I will reveal my own difficulties in conceptualizing group interactions and individual behavior as more than the manifestation of structural and cultural processes. Nevertheless, I note that their theoretical status and empirical perception raise issues deservant of attention distinct from the other two dimensions.

The concern for immigrant integration as a *process* implies a formal distinction in three dimensions, if only to distinguish between and compare theoretical premises about the ongoing dynamic (cf. Peters, 1993:77ff). With reference to the market metaphor, it is presumed that individuals from divergent ethnic categories, in their occupation of specific market positions, are not compelled to interact with each other. Imagine all these individuals competing for strategic locations on the marketplace, their minds filled with ambitions and anxieties. Who talks with whom? Are they congenial or hostile toward each other (and do they agree upon the difference between congeniality and hostility)? Who regulates the access to the most lucrative locations? Is the control realized with communication or with apparent silence? Which individuals are ignored, and virtually isolated? With knowledge of the market structure and culture, a great deal could be predicted about individual behavior, but the ongoing dynamic between market individuals continuously alters structure and culture.

In this section the parameters of this interactive dimension are explored, introducing again central concepts at local and individual level. First the concept of *interaction* is considered, and its individual complement in a concept of *contacts*. The interactions between ethnic categories can be characterized in quantitative terms - by referring to their place, duration and purpose - and in qualitative terms - concerning their legitimacy and harmonious transition. These characteristics will be discussed in the second sub-section, along with complementary conceptions for the contacts between individuals. While in all these notions integration is acknowledged as a dynamic process, they all allude directly to a state or context. Central to issues of immigrant integration is the question whether interactions should be encouraged at all costs, or should harmony be preserved by keeping such interactions to a minimum.

Ethnic Interaction: Real and Potential Contacts

Few sociological concepts compete with *structure* and *culture* as to their abstract nature, but *interaction* is unquestionably one of them. Literally, interaction means nothing less than two entities acting upon each other. Sociologically the concept may cover the entire gamut of circumstance in which individuals, groups or societies exert and undergo external influence. It refers in this study specifically to the interactions between ethnic categories. This limitation is not intrinsic to the formal conceptual model, but is determined arbitrarily by the nature of the empirical (Haarlem) study. An adequate measurement of (potenital) interactions does however require that these attributes of the *actors* in the inter*action* be decided upon beforehand.

Here I am not directly concerned with the effect an ethnic category exerts upon other groups purely on the basis of the location they occupy in a given market, which is a structural issue. Instead my concern is the nature and intensity of their interaction with other categories. Interaction implies the exchange of information and other social goods but - due in part to the ambiguity of culture - it cannot be assumed that the goods received correspond with the goods sent. It will only be assumed here that, through interaction between ethnic categories, social goods are exchanged. There are however expectations or norms, derived from the cognizance of social structures and cultures, that lead actors to expect interaction of a specific intensity or nature. Such expectations are referred to when I speak of *potential interaction* or (at a micro level) *potential contacts*.

Permit me to illustrate these notions briefly. Imagine a locality with a single job placement office, in which indigenous mediators counsel a selection of job-seekers from all ethnic categories. In principle, the percentage of job-seekers counseled from a given category is proportionate to their percentage of all the job-seekers. This may be considered the *potential* interaction between job counselors and job-seekers; for the individual job-seeker it corresponds with the *prospect* of being mediated. With this potential, we then observe that a specific category of job-seekers has little interaction with the placement mediators. The explanation for this lack of access could be structural (e.g., the category has a marginal location in the office's data base) or cultural (e.g., the office harbors negative convictions concerning the category's placement prospects). The actuality is, the category is not receiving its potential share of the job mediation.

Interaction refers here explicitly to processes at local level between ethnic categories. At the individual level the notion of *contact* denotes communications between individuals. In this study the focus is accordingly the comparison of contacts (within and) between individuals of divergent ethnic origin. Actual contact between individuals can be observed and mutually confirmed by the actors concerned. Potential contact is again the chance of two actors communicating. Whether the potential is realized is a direct function of the separate actors' *behavior*, i.e., one or both may avoid contact. Like positions and orientations, social behavior is an individual attribute. For this reason the parameter at individual level is denoted more formally as the behavioral (as opposed to the contactual) dimension.[9]

The Nature of Contacts: Functionality and Intimacy

Assuming that local interactions can be observed and measured, what parameters further qualify their nature? First there is their location. The example above referred to job placement offices and, with reference to the market metaphor, a distinction can be made in various domains of interaction. Relevant to a concept of interaction is the precursory observation that domains differ in their nature. Some have a spatial character; others are characterized more by the social good being exchanged.

The second parameter pertains then to the goods being exchanged. What is the functional (i.e., intentional) nature of the interactions? Can the actual consequences for the separate categories be discerned? This parameter is explicitly tied to the structural dimension, but it is also bound intrinsically to cultural parameters. The categories may differ in the cultural components that characterize their market perspective; they may harbor divergent ideals and expectations as to the significance and objective of interaction. Consequently, they diverge in their appraisal of the actual exchange. Where the one group expresses satisfaction with the arrangement, the other finds it is entitled to a better deal.

This brings me to a third and most problematic parameter, namely whether the interaction can be characterized by *harmony* or *conflict*. Conflict is observed when the interaction results in physical harm or the destruction of material goods within either group. There are however less visible forms of conflict, for instance: the cultivation of grievances within a group (i.e., dissatisfaction) or the refusal to exchange necessary social goods with the other group (i.e., exclusion). These two examples illustrate the theoretical difficulties bound to this parameter. When grievances are expressed, they take the form of observable interactions. They might also smolder within the respective groups and either dissipate or manifest themselves through interactions with third parties. The example of a group withholding goods is similarly academic in its conception: the lack of interaction can only be observed in theory as 'unfulfilled potential.' The issue here is the range of causal reasoning used to observe and explain ethnic conflict.

To resolve these conceptual problems is the substance of (less formal) theory, and will not be dealt with here (see, e.g., Horowitz, 1985; Brown, 1993, 1997). Their significance for the appraisal of local integration is nevertheless crucial. The perceived culpability of one group for the other's deprivation raises issues of *legitimacy*: the extent in which a group's objectives and activities are construed as morally just (cf. Schermerhorn, 1970:68-71). For Schermerhorn legitimacy was central to the distinction between integration and other processes with a more coercive character (1970:77-85). Differences between indigenous and immigrant groups may be perpetually characterized by social inequality and cultural polarities. However, as long as the groups concur concerning the legitimacy of their interactions, then the (centripetal or centrifugal) process maintains - by definition - an integrative character.

How are these distinctions observed at the micro level of immigrant integration? There we observe individuals with their reciprocal contacts. Were all these contacts formal and fleeting, then discrepancies between potential and actual interethnic contacts might be minimal. However, individuals tend to develop *ties* with significant others; i.e., they rely on a network of family, friends and acquaintances for their ongoing social exchanges. A particular contact or tie with another individual varies along parameters of functionality and intimacy. *Functionality* pertains to the social goods exchanged or shared. The boss who only hands out directives and salary is a tie whose functionality is limited to one domain; the partner at home can be functional in all local domains. *Intimacy* pertains to the emotional affection entrusted in the tie; indicative for intimacy is for instance a notion of 'significant others' who are part of and partial to the individual's own identity. Important for my purposes is the observance of ties across ethnic boundaries. Do individuals' interethnic ties differ perceptibly in their functionality and intimacy?

Complementary to the difficulties observed at a macro level concerning the parameter of *harmony* and *conflict*, distinctions between *congenial* ties and those characterized by *hostility* are similarly ambiguous. Two individuals of divergent ethnic descent can maintain intimate ties without being conscious of any ethnic disparity; the relation might even end in hostility without differences in ethnic orientation being perceived. Contrarily, an individual may attribute a lack of ties, or a cessation of ties, to the intolerance of the *other* group. It remains open to conjecture whether the person is a victim of discrimination.[10]

Contact Diversity: Seclusion and Sociability

Four parameters have been differentiated concerning individuals' behavior: *ties* refer to the relative frequency of contacts, *functionality* refers to their positional range and *intimacy* their orientational affection, while *congeniality* and hostility allude to tension that characterizes the contact. Particularly the last parameter is ambiguous and encompasses several other parameters, dependent upon the perspective used to observe the contact.

The focus upon interethnic contacts reveals the difficulties involved in perceiving and interpreting the dynamics of integration. To illustrate the dilemmas they entail, let us consider again the predicament of a newly arrived, solitary immigrant. Solitude signifies social isolation, with no local ties to facilitate functional and intimate contacts. Perhaps he or she is willing to endure the paucity of contacts for the time being, not expecting the locals to include *others* automatically into their established networks. However in time, the uncertainty arises whether the continued isolation should be attributed to the immigrant's orientation (that may have no recognized value on local markets), or to the intolerance of the locals. The immigrant who decides not to acquiesce in the solitude can seek contact with indigenous locals and risk either the indignity of their hostility, of their token embracement of diversity, or their insistence on conformity. Alternatively, the immigrant could seek contact with other immigrants. Besides the risk that such contacts lead to similar indignities, such contacts are generally seen to inhibit endeavors to become part of the new environment. Moreover, in an urban environment where privacy is a scarce good, and the affluent appear more oriented toward global than toward local culture, the immigrant may wonder whether local contacts are all that necessary. In short, the immigrant must determine whether the source of the solitude is personal or environmental, and whether its alleviation is fostered by contacts with indigenous locals or with fellow immigrants.

Random interviews with local residents are not an adequate method to detect whether local interactions are characterized by harmony or conflict (this assertion will be clarified in chapter three). Nor can individual respondents, as actors with their subjective perspectives, attest to the reciprocal significance of their contacts for the *other* actors. The survey method does however provide possibilities to monitor how individuals seek resolutions to the behavioral dilemma of *solitude* or *sociability*. To this end I adapt and modify the interactive concepts of *exclusion* and *inclusion*. In contrast with (relatively) isolated individuals characterized by their paucity of contacts, a distinction can be made along ethnic lines in three types of contacts:

- *seclusive* contacts refer to communications with individuals from the same ethnic category;
- *inclusive* contacts refer to communications with indigenous individuals (or, for indigenous individuals, communications made with immigrants; and
- *eclusive* contacts refer to individual immigrants' communications with individuals from *other* immigrant categories.

The notion of eclusion (derived from the term eclectic) reflects my observation that in most European cities, contacts *between* immigrant categories represents an alternative form of sociability and a potential realm of conflict. The operationalization and measurement of these conceptual distinctions will be a central theme of chapter six.

Domains of Local Integration: Private and Public Space

In the previous sections three primary dimensions of immigrant integration have been circumscribed. These three dimensions bear upon the relations between ethnic categories, and between individual immigrant and indigenous residents. The formal outline of these relations has been quite abstract, even with occasional excursions into hypothetical job markets. In this section I slightly dissipate the abstract character of the conceptual framework. This is done by associating the framework with several *domains* of individual and local process. The notion of a domain used here refers to an entity in which social goods of a specific nature are produced and exchanged (cf. Hortulanus et al., 1993:62; Engbersen and Gabriëls, 1995b:23).

Any classification of local life into domains is arbitrary as to the choice of goods upon which is focused. The differentiation in six domains presented here is based upon a combination of three criteria: a theoretically adequate distinction that illuminates and eventually ranks a variety of concrete social issues; a distinction that corresponds with the policy sectors of (many Dutch) local administrations; and a distinction that individuals conceivably use to order and comprehend the various facets of their local life.

Allowing for these three criteria, six domains of local integration are distinguished: civic life, neighborhood environment, health and welfare, work and material security, education and upbringing, and a private domain. In the coming sub-sections, these will be delineated. In the process, various theoretical and social issues pertinent to immigrant integration will be cited. The - primarily Dutch - examples cited serve to illustrate the diversity of perspectives projected within the conceptual model.

Civic Life

This is the most abstract domain, as it ultimately excludes only those activities that take place in a *private domain* (cf. Choenni, 1992:88; Rex, 1996:18). It concerns all local activities in which an individual may meet previously unknown others. Civic life refers to a spatial realm, such as a shopping mall or public park, where a real possibility exists to encounter strangers. It also includes a less tangible communicative realm, in which interaction occurs through less observable media.

Within the domain of civic life (parts of) four other domains can be distinguished; all of them concern activities and situations outside the private circle of household and family. In this sense the civic domain could be regarded as a rest category: aspects of immigrant integration are perceived here that are not located in other domains. I prefer to consider this domain the basis from which other domains are distinguished. As a basis its boundaries vary from person to person, and from one group to the next. A Moroccan woman's perception of the limits to her civic life can differ radically from that of a Antillean man, and these imagined limits affect their respective perceptions of other domains. Taking into account the civic issues dealt with more directly in other domains, three facets of civic life are distinguished here.

- The first facet is the *differential access of public space*. The (in)accessibility of public localities for specific ethnic categories can be construed as a structural issue. Distances from particular neighborhoods and the quality of public transport may limit the opportunity to enter a given area. It is also a cultural issue. That Muslim women more readily avoid the company of strange men is an acknowledged norm in the Netherlands, but many cities have public areas where any woman's access is limited (cf. Rublee and Shaw, 1991). The issue of crime and public safety unveils an interactive component. There are divergent reasons why juvenile immigrants are regarded as a greater threat to public safety (cf. Hall, 1978; Bovenkerk, 1994a). In Dutch cities their prospects for contacts with local police have become in any event inordinately large (Junger, 1990; Junger-Tas et al., 1994; Haan and Bovenkerk, 1995; Haan, 1997).
- *Civil society and participation in social-cultural activities* refer to the institutional realm between the occupational, political and private life. It concerns the demand for, and uses of, cultural arrangements and events in public areas. Cultural expression is regarded here as a marketable social good regulated by processes of supply and demand (Ganzeboom, 1989; Knulst, 1989). This facet of civic life concerns issues rooted in the cultural dimension: what rights and privileges have immigrant groups to public podia and arrangements for the dissemination of their cultural heritage? Where such arrangements are available

- as podia and meeting rooms, parks and sport halls - when have the privileged the right to exclude other (ethnic) groups?
- *Public communication and political debate* form a third facet of the civic domain. There is a wealth of literature pertaining to (national) issues of citizenship acquisition and immigrant judicial rights (e.g., Bauböck, 1994; Kymlicka, 1995; Saharso and Prins, 1999). A focus upon local political processes considers the dissemination of information to immigrant groups, the participation of these groups in electoral processes (Rath, 1988; Gilsing, 1991) and their further prospects to influence local policy (Rath, 1991; de Haan, 1995).[11]

Neighborhood Environment

This domain provides, in a spatial sense, the intermediary boundaries between civic and private life. Does the frontier begin in the living room, beyond the front door, or out in the street? In other words, where, when and with whom are the privacy rights of individuals and families transformed into public constraints? Neighborhoods vary in the social goods that residents exchange and the affinities that they engender (Warren, 1977, 1978). Due in part to this diversity, the outer limits of the neighborhood environment are as much a cultural as a spatial entity. A wealth of literature has focused on neighborhood processes and their significance for immigrant integration. Four sociological studies deserve particular note, for the divergency of their theoretical approach and their influence upon (Dutch) empirical research. Park and Burgess (1925) originally proposed the 'contact thesis' in which the importance of (neighborhood) interactive processes is emphasized to alleviate structural inequalities and cultural intolerance (cf. van Niekerk et al., 1989). Elias and Scotson (1965) focused upon the shifting cohesion and toleration in working class neighborhoods (cf. Bovenkerk et al., 1985). Rex and Tomlinson (1979) examined the effect of local policy and other structural processes upon immigrants' housing position (cf. van Kempen, 1991). Finally, Wilson (1987) has dissected the complex interaction of structural and cultural factors that lead to urban ghettos, and the ghetto's capacity to stifle individual opportunity (cf. Engbersen, 1990). Here a distinction is made in two central facets of this domain.

- *Housing* is - next to education and labor - the central social good acknowledged and monitored as indicator of immigrant detachment in the Netherlands (Penninx, 1988; WRR, 1989; van Dugteren, 1993; Tesser et al., 1997). As a structural issue, it concerns immigrants' opportunity to secure the housing of their preference, and the possibilities for local authorities to regulate housing supply and distribution (Kornalijnslijper, 1988; Burgers, 1995). A cultural issue concerns the divergent housing needs and desires across ethnic categories (van Amersfoort, 1987). As for the contact thesis, one may wonder whether interethnic conflicts occur in spite of, or due to, government interventions that allocate social housing to immigrants (van Kempen, 1997). With this last issue - conflicts between (building) residents - housing issues merge with those of the surrounding neighborhood.

- The *neighborhood* can be considered spatially as a miniature locality with a diversity of markets; or symbolically as a social good in itself whose value is subject to market competition. Are there ethnic variations in the functions of the neighborhood environment,[12] and do these functions correspond with the concentration of immigrants in specific neighborhoods? Are interethnic tensions a manifestation of discrepancies in local positions, polarities in neighborhood cultures, or a failure to communicate (Vermeulen, 1990)?

Health and Welfare

This domain is concerned with those social processes that evolve around individuals' endeavors to realize 'health and happiness,' inasmuch as these are not acquired with a 'roof above one's head' (neighborhood environment) and a 'wad of bills' (work and material security). It encompasses more general issues of physical, mental and social welfare, rather than the (more limited) prevention of, and struggle against, sickness and disabilities. The possession of welfare is commonly construed as a private affair, but since Durkheim's studies on suicide (1897) sociologists have acknowledged its social significance. The concern here is with the local character of health and welfare services. Analogous to the three dimensions of integration, an analytical distinction is made between: 1) the supply and demand of health and welfare facilities, 2) ethnic-specific divergencies in personal health and welfare, and 3) individuals' informal network of ties, and how these relate to other aspects of health and welfare.

- Every society has standards of health, and these affect the ways in which individuals' ailments are manifested. Littlewood and Lipsedge (1989) for example specify obesity, anorexia nervosa, and agoraphobia ('housewives-disease') as typically Western, culturally-bound syndromes. Dutch empirical research has shown that immigrants, particularly those of Turkish and Moroccan origin, not only experience their health differently than indigenous Dutch. They generally experience their health as worse (Uniken Venema, 1989; ACOM, 1991; Uniken Venema and van Wersch, 1992). This raises issues regarding immigrant access to local facilities, the notion of welfare market position, and the significance of this position for individuals' position upon other markets.

- In this study variations in personal welfare are associated with notions of self-reliance and (dis)satisfaction. In the forthcoming section these notions will be allocated central locations in the conceptual model. Measures of public welfare use, and individuals' satisfaction with their local circumstance, are accordingly central criteria for the designation of individuals' degree of integration (see chapter three). A policy issue pertinent to local integration is whether minority categories are entitled to their own separate welfare facilities. In chapter five Haarlemmer residents' views concerning this issue will be addressed.

- Personal ties serve as a safety-net that relieve reliance upon local welfare services, provide personal satisfaction, and suspend social isolation. These three - causal - presumptions however can be reversed: a scarcity of public welfare services increases reliance upon personal ties; their function as source of satisfaction reflects a more general lack of affluence; and they may embody (seclusionary) processes that inhibit contacts with other locals. In chapter six I focus upon such issues, not to unravel their theoretical knots but more the measurement obstacles.

Work and Material Security

Work and material security are considered two central facets of the same domain. Work refers to individuals' physical and mental activities that result in the production or distribution of social goods; material security refers more generally to individuals' prospects for material wealth. The two are intrinsically related as work generates material security. They are central to a conception of immigrant integration since both are considered, in theory or policy, as indicative of individuals' positional engagement.

The boundaries to this domain are delimited by the market for material security: individuals must in one way or another have prospects for food and shelter. A salary received in exchange for one's labor is one source of material security. It can be augmented or substituted by many real and imaginary sources: business contacts and investment, knowledge and skills, welfare benefits and pension rights, marriage contracts and dowries, or a fundamental belief in humanity. Such alternatives allude to divergent theoretical clarifications for the marginalized positions immigrants occupy on the labor market and the poverty observed within particular immigrant categories. The three dimensions are briefly traversed to note divergent perspectives on immigrant integration rooted in this domain.

- An unequal distribution of material security reflects the inadequacy of market regulations and state interventions to ensure a minimum income for all. That immigrants are currently overrepresented among the so-called 'minima' can be clarified by their relatively weak judicial position. Market mechanisms that compel them to compete for positions with overqualified indigenous residents present further clarification. Evidence to the inadequacy of market interventions is the growth of an informal job market that capitalizes upon less legal (immigrant) labor (Kloosterman et al., 1997).
- That immigrants are inordinately dependent upon welfare benefits and other state sources of material security can be construed as a cultural 'deficit' or 'mismatch,' i.e., their orientation does not conform to the demands of European labor markets (cf. Cross and Waldinger, 1997:17ff). A 'culture of poverty' however, when it is perceived, is not necessarily the cause but the consequence of immigrants' marginalization (cf. Niekerk, 1993). Many immigrants apparently lack the knowledge and skills to compete beyond narrow and lower segments of the labor market. Or is the cultural divergency rooted more in the imagery held by indigenous employers, incapable of appreciating the divergent qualifications immigrants import (cf. Essed and Reinsch, 1991; Gowricharn, 1993b; Essed, 1994)?
- The actual interactions between indigenous employers and immigrant job-seekers are not commonly construed as hostile. However, considering the relatively high unemployment observed among immigrants, the interactions don't conform to potential. The problem may be in part a 'behavioral mismatch,' i.e., employers tend to seek labor along channels divergent from those used by immigrants in search of jobs (Hooghiemstra et al., 1990). However, various Dutch surveys and experiments also confirm that among comparably qualified applicants, employers favor indigenous to immigrant candidates (van Beek, 1993; Gras et al., 1996). In any event, the option for immigrants to establish their own businesses, or entire markets, has become an increasing focus of study (Choenni, 1997; Rath and Kloosterman, 1998).

Education and Upbringing

This domain encompasses activities in schools and other educational or day-care facilities. Conceptually however it concerns more general issues of socialization (cf. Hurrelman, 1975), and it involves a greater variety of actors and locations (cf. Rex, 1996:21). In the Netherlands - as anywhere else - the various means and ends are the subject of continual and fundamental debates. The issues raised can be ordered according to the three dimensions of integration differentiated in this chapter (cf. Veenman, 1995:117ff).

A century ago, the Dutch state acknowledged the right of private institutions to provide educational facilities with public funds. This act signified the establishment of a segmented educational market, in which facilities for Protestant or Catholic education formally became (separate but) equal to those of public education. It also signified national objectives of cultural diversity, i.e., divergent pillars were sanctioned to transmit cultural differences from one generation to the next. That education fulfills an important role by the distribution of labor has been acknowledged even longer. In the past the function of education could be conceived more as class *allocation*: children were equipped for the economic and social tasks they were destined to fulfill. Nowadays this function is seen more in meritocratic terms of *acquisition*: education is instrumental if not decisive for the position that individuals acquire on the labor market. Finally, education's compulsory nature can be considered with *interactive* concepts. When first regulated in the Netherlands, compulsory education served to protect the younger generation against the social injustices bound to child labor. It is now more generally seen to provide children with contactual skills and a network of peers. While correcting for potentially destructive excesses in parental upbringing it furthermore keeps delinquents off the streets. This brief historical sketch (based upon Brands et al., 1977:31ff) introduces three facets that focus more specifically upon issues of education and immigrant integration.

- Structural issues of *education and social mobility* concern on the one hand the determinants of educational opportunity and achievement. On the other it concerns the role of education for individuals' prospects for paid work and other channels of local engagement. Why (first and second generation) minority children achieve relatively little in Dutch schools has been the topic of an ongoing theoretical debate, in which the deprivations of working class background are pitted against the constraints of immigrant cultures (Driessen, 1990; van 't Hof and

Dronkers, 1993; Kloprogge et al., 1994; Pels and Veenman, 1996). That more education corresponds with better prospects for a job also applies for Dutch immigrants (cf. Dagevos and Veenman, 1992; Veenman, 1994; Veraart, 1996). When I note however that immigrants' current prospects are significantly lower than those of indigenous Dutch with comparable educational levels (Dagevos et al.; 1996:50ff), then individual opportunity and social mobility are obviously affected by other factors (cf. Veenman and Martens, 1995:39ff).

- The *transmission of cultural orientations* pertains to issues of cultural reproduction (Bourdieu, 1977) from generation to generation, and from school to individual. A basic function, e.g., of (primary) education is to imbue pupils with common knowledge and morals. Around this objective young minds are exposed to particular cultural beliefs for years on end. The diversity of school types (e.g., Public, Christian, Islamic) and curricular streams (e.g., intercultural, immigrant languages), and their effectivity in fulfilling the needs and expectations of parents and pupils, allude to issues at a local level (cf. Fase, 1994).

- The *cultivation of contacts* has served, for instance, as individual integration objective to legitimate the cancellation of Dutch curricular programs in immigrant languages and culture. Namely when local officials find that the (seclusive) time immigrant pupils invest in these programs can better be spent with *other* classmates, they now have the authority to intervene. Such interventions lay bear the divergent principles and priorities held by residents as to the nature and objectives of local integration. They also allude to the exclusion-inclusion dilemma that characterizes ethnic interactions.

Private Life

The sixth and final domain falls outside the public domains that directly pertain to local integration. Although like other domains the boundaries of private life are culturally flexible, there is presumably a spatial and social realm in which individuals' position, orientation and behavior are not legitimate concerns of state intervention. In other words, local integration objectives do not dictate the way individuals live their private lives (within certain judicial limits). My motive for monitoring this domain is that various theoretical perspectives consider private life indicative of, if not restrictive for, immigrant integration in other domains (cf. Ellemers, 1995:259). In the forthcoming chapters this domain will correspond with the spatial notion of a household or residential unit. The boundaries could be drawn along more sociological notions of (nuclear) family, or even along interactive lines of (in)formal exchanges. Such distinctions would however clearly overlap various public domains in a spatial sense. Moreover, they could not be sustained when considering the Haarlem data.

- In chapter four the variety of social goods exchanged within households and families will be considered. The focus will be primarily upon Haarlem variations in household size and composition. The literature suggests several structural obstacles to integration. Does a profusion of dependents correspond with diminished material security? Does the position of household dependent correspond with social solitude? What indications are there that single parents are more estranged? And when household composition conforms more to indigenous norms, is there more public evidence that the members are more integrated?
- Within this domain cultural issues concern in the first place the potential polarities between immigrant and indigenous 'family.' The Haarlem survey did not address such issues. Instead, the more general theoretical issue of ethnic orientation will be considered (in chapter five) as an essentially private matter (cf. Rex, 1996:14ff). Regarding the ambiguities characteristic of ethnic orientation measurement, I will consider how the notion can be understood in its relation to cultural polarities characteristic of other domains.
- Finally, a behavioral issue concerns the interethnic mix within households. Marriage outside one's (ethnic) group has often been viewed as a central indicator or even instigator of immigrant integration (cf. Lieberson and Waters, 1988; Hondius, 1999:40ff). In chapter six the Haarlem evidence on intermarriage will be sifted, to detect whether the individuals involved display other attributes indicative of their integration.

First the various objectives that constitute local integration processes will be reconsidered.

Integration Visions: Local Objectives and Individual End-goals

Until this point, integration has been understood as a process, although it has not been divided into possible phases. A figurative cube has been sketched, delineated by dimensions and domains, layered by individuals associated with variant categories, in the context of an urban locality. The cube remains a formal model *of a theory* as little effort has been made to clarify the relation between levels, dimensions and domains.

The model is constructed around the qualification that the integration of individuals and groups is perceived and evaluated as to their compliance with local objectives. Various objectives have been referred to in the previous sections that embody centripetal or centrifugal processes within specific dimensions. In this section these objectives will be reconsidered, combining them to sketch the contours of eight ideal-typical localities. For each objective a corresponding end-goal is also postulated, that signifies personal ideals at the micro-level of individual integration. This exercise serves to illustrate the normative aspects and empirical range of the integration concept. The various objectives and end-goals will be referred to regularly in the coming chapters to evaluate integration criteria.

Several terms must be qualified first. The notion of *local vision* refers to the ideal-typical combination of structural, cultural and interactive objectives. It signifies, at least for six of the eight combinations, a conceivable (i.e., viable) though imaginary urban environment. Visions are imaginary since they exist only in our minds, but they do represent social ideals that infuse meaning into local processes. The individual integration criteria derived from these local objectives are called end-goals. An *end-goal* is not quite a pleonasm, for it refers to the desired direction a process should take without presuming that the process is teleological (i.e., that it proceeds for that purpose), nor that the process will end should the goal be reached. I have alluded to the local objectives and their corresponding end-goals in the previous sections, often as a dilemma characterizing a given dimension. They are summarized as follows:

- In the structural dimension, *social equality* concerns the distribution of material and immaterial social goods. It is opposed to objectives of *civil liberty* since the realization of social equality presumably requires state interventions, while civil liberty refers here to a minimum on governmental constraints. The positional end-goal by objectives of civil liberty is the realization of *self-reliance*, i.e., a minimal reliance upon state programs, facilities and other forms of intervention. By objectives of social equality, with the corresponding dearth of variation in (im)material wealth, personal end-goals are embodied by ideals of *selflessness*.

- The cultural dimension is construed as a spectrum between objectives of *cultural unity* - the compatibility of cognitive, moral and expressive components within public domains - and *cultural diversity*, which signifies conflicting or polarized symbolic cultural patterns within public domains. For individuals, these objectives correspond with end-goals of either *conformity* or *personality*. The former signifies an orientation prevalent among (predominant) others, while the latter signifies an orientation unique in its combination of knowledge, beliefs and affections.

- Interactive objectives pertain specifically to the relation between immigrant and indigenous categories. Centripetal processes, characterized by increasing interactions and a gradual dissolution of ethnic boundaries, are denoted as *inclusion,* while centrifugal processes of decreasing interaction correspond with objectives of *seclusion.* At the individual level, these objectives correspond with end-goals of *sociability* or *privacy,* when these qualifications refer to a profusion respectively a paucity of contacts with individuals from *other* ethnic categories.

When each of the diametrically opposed objectives is combined with objectives from the other two dimensions, a total of eight local visions results. These eight combinations are presented in table 2.1. Each represents a discrete set of criteria: for the determination of local processes as integrative or coercive (dependent upon the compliance of indigenous and immigrant groups), and for the evaluation of individuals' situation within this context (as integrated or estranged).

The adequacy of these visions as reflections upon distinct and viable objectives is of course debatable. They are based upon the presumption that the correspondence between end-goal criteria applicable for the evaluation of individuals' circumstance, and objectives that characterize entire localities, is *direct* and *enduring*. Were the relation indeed direct, then visions would become more manifest with each individual that meets end-goal criteria. This presumption reduces localities to the sum of their separate inhabitants, a non sociological premise but necessary given the (democratic) principle of compliance central to the integration model. Was the relation enduring, then centrifugal processes of market liberalization or cultural diversification would not alternate with processes of a more centripetal nature. This presumption signifies a rejection of sociological perspectives in which the pursuance of social objectives is characterized more by conflict than by consensus. The idea of a gradual and enduring consensus concerning local objectives may be unrealistic, but an alternative viewpoint would require less formal (i.e., more substantive) theories concerning the successive phases in the local integration process, and concerning the (incongruent) objectives and end-goals of the conflicting groups.

Table 2.1 Eight visions of local integration and their corresponding end-goals for individual integration

structural objective	cultural objective	interactive objective	local vision
social equality	unity	seclusion	mechanic
social equality	diversity	seclusion	organic
civil liberty	unity	seclusion	racialized
civil liberty	diversity	seclusion	pillarized
social equality	unity	inclusion	communistic
social equality	diversity	inclusion	egalitarian
civil liberty	unity	inclusion	assimilated
civil liberty	diversity	inclusion	tolerant

positional end-goals	orientational end-goals	behavioral end-goals	local vision
selflessness	conformity	privacy	mechanic
selflessness	personality	privacy	organic
self-reliance	conformity	privacy	racialized
self-reliance	personality	privacy	pillarized
selflessness	conformity	sociability	communistic
selflessness	personality	sociability	egalitarian
self-reliance	conformity	sociability	assimilated
self-reliance	personality	sociability	tolerant

Comparable typologies are widespread in the field of ethnic studies. This one is derived from the two-dimensional typology presented by Schermerhorn (1970:83, see figure 1.1), in which cultural and structural distinctions are crossed with (shared) centripetal or centrifugal objectives (cf. Portes and Manning, 1986). Schermerhorn's focus upon shared objectives was an explicit response to the typology formulated by Wirth (1945), in which four basic objectives were formulated (only) from a minority group perspective: assimilation, pluralism, secession, and militantism. A derivation upon Wirth's four types is prevalent in social psychological literature concerning (minority) individuals' end-goals. At individual level general distinctions are then made (e.g., by Berry et al., 1986; see table 6.1) between the assimilated, acculturated, separated, and marginalized. Essentially, Schermerhorn recognizes four trends, all of which can be construed as *integrative*, where two of the four identified by Wirth (i.e., secession and militantism) tend toward *conflict*.

The added complexity of the three-dimensional typology presented here provides necessary nuances in at least two ways. First, it reveals the formal distinction within so-called pluralistic visions, between localities with either a paucity or a profusion of interactions between culturally divergent groups. Secondly, the inclusion of egalitarian visions alludes to the possibility of (culturally diverse) localities, in which the primary objective is not so much the cultivation of ethnic differences. Instead the emphasis is upon the realization of equitable differences. This latter nuance is based upon the presumption that culturally diverse communities are not necessarily characterized by processes of ethnicization. Residents without ethnic affinities in such localities may meet end-goal criteria even though - according to the typologies prevalent in social psychology - they are ethnically 'marginalized.' Of course, many others have noted and conceptualized these nuances (e.g., Mullard et al., 1990:50ff; Marger, 1991:113ff; Rex, 1996:14ff). Here they are more explicitly derived from Schermerhorn's framework. I will briefly describe each vision with references to theoretical and social traditions.

Mechanic and Organic Visions

The first two visions are the most difficult to visualize. Social environments with a paucity of interactions between ethnic categories, nevertheless sufficiently regulated as to assure social equality between and within the categories, may be ideal-typical. They remain, however, perpetually fictitious. Presumably a species of insect exists (e.g., a colony of snails) who have similar productive tasks, consume from a common cache, and conscientiously pursue communal objectives, yet conduct their activities in spatially exclusive groups. As a homage to sociology's first typology of integrated societies (Angell, 1968:381), Durkheim's concept of *mechanical solidarity* is adapted here to denote this culturally homogeneous anomaly.

Durkheim's typology (1893) did not refer to localities characterized by egalitarianism and ethnic seclusion. Nor did his concept of organic solidarity pertain to cultural diversity, more to a diversity of functions (and corresponding positions) that complement each other in realizing common objectives. It is adapted here, instead of more contemporary distinctions, to help visualize an array of groups, all variant in their cognitions, morals and expressions, who coordinate their separate qualities and activities to be harmonious and equitable. Again allusions to the insect world (e.g., a contingent of bees) appear more appropriate than references to the social world.

Racialized and Pillarized Visions

These two visions lack, in contrast to the previous two, objectives of social equality between individuals and ethnic categories. A minimum of market constraint is more the common characteristic, prosperity guaranteeing the security of a fortunate few. The visions are consequently more abstract (i.e., mechanic and organic could be considered sub-visions) and at once more viable. They differ again in the appreciation of cultural diversity. Racialized visions characteristically propagate the superiority of a specific culture, a *way of life* appropriate for all though some categories are innately better equipped. Such innate differences, according to many 19th century social-evolutionists and European colonial regimes, could best be respected through practices of seclusion (cf. Furnivall, 1948). The segregation of Afro-Americans in the US Deep South prior to the Civil Rights movement also reflected a racialized vision (cf. Rex, 1996:16), assuming for expository purposes that Afro-Americans actually complied with this vision.

Pillarized visions disregard the premise of an imperial culture, superior above others and appropriate for all. In a more organic social conception, the potential for separate ethnic categories to coexist and even collaborate by the realization of structural objectives is acknowledged and accentuated. This *separate but equal* vision also served to legitimate seclusive processes in colonialized environments (e.g., South Africa, see M.G. Smith, 1965, 1986), and in early 20th century Dutch society (Lijphart, 1968; Bagley, 1973).

The associations made here with South African and Dutch society illustrate nuances that 'seclusionary' visions necessarily contain, regarding the specific domains in which interaction between ethnic categories is condoned. In South African Apartheid, local interactions occurred primarily on the labor market, though it too remained segmented along ethnic lines (Bonacich, 1972). The Dutch experience called for seclusion consistent with religious orientations in various educational, labor, political and leisure institutions. Yet it was less pervasive in the more spatial domains of neighborhood environments and civic life. Were these nuances not evident, then the visualization of a given urban environment as a single locality would be difficult.

Communistic and Egalitarian Visions

Moving to visions in which the interactions between ethnic categories are viewed less apprehensively, the first two highlight collective objectives of collaboration and structural equality. The communistic vision finds its primary philosophical foundations in the work of Karl Marx, who envisioned a community of man so unified in purpose and perspective that the need for state intervention would eventually disappear. Millions in Eastern Europe and Asia have experienced less visionary manifestations of communistic objectives of cultural unity, namely the dissipation of the private domain.

A fundamental characteristic (or flaw) of the communistic vision is the presumption that a locality of responsive and responsible individuals can all share the same orientation, i.e., think the same way. Egalitarian visions, at least the more democratic variants, retain an emphasis upon objectives of social equality while acknowledging the vitality of cultural diversity. A characteristic egalitarian theme is for instance that individuals entering a given market have *equal opportunity* to acquire the social good, e.g., the realization of equitable starting positions upon the labor market via state regulated educational facilities. Concerning this objective, egalitarian visions focus upon the excesses of free market processes, and upon the inequalities resulting from exclusion (cf. Habermas, 1988; Cohen and Arato, 1992; Giddens, 1994:190ff). The past several decades they have served in many Western countries, including the Netherlands, as ideological bases for affirmative and positive action policies (cf. Bovenkerk, 1986).[13]

Assimilated and Tolerant Visions

In contrast to the state interventions characteristic of communistic and other egalitarian visions, in these last two visions state constraints are liberally minimized. Assimilated visions focus upon the potential to fuse a (new) unity out of a diversity of cultures, the *melting pot* being an emblematic metaphor. In the Netherlands the notion of assimilation is commonly associated with the oppression of cultural difference by a dominant (indigenous) group (cf. Mullard et al., 1990:32ff) but, as I have emphasized, where subordinate groups also comply with objectives of cultural unity, the local process is integrative rather than coercive.

The tolerant vision has no unifying cultural objective, and is therefore dependent upon other qualities to entice and retain its 'adherents.' These characteristics concern an appreciation - or glorification - of difference for its progressive value.[14] The foundations to this vision in social theory are as diverse as the cultures it celebrates. The idea of social interaction (and ultimately, history) having no purpose more lofty than the interaction itself can be linked with the phenomenological sociology of Schütz and Elias. I associate this vision most with the philosopher Walzer, whose work has focused upon the possibilities to combine cultural diversity with ideals of civil liberty and social justice (Walzer, 1983, 1991, 1997; Trappenburg, 1993; van den Brink, 1994).

A more detailed consideration of the eight visions goes beyond the focus of this study. They are introduced here to illustrate the potential provided by the parametric distinctions to sketch the contours of divergent processes of local integration. Along with the innovations, the distinction in eight visions has its weaknesses. As pointed out in opening this sub-section, the correspondence between local visions and individual end-goals presumes a one-on-one correspondence between processes at local and individual levels. Nor are these visions infused with *local* qualities that distinguish them from visions concerning the nation-state.

Most pertinent for the investigations in the forthcoming chapters is whether the notions used to designate individual end-goals indeed possess sufficient clarity to generate valid measurements of individual integration. By the examination of the Haarlem data, my intention is to focus upon the possibilities to perceive local processes according to criteria associated with a tolerant vision. This normative concession is made not only for purposes of simplicity and consistency, it is motivated by personal convictions concerning the desirability and viability of tolerant objectives. Before moving to these issues, I consider more generally the potential and problems of the conceptual framework.

Assessment: Theoretical and Normative Tensions

Awed by the diversity of normative criteria, theoretical perspectives and empirical focal points encompassed by a notion of immigrant integration, in this chapter I have devised a framework. With this formal model my intention is to:

- order and evaluate the adequacy of survey measurements made in one locality,
- elucidate criteria that differentiate between the integrated and the estranged, and

- consider the possibilities to measure various parameters and estimate their potential to clarify differences in individuals' integration.

In closing this chapter the central parameters contained in the model will be reviewed while I note the more obvious obstacles that inhibit my three analytical intentions.

For the reader's convenience, the central parameters that make up the model are displayed in figure 2.1, at the end of this chapter. The scheme shows two sets of cubes, the upper one representing parameters of local integration, the lower one parameters of individual integration. Not visible in figure 2.1 are two other parameters introduced in this chapter, namely the distinction in observational perspectives and the parameter of time. Moreover, concepts associated with a (meso) focus upon processes of group integration are not displayed in the figure, nor have they been developed in the sections above. Criteria for group differentiation serve nevertheless as a parameter within the formal model: distinctions for instance in (cultural) toleration and (interactive) exclusion presume in- and out-groups. In this study these groups are so-called ethnic categories, differentiated according to individuals' (parents') geo-political regions of birth.

Can the Model Help Order and Evaluate Survey Observations?

The coming chapters provide substantive testimony in answer to this query. A preliminary assessment of the models' lucidity and validity elicits two central criticisms.

First, in the parsimony and symmetry of its cubic image (i.e., parametric distinctions in levels, dimensions and domains of integration), the model's abstraction leads to ambiguities. This problem is discernible in various areas of the figure. It has been noted by parameters within specific dimensions, for instance the distinction between *regulation* and *intervention*, or the spectrum between *harmony* and *conflict*. Also the divergent nature of domains, as spatial or more imaginary realms structured around markets for (arbitrarily designated) social goods, is a priori ambiguous. The possession of a job for instance is indicative of an individual's position in the domain of work and material security. Yet most jobs also have a spatial quality, i.e., they are held within a household or neighborhood, within or outside the individual's home locality. The 'vertical' parameter of the cube is arguably the least lucid, namely a distinction in (e.g., micro and macro) levels of focus. That the one level fixes upon individuals within the local context, and the other upon the locality as more than the totality of its inhabitants, suggests more the intrinsic bond than the distinction between the two levels.

The second problem concerns the parameter of time. Integration is a process, but with certain exceptions (e.g., *mobility* and *contacts*) the model's parameters pertain to static attributes, i.e., individual and local circumstance that can be observed in the same moment. This quality is intentional, as the model has been primarily designed to order survey data gathered from individual respondents, and surveys are almost by definition ephemeral observations. Presumably the integration dynamic could be observed with a series of (panel) surveys, in which the model is used to monitor individuals' process through given intervals. There are however too many parameters to derive a lucid explanation why an individual's integration proceeds as it does. Particularly the problems bound to the measurement of parameters at group and local level, and the estimate of their effect upon processes at individual level, undermine the prospects of clarifying individual integration (solely) by means of repeated survey measures. These issues are methodological, and apply more generally to observations limited in focus and time span. Nevertheless, I must remain wary of the presumption that the process of integration is simply a sequence of separate moments.

Does the Model Clarify the Normative Criteria that Designate Who Is Integrated and Who Is Not?

Only to a limited, ambiguous extent. For instance, objectives of cultural diversity and toleration do little to delineate a normative criterion of *personality* (i.e., nonconformity). Do they imply that immigrants acquiesce in their estrangement, or that indigenous residents respect and respond to immigrant dissatisfaction?

This example illustrates a more general normative issue concerning the interpretation of (dis)satisfaction. Where individual integration is defined as the 'active and coordinated compliance with the ongoing activities and objectives of other local resident,' any observed failure to comply means that the individual is not integrating. Moreover, it implies a lack of consensus concerning the accepted activities and objectives. Considering the diversity of activities and objectives characteristic of urban localities, the possibility of a consensus concerning any given issue is - by definition - zero. When then does dissatisfaction designate a local crisis in legitimacy, and when an individual failure to integrate? The issue pertains to the conceptual distinction between processes of integration and processes of coercion. In social reality, it is not resolved with the realization of a consensus shared by all, but a consensus rooted in the democratic legitimacy of authority. In the coming chapters a variety of interpretative problems will be considered, bound to the observation of integration criteria in specific domains.

Does the Model Facilitate the Measurement and Comparison of Various Parameters as to Their Significance for (Individuals') Integration?

This again is an attribute that will be illustrated in the coming chapters, although the systematic comparison of Haarlem survey measurements will focus more upon methodological problems than upon theoretical clarifications. The model is designed to provide a framework in which, e.g., the possession of educational diplomas or a profusion of indigenous contacts can be compared for their potential to clarify immigrants' degree of integration. To assume however that the model offers an unbiased platform for the comparison of theoretical perspectives would be naive. As pointed out in the first sub-section directly above, perspectives that focus for instance upon *time*, i.e., integration as a historic and interactive process, are not taken sufficiently into account.

The limitations are ultimately bound to the functionalistic nature of the integration concept. I have relied heavily upon Schermerhorn's conceptual framework to devise the model, in part because his framework (also) foresees integration in the (centrifugal) processes of diversification. Nevertheless in Schermerhorn's approach, and in the model presented here, integration is presumed to be a process delineated less by the (historical) past, than by the (future) objectives. Integration is not so much the resolution of (current) social problems and conflicts, but more teleologically the realization of (shared) objectives. Consequently, where two perspectives on a specific social problem are compared, the perspectives are evaluated less for their potential to *explain* the problem, and more for the integration obstacles the problems *imply*. The problem of inordinate immigrant unemployment can be perceived for instance as a (structural) process of diminished labor market demand or as a (cultural) process of deficient immigrant ambition. That immigrant unemployment forms a problem is a presumption implicit to both perspectives. However, when perceived for instance from a *tolerant* local vision, the former implies that immigrants acquiesce in their deprivation, while the latter perspective implies their supposed aversion to work be respected. This example illustrates the value of the integration concept, as it forces one to articulate the normative criteria used to perceive a given phenomenon as a social problem. It also shows the (cultural) bias contained in the concept to perceive phenomena as to their significance for the realization or retention of a shared consensus.

With this observation, on the relative value of conceptual definitions and democratic consensus, I am about to embark on more empirical ventures. Let us now consider more concretely the problems and possibilities of distinguishing the integrated from the estranged.

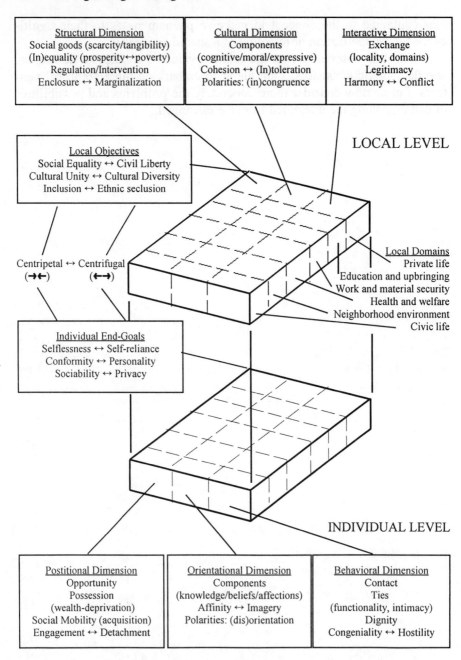

Figure 2.1 Parametric concepts within the construct of immigrant integration

3 Contextual Considerations

A conceptual framework has been presented in the previous chapter, designed to comprise the process of immigrant integration. Two parallel sets of concepts were introduced, referring to the perception of integration processes at individual and at local level. Where my goal was to derive and describe a coherent model, in the forthcoming four chapters I will examine its utility. In the process a range of methodological issues will be encountered that inhibit comprehensive and valid measurements of individuals' integration. The focus will be upon survey data collected from inhabitants of the city of Haarlem. However, in the search for more adequate measurement tools a broad range of empirical research will be considered.

To commence these observations, I first reflect in this chapter upon the epistemological limitations bound to survey methods. The insights and illusions derived from survey observations have been extensively documented, and it is not my intention to oversee this literature here. My more specific purpose is to consider various aspects characteristic of surveys among immigrants that render such observations suspect. In the process, some contexts and characteristics of the Haarlem survey will be conveyed. These observations revolve around the following question:

What factors limit the adequacy of empirical observations derived (solely) from survey interviews with immigrant (and indigenous) individuals?

First the local context is considered in which the survey is situated, i.e., how at local level the research activity affects and is affected by the process it is meant to measure. Issues of categorization and survey sampling are touched upon in the second section. Some general characteristics of the Haarlem (sub)samples are herewith presented. In the third section the step from categories to individuals, and from subjects to respondents is made, as I consider communication problems bound to interviews with individuals of divergent (linguistic) origin. Particularly the interviewer-respondent relationship is an object of concern. Then in the fourth section central criteria are presented with which the individually integrated are distinguished from the estranged. More specifically five measures are selected from the data and combined to rank individual respondents along a single index. The derivation of this index is steeped in theoretical, methodological and ultimately normative presumptions. Having introduced the

index, it will subsequently serve in the forthcoming chapters as a (normative) standard, with which other measurements of individuals' attributes are
compared and evaluated.

The Research Context: Environments and Agents

With the distinctions drawn between dimensions, domains and objectives
of integration, I intend to observe and evaluate the relations between individuals and ethnic categories within an urban environment. Considering
the reliance upon structured interviews, I first reflect upon the particular
perspective provided by individual residents. In the process, some characteristics of the Haarlem locality will be presented.

The Haarlem Context: Historical Town within an Urban Conglomerate

In chapter two, the terms 'locality', 'urban environment', 'city', and 'surrounding' have been used synonymously. They refer to any area characterized by a near continuous sequence of buildings, where a predominantly
non agrarian collectivity resides. The buildings are grouped around - and
the residents may be oriented toward - a center of commercial, service,
artistic or academic activity. This description may seem straightforward
but it is rarely clear where the locality ends, in relation to surrounding
rurality or to bordering localities.

The city of Haarlem is a distinct geo-political entity with legal limits
enclosing 30 square kilometers of land. Essentially all this land is cultivated; with 5026 inhabitants/km² it is eleven times more densely populated
than the nation as a whole (Haarlem, 1995:7). The city was founded more
than 750 years ago and has functioned for centuries as a commercial center, as the provincial capital of North Holland, and as a center for the arts
(cf. van Turnhout, 1995). Of the 150,000 residents - a number, tallied at the
end of World War II, that has remained essentially stable the past decade
(Haarlem, 1995:15) - 82% of the adults are indigenous Dutch, 32% of
whom are native to the city.[1] I note, before considering immigrant residents' relation to their locality, that a majority of the indigenous inhabitants
have also moved to the city from elsewhere in the Netherlands.

The city provides commerce and services for its inhabitants and those
of the surrounding region. It also serves as a sea of relative tranquility for
commuters to cities and industries elsewhere in the surrounding urban
conglomerate. Pastureland to the east separate it from Schiphol airport and
Amsterdam's industrial areas; dunes to the west lead to the coastal resort of

Zandvoort and the North Sea. To the north Haarlem residential districts merge with those of neighboring towns, with Ijmuiden's harbor and steel industry looming in the distance. To the south similar mergers occur, only these districts gradually unfold into the heart of Holland's flower industry. I note, before examining whether immigrant residents are sufficiently part of their new locality, that the more integrated among the indigenous residents could very well display greater affinity toward markets and ties in The Hague, Amsterdam, and beyond.

Urban environments obviously differ in size, population density, the commuter and migratory routes to surrounding and distant regions, and the extent in which they function and have functioned as an economic, political, and cultural center. These factors and more render comparisons between localities regarding the integration of immigrants problematic.

The Survey Context: Client Directives and Sensitive Issues

The decision about which locality forms the research context is rarely left to the (dice roll of the) empirical researcher (cf. Penninx, 1992). Should research lack the restriction that an urban environment is randomly selected, then the availability of funds and clients affects the choice of research context - and the research content.

The research in Haarlem was initiated by local civil servants, who arranged subsidies from the municipality and two state ministries. We were not commissioned to measure immigrant integration and it was not our objective to do so. Our task was to devise criteria with which local policy initiatives could be evaluated for their potential to encourage local integration (cf. Reinsch et al. 1995:263). More generally, local authorities wanted to revise existing minority policies, and commissioned us to order and interpret the views and experiences of local residents. Within this context we focused upon the (local) issue, 'what local integration policies do residents want'? We were only indirectly concerned with the issue, 'which residents are integrated and which ones not'?

Local officials also monitored the research process. Such collaboration helps narrow the range of local issues measured and evaluated. On the one end, they may advise researchers to ignore a range of topics because local experts consider them *nonissues*. The advice is well taken as researchers prefer to measure pertinent parameters as opposed to less sensitive constants. However, when measuring local integration, it can be crucial to record the views that everyone shares. On the other end, a range of topics may be found too sensitive within the local context, as they may strain the researchers' relationship, either with respondents or with local officials.

The Respondents' Context: A Pattern of Subjective Viewpoints

The study of Haarlem integration processes is based primarily upon data derived from survey interviews with individual residents. Although I will illustrate the wealth of theoretical and empirical insights that can be derived from survey research, it has its limitations. These are bound to the reliance upon standardized interviews to observe the diversity of perspectives, and upon the subjective nature of these viewpoints. Why can't I rely on randomly selected individuals to detect local objectives, and qualify those who comply with them?

First, because in their particular *positions*, individuals cannot oversee the social processes that converge within the locality. Those occupying higher positions (in a literal sense) can look beyond the immediate surrounding, but even they cannot perceive all the processes taking place. Individuals - and survey respondents - may perceive a visible *other* as their adversary, while the source of deprivation and hostility is a social process occurring faraway.

Besides position, individuals differ in their *orientations*. Their social expertise and affinities may all vary immensely. A central issue in this context is the disparity between the end-goals of individuals - aspiring to variant degrees of wealth, happiness and congeniality - and the objectives of entire localities. Even when all residents express congruent convictions concerning personal and communal goals, this does not imply that the goals are viable. The designation and pursuit of local objectives are all the more problematic where orientations diverge.

In completing this brief round, the interpretation of individuals' expressed behavior is ridden with ambiguity. Many indigenous residents may never converse with their immigrant neighbors (e.g., out of respect for personal privacy). Others might regularly seek such contacts as a matter of principle (and curiosity). To conclude that the latter are better suited for residence in a *tolerant community* requires many presumptions. My point is allusively simple. It is quite difficult to predict how the contact between two individuals will proceed, based upon knowledge of their behavioral characteristics and intentions. To do so for entire groups, based on random interviews with individual members, presumes that social process varies with the relative (will)power of individual participants. This would mean that the interaction evolves according to the collective purpose of the more powerful group. The outcome of even the most innocuous political debate is - fortunately - difficult to predict. This applies even more for interactions between local groups, indigenous and otherwise.

What can be learned from interviews with individual urbanites? They provide an indication as to how residents perceive and evaluate their relation to their local environment. This information is partial to the individual; it is limited in its potential to identify integrative factors beyond the concrete historic, geographic and personal context; and the information is temporary in nature. Let us now briefly consider how the specific context of survey interviews raises more doubts as to the adequacy of the measurements.

The Interview Context: Diversity and Survey Standards

To realize a representative measurement with a maximum potential for generalizations, the cooperation of individuals is essential. This means that time and information must be solicited from a wide range of respondents. We had to reckon with an unknown number of respondents who were, for instance: unaware of local integration issues, longing for personal attention, wanting to learn how we knew their name and address, and reluctant to have local authorities intrude in their private affairs. Accordingly, these reactions raise the issue whether *problematic* and *ideal* urban environments exist for the measurement of immigrant integration.

The social sciences have acknowledged professional codes meant to protect survey respondents. We could assure respondents for instance that their answers would remain confidential and their participation unknown to public officials (see Kidder and Judd, 1986:500ff). Certainly after we informed them - again according to professional codes (Kidder and Judd, 1986:495ff) - that our objective was to advise local authorities of their experiences and perspectives. Where the objective is to measure individual integration, finding and interviewing the estranged lower end of the sample is particularly problematic (cf. Visscher, 1997).

In a forthcoming section the interviewer-respondent relation is considered more in depth, particularly where (immigrant) respondents require interviewers who speak the same language. Language differences relate however to other ethical issues worthy of mention here. Kidder and Judd differentiate ten categories of 'questionable practices' encountered in social research (1986:461ff). In formulating questions and structuring answer categories, even in a language native to the respondent, the researcher potentially engages in half these practices, namely: 1) invading the privacy of the participants; 2) leading the participants to commit acts that diminish their self respect; 3) exposing the participant to physical or mental stress; 4) failing to treat participants fairly and to show them consideration and respect; and 5) violating the right to self-determination. The researcher can reduce the problematic nature of these practices by:

- striving for *brevity* in the survey interview;
- formulating questions that in their *simplicity* do not form an affront to individuals' dignity; and
- using universally acknowledged response categories that facilitate *comparability*.

These three criteria complement two other criteria commonly considered intrinsic to the measurement process, namely:

- *reliability*, which here refers to the consistency of response when interviewers and interview procedures vary; and
- *validity*, which pertains more generally to the congruity between the theoretical concept meant and the empirical measurements made.

In the forthcoming chapters I will use these five criteria by the evaluation of survey operationalizations and measurements. The conclusion can already be divulged that rigid application of these five criteria severely limits the possibilities to measure immigrant integration. The *brevity* criterion implies that not all relevant parameters can be measured via the random survey interview. The *simplicity* criterion implies that items should be avoided that tax individuals' (cognitive and emotional) capacities, although within given theoretical perspectives these are essential qualities of the individually integrated. Finally, the *comparability* criterion ultimately casts doubt upon the possibility to measure respondents' integration into those (ideal) localities characterized by cultural diversity.

Local and individual integration are sensitive issues. The urban environment where their measurement would not be met with problems and protest is difficult to imagine. Local boundary problems can be seen to reflect the shifting affinities that confront any individual or locality (except perhaps those ideal-types - delineated in chapter two - encountered in social vacuums). Here I have noted the intervening interests of research beneficiaries. I accordingly noted that few beneficiaries would subsidize social research without a social problem. Turning to the respondents' context I observed that residents, as participants within the local process, are limited in their capacity to denote its direction. The ethical issues touched upon in the previous sub-section suggest that those individuals who are *estranged*, according to a given integration criterion, may be the least accessible of interview subjects. The concept of integration signifies in short the tensions between local harmony and conflict: the more processes are characterized by conflict the more problematic the individual measurement; the more processes are characterized by harmony the less necessary the individual measurement.

Within this perennial paradox, I have identified in this section five criteria that will be used in the forthcoming chapters to evaluate the *adequacy* of empirical measurements: validity, reliability, brevity, simplicity and comparability.

The Survey Subject: Categorizing Immigrants and Indigenes

At this point in the research process, the locality has been selected. The categorical distinction between immigrants and indigenes has also been determined. *Immigrants* are all those residents born outside the Netherlands (first generation) or with at least one parent born outside the Netherlands. Before the random inhabitants are approached, I need to consider the potentially relevant sub-populations, and whether stratified samples need to be selected. The conceptual confusion existing between *immigrants, foreigners, ethnic groups* and *minorities* was touched upon in chapter two. Here this issue returns, as I consider problems that arise when surveys focus upon specific immigrant populations. The focus is more specifically upon sampling activities, and how these limit the research reliability with the measurements made. Then I present several demographic characteristics of the Haarlem survey. These are individual attributes that are not represented in the conceptual framework, and are largely insensitive to state interventions. They are however attributes - such as age, sex, and migration motives - that may go further than the distinction between immigrants and indigenes in clarifying who is integrated, and who is not.

Stratified Samples and Urban Representation

With the operational (and gradual) distinction between immigrants and indigenous residents, the boundaries between survey populations can be drawn. Considering the specific attributes of immigrant populations, how should representative survey samples be drawn. Such issues concern the source from which the sample is drawn, the number and variety of respondents needed, and the technique used to make selections.

Cities in most European countries have registry offices, where vital statistics on all (documented) residents are kept on file. In the Netherlands, practically all these offices can indicate which registered residents are first or second generation immigrants. Other sources can be tapped, each with their corresponding penchants: e.g., ethnic organizations for the ethnically oriented, police dossiers for the criminal suspects, and unions for the organized laborers.

With this I touch upon issues of sample size. To draw conclusions for an entire population, the rules for necessary sample size are rarely cut and dried. These are dependent upon the number of parameters being monitored, and the statistical techniques used to unravel their relations.[2] Important in this respect is the designation of categories that are each perceived as sub-populations. In Haarlem we were not only concerned with differences between immigrants and indigenous residents; within the immigrant population we focused upon specific groups subject to minority policies. Consequently five sub-populations were differentiated: Turks, Moroccans, Surinamese/Antilleans,[3] 'Other' immigrants,[4] and indigenous Dutch.[5] For each of these *ethnic categories* representative samples of ± 125 respondents were drawn, although their proportion of the adult Haarlem population diverges substantially.

The decision to focus upon these five categories, and to draw samples per category, infers the use of a stratified sampling technique. Stratification has consequences for the analysis of, and comparisons made from, the data. For instance, the technique we used implied that:

- The original odds for sample selection among adult residents varied from one in 16 to nearly one in 700, dependent upon the ethnic category in which individuals are classified.
- The samples are not entirely random, as we worked with quotas to ensure proportionate district representation, while a given resident could be selected only once.
- Prior knowledge of the interview objective and questionnaire is probably more prevalent among minority categories, due to the greater proportion interviewed during the four-month survey period.
- By data analysis, weighting factors are required to derive generalizations concerning all minorities, all (first generation) immigrants, or all local residents.
- The range within weighting factors, with the corresponding margin of error, limits the reliability of generalizations, particularly those referring to *all* residents.

These implications may sound technical, but they signify distinct limitations. For instance, with the Haarlem sample the relative significance of religious affiliations for individuals' integration can be estimated within specific ethnic categories. Yet not only are estimates of their significance for all immigrants less reliable, the potential to draw alternative categorical lines are limited by the stratified sample. A search for factors that affect the integration of all 'Muslim' immigrants, or all 'political refugees', is statistically precarious. In short, sampling techniques used within a given survey framework limit the comparability between, and particularly across, ethnic categories.

Table 3.1   Generation and citizenship of the five sub-samples

	Moroc-cans	Turks	Surinamese Antilleans	'Other' immigrants	Indigenous Dutch
Generation: 1st (arrival age>13 years)	87%	80%	68%	39%	-
'between' (arrival age<13 yrs)	12%	13%	16%	8%	-
second (born in NL)	1%	7%	17%	53%	-
Citizenship: land of origin	97%	95%	17%	36%	-
Dutch	3%	4%	82%	62%	100%
n = 100%	93/92	159/158	77/76	100/94	- /170
% local adult sub-population	5.59%	5.19%	4.46%	0.65%	0.17%

An initial overview of the survey respondents illustrates several distinctions made in this sub-section. The columns in table 3.1 differentiate the five ethnic categories from which sub-samples were drawn. The bottom row displays the degree of sample stratification, showing, e.g., how much greater is the percentage of Moroccan residents who took part in the survey (5.6%) compared with the percentage indigenous residents (0.2%). The other rows illustrate the diversity within and between sample categories regarding respondents' immigrant status. One may note for instance that few second generation immigrants are encountered among the minority categories, and that most of the 'Other' immigrants have (acquired) Dutch citizenship.

Demographic Estrangement: Generation and Gender Gaps

Several limitations in context and perspectives were reviewed in the previous section that restrict explanations as to why some immigrants are more integrated than others. Before proceeding, several individual attributes are presented here that broaden the scope and are readily measured. These are attributes that are not explicitly reflected by concepts within the three dimensions of individual integration, and might therefore be overlooked by the presentations in chapters four through six. The number of such attributes is theoretically endless. Those few treated here are either demographic variables commonly measured in survey interviews, or they pertain to personal histories that help clarify immigrants' end-goals.

Table 3.2   Demographic attributes of respondents

Attribute		Moroccans	Turks	Surinamese Antilleans	'Other' immigrants	Indigenous Dutch
Age:	18-34	59%	54%	46%	30%	29%
	35-54	28%	37%	36%	45%	41%
	55 and older	13%	10%	18%	25%	31%
Local resident	< 10 yrs	51%	38%	44%	36%	19%
	10 thru 19 years	29%	41%	30%	20%	11%
	20 years and more	20%	21%	26%	43%	71%
Haarlem Quarter*:	East	19%	22%	1%	11%	15%
	North	16%	22%	18%	34%	39%
	Center-South	14%	17%	31%	30%	26%
	Schalkwijk	51%	39%	49%	25%	20%
Migration motive:	work	24%	28%	2%	9%	-
	family reunification	44%	35%	32%	27%	-
	family formation	15%	30%	9%	36%	-
	other motives	17%	7%	58%	29%	-
n = 100%		93/93	158/159	77/77	100/99	170/170
		93/91	158/138	77/59	100/45	168/ -

* Haarlem is administratively divided into 12 districts or 40 neighborhoods. In the overview presented here the following districts are combined: *Haarlem-Oost* is the East quarter; *Westoever Noord Buitenspaarne, Ter Kleef en Te Zaanen, Oud Schoten en Spaarndam,* and *Duinwijk* comprise the North quarter; *Oude Stad, Leidse Spoorbaan,* and *Haarlemmerhoutkwartier* comprise the Center-South quarter; and *Europawijk, Boerhaavewijk, Molenwijk,* and *Meerwijk* comprise Schalkwijk in the south-east.

The demographic attributes could be construed as positional attributes. I am referring to factors such as *age, sex, residential district* and *residential duration*. Such attributes refer more indirectly to positions upon a particular market for social goods; moreover their distributions are not legitimately affected by state interventions. However, when demographic differences vary across ethnic categories, they may point to imbalances in the integration measurement. Table 3.2 shows for instance that most of the Moroccan and Turkish residents are younger than 35 (59% resp. 54%), while only 30% of the 'Other' immigrants and indigenous Dutch are in this age cohort. Such categorical discrepancies may help clarify why indigenous residents tend to earn more. They can also suggest why specific cultural polarities correspond more with 'generation' than with 'ethnicity'. For instance, the minimal interest among Haarlem minorities for local museums, theaters and other manifestations of 'high' culture may have more to do with their youth than with their ethnicity.

The significance of another demographic factor presented here - duration of residence in the municipality - pertains to the parameter of *time*: the longer individuals reside the more likely their integration has indeed progressed (cf. Sampson, 1991). One sees in table 3.2 that few immigrants in minority categories have resided more than 20 years in Haarlem, while this applies for a large majority of the indigenous Dutch. Many potentially relevant factors by in integration pertain to *duration*. However, methodological obstacles arise when isolating the particular significance of a given duration factor, as time factors tend to correlate.[6]

Residential distribution is a third demographic factor summarized in table 3.2. An inordinate percentage of the three minority categories are seen to reside in the local quarter known as *Schalkwijk*, characterized by high-rise tenant apartments. Because residence in specific neighborhoods or districts may signify a personal end-goal, this factor differs from age or sex in its social significance. In the forthcoming chapters it will reappear regularly.

The other category of demographic attributes revolves around individuals' attachment to their land of origin and their motives for migration. Family or possessions elsewhere could be regarded as an indication of estrangement (CBS, 1985; Friedberg, 1993). As themes in Dutch survey interviews though, they annoy respondents (Meloen and Veenman, 1990: 154ff) while the number of possible themes indicative of individuals' orientation toward the wider world is infinite. More theoretically pertinent, and less problematic in practice, are indications as to why individuals choose to move. Migration is rarely an individual and voluntary decision (Petersen, 1975:321ff; Esveldt et al., 1995; Springers, 1995). Ogbu (1996) argues for instance that a distinction between voluntary and involuntary immigrants goes far to explain differential integration in the United States. In Haarlem, we were curious whether individuals who came primarily in search of work (such as ± 25% of the Moroccans and Turks) have orientations and contacts divergent from those who came for schooling (such as 22% of the Surinamese and Antilleans) or for family formation (such as 36% of the 'Other' immigrants). We neglected to ask the indigenous Dutch why they came to Haarlem.

In this section two issues surrounding immigrant survey samples were presented. First sampling techniques were considered, noting sources of sampling bias and the demands of sample size. A combination of two elements entails that surveys readily require hundreds of respondents: the number of factors being analyzed for their interrelationship, and the number of (ethnic) categories being compared. When specific categories are numerical minorities, they require stratified samples to select potential respondents. The use of these techniques further confuses the (statistical) context in which comparisons are made.

In the second sub-section, several demographic factors were presented. Differential distributions of age and sex not only provide an indication that survey samples are representative.[7] They and other demographic factors may suggest that ethnic categories are in divergent phases of their integration. However, before *age* can be construed to indicate those immigrants subject to a generation gap, and *sex* becomes indicative of those immigrants oppressed by gender gaps, a variety of theoretical, statistical, and normative issues must be resolved.

The Survey Interview: Appreciating Communicative Agents

The previous two sections have been concerned respectively with the survey context of cities and of sample populations. In this section I turn to several communicative issues pertinent to interviews with immigrants. I will focus upon three *media* of communication.

Immigrants tend to have less command of predominant local languages when compared with more indigenous residents. Does a diversity of languages require a variety of questionnaires? How can researchers know whether questions formulated in one language elicit valid responses in another language? I first touch upon the issue of language as a communication barrier. Then the role of the interviewer as medium between respondents and researchers is considered. The focus is specifically upon the survey practice of matching the interviewers' immigrant descent - and gender - with that of the respondents. A third issue concerns the respondent as medium. The ideal interview context calls for the isolation of respondents, to minimize the influence of others. This requirement is problematic in households characterized by a premium on space. Can the effect of this bias be measured? Is bias an appropriate qualification?

Language as a Medium

All these letters form symbols, relating in (American) English the misunderstandings that arise when questions, originally formulated in Dutch, are posed to respondents with a variety of linguistic backgrounds. How much will be lost in translation, and how much is related to the ambiguity of symbols in any context? Ultimately we have no certainty that two actors involved in a communicative process know when the same symbol signifies different entities (e.g., we only agree these letters are 'black'), or when different symbols signify the same entity (e.g., we might also agree that these letters are 'zwart,' 'negro' or 'noires').

A broad range of academic debates focuses upon this linguistic dilemma (e.g., Brislin et al., 1973; Berry, 1989), and a large body of cross-cultural research is fixated upon the communication gap between languages and cultures (e.g., Asante and Gudykunst, 1989; Gudykunst, 1994; cf. Shadid, 1998:122ff). Dutch envoys of the latter tradition (e.g., Eppink, 1981; Pinto and Pinto, 1994; Hofman, 1994) tend to overemphasize the gap by dissecting the inter-cultural ambiguity encountered in even the simplest of exchanges. Alternatively, researchers may downplay the linguistic gap in which they find themselves, or limit their observations to immigrants (presumably) fluent in the indigenous tongue. The one perspective sees surveys as inherently flawed due to the culturally specific meaning of concepts and categories; the other sees that surveys can quantify the universal essence of individual views and experiences.

Meloen and Veenman, placing themselves between these two poles (1990:109), produced the first comprehensive Dutch study on the types of interview distortion encountered in surveys among immigrants. They emphasize, for instance, the importance of transcribing questionnaires with a translate-retranslate method (1990:101). For the Haarlem survey, the questionnaire was translated into Moroccan-Arabic and Turkish, without the added certainty of a retranslation. We did employ multilingual interviewers who not only could cater to respondents' language preference. They would improvise upon insensitive and complex formulations, and could inform us and each other about linguistic ambiguities. Most of the Moroccans (57%)

and a broad majority of the Turks (75%) opted for interviews solely in these respective languages. The comparison of their response patterns with those who chose to speak in Dutch reveal the interpretative difficulties bound to multilingual interviews. They arise for instance where respondents are asked to express their views on local integration objectives (see chapter five). However, the most significant differences in response patterns concern questions pertinent to the respondents' positions: those immigrants who do not speak Dutch qualify their various social positions as decidedly more detached. To what extent can categorical differences be attributed to subjective proclivities anchored in particular linguistic systems, and to what extent do they realistically reflect the detached social position occupied by immigrants who do not speak Dutch?

Another Haarlem result helps to crystalize the issue. The number of missing responses to questions, the so-called item non response, provides an indication of communicative problems. Exactly 100 survey items could be answered by all respondents, regardless of the interview route. Of these, 26 concern respondents' positions in various domains, 43 pertain to their orientations, and 31 to their contacts and activities. The mean percentage of missing responses ranges minimally but significantly from 8.9% (for indigenous Dutch) to 11.3% (for Moroccans) (see table 3.3 rows four through six). More noteworthy are the types of questions specific ethnic categories avoid. More than half the non response by indigenous Dutch could be attributed to their unwillingness or inability to provide information on their social positions (mean=5.1). Such questions elicit a significantly lower non response by all immigrant categories - particularly by respondents interviewed in Turkish (mean=2.5). On the other hand, indigenous Dutch respondents have relatively little problem expressing their cultural orientations (mean=3.5). Such orientational items form a large majority of the non response among minority categories - particularly by respondents interviewed in Arabic (mean=8.4). Other researchers have signaled the high item non response when questions refer to immigrants' values and perspectives (see Zusman and Olson, 1977; Meloen and Veenman, 1990:51). It remains (forever) unclear how much this stems from *linguistic incongruence* between the instrument and the immigrant (i.e., the ability to express particular values and perspectives), and how much stems from immigrants' *limited orientation* (i.e., limited opportunity to acquire and convey universal values and perspectives).

Should the researcher cater to the immigrant respondents' linguistic competence? This is obviously dependent upon research objectives, available funds and the linguistic diversity present in the local population. More fundamentally, it is dependent upon the local integration envisioned.

Where linguistic competence is considered a necessary attribute for local orientation and participation, language proficiency is a requisite end-goal of individual integration. Adapting this viewpoint, multilingual measurement instruments become essentially superfluous, as immigrants are by definition estranged if they are unable to respond in the indigenous tongue (cf. Esser, 1980:179ff).

How about local visions characterized by objectives of cultural diversity? How does one traverse linguistic polarities in order to measure individuals' integration into such ideal environments? It is my conviction, in accordance with such visions, that the focus should be less upon languages as barriers - as sources of misunderstanding - and more upon their potential to mutually enlighten values and perspectives (Mok and Reinsch, 1996: 15ff). After all, we need not agree upon *what* we learn, to agree we all *learn* from our experiences. For measuring individual integration, this implies the relaxation of research goals to encapsulate universal ideas and categories. The researcher and the respondent should tolerate the ambiguity of ideals, savor the plurality of viewpoints, and accept the transiency of cultural orientations. Even in the survey interview the communicative goal is not so much to establish a consensus, but to encounter variation.

Interviewers as a Medium

Besides linguistic symbols, interviewers are positioned between the researcher and the (oral) survey respondent. To bridge linguistic and cultural gaps, a common (Dutch) practice is to match the ethnic background of interviewers with that of respondents (cf. Meloen and Veenman, 1990:103; Kemper, 1998:45ff). By a survey concerning the *ethnic-cultural position* in which (300) second generation Amsterdam Surinamese situate themselves, van Heelsum compared the answers gathered by eight Surinamese and eight indigenous Dutch interviewers. She observes that specific interview themes are particularly sensitive to matching practices, namely *ethnic specific* themes (e.g., ethnic self-identification, subjection to exclusionary practices, importance of language and culture, preference for Surinamese contacts) and more general *interpersonal* themes (e.g., experience with and views on loneliness). These findings correspond with her conclusions from a general literature study on immigrant surveys (van Heelsum, 1993:20).

For the Haarlem survey we matched interviewers and respondents in the three minority samples, while primarily indigenous interviewers approached the 'Other' immigrants and indigenous Dutch. Systematic comparisons of ethnic matching affects can therefore not be made. As for gender, we carried out matching practices within the Moroccan and

Turkish samples, as male interviewers mediated mainly with male respondents. This was done in accordance with a widely acknowledged Dutch adagium, that in Muslim households women should not be left alone with male 'guests'. Several possible effects of gender combinations can be discerned in table 3.3, which provides an overview of four sets of response variations, differentiated by respondents' gender (columns) and by interviewers' gender (rows).

Table 3.3   Response variations between female and male respondents, differentiated by interviewers' gender*

		Moroccans		Turks		Surinamese Antilleans		'Other' immigrants		Indigenous Dutch	
interviewer gender ⇓		♀	♂	♀	♂	♀	♂	♀	♂	♀	♂
Interview participation	♀	79%	68%	81%	78%	54%	64%	49%	73%	64%	59%
	♂	-	54%	76%	72%	16%	37%	33%	42%	39%	47%
mean (=Σn)	Σ	73%		79%		57%		55%		54%	
Item non response	♀	14%	11%	10%	7%	10%	10%	10%	10%	9%	9%
	♂	12%	5%	9%	10%	12%	10%	9%	11%	9%	8%
mean	Σ	11%		9%		10%		10%		9%	
Interview duration (min)	♀	71	90	76	79	94	88	103	94	83	79
	♂	90	98	84	81	89	95	63	71	67	70
mean	Σ	82		79		91		88		77	
Interviews with others present	♀	66%	74%	55%	70%	37%	33%	27%	48%	15%	48%
	♂	0%	47%	42%	70%	50%	25%	30%	41%	52%	35%
mean	Σ	65%		62%		36%		35%		34%	
n =	♀	42	35	54	44	38	29	39	26	57	60
	♂	1	15	21	40	6	4	19	15	23	30

* Underlined statistics vary significantly (Student's t < 5%) from those attained with interviewers from opposite gender.

The first set (rows one to three) pertains to the actual survey response, i.e., the percentage residents who, once in contact with interviewers, eventually agree to an interview. This actual response is seen to vary from 42% among female 'Other' immigrants to 80% among female Turks.[8] A comparison of the column percentages between rows one and two shows that, regardless of ethnic category and gender, female interviewers are more successful in realizing the participation of potential respondents. For three of the five ethnic categories, these differences are statistically significant (underlined in the table).[9]

These results would warrant the use of female interviewers within all sample categories. But how did the interviewers proceed, once they had permission to enter? In table 3.3, rows four to six, mean percentages for the item non response are presented, i.e., the average number of questions that respondents did not answer. The differences per column are largely insignificant. One observes however that Moroccan men are significantly *more* responsive toward male interviewers while Turkish men are significantly *less* responsive toward male interviewers.

Table 3.3 displays two other indications as to the possible effect of interviewers' gender. The first, presented in rows seven to nine, pertains to the average duration of interviews. The other concerns the presence of other persons during the interview. Presumably specific interviewer-respondent combinations prompt respondents to arrange the attendance (i.e., 'support') of household members and friends. The only significant differences occurred among indigenous female respondents: others were rarely present with female interviewers, and usually present with male interviewers (15% resp. 52%).

These results do not lend credence to strict schemes of gender matching by interviews with immigrants. They do show how the interaction between an interviewer and (potential) respondent lends itself for comparative analysis. The analyses suggest that the interaction affect response within ethnic categories in a variety of ways. The variety of response patterns encountered in surveys among immigrants, and their clarification, remains largely unchartered (van Heelsum, 1997:158).

Respondents as a Medium

Before closing this section another characteristic of the interview situation deserves attention. Survey interview protocol commonly calls for an environment, in which the influence of other persons or objects upon the respondents' answers is kept to a minimum (cf. Kidder and Judd, 1986:225). It is unclear when and to what extent immigrant survey research violates this protocol, in part because researchers rarely mention it as an extenuating factor (Meloen and Veenman, 1990:54). However, as displayed in table

3.3, the Haarlem interviewers noted that other persons were often present during interviews. For the interviews among Moroccan and Turkish residents this applied to most interviews, while in the other three survey categories more than a third of the interviews were held in the presence of others.

No simple method can effectively discern how these friends and household members affect the respondents' answers. Interviewers could supply their estimates about whom was influenced and by which questions,[10] but such evaluations are a poor basis for general measurement corrections. Upon comparison of the response patterns provided by those interviewed alone, with those interviewed in the presence of other persons, an interesting but ambiguous distinction appears. Within all ethnic categories, those interviewed alone tend to estimate their positional attributes, such as educational level and household income higher than those with witnesses. Before concluding that witnesses help temper respondents' self-appraisals, one must take into account that those with higher social positions may have generally more opportunity to seclude themselves from other members of the household.

Given the presence of others in the crowded and sociable quarters of respondents' households, should steps be taken to minimize their influence upon the interview? Various interview techniques help curb third party interference (see Kidder and Judd, 1986:226; Meloen and Veenman, 1990: 107), but other practical problems accompany their use. In the end, the decision hinges upon the research objectives. In Haarlem, our central and explicit purpose was to compile ideas and perspectives for local policies. Within such a context noting the partner's opinion may be opportune as well. The alternative is to take efforts to simulate a clinical environment, with as possible consequence respondents who no longer have a view to convey. More generally, surveys concerned with the relative position of households or categories, which rely upon random respondents to provide representative information, use the respondents' perspective as a medium. The researcher's dilemma represents a double paradox: one must rely upon either isolated representatives, or sacrifice survey representability by allowing representatives to consult with their constituents. In Haarlem, we opted for the latter.

The Local Index: Denoting Integrated Individuals

The final contextual consideration, arguably the most central to research on integration, is the choice of normative criteria. To denote integrated individuals, and to examine the factors that account for differences in degree, one or more criteria must be chosen. Various normative, theoretical and methodological considerations that accompany this choice are presented below. The index used in the coming chapters to illuminate integration processes is then introduced. A quick preview reveals an index that ranks respondents with reference to an 'average' (adult) resident. After introducing the index in the second sub-section, some presumptions associated with the end-goals of individual integration, and their (statistical) interrelationship, are assessed. The (statistical) relation is then considered between factors discussed in the previous sections - differences in interview context and respondents' demographic attributes - and respondents' integration scores.

The Various Qualities of an Integration Criterion

To denote integrated individuals is ultimately a normative activity, in which any number of criteria are combined. Considering the divergent end-goals perceived in individual integration processes, the criteria could be either complementary or disparate. Various theoretical and methodological restraints must be taken into account, while the ideal index should also be generally applicable, brief and simple, reliable and unambiguous.

Take for instance a criterion used to denote the inclusion of immigrant groups: marriages with indigenes (cf. Lieberson and Waters, 1988; Harmsen, 1998). At the micro level of individual immigrants this criterion serves at best as an indication (cf. Hondius, 1999:305). As an index it would categorically exclude all individuals without (marriage) partners. A similar limitation applies to another criterion often encountered in research on social mobility: the social status attributed to individuals' occupations (cf. Dagevos and Veenman, 1992). Those individuals inactive upon the labor market have no (i.e., zero) rank upon a professional status index.

Other criteria will be considered in the coming chapters that are applicable for all adults, but exhibit particular normative and theoretical limitations. For instance, level of education or degree of fluency in the indigenous language play key roles in theories on individual integration (eg. Esser, 1980). In principle, any individual could be ranked along a continuous scale representing either of these criteria. However, I find the designation to be normatively 'intolerant' that by definition the poorly educated or the inarticulate are locally estranged. As criteria they hardly reflect end-goals of the tolerant vision that serves as normative basis to this study. These factors may *suggest* possible obstacles to integration, but they *should* not *denote* estrangement.

Education and language, and also professional status, call attention to another consideration: social policy. Such factors refer to various domains of state intervention used to advance immigrant integration. In this context they represent various *means* rather than *objectives* of the integration process. Ideally, integration indices should reflect the objective or end-goal of a process in terms that can be used by local authorities to evaluate their policies and programs.

That integration criteria are preferably simple and concise in their compilation (i.e., not tax survey respondents unduly with a barrage of questions) and interpretation (i.e., not require vast statistical expertise) amplifies the challenge. The decision made here to combine various criteria into one index is above all a question of convenience: e.g., the discussion of Haarlem data in the forthcoming chapters will focus upon one rather than a variety of dependent variables. To this end, I presume that individuals' degrees of integration within a given geo-political or social context can be projected upon a single spectrum. Moreover, the intervals along the spectrum are portioned so that the distribution of local residents' scores along the spectrum resembles a normal or bell curve (i.e., 68% of the individuals are within one standard deviation of the median point on the spectrum, and 95% within two standard deviations). This presumption increases the potential to use statistical techniques that can illuminate and account for individuals' variant processes. The problem then is to project the spectrum.

With these various considerations in mind, items were sought in the Haarlem survey data that, in their singular characteristics and correlations, optimize the probability that an adequate spectrum is drawn. Five sets of response-items or *components* were selected that combine to represent theoretically and mathematically a single 'integration' index. The five separate components will be considered more in detail in the coming chapters. I suffice here with a brief introduction:

- *Per capita income* An indication of respondents' material wealth was calculated by relating their net monthly household income to the composition of their households (see chapter four, section three).
- *Welfare independence* Individuals may be seen to vary in self-reliance as one is more dependent upon public *services* (e.g., labor exchanges or legal assistance) provided by local authorities while another uses only municipal leisure *arrangements* (e.g., libraries and sports facilities). Based upon respondents' use of nine local services, their relative position on a service-arrangement spectrum was estimated (see chapter four, section four).

- *Perceived opportunity* Respondents were asked to compare their opportunities for education, labor and housing with the average resident. Their estimates upon the three scales were subsequently combined (see chapter five, section three).
- *Local satisfaction* Respondents were also asked to appraise various aspects of their Haarlem experience: their personal life, their home, their neighborhood and the city overall. These scores were also reduced to a single component (see chapter five, section four).
- *Cultural participation* The chance to meet and speak with 'strangers' increases with the use of public areas. The frequency in which respondents visit various Haarlem localities and events such as markets, cafés, parties, theaters, and festivals were transformed into a principal component (see the penultimate section of chapter six).

How do these five components conform to theoretical and normative criteria? To begin with, each is applicable for all adult residents. Theoretically, they represent criteria associated with all three integration dimensions and with various domains differentiated in the previous chapter. Normatively they can be seen to represent end-goals associated with the tolerant vision, as will be clarified in the three paragraphs below.

The first two components are indicative of individuals' social positions. Per capita income is a measure of material wealth, while welfare independence reflects more generally end-goals of *self-reliance*. Besides serving as individual criteria, they also embody tolerant objectives of local integration. Here I presume that in a tolerant community, immigrants as (aggregated) categories should not differ from indigenous groups as to their *civil liberties* (i.e., the reliance on state interventions is no greater among immigrants). Moreover, I presume a certain degree of *social equality* within this ideal community, namely that immigrants and indigenes as (aggregated) categories have comparable opportunity to accumulate material wealth (i.e., poverty is not more pervasive among immigrants). More concretely, the criteria are based upon the presumption that the greater the income, and the less reliance upon government services, the more engaged an individual is. In short, these criteria are specific and concrete measures of the 'differential participation in institutional and associational life' (Schermerhorn, 1970:16).

The third and fourth component, perceived opportunity and local satisfaction, concern expressive aspects of individuals' cultural orientation. They too represent normative end-goals where they reflect individuals' 'extent of satisfaction or dissatisfaction with the different patterns of participation' (Schermerhorn, 1970:16). The normative presumption that individuals are more integrated the more they express satisfaction with their local situation is obviously limited in scope. Knowledge and belief components of individuals' orientation (e.g., communicative skills and religious convictions) are overlooked. But then, according to end-goals of *personality*, I presume that beyond compliance with local objectives no other orientational criteria apply to which residents must conform. Within a *tolerant* vision, immigrants may - even *should* - differ from indigenes in their cognitive and moral orientations. The two criteria do service here for lack of more adequate measures within the Haarlem data (see further chapter five), and for their embodiment of *local* integration objectives. Presumably, a necessary condition for local objectives of cultural diversity is that immigrants (as aggregated categories) compare with indigenes as for their (variant but sufficient) *appreciation* of their local circumstance.

The fifth component, cultural participation, represents individuals' potential to realize local contacts. It is based on the presumption that the more individuals participate in local activities, the more they have resolved the behavioral dilemma of *solitude* or *sociability* in favor of the latter. In itself, the criterion fails to distinguish between local integration objectives of seclusion (i.e., minimal interactions between ethnic categories) and inclusion (i.e., optimal interethnic interactions).[11] In other words, participation in local cultural activities signifies greater integration, regardless of the locals encountered. This component should be complemented by respondents' actual frequency and quality of (interethnic) contacts for it to reflect 'overt or covert behavior patterns of conflict and/or harmonious relations' (Schermerhorn, 1970:16). Unfortunately, the survey data did not contain more adequate behavioral measures. The possibilities to realize such measures will be considered in chapter six.

Before presenting the index made up by these five components more in detail, let me consider its general limitations. First, the index is a statistical artefact extracted from survey data, replete with measurement bias and local idiosyncracies. Consequently, although the separate components are measurable in other localities, they would not necessarily combine to form a comparable and reliable index. To sustain the spectral presumption, a statistical restriction was applied that all components significantly correlate with the index so that each component contributes to individuals' integration score. Due to this restriction, several potential criteria available in the Haarlem data were excluded from the index.[12]

The empirical basis of the index calls attention to its limited theoretical status. It is not derived from a theory of integration; the components do not represent divergent phases of individuals' local 'entry' process (cf. Gordon, 1963; Esser, 1980; Baker, 1983). To reflect more directly the parameters of the formal framework presented in the previous chapter, the interaction between dimensions, domains and levels of analysis through time would require the designation of several indices. In this respect, the presumption that individuals' integration can be designated by a single (albeit combined) score relative to other local residents is most problematic. To keep the presentation simple I nevertheless embrace the presumption, rather than seek more nuances in a deluge of indices and their corresponding components.

Because the alignment with parameters of the formal model is not clear cut, and the selection of end-goal criteria incomplete, the index remains ambiguous. In other words, the index does not ostensibly reflect end-goals associated with the tolerant vision listed in table 2.1. This ambiguity has its reasons, and advantages. A strict application of these end-goals would imply that respondents are being ranked according to (tolerant) criteria that are not widely shared and pursued as local objectives. It is possible however to examine whether those respondents who do support such objectives are indeed more integrated, a survey finding I will discuss in chapter five.

A final limitation pertains to the relative intangibility of statistical artefacts. Because of the presumed (interval) level of measurement and normal distribution of respondents, the principal component factor used to form the index ultimately offers more statistical potential to analyze and interpret the effect various factors have upon individuals' integration. However, hypothetical comparisons to the average resident might appeal less to one's imagination than more nominal indices, for instance residents' subsistence above or below poverty level or their partner preference.

Constructing a Statistical Standard

To derive the index, first the survey data was re-weighed so that as to geopolitical origins the 600 respondents could be considered representative for the population of adult residents. This meant that the (170) indigenous Dutch respondents counted for approximately 100 times as many residents as the (93) Moroccan respondents.[13] A diversity of factors was then entered in a principal component analysis, based on the combination of (theoretical and normative) criteria discussed directly above. The five components contained within the index are seen to be significantly aligned to the principal component (i.e., the factor loadings are at least .50), while the addition of more factors reduced the principal component's reliability.[14] The results of the analysis are summarized in the second column of table 3.4 (under *local index*). One may observe that, in comparison to the other four components, *perceived opportunity* is more centrally aligned with the principal component (i.e., a correlation of .69). The column also shows that the principal component accounts for 32.6% of the variance within the five contributing components.

Table 3.4   Five component 'loadings' upon the local index (for entire Haarlem population) and for separate ethnic categories

Components	Local Index	Morocc- ans	Turks	Surinam- ese/Antil- leans	'Other' immi- grants	Indige- nous Dutch
per capita income	0.51	0.08	0.29	0.7	0.65	0.45
welfare independence	0.56	0.69	0.63	0.31	0.59	0.51
perceived opportunity	0.69	0.55	0.66	0.66	0.65	0.72
local satisfaction	0.56	0.37	0.22	0.61	0.06	0.59
cultural participation	0.51	0.63	0.69	0.41	0.54	0.5
percent of variance	32.6%	26.6%	28.8%	31.3%	29.9%	31.7%
mean (and standard deviation)	0.0 (1.0)	-1.49 (0.88)	-1.22 (0.94)	-0.38 (0.94)	-0.11 (0.93)	0.08 (0.97)
n =	599	93	159	77	100	170

The resulting index distributes respondents on a spectrum around the 'average' resident, whose integration score is set at zero. For purposes of comparison, a principal component specific to each of the five ethnic categories was then derived from the same five components, but limited to data from respondents within each of the five survey sub-samples. The component structures of these so-called ethnic indices are also summarized in table 3.4 for each of the respective categories. One may note that the loadings within the ethnic indices do not all meet the statistical criteria set for the local index (i.e., greater than .50). Comparable to the search for valid and statistically significant components for the entire local popula- tion, components with consistently high correlations could have been sought for each ethnic category. However, such a procedure would eventu- ally result in ethnic indices of divergent constitution. I fail to recognize solid theoretical grounds that legitimate why a given criterion represents a relevant integration end-goal for one ethnic category and not for another. Stated euphemistically, comparisons between ethnic categories become complex when individuals within them are ranked according to disparate criteria. Here the ethnic indices serve to illuminate the spectral quality of the local index by revealing those components that do not display significant loadings within the separate ethnic categories.

One may note that the *perceived opportunity* component retains a consistently high correlation within each of the ethnic indices. The other four components are less consistent. In particular, the *per capita income* component among Moroccans and Turks, and the *local satisfaction* component among Turks and 'Other' immigrants, correlate minimally with other components within the index. A logical consequence of the diminished loadings is that less variance within the separate components is accounted for by the ethnic indices. This is most apparent for Moroccans (only 26.6%). For this ethnic category a second principal component would account for nearly as much variance within the five contributing components (namely 24.1%). In appendix II, correlation matrices of the local index and its contributing components are presented for each of the five ethnic categories, as well as other statistics concerning the contributing five components.

Considering the limited variance clarifed by the local index, how does it reflect upon respondents' (linear) degree of integration? Once one presumes that all five components are valid end-goals of individuals' integration, it shows the local diversity of integration processes. It offers a measure of the five components' interrelation within a specific local context. Should the local index account for nearly 100% of its components' variance, then individuals' degree of integration is reliably reflected by their score on any single component. In literal terms, the more integrated residents would all be self-reliant, they would all express greater satisfaction concerning their local situation and prospects, and they would all frequent a spectrum of local activities more often than other residents. When individuals' integration according to one criterion displays little relation to their integration according to the other four criteria, the variance within the contributing components that the index accounts for approaches a minimum (e.g., 20% for five components). Where individuals score 'low' on one component, this can be 'compensated' by their scores on others. In short, the low percentages show the diffuse relation between integration end-goals among the residents surveyed, and particularly among those of Moroccan origin.

The next-to-bottom row of table 3.4 presents the mean scores (and standard deviation) for individuals in separate ethnic categories upon the *local index* (the mean scores upon the *ethnic indices* are - by statistical design - zero). With the help of a z-table for normal distributions, these statistics help estimate the percentage individuals within a category with a given degree of integration. The Moroccans can be regarded as the most estranged category: only 7% of all residents score less integrated than the average Moroccan.[15]

In figure 3.1 the distribution of respondents along the local index is graphically portrayed. The horizontal axis displays the index scores in standard deviations around the zero-point of the average resident. The vertical axis displays the cumulative percentage per ethnic category that has *not* realized a specific degree of individual integration. One notes that the lines representing the four immigrant categories remain to the left of the thick solid line representing the indigenous residents. This means that for any given degree of integration, the percentage immigrants who are more estranged is always greater than the percentage indigenes. Particularly the (thin) line representing the Moroccans, and the (dashed) line representing the Turks ascend steeply to the left, with more than half of both categories scoring lower than -1.0 (i.e., the most estranged 16% of all residents). The (dotted) line representing the Surinamese/Antilleans and the (dash-dot) line representing the 'Other' immigrants resemble more - and occasionally touch - the cumulative curve of the indigenous Dutch.

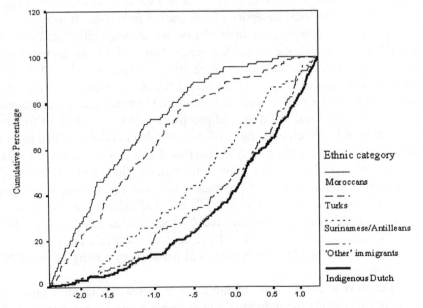

Figure 3.1   Local index scores, cumulative percentages per ethnic category

Of course other statistical techniques can be used to derive an integration index. One could, for instance, decree that the separate components contribute equally to the index, i.e., that it is a simple average of respondents' (standardized) scores upon the five components. More explicitly, the precise import of the separate components could be stipulated, e.g., that per capita income is double the weight of individuals' perceived opportunity. Reasoning more in theoretical phases, separate components could contribute conditionally to the index, thus forming an additive scale. For instance, that individuals must realize a specific welfare market position (e.g., zero reliance upon welfare services) before per capita income scores are indexed. All these alternatives require presumptions concerning the empirical relation between components that I consider inappropriate for the exploratory nature of this study.

Nevertheless, the relation between the separate components should not be construed as simple. Beyond the presumption that in their cumulative (i.e., additive) effect they denote individuals' degree of integration along a single spectrum, their interrelations raise more issues. The inclusion of immigrant and indigenous residents in the analysis bypasses normative presumptions in which only indigenous residents set the norm to which immigrants should conform. It then relies upon a similarly disputable presumption that average residents set the standard, and not the most estranged or integrated ones at the outer ends of the spectrum. Would it not be more appropriate to presume that the integrated status should be attributed to most local residents, without reference to an average resident, so that more limited numbers are stigmatized as estranged? In statistical terms, shouldn't a skewed left distribution be presumed instead of a bell curve around a zero point (cf. Gould, 1996).

A final issue in this regard concerns the variant weights allocated the five components within the local index, a consequence more of statistical than theoretical reason. Considering their loadings within the index, orientational components affect individuals degree of integration more than positional or behavioral ones. Particularly variations in perceived opportunity differentiate within all ethnic categories between the integrated and the estranged. That this component should occupy a crucial position within the index may meet with the approval of affirmative action advocates. However, as I will later discuss, the reliability of the component is questionable, and reliable measures of perceived opportunity should be complemented by more valid measures of individuals' actual opportunity.

Effects of Interview Context and Demographic Attributes

Having introduced an index that represents individual variations in integration, I will now examine whether various factors introduced in the previous sub-sections - variations in interview circumstance and respondents' demographic attributes - correspond with index scores. In appendix I measures of statistical association are displayed for respondent attributes, discussed in this and the coming three chapters, that correspond significantly with variations in respondent scores upon the local index. Two measures of association are used: the *eta* (η) for attributes measured at nominal or ordinal levels, and Pearson's correlation (R) for attributes measured at interval level. Characteristic for both statistics is that when squared, they designate the proportion of the variance in the dependent variable (i.e., the local index) accounted for by the independent variables (e.g., in this sub-section variations in interview context and demographic attributes).

The first section of appendix I presents factors bound to the interview context. Most of these factors allude to rather spurious relations, i.e., the factors in themselves can hardly be construed as determinants of individual integration. They are related instead to other attributes - respondents' Dutch linguistic skills in particular - that more directly effect individuals' integration. One sees that interviews with more estranged immigrants tend to last longer (R=-.27); they tend to be described by interviewers as 'difficult' (η=.21); and (particularly among Moroccans and Turks) they are not conducted in Dutch (η=.48).[16] One rather curious result is that interview items designed to measure cultural orientations are met with a greater non response from more estranged immigrants (R=-.22). This correlation however is not observed within the Moroccan and Turkish categories. In short, several indications of interview bias are apparent; most I consider exemplary for the interpretative problems signaled in section three concerning survey interviews in a multilingual context.

An interpretative problem of a different nature pertains to the fact that one-third of the interviews (197 out of 600) were conducted in so-called clusters. These are ten neighborhoods spread throughout the city, characterized by a greater 'concentration' of immigrants. We were concerned in the original research project whether such neighborhoods are confronted with specific problems (see Reinsch et al., 1995:105ff). Although the inclusion of cluster residents in the survey did not alter the general representability of the sample (as to age, sex, district distributions and residential duration), their greater chance of selection does not conform with the strictures of a-select sampling techniques. Not only indigenous residents, but to a lesser extent immigrant residents of such clusters, are more estranged than other respondents (η=.21 resp. .13). The removal of these respondents' data from the analysis was contemplated. However, considering their minor (though statistically significant) variations in integration, and the exploratory character of the study, I decided that the added value of their responses outweighs the relative loss of sample randomness.

The second section of appendix I presents nine demographic attributes that account for significant differences in individual integration. 'Region of origin' pertains within the various ethnic categories to divergent classifications. Among the 'Other' immigrants it refers to a distinction between Western Europeans, Eastern Europeans, Indonesian Dutch, and (poor world) *others*. Indonesian Dutch are more integrated, the poor world *others* much less than the average resident (η=.36). For the Surinamese and Antilleans the indicator monitors whether the (24) respondents originating from the Dutch Antilles vary significantly in their degree of integration from the (53) respondents of Surinamese origin. They don't. For the other three ethnic categories more specific inquiries into (e.g., provincial) region of origin were not made. A rough re-division of all immigrant respondents into four categories - Western Europeans, Indonesian Dutch, Minorities and *others* - is seen to account for significant variations along the local index (η=.39).[17]

A second demographic factor pertains to differences in gender. The poor position and limited participation of immigrant women - particularly Muslim women - are recurring topics of social concern (cf. Hooghiemstra and Niphuis-Nell, 1995; Jones-Correa, 1998) and political debate (cf. Cherribi, 1994) yet Haarlem differences in integration scores between immigrant men and women are negligible. Only among the indigenous Dutch do men score significantly higher on the local index (η=.21). A more detailed analysis, focusing upon the five components within the index, shows that *per capita income* (η=.16) and above all *perceived opportunity* (η=.24) are lower among indigenous Dutch women. These results illustrate the nuances necessary when signaling obstacles to individual integration. They are observed within a specific (local) context, measured according to specific criteria, and they fail to take the (interactive) effect of other social indicators into account. Given these conditions, gender obstacles to individual integration are more an indigenous phenomenon.

Four demographic factors are in one way or another related to the parameter of time. Among Haarlems' indigenous Dutch, one can observe that integration decreases with increasing age and residential duration (R=-.25 resp. -.29). In search of clarification, two components of the local index are seen to be particularly sensitive to differences in age: the elderly Dutch find they have (had) less *opportunity*, and they are less inclined to traverse the public domain for *cultural participation*. A similar relation between age and integration is found among Moroccans (R=-.40) and Turks (R=-.28). Besides (diminished) opportunity and cultural participation, an individual's *welfare independence* is seen to increase with age among the Moroccans and Turks. For immigrants overall the diminished opportunity and cultural participation among the elderly are compensated by their higher income and greater satisfaction, so that the net effect of age upon integration scores is insignificant (cf. Walker and Maltby, 1997). Two other time parameters specific to immigrants - age at migration and years since migration - also correlate with differences upon the local index (cf. Guest and Stamm, 1993). Within all three minority categories one can observe that the older immigrants were upon arrival in the Netherlands, the less *perceived opportunity, cultural participation and per capita income* they convey.

Local index differences between men and women, or the old and the young, are not necessarily linked to the immigration experience. Two other demographic factors however are more specifically tied to immigrants, namely the primary *motives for immigration* and the *generation* since migration. The first of these two factors is particularly significant among Moroccan immigrants, and to a lesser extent among Turks (η=.53 resp. .24). Within these two ethnic categories, respondents who came to the Netherlands either for reasons of 'work' or 'family formation' are particularly estranged. With a mean degree of integration score of -2.04 (i.e., more estranged than 98% of the city's residents), the Moroccans who expressed such motives may be seen to embody the disillusionment of the 'guestwork' experience. That the generation attribute accounts in part for integration differences among the city's immigrants provides a sign of hope. However, the number of second generation minorities is too small to suggest that their integration is simply a matter of time.[18]

The demographic attribute that corresponds most with integration scores pertains to the district in which respondents reside. For all immigrants, 26% of the variance in the local index can be attributed to such differences (for the indigenous Dutch 14%). This implies that the local district in which one resides is a better predictor of an immigrant's integration score than the geo-political region from which he or she arrives. However, when the focus is specifically upon Moroccans and Turks, district differences in index scores are statistically insignificant. These findings are illustrated in figure 3.2, where mean scores for the five ethnic categories are graphically displayed for the twelve Haarlem districts. One can see that the mean scores for Moroccans (represented by the thin line) show relatively little variation per district. Along with the Turks (the dashed line)

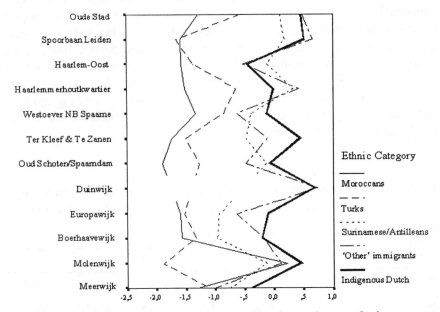

Figure 3.2   Mean index score per local district and per ethnic category

their mean scores are also consistently lower than those for the other three categories. Inordinately few Moroccans and Turks reside in those exclusive districts more generally populated by residents with high integration scores. Those that do are not necessarily more integrated (excepting the two Moroccan respondents in *Molenwijk*).[19] Nor are those Moroccans and Turks more estranged who are 'concentrated' in districts characterized by high-rise tenant flats (*Haarlem-Oost* and three of the four districts of *Schalkwijk*: *Europa-*, *Boerhaave-* and *Meerwijk*). In the fifth sub-section of the next three chapters, clarification will be sought for these residential differences.

Assuming these indicators to be (statistically) interrelated, the combined effect of selected demographic attributes upon local index scores was analyzed with multiple regression techniques. The results are summarized in table 3.5. In the bottom two rows of the table, two percentages are presented per ethnic category: the top one displays the index variance accounted for by all indicators combined, the bottom one the variance accounted for by those indicators marked with an asterisk. One can note for instance that among Moroccans approximately 16% of the variance is 'explained' by one attribute, namely differences in respondents' age. For the other ethnic categories the variances explained in the local index ranges between 13% and 18%, except among 'Other' immigrants by whom 'region of origin' and 'residential district' account for 26% of the index variance. When demographic effects are considered for all immigrants combined, the significance of 'residential district' overshadows variations in 'region of origin' and age. The variance accounted for by these three factors combined is a substantial 35%. In the final section of the forthcoming chapters comparable analysis results will be presented for positional, orientational and behavioral attributes respectively.

Table 3.5 **Percent of variance in local index scores accounted for by demographic attributes, controlling for other attributes**

Demographic attribute	Moroccans	Turks	Surinamese Antilleans	'Other' immigrants	All immigrants	Indigenous Dutch
gender	n.s.	n.s.	n.s.	n.s.	n.s.	2%*
age	10%*	10%*	n.s.	n.s.	2%*	n.s.
residential duration	n.s.	n.s.	n.s.	n.s.	n.s.	4%*
residential district	n.s.	5%*	n.s.*	13%*	17%*	8%*
region of origin	-	-	n.s.	n.s.*	10%*	-
combined (adj.) R^2	17%	14%	10%	25%	35%	18%
* indicators R^2 only	16%	14%	13%	26%	35%	18%
n (listwise deletion)	93	158	77	98	421	168

* = probability < .05, n.s.= not independently significant, p > .05.

In this section a *local integration index* has been introduced, derived via principal component analysis. It distributes Haarlem survey respondents around hypothetically average adult residents. The distribution is designed to resemble a standardized bell curve, with the zero point in the middle. Five components contribute to a respondent's score upon the index: *per capita income* and *welfare independence* pertain to local positions, *perceived opportunity* and *local satisfaction* pertain to the orientational appreciation of local circumstance, and *cultural participation* provides an indication of local behavior. The components reflect end-goals of individual integration that are not only applicable to immigrants but rank all local adults.

Statistically, the index is not particularly reliable: a person's score on a particular component has little potential to suggest their degree of integration based upon all five components. Reliability is in this sense a normative criterion, embodied by a vision of integration in which individuals' position, orientation and activities all closely correspond. The local index is itself all a normative criterion, based in part upon the presumption that a person's estrangement according to one component may be compensated by a higher score upon other components.

The index is essentially a statistical tool that combines in one number a respondent's position, orientation and behavior compared with other residents. It offers a simple and compact means to consider the effect various factors have upon individuals' integration, once the 'compensatory' normative presumptions are accepted. Having ranked the survey respondents along this index, it was subsequently used to consider the possible effect of interview context and demographic attributes. In the forthcoming chapters, a broad range of respondents' attributes will be considered in their relation to the local index.

Assessment: Individual Processes and Survey Tones

Starting with the conceptual framework various steps have been considered that researchers take to meet immigrants and monitor their integration. My purpose was to identify some epistemological limitations when survey techniques of standardized interviews are relied upon to observe individual integration processes. The observations will be summarized as a response to the following query:

Can I predict via a survey of local residents, which ones are most likely to underwrite and pursue local integration objectives?

When I focus upon integration as an *individual* process, without comprehending the broader range of phenomena that affect local prosperity and cohesion, the random respondents are essentially isolated from the context in which their process transpires. My viewpoint is fragmentized when integration is perceived only through the eyes (minds and mouths) of individual residents. Research tools are available that help combine these fragments into more coherent images of the city. Yet I should be wary to assume the images adequately capture the city's location within historic, spatial and social contexts. Despite the multifaceted view, any conclusions as to the nature and determinants of local objectives are suspect.

The fundament for my doubt is set down in the first section. There I observe first that the city's boundaries are rarely clear. Even if they are clear for the researcher, the individuals conveying fragments of their local experience do not necessarily enclose their images within the same frame of reference. The interests and concerns of research patrons were considered, which led to the realization of a research paradox: the more the locality is characterized by in-groups and out-groups (i.e., *social inequality*), by disagreement concerning integration objectives (*cultural incongruence*) and by outright conflict, the more problematic the realization of representative interviews. In short, the more integration is an issue, the less adequate survey techniques are liable to be. Meanwhile, five criteria for measurement *adequacy* were derived - validity, reliability, simplicity, brevity and comparability. With reference to these criteria a variety of survey measures will be evaluated in the forthcoming chapters.

In the second section several problems were reviewed regarding the size and structure of survey samples. I observed that the selection of (sub)-samples, which enable the comparison of residents according to a diversity of personal attributes, may in itself distort the perception of pertinent integration characteristics. Demographic attributes such as gender, age and initial motives (to migrate to Haarlem) were considered. By varying the focus upon these attributes, obstacles to integration could be seen in gender differences, generation differences, as well as ethnic differences.

The third section focused upon three media of communication that the researcher relies upon to understand and measure integration. The medium of language presents central interpretative dilemmas, particularly when the survey is held among residents with divergent linguistic backgrounds. Ultimately the researcher must decide whether linguistic symbols (e.g., *freedom*, *diversity* and *sociability*) denote local objectives with which all integration issues can be conceptualized. They may just as well serve as symbolic hat racks that reflect the ambiguity of individuals' views and expectations. In focusing upon the interviewer as medium, the potential effects of interviewers' (ethnicity and) gender upon respondents' answers were considered. The researcher must unravel that part of the survey response affected by the interviewer-respondent interaction from the part pertaining to integration issues. Thirdly, the consideration of the respondent as medium pertains to the paradox of finding random residents and realizing representative interviews, while controlling for the effect other residents have upon the respondents' responses.

The previous section focused upon the possibilities as researcher to present the survey results. Predictions could be presented about which (types of) residents would probably comply with a series of objectives. A theory could eventually be formulated that describes the sequential phases of individuals' integration, and estimates how many would experience estrangement in any given phase. However, with measurements made only once among residents, the data are inadequate to monitor mutations in integration objectives and to substantiate predictions. To simplify and therewith symbolize the measurement process, an index has been devised. It ranks the (600) Haarlem respondents according to a set of criteria that allude to the so-called tolerant vision: *per capita income, welfare independence; perceived opportunity; local satisfaction;* and *cultural participation.* The index combines, via the statistical technique of principal component analysis, respondents' scores upon these criteria to rank local adults in a normal distribution around zero score of the 'average' resident. Various theoretical, methodological and normative presumptions are necessary to regard this index as an adequate ranking of residents' integration. Most fundamental is the (normative) presumption that these five criteria represent ideal attributes of individual residents; they represent not so much the means but the end-goals of integration. This index provides a compact instrument to help explore those (positional, orientational and behavioral) attributes that characterize individuals and groups who (fail to) meet the five integration criteria.

Reviewing this assortment of limitations I note two issues in particular that, in their persistence, continually bring the adequacy of survey measurements into question. The first refers to the perspective of the individual respondents. It is the ongoing relation of these individuals to other individuals that forms the object of research. The presumption that these processes can be understood simply by comparing the various positions, orientations, and activities of the individuals involved, as related by the individuals themselves, is untenable. Even if interviews are held with all residents, their combined perspective may remain blind to historical and global factors.

The second issue concerns the divergent objectives attributed the integration process, by residents and researchers. It is an individual's active compliance with shared objectives that, by definition, differentiates the integrated from the estranged. Do the five criteria that comprise the index adequately encompass the various local objectives and personal end-goals upheld by residents? Could a shared consensus be found among residents as to the literal meaning and the social significance of these criteria? Would the consensus only commence in response to structured questions, or does it already exist within the local culture? The challenge is to design a survey instrument that will not only clarify differences in residents' *degree of integration*, but also identifies the shared objectives that legitimate the integration process. In the next four chapters, I will try to meet this challenge.

4 Perceiving Positions

In chapter two the notion of *position* was presented to denote the location an individual has upon a given market in social goods. The abstract nature of this notion was slightly confined by the distinction made in six domains of local integration. My purpose in this chapter is to examine more concretely the nature and potential significance of the various positions that individuals occupy in a locality. The examination will follow two central lines of inquiry.

First I explore the positional dilemmas with which individuals are confronted in their local actions. These are construed as oppositions between *deprivation* and *dependency*: market engagement alleviates deprivation in exchange for dependency upon other market actors. The pertinence of this dilemma will be considered within the various domains. To alleviate the speculative character of this exploration, references will be made continually to the Haarlem survey data. The data serves not only to illustrate variations in market positions; it will also depict the potential theoretical significance that can be attributed to these variations for individuals' integration. To this end, the positional differences observed among respondents will be compared with their scores on the so-called *local index*, introduced in the previous chapter. The presentation evolves around the query:

What significance may be attributed to individuals' various social positions as indicators of their integration within the local (Haarlem) context?

This brings me to the second line of inquiry central to the presentations in this chapter. While considering the potential normative and theoretical significance that can be attributed to individuals' market positions, the focus will also be upon the methodological possibilities and problems bound to their measurement. More specifically, I will appraise the problems that arise when positional comparisons between immigrants and indigenous Dutch are based upon survey measurements. The problems will be evaluated using the criteria introduced in chapter three: comparability, simplicity, brevity, reliability and validity. These criteria will not be wielded curtly and obsessively; the concern is more to reveal measurement issues that require further attention. This presentation revolves around the issue:

What methodological obstacles, pertinent to the operationalization of individuals' social position, render the measurement of immigrant integration particularly problematic?

An answer to the two questions is wrought with presumptions concerning the variety of normative criteria, integration processes, and market positions. Rather than investigate the validity of these presumptions, my purposes are more austere. I will order the Haarlem data, in this and the forthcoming three chapters, in a singular attempt to qualify the manifest (i.e., statistical) relation between various integration indicators encountered in the literature, and end-goals of individual integration embodied by the local index. The resulting order presumably will provide a more secure basis from which more adequate measurements of individuals' integration into their surrounding locality can be undertaken.

The chapter consists of seven sections, as the six domains of local integration will be traversed before arriving at a preliminary assessment. The order in which the domains are brought into focus is not entirely arbitrary, and will be repeated in the following two chapters. First the notion of household positions, and the dependencies they entail, will be considered. Then testimony will be presented for the importance of individuals' educational positions. A comparable presentation will be made in the third section for job market positions, along with a consideration of the end-goal criterion of *per capita income*. The other positional criterion contained within the index, *welfare independence*, is presented in the fourth section. The notion of segmentation will be used in a fifth section to illuminate housing market positions, before I qualify respondents according to the neighborhoods in which they reside. Finally, the notion of individuals occupying public positions in the domain of civic life is considered. Predictably, the closing section offers a summary of important findings.

Private Intimacies and Household Dependents

The private domain is an aberration when considering the local engagement of individual immigrants. By definition the domain does not pertain to individuals' public affairs, and identifying a specific social good exchanged only within its bounds is difficult. I note at least two reasons however to consider individuals' private positions. First, the distinction between public and private domains varies with the (normative) perspective taken. Secondly, the significance attributed to individuals' private positions for their public engagement varies accordingly. Given these issues, what are private *dependencies* and *deprivations*, and can they be measured with survey instruments?

Let us begin by considering the contours of, and the commodities exchanged within the private domain. When I presume the institution of the family to be central for private relations, I note that the contours fluctuate with the distinction between nuclear and extended families. The commodities also vary along the entire spectrum of social needs. Distinctive for private exchanges is - it is almost tautological - the potential for intimacy, i.e., exchanges that are (preferably) not subject to the perusal of an unknown public. Besides as spatial context, intimacy can be conceived as a social good that individuals *acquire* in their contacts with (significant) others. Not all private relations however are intimate; nor is a lack of intimacy characteristic of 'public' personalities.

How can I conceptualize individuals' private positions as to their prospects for intimacy? One way is to consider their capacity to avoid public perusal, in combination with their prospects for personal ties that prosper within the available private space. Occupants of single family homes generally have more privacy than those in hospitals or prisons, but they are dependent upon friends and family to realize intimacy within it. This dependency upon others denotes the elastic contours of the private domain: the more occupants of a home, the greater number of intimate ties each resident potentially maintains. However, with more occupants the prospects to relate intimately on a one-to-one basis diminish.

With this premise the dilemma between *deprivation* (of intimacy) and *dependency* (upon others) is unveiled: individuals are dependent upon (significant) others for intimacy, but too much intimacy may diminish prospects to acquire positions and maintain contacts outside the private domain. Problematic resolutions to this dilemma, according to prevailing (Dutch) norms, are seen for instance in the single parent household with only one adult to provide intimacy and other commodities to young dependents (cf. Ryan, 1976:63-116; Tesser et al., 1995:175ff), in households with an excess of young dependents (AFS, 1993:20ff; Mok and Reinsch, 1993:5; Brief et al., 1997), and in households with strict divisions between public ($\male$) and private ($\female$) duties (cf. AFS, 1993:39, CTHOA, 1995; James et al., 1996).

That such distinctions form a *potential* impediment for immigrants' integration is illustrated in table 4.1, where differences in mean household size can be observed between Haarlem ethnic categories. Comparable to national findings (van Dugteren, 1993:25), the average Moroccan or Turkish household is one-and-a-half times larger than that of the indigenous Dutch. The five categories used to display differences in household type suggest that few Moroccan and Turks live alone (6%). Most reside instead in nuclear families with a partner and young children. 22% of the Moroccan and Turkish respondents reside in households with three or more children younger than the age of 18, compared to less than 10% of the respondents in other ethnic categories. The comparison of household types between categories illuminates at least two other ethnic-specific attributes commonly observed in the Netherlands: more Surinamese and Antillean respondents head single-parent households (Tesser et al., 1995:177; Veenman, 1997), and 'minorities' reside more often in (extended) households with other occupants besides partner and young children (cf. van Dugteren, 1993:22).

Table 4.1   Variations in household size and type

Household size/type	Moroc-cans	Turks	Surinamese Antilleans	'Other' immigrants	Indigenous Dutch
mean household size	4.8	3.9	3.1	2.6	2.6
single persons	6%	6%	15%	22%	26%
couple (married or not)	21%	22%	28%	39%	34%
couple with kids < 18 years	47%	58%	33%	28%	30%
single parent, kids < 18 years	1%	3%	10%	2%	1%
other (extended) household	25%	11%	14%	9%	10%
n (=100%)	91	156	72	98	169

Do these variations in the size and composition of households correspond with differences in their occupants' integration? In appendix I, where an overview of integration indicators is presented, two measures concerning respondents' households are displayed. The first, *household type*, shows whether differences in index scores vary with the five household categories distinguished in table 4.1. One may note that significant differences are only observed among the Turks (η = .29) and indigenous Dutch (η = .25). The pattern varies per ethnic category, but generally those immigrants residing in households with (many) young children are more estranged. Particularly 'single parent' households appear problematic, although with only 16 respondents in this category the results are particularly sensitive to sampling bias. Within the Turkish sample, all five sub-components comprising the local index are seen to vary with differences in household type. Particularly those Turks who reside in extended households are more satisfied with and active in their local surroundings. In other ethnic categories, the patterns are more diffuse. The only index sub-component that consistently corresponds with household type is *per capita income*: generally respondents residing alone or with only a partner have access to more monthly income. This statistical relation however is foreseen, as the per capita income criterion takes household sizes into account.

Table 4.2   Primary responsibility for household incomes

Responsible	Moroccans	Turks	Surinamese Antilleans	'Other' immigrants	Indigenous Dutch
respondent self	38%	39%	24%	39%	42%
partner	31%	29%	45%	45%	39%
respondent and partner	3%	20%	10%	7%	11%
someone else	28%	12%	22%	9%	8%
n (=100%)	81	136	51	69	118

During the interviews, the only inquiries into individuals' household positions concerned the question who is primarily responsible for the household income. The valid responses, reduced to four categories, are presented in table 4.2. The table displays several modest variations across ethnic categories, namely that few Surinamese or Antillean respondents consider themselves the primary 'breadwinners', while they and Moroccan respondents often convey that 'someone else' besides the partner is primarily responsible. Only among Moroccans and Turks could respondents' classification in one of these four categories be seen to correspond with their degree of integration. For immigrants there is then little evidence that *breadwinners* are more integrated than the *dependent* partners. One could at best conclude that breadwinners perceive their *opportunity* more favorably, but they do not express more *local satisfaction*, nor *cultural participation*. These results fail to substantiate the premise that the position of household dependent isolates immigrants from contacts with the local environment (cf. Spain, 1988; Hutton, 1991).

Rather than elaborate upon these theoretical issues, my more immediate concern are the measurement issues related to these distinctions. They begin with the presumption that the contours of individuals' private domain are better captured by a (spatial) notion of *household* than, for instance, by a (social) notion of *family*. The Dutch Central Bureau of Statistics (CBS) commonly observes households as the private context, presumably because it provides a more cogent basis for comparisons on individuals' housing and finances. An evaluation of CBS survey inquiries has suggested however that Turks and (particularly) Moroccans are ill acquainted with the Dutch notion of household (*huishouden*), while Surinamese and Antilleans differ in the meanings they give it (Meloen and Veenman, 1990:155ff). The notion of a household as a financial unit is particularly problematic, and overlooks the complex economic ties that immigrants maintain with family elsewhere (cf. Esveldt et al., 1995:119ff).

Problems of comparability associated with *household* measurements are complemented by an element of respondent distrust. Many welfare and tax regulations are contingent upon household composition. These lead to discrepancies between the *formal* household known to governmental offices, and the *informal* household of temporary and more permanent members who actually share rooms, meals and funds. The attributes just alluded to (i.e., time, space, activities, budget) suggest how multifaceted household boundaries are. The potential to perceive reliably this informal household is dependent in part upon the respondents' faith in the confidential nature of the survey.

The distinction between *breadwinners* and *dependents* is a further source of ambiguity within the household context. We observed in multiple-adult households that 62% had at least two members currently holding paid jobs. Would we have tallied as many breadwinners had we directed our inquiries, as is customary in survey research, to the 'head' of the formal household? How many of these breadwinners are younger than 18 and consequently dependents according to Dutch norms (cf. Schiepers et al., 1993)? When does a profusion of children form more than a financial obstacle to immigrants' integration? These questions may be considered fastidious and tendentious, but they are all pertinent to normative and theoretical perspectives in which immigrant households are considered an obstacle to their members' integration.

Thus far, I have concentrated upon the contours of the private domain, neglecting the individuals' positions within this domain. With the use of a crude labor market distinction between breadwinners and dependents, I have barely alluded to individuals' intimate responsibilities and privileges. More extensive survey protocols monitor individuals' positions within households. Generally they follow one of two monitoring lines: either they establish the respondent's kinship relation to the household 'head', or they map the entire household's affiliation to the selected respondent. The first

technique, may be adequate for purposes of monitoring dependency relationships between genders and generations. However, it bears the ambiguity that households may be characterized by a plurality of 'heads', and the
normative presumption that a 'head' is the household member with the largest income. The second technique uses a more inductive approach that may
help avoid such categorical problems but, certainly in large households
characterized by intricate networks of affiliation, its measurement is time-
consuming and intrusive. Wallman combined the second technique with an
extensive inventory of 'household machinery' to deduce the divergent tasks
and duties of household members (1982:214). Her study is as an examination of how positions and activities in the private domain may inhibit individuals' engagement in more public domains. It also serves to illustrate the
practical problems - of interview brevity and comparability - required to
examine this theoretical link.

This section has focused upon the household as private domain. I have
considered whether specific household types, particularly large households
with an inordinate number of dependents, are a detriment to individuals'
local integration. We observed in Haarlem that individual members of such
households tend toward financial deprivation, but we uncovered no manifest indications that these individuals are less satisfied with, or more isolated from, their local surroundings. A distinction between *breadwinners*
and *dependents* provided a rudimentary approach into the intimacies of
household positions. It served more to raise general methodological issues
as to the vague and variant boundaries of households, families and private
domains within divergent contexts. The household threshold signifies for a
Turkish woman with four children a greater barrier to local opportunity
than that experienced by the average resident. But the barrier appears to be
equally formidable for the single Turk without household intimates.

Diplomas: Time, Tuition and Tutorial Investments

The domain of education and upbringing was characterized in chapter two
as a market in *socialization*. I differentiate here between those (educational) exchanges that take place within the institutional confines of
schools, and child-rearing processes considered the responsibility of parents and other guardians. A strict distinction between the two commodities
is in itself a normative issue. For instance, seen from a (communistic) vision in which both commodities are best provided by the state, the distinction between education and upbringing is less manifest. The focus in this

section will be upon the measurement of educational differences, upbringing being considered briefly in closing.

Education

To what does the notion of educational position refer? When an image is drawn up of *knowledge* as a social good exchanged in educational markets, it refers to individuals' variant potential to teach and learn. However, if it is viewed in such general terms, it becomes a personality trait that is continuously manifested and altered by behavior. To simplify its measurement, the notion is limited here by references to (state regulated) markets in formal education. The dependency dilemma then helps to clarify the commodity exchange: individuals *acquire* (formal) educational degrees in exchange for their investments in conscious time and tuition. Moreover, they are *dependent* upon the various qualities of their teachers and schools, and the patience and trust of parents and benefactors, to ensure that their potential is optimally cultivated.

The interplay of these factors, in determining the quantity of formal education an individual ultimately acquires, reveals the difficulties bound to measurements of educational position. Unlike formal education in the United States for instance, where the designation of grade levels seemingly simplifies the task of tabulating the quantity of education an individual has acquired, Dutch education levels are more manifestly inordinate. This is due in part to variations in educational curricula and school denomination, so that age cohorts in Dutch secondary schools and colleges are more spatially segregated. Despite these factors, social researchers recognize a stable rank order - based on the legitimacy of centralized state examinations.

Following these presumptions, respondents are classified in table 4.3 into four educational positions, or levels. A distinction is made between educational levels attained in the Netherlands - a position many immigrants fail to acquire - and general (estimates of) levels completed regardless of where (the percentages in bold face). One sees that a large majority of Moroccans and Turks have completed some form of primary school at best, and that most of the other three ethnic categories have completed higher forms of secondary education. Variations in educational position among Surinamese and Antilleans largely parallel those of indigenous Dutch; while 'Other' immigrants have as a category completed even higher educational levels. The percentile distributions within ethnic categories correspond roughly with 1994 national survey measurements (Martens, 1995:48; Tesser et al., 1996:156), albeit that Haarlem residents (particularly Surinamese and Antilleans) have attained slightly higher levels.

Table 4.3   Variations in level of formal education completed

Educational level	Moroccans		Turks		Surinamese Antilleans		'Other' immigrants		Indigenous Dutch	
	NL	∩	NL	∩	NL	∩	NL	∩	NL	∩
primary at best	24%	67%	24%	66%	4%	20%	12%	16%	13%	16%
lower secondary (*lbo/mulo/mavo*)	56%	22%	48%	20%	21%	25%	22%	24%	30%	29%
upper secondary (*mbo/havo/vwo*)	16%	9%	20%	12%	49%	38%	41%	36%	34%	32%
collegiate (*hbo/wo*)	4%	2%	9%	3%	26%	16%	25%	24%	24%	23%
n (100%) =	25	88	46	154	47	68	68	88	157	163

* NL = education completed in the Netherlands, ∩ = education completed anywhere.

The relevance of these differences in educational position for individuals' integration can be discerned in appendix I. Within all five samples local index scores vary significantly with differences in educational level completed. The eta statistic for all immigrant categories combined is an impressive .61, signifying that differences in educational position account for 37% of the index variance. A brief review of the results displayed in appendix I reveals that no other indicator considered in this and the forthcoming chapters accounts for so much variance, nor is any indicator so consistently significant within all five ethnic categories. This observation remains valid when the focus is limited to those immigrants who have acquired Dutch formal education. It also applies when the analysis is expanded to immigrants' scores upon the five components that form the local index. Educational background is the most reliable predictor of a Haarlem immigrant's integration.

Nevertheless, even these results do not warrant the conclusion that integration is merely a matter of time, namely the time immigrants invest in formal education. An analysis of the five components that contribute to the index serves to reveal some discrepancies. While *perceived opportunity* generally corresponds (linearly) with an individual's educational level,[1] *per capita income* and *local satisfaction* do not. For Moroccans and Turks the correlations between educational level and per capita income remain insignificant. For 'Other' immigrants, and for Haarlem immigrants overall, the income variance accounted for by Dutch educational achievements are modest, namely less than 10%. In short, if material wealth is the end-goal of immigrants' integration, education is not necessarily the means.

More perplexing is the relation between educational position and *local satisfaction*. Among those Turks and Surinamese/Antilleans who have acquired Dutch diplomas the correlation is highly significant - and among the Turks quite negative. The observation that the more Dutch education, the less Turks are content with their local situation, alludes to the dependency dilemma. Has their schooling cultivated a conscious estrangement, disaffected from local immigrants and indigents? Or have they simply learned to be more critically outspoken? Clarifications for the discontent among these more educated Turks are wrought with statistical uncertainty, as it concerns only fourteen respondents who have completed higher secondary or collegiate levels. Nevertheless, in comparison with other Turkish respondents they are markedly more critical of their neighborhoods, and half have an outspoken preference for remigration to Turkey or to other countries. They do not differ appreciably in their ethnic orientations, in their perspectives on local integration objectives, or their local ties.

These measurements illustrate the crucial but complex role education plays in immigrant integration. The designation of educational positions entails presumptions concerning three issues:

- rank order differences in educational background,
- the social-cultural antecedents of educational inequality, and
- their potential significance for individuals' later integration as adults.

To measure how much education individuals acquired, differences in the time parameter must be brought in conjunction with spatial and curricular variations. For instance, equivalencies between Moroccan and Dutch levels, and between technical and social curricula, must be presumed.

Three factors are then the focus of Dutch debates on the determinants of educational position, namely: individuals' social economic background, their cultural upbringing, and the stimulation they receive in the school environment (cf. Veenman, 1995:100ff). These three factors are complemented by (market) processes at local or national level that influence the supply of educational opportunity. The measurement of these factors, to unravel their interactive influence, requires an impressive list of theoretical and mathematical presumptions. Ultimately, presumptions and premises concerning the potential significance of individuals' education must guide the researcher in the selection of components to be measured.

Upbringing

This leads me, briefly, to a few observations on child-rearing. They are succinct in part because within the Haarlem survey child-rearing as a local issue was largely overlooked, providing little empirical material. Research on child-rearing within immigrant households may focus upon problems of educational orientation (cf. van der Hoek, 1994; Pels, 1998) or juvenile delinquency (cf. Bovenkerk, 1994:9; van Gemert, 1998) among immigrant youth. More generally, it concerns the transmission of divergent cultural orientations from one generation to the next (cf. Pels, 1994; Rispens et al., 1996). Such issues may be seen to have 'immediate' relevance for processes of local (e.g., public safety) and group integration. However, the long-term effect of upbringing for the *individual* integration of future adults is a topic that does not lend itself for - brief, simple and comparable - survey research.

The importance of the child-rearing role for the individual integration of parents or guardians forms a more immediate research topic. What investments in time, money and dignity does the child-rearing position entail? How much (and why) do immigrants vary in their fulfillment of upbringing tasks? What effect does child-rearing have for immigrants' other positions, their orientations and behavior? Again, these questions cannot be adequately examined with brief and simple surveys, and I am unaware of initiatives in this research direction.

The attention given to upbringing issues is dependent upon the more general purpose of the survey. If one is concerned with immigrants' differential engagement in local activities, then is the child-rearing position largely a mitigating circumstance. If the focus is more upon (cultural) polarities transmitted from one generation to the next, then more precise attention must be paid to those respondents in child-rearing positions.

These simple precepts point to more general considerations that demarcate measurement obstacles in the domain of education and upbringing. Where one is in search of immediate indications for respondents' degree of integration, then educational position is primarily a background (i.e., antecedent) indicator instrumental for individuals' position and orientation in other domains. With this observation the divergent opportunities individuals have and use as adults to alter their educational position is neatly overlooked. However, where the purpose is to comprehend immigrant integration more fundamentally as a process, one is confronted with the broader issues concerning educational opportunity as it varies from one (immigrant) generation on to the next. Within such research contexts, the upbringing individuals provide should be more integrally linked with the schooling they have (had). This is one reason child-rearing activities have not been relegated to the private domain (cf. Rex, 1996:21ff). Yet to monitor this process, one must rely upon the memory, patience and trust of survey respondents. Coupled with the difficulties of international school comparisons, these obstacles form a considerable challenge for those seeking to establish education's significance for immigrants' integration.

Financial Security: Labor and State Benefactors

The domain of work and material security links two metaphorical markets, one on which human labor is exchanged, and another on which material means of existence are exchanged. Paid labor provides the common link, there where an individual makes or provides products or services in exchange for material benefits. The markets diverge in that work is not necessarily reimbursed in material terms, and material wealth is not necessarily acquired through productive labor. Both markets are subject to intensive analysis and regulation, exemplified by the wide range of concepts used to comprehend market dynamics and the ongoing discrepancy between formal and informal market relations. In this section various attributes bound to individuals' market positions will be briefly sketched, while outlining various issues bound to the allocation and measurement of categorical distinctions. Several issues concerning immigrants' positions on the two markets will receive particular attention. The status associated with individuals' labor market position and the estimate of labor opportunity are first considered. The formal norms and cultural taboos bound to the calculation of *per capita income* are then considered in the second sub-section.

Paid, Potential and Underclass Labor

To unravel the complex lacework of attributes that circumscribe an individual's labor market position, I consider again the potential relevance of this position with the dilemma between deprivation and dependency. This leads me to focus upon issues of (material) reimbursement and (self)regulation. The former is concerned with the nature of the activity perceived as an occupation (the production or provision of a good or service) and the payment in return (the immediate provision or promise of wages, products and services). Market regulation refers to distinctions between (self-employed) entrepreneurs, employers and employees, and the extent in which such positions are created, supported and controlled by state, public and private organizations. In everyday terms, one is interested in monitoring whether an individual has a job (paid or voluntary), what the job entails (function and sector), how much is earned, and to what extent the position and earnings are secure (e.g., piecework or formal contract).

Labor market engagement has been consistently identified as the key to immigrants' integration (Gordon, 1963; Esser, 1980; WRR, 1989; RMO, 1998). How can its significance be perceived within the local context? In the Haarlem survey, we focused on whether respondents had 'paid' positions. Based on two responses respondents were categorized into one of five labor market positions. The percentages per ethnic category occupying each position are presented in table 4.4.[2] The table displays several obvious market differences between the ethnic categories. Focusing upon those respondents currently *active* on the labor market (i.e., the first three rows), one may note that cumulative percentages vary from half the Moroccans to three-fourths of the 'Other' immigrants. The percentage 'jobless seeking work' among this *active* labor force ranges from 4% of the indigenous Dutch to 24% of the Moroccans and Turks. A couple noteworthy distinctions, concealed within the percentages for respondents not active on the labor market, concern the percentage inactive Moroccan women (63%) and the percentage Moroccans and Turks who name physical disabilities as the primary reason for their inactivity (16% resp. 13%).[3]

Table 4.4   Variations in labor market position

Labor market position	Moroc-cans	Turks	Surinamese Antilleans	'Other' immigrants	Indigenous Dutch
full-time work (> 32 hrs/wk)	26%	43%	31%	41%	47%
part-time work	12%	10%	21%	21%	23%
jobless seeking work	12%	17%	8%	12%	3%
inactive with job potential	33%	15%	27%	12%	8%
inactive retired or disabled	17%	15%	13%	13%	19%
n (=100%)	93	157	77	99	170

Do these variations correspond with respondents' degree of integration? Continuing the simple but systematic comparison, one can see in appendix I that the distinction in five labor market positions accounts for significant variations in all ethnic categories. For Haarlem immigrants overall, 15% of the variance in the local index is accounted for by differences in labor market position. These results should not be purely construed as testimony for the premise that the more active are more integrated. The relation is more nominally diffuse. Among indigenous Dutch those with 'full-time work' are the most integrated and the 'jobless seeking work' the least. Among immigrants the index range varies from the 'part-time workers' on the one end and the 'inactively retired/disabled' on the other. Particularly among Moroccans and Turks one can observe those in the latter position - primarily disabled men - to be particularly estranged. In short, the most estranged immigrants are not the job seekers dependent upon market fluctuations in supply and demand, but those more permanently excluded from the labor market (cf. Roelandt, 1994).

The differentiation in (five) labor market positions offers only a nominal distinction between respondents. Hierarchical distinctions can be made among those individuals with paid work, by considering their occupation or function. Research has focused upon these attributes to identify 'successful' immigrants (Dagevos and Veenman, 1992). The occupational prestige scale used in Dutch studies is based upon the rank allocated a select number (116) of occupations (see Sixma and Ultee, 1983). Besides its merits, this scale has several limitations. Two are intrinsic to such scales: they exclude those survey respondents without recognized occupations, and their validity diminishes with historical shifts in the occupational structure (Bakker, 1994). Other limitations are more specifically related to dilemmas of immigrant integration. A unidimensional prestige scale combines occupational *dependencies* concerning time investments (e.g., those factors sensitive to education and training) with those concerning job autonomy (e.g., employee or entrepreneur positions) and other social criteria (e.g., isolated or cooperative activities). Succinctly stated, the scale 'homogenizes' the value attributed a given occupation according to divergent cultural norms.

These limitations allude to the difficulties encountered when measuring labor market *mobility* as an indication of an immigrant's successful integration (cf. Dagevos, 1998; Liem, 2000). Similar problems pertain to the estimate of labor *opportunity*. Can one compare an individual's *prospects* of climbing the occupational ladder with those of other market participants? Dagevos and others (1996:50ff) calculated standards for immigrant joblessness based on the percentage jobless encountered among indigenous Dutch with similar age, gender and educational levels. The measures were presented as aggregates per minority category, but more precise measures could be given for specific cohorts, and they could conceivably be further specified according to the labor sector where work is sought. Such measures retain a quality of 'color blindness', as they presume geo-political origins to be irrelevant when considering individuals' qualifications. A more practical limitation resides in the number of respondents required to make relevant comparisons across ethnic categories.

Table 4.5 illustrates the possibilities and limitations bound to such measures. In the table percentile estimates are presented for respondents with paid work, differentiated according to minority status and level of education completed (omitting respondents older than 65 or currently enrolled as full-time students). The table offers the possibility to compare (horizontally) the labor prospects of individuals in various ethnic categories with a comparable educational background. Various types of immigrants are differentiated, namely:

- 'Minorities' with Moroccan, Turkish, Surinamese or Antillean geo-political origins (column 2),
- any respondent (one of whose parents was) born outside the Netherlands (column 3), or
- any (first or second generation) immigrant who has attended Dutch schools (column 4).

Table 4.5   Percentage of educational cohorts with paid work

Educational level completed	Immigrant 'minorities'	All immigrants	Dutch educated immigrants	Indigenous Dutch
primary education (*bo*) at best	41%* (155)	42%* (92)	46%* (22)	71% (14)
lower secondary (*lbo/mavo*)	67%* (49)	67%* (69)	69%* (48)	82% (39)
higher secondary (*mbo/vwo*)	74% (38)	71%* (96)	75% (80)	84% (37)
collegiate level (*hbo/wo*)	77% (13)	95%* (56)	98%* (40)	85% (34)
all levels combined	53%* (255)	66%* (313)	75% (190)	82% (124)

* Chance that population % does not differ from survey estimate for indigenous Dutch is less than 5%.. In parentheses the number of respondents are presented upon which the estimates are made (n=100%).

The comparison reveals that the labor prospects are much less than those for indigenous Dutch residents, except for college educated immigrants. Before concluding that the differences are due to exclusionary practices one should, following Dagevos and others, differentiate further according to age, gender and occupational sector. Yet already the number of respondents, upon which specific percentages are calculated, is so low that several percentile differences lack sufficient sample reliability. To differentiate for these additional three factors, literally thousands of respondents per ethnic category are required. In cities the size of Haarlem the number of possible categories (i.e., control factors) are severely limited. Moreover, in large surveys that enable differentiated measures for job opportunity, one must still interpret the measures' theoretical significance. Not only might they reveal the effect of immigrant exclusion, they ambiguously suggest exclusionary practices revolving around age, gender, schooling and labor market segmentation.

With these observations the contours of the labor market have been briefly scrutinized to identify several primary measurement obstacles. Particular issues associated with the position of entrepreneur have been neglected (cf., Choenni, 1997); references to the segmentation (and categorization) of market sectors have been minimal (cf., Niesing, 1993); and only with the 'part-time' qualification are there allusions to time and duration in job acquisition and mobility processes (cf., van Eekert and Gelderloos, 1990). The distinctions between paid and voluntary work, between formal and informal relations, and between job deprivation and job mobility testify to the dilemmas that confound job market processes, and to the categorical ambiguities associated with market measurement.

Per Capita Income and State Dependency

To situate individuals' position on the material security market, three questions could be posed. What are the various sources of material security? How much security does an individual possess? What dependencies are tied to the securities acquired? Such survey questions would presumably elicit a wide range of philosophical, puzzled and non responses. The sources, manifestations and processes of material enrichment are nevertheless crucial to conceptions of the immigrant minority (van Amersfoort, 1974), the underclass (Roelandt, 1994), and the poor (Engbersen et al., 1997) that have fueled Dutch debates on immigrant integration. Such goods are difficult to measure with survey instruments, which is one reason that the standard unit in the Netherlands is the currently stable guilder (equal to €0.45). With this unit, finding individuals on the material security market is reduced to estimations of their *financial position*.

Measuring financial position, despite the prospects of rational level indicators, is wrought with unreliability (cf. Meloen and Veenman, 1990: 176ff). Even should researchers have access to individuals' tax records, discrepancies remain between formal and informal transactions. Though respondents may be found willing to convey their actual situation, positions may fluctuate acutely over time, subject not only to variations in income and expenditures but also to respondents' memory. Moreover, the respondents' position may be integrally related to the activities of family or household members in ways that the respondent self is unaware. The size of this measurement error is dependent in part upon the survey context (e.g., the capacity to penetrate eventual privacy norms about personal finances), and upon the normative or theoretical perspective that delineate measurement categories. Income sources for instance may be classified under: ethnicity, legality, regularity, dependency and services rendered in exchange.

Table 4.6   Mean estimated monthly household income*

Primary income source	Moroccans	Turks	Surinamese Antilleans	'Other' immigrants	Indigenous Dutch
Employment	ƒ 2674 (44%)	ƒ 2867 (65%)	ƒ 2971 (59%)	ƒ 3177 (64%)	ƒ 3255 (60%)
Business profits	-	ƒ 4000 (1%)	ƒ 3450 (3%)	ƒ 2308 (5%)	ƒ 3293 (10%)
Old age pension/*aow*	-	ƒ 2332 (6%)	ƒ 2100 (3%)	ƒ 2055 (11%)	ƒ 2256 (14%)
Other (state) benefits	ƒ 2051 (49%)	ƒ 2035 (18%)	ƒ 1300 (33%)	ƒ 1629 (16%)	ƒ 1924 (12%)
Other/mixed sources	ƒ 2800 (8%)	ƒ 2119 (10%)	ƒ 1300 (2%)	ƒ 2121 (5%)	ƒ 3161 (3%)
Mean for all cohorts	ƒ 2380	ƒ 2622	ƒ 2381	ƒ 2725	ƒ 2963
Per capita income	ƒ 1163	ƒ 1453	ƒ 1474	ƒ 1885	ƒ 1999
n (=100%)	80	145	58	88	144

* The numbers in parentheses indicate the percentage of respondents with this primary income source.

In the Haarlem survey, we focused upon (*state*) *dependency* categories to differentiate between *primary sources of income*. Respondents were asked to estimate the net monthly household income by designating one of nine (ordinally-ranked) income categories. The responses are summarized in table 4.6, where household income is differentiated for each of the five ethnic categories according to primary income sources. The table displays several substantive differences and methodological obstacles. Focusing first on the bottom two rows, one observes that the mean household income ranges from f2380 for the Moroccan and Surinamese/Antillean categories to f2963 for indigenous Dutch. The funds for an adult household member, one of the five criteria that make up the local index, displays a broader mean range between ethnic categories (from f1163 to f1999). Again, the statistic for household income is not based upon monetary figures explicitly conveyed by respondents, but upon their more passive designation of a broad income category.[4] The *per capita income* statistic is the quotient of this estimate when weighted by information concerning household size, calculated according to CBS equivalency scales.[5] These statistics are therefore derived using common measurement techniques, and are comparable to other local and national estimates (cf. Gemeente Haarlem, 1996:122; Martens and Veenman, 1996:75). However, the use of CBS equivalency scales is based upon the presumption that immigrant households display the same budgetary behavior as indigenous Dutch (cf. NIBUD, 1997:65), while the use of standard income categories prohibits for instance the identification of households that subsist below poverty levels (cf. Veenman, 1997:214).

The primary income sources, summarized in the upper five rows of table 4.6, reveal several significant distinctions: immigrants earn less via employment; they vary greatly in the mean amount of monthly state benefits received (due in part to differences in household size); and more immigrant households are dependent upon state benefits as a primary source of financial security. Moroccans in particular are likely to be state dependents; only 44% designate paid work as a primary income source.

Does this differentiation between respondents according to the primary source of their household income help distinguish the integrated from the estranged? In appendix II.2 it can be noted that for four of the five ethnic categories (the exception being the Surinamese and Antilleans) differences in primary income source correspond with variations in the local index. The relation is partly one of design, in that the (state) income sources help determine the amount of per capita income, one of the five components of the local index. Nevertheless the findings display again a categorical diversification that prohibits broad generalizations on the state dependency of estranged immigrants. For instance, those Haarlem immigrants dependent upon 'business profits' score highest on the local index (according to the other four components) while those dependent upon 'other (state) benefits' the lowest. These findings display subtle distinctions with the indigenous Dutch, among whom those dependent upon 'employment' score highest on all index components, while the lowest scores are found among the elderly dependent upon pensions and state benefits.

After first correcting for sampling stratification, the differences in per capita income within the adult Haarlem population could be derived from the survey respondents' estimates. Table 4.7 summarizes the distribution of ethnic categories along this (standardized) income spectrum, by presenting the category percentages in each of four quartiles. Nearly 95% of all Moroccans subsist on less than the *average resident*, three-fourths belonging to the poorest local quartile. A large majority of the other three immigrant categories are also seen to subsist on less than the *average resident*, the income distribution among Turks roughly paralleling that of Surinamese and Antilleans. In the forthcoming section and chapters, comparable tables will be presented for the other four components of the local index. None however will display such discrepancies between immigrant and indigenous Dutch residents as shown here for their income distributions.

Table 4.7   Quartile distribution along per capita income spectrum

Quartile	Moroccans	Turks	Surinamese Antilleans	'Other' immigrants	Indigenous Dutch
poorest 25%	76%	47%	43%	27%	22%
25% - 50%	18%	32%	35%	40%	18%
50% - 75%	3%	15%	14%	7%	29%
richest 25%	2%	6%	8%	26%	30%
standardized mean	-1.12	-0.72	-0.67	-0.1	0.07
stanard deviation	0.66	0.79	0.89	1.03	0.99
n (=100%)	93	159	77	99	170

To devise a more adequate measure of individuals' financial position, as criterion for their degree of integration, one would ultimately need to calculate personal *wealth*. Reasoning in budgetary terms, this amounts to a 'balance' between individuals' assets and liabilities. I am unaware of survey attempts to perforate prevailing norms so rudely, but in principle personal savings and debts could serve as rough estimates. More comprehensive means to monitor the dynamics of personal wealth and financial opportunity would be to compare household income with expenditures. The NIBUD survey (1997) provided the first such Dutch overview of immigrant household budgets. The number of survey questions necessary to derive such budgetary overviews is prohibitive, but specific budgetary posts have done service as indicators of immigrant households' financial position (cf. Meloen and Veenman, 1988:app2/40).

In this sub-section per capita income has been focused upon as indicator of financial position. Besides noting the brief but unreliable survey techniques used for measurement of income variations, the more general problem of estimating financial position and material wealth has been briefly considered. Before designing lengthy and intrusive measurements of household assets and budgets, a return to the more normative issue seems prudent: which positions on the material security market are relevant for local and individual integration? Reasoning within a *tolerant vision*, I presume that as long as large groups of immigrants require state benefits to realize a minimum of material security, objectives of civil liberty have little legitimacy. Accordingly, research does not need to monitor the many nuances in local prosperity. It should focus instead upon measures that locate those individuals and groups who are deprived of a minimum on material wealth necessary to agree and comply with local objectives.

Welfare Independence and Personal Well-being

The previous section focused upon per capita income as criterion of material wealth, and the importance of paid work in acquiring it. The domain of health and welfare can be considered its metaphorical complement as the central market for the acquisition of immaterial wealth. In this section the welfare independence criterion is presented that together with per capita income serve as positional components in the local index. More generally I reflect upon the possibility to survey the social welfare market.

First I should note that the conceptual distinction between individuals' physical health and psychic welfare, when measured via the self-evaluation of individual respondents, does not encourage empirical clarity. The two are here contained in a notion of *personal well-being*, which on its part has a spectral character. The domain consequently encompasses a market for social welfare where individuals with their variant well-being seek nourishment (cf. Hortulanus et al., 1993:61ff).

This being said, how can the premise be substantiated that individuals' well-being signifies not only a personal quality, but also denotes a degree of integration? An inability to cope with the demands of local life would presumably manifest itself in chronic disorders, particularly in the sub-domain of psychic welfare. Survey measurements like this, which enable the comparison of immigrants with indigenous Dutch, are rare (cf. Bollini and Siem, 1995). Uniken Venema, in a survey of Rotterdam Turks and indige-nous Dutch, probed respondents' chronic ailments and mental stress, using instruments that serve in more general health surveys conducted by the Dutch CBS. Turkish respondents express a greater occurrence of chronic disorders, but only two social attributes clearly correspond with the occur-rence of such disorders: unsatisfactory contacts with indigenous residents, and the desire to re-migrate (Uniken Venema, 1989:201). The fact that these measurements fail to reveal relations with other attributes raises doubts concerning the validity of the instruments (cf. Uniken Venema, 1995). Particularly the instrument used to measure 'psychic stress', the so-called 'VOEG' questionnaire (Dirken, 1969), has been found unreliable (Meloen and Veenman, 1990:189) and ambiguous (Furer et al., 1995:55ff). Systematic evaluations of survey instruments have been recently con-ducted, for the measurement of psychic welfare (Furer et al., 1995) and for physical health (König-Zahn et al., 1995). Dutch researchers thus have more ready access to instruments with proven validity across national bor-ders. However, a brief, valid *thermometer* is not among them. One can bet-ter first consider more theoretically which ailments suggest an individual state of detachment.

In the Haarlem study, we did not delve into respondents' personal well-being. We did ask about their use of social services. Our purpose was to examine potential problems with the accessibility of those services, but the data also provides rough indications of individuals' position on a more gen-eral social welfare market. Respondents were namely asked which of nine types of social services had been used during the year prior to the survey.[6]

In table 4.8 the percentages per ethnic category are presented for each of the nine types of social service used. One may note that, while only sport facilities and libraries are used by most of the indigenous Dutch, most respondents in the other four ethnic categories use a variety of other service types. This is most immediately reflected by the figures in the bot-tom row of the table, which display the mean number of service types used by respondents.[7]

These initial observations presume that various types of social services have a similarly essential value: the more services an individual uses, the more *engaged* an individual is upon the social welfare market. The various services allude however to qualitatively divergent commodities. For in-stance, an individual who frequents welfare or legal offices is generally in more dire straits than one who only uses sport facilities and libraries. When these notions are transposed to the local level, a segmented market for social welfare is observed. On the one end *necessary services* are provided to those individuals required (by the state) to solicit for specific social goods in other domains: labor exchanges for job seekers, welfare bureaus for social security recipients, housing offices for the homeless, police and lawyers for legal assistance. At the other end one encounters *arrangements* where social goods are offered, not so much to the needy but to the residents voluntarily in search of recreation: libraries, sport and educational facilities, and activity centers (cf. Hortulanus et al.; 1993).

Table 4.8   Use of local social services the previous year

Type of social service	Moroccans	Turks	Surinamese Antilleans	'Other' immigrants	Indigenous Dutch
Labor exchange, welfare, other social security offices	52%	57%	51%	31%	29%
Municipal or cooperative housing	50%	46%	42%	27%	23%
Legal services, police or fire department	46%	56%	31%	37%	24%
Health or nursing services	56%	62%	51%	50%	38%
Day-care or nursery centers	13%	24%	20%	18%	6%
Neighborhood activity centers	18%	26%	25%	17%	16%
Educational services	46%	55%	46%	44%	26%
Sport facilities	33%	53%	57%	59%	58%
Libraries	32%	39%	68%	50%	60%
Mean # service types used	3.4	4.1	3.8	3.3	2.8
n (=100%)	89	155	72	96	168

The welfare independence component within the local index is based upon this distinction. I have adapted the normative viewpoint that personal well-being is essentially a private matter, and have presumed that only those deprived of such well-being become dependent upon *necessary services*. The distinction is not only based upon the presumption that the necessary services are adequate and accessible 'from the cradle to the grave'. It also presumes that those who do not frequent necessary services are not in need of them.

This qualitative distinction is reflected by the order in which the social services are presented in table 4.8. The specific order however is not only grounded conceptually; statistical analyses show a tendency among respondents either to use service clusters at one end of the spectrum, or arrangement clusters at the other.[8] Stated concretely, those respondents who used labor or welfare services the previous year are least likely (among social service clients) to have frequented public libraries.

The distribution of respondents along this statistical spectrum is summarized in table 4.9. If absolutely no differences existed between ethnic categories, then equal percentages (namely 25%) would be observed in all table cells. Instead one observes that most of the Moroccans and Turks are found at the dependent end of the spectrum, in the resident quartile most in need of local services. More than 60% of the other two immigrant categories also score lower than the 'average resident,' but the mean scores for these two categories are much closer to the local mean (zero) than those for the Moroccans and Turks.

Table 4.9   Quartile distribution on welfare independence spectrum

Quartile	Moroccans	Turks	Surinamese Antilleans	'Other' immigrants	Indigenous Dutch
dependent (lowest 25%)	56%	57%	33%	28%	24%
relatively dependent	29%	29%	31%	34%	23%
relatively independent	12%	6%	22%	18%	21%
independent (highest 25%)	3%	9%	14%	19%	32%
standardized mean	-0.96	-0.91	-0.3	-0.17	0.07
standard deviation	0.98	1.01	0.87	0.99	0.98
n (=100%)	93	159	77	99	170

How well do respondents' positional scores along this spectrum correlate with their scores upon the other four components within the local index? One can observe (in appendix table II.1) that the overall correlations (i.e., for all immigrants) are all significant. Particularly that the correlation with per capita income (R=.28 for all immigrants) attests to the component's (concurrent) validity as a measure of *welfare independence* (cf. Kidder and Judd, 1986:55). However, as central measure of personal well-being, these scores allude to an interval precision that cannot be validated. The problem is in part the categorization of theoretically and locally relevant social services (cf. Roelandt and Veenman, 1989). Moreover, a more precise tabulation of service use (i.e., ordinal level or higher) would enable the application of more powerful statistical techniques. The scores presented here for instance remain (too) sensitive to differences due to sample stratification. Nevertheless, the results illustrate how even nominal measurements can be used to estimate individual rank-positions along a social welfare spectrum.

With the decline of the welfare state (cf. van de Swaan, 1988; Esping-Andersen, 1990), the notion of self-reliance (*zelfredzaamheid*) has come increasingly into vogue in Europe. With deference to this notion, a measure of *welfare independence* has been designated a central criterion within the index for individual integration. In this section the adequacy of the component, based upon respondents' use of divergent types of social services, has been considered. The presumptions needed to perceive the component as a measure of personal well-being, i.e., individuals' *position* along a spectrum of immaterial wealth, have also been examined. Along these lines, complementary measures for individuals' evaluation of personal health (cf. Uniken Venema, 1989:10ff) are needed for the realization of more valid measurements.

Neighborhood Environments: Visibly Overlapping Markets

The previous sections have all focused upon abstract commodity markets. The goods being exchanged - except perhaps financial securities - are quite intangible and imperceptible. The neighborhood environment domain, due to its spatial character, contains more observable commodities: residential dwellings. Moreover, neighborhoods themselves have other tangible qualities that motivate residents to remain or to move. This would presumably simplify observations within this domain but, when the purpose is to specify immigrants' position on housing and neighborhood markets, spatial realities are not that simple. Perhaps because they are so clearly multidimensional. Let us take a look.

Homes: Investments and Interventions

First I consider ways to rank immigrants' integration according to their position on the housing market. The nominal distinction between the haves and the homeless immediately presents itself. The furtive image of the homeless vagabond, as counterposed to sedentary ideals, is a symbolic scapegoat of European culture (Preiswerk, 1980:137). It also fits neatly within the notion of local detachment (cf. Burgers, 1995:137). However, opportunities to examine the tenability of this observation are limited. Homeless urban residents are arguably the least accessible subjects for survey samples (cf. Korf and Deben, 1997). They are excluded de facto from most surveys - including the one in Haarlem - that refrain from randomly approaching 'men-in-the-street.'

How could one sensibly rank residents with homes to show their market position? Exploiting the spatial characteristics, the size of the home could be noted: square meters and number of rooms are common measurement units (SCP, 1998:257). These may subsequently be considered in relation to the number of household members, and to the housing costs. In Haarlem for instance, the mean room occupation (i.e., inhabitants/rooms) ranges from 0.7 for indigenous Dutch and 0.8 for Surinamese/Antilleans to 1.1 for Turks and 1.2 for Moroccans. These ratios correspond with national estimates (cf. SCP, 1998:257). One could conclude that Moroccans have scarcely half as many rooms at their disposal as indigenous Dutch, but we could also observe that their housing expenses, even per room, are less. This is where the dilemmas surface. Does inexpensive housing signify immigrants' successful market penetration, or have they simply cornered a less prestigious segment of the market? To deal with this diversion, the housing size/expense ratio could be considered in relation to the housing quality. For this latter attribute, survey indicators range from building age (which is seldom a linear function as to building value) to entire home-quality scoring systems (e.g., van Dugteren et al., 1993:131ff). We sufficed with a distinction in housing types, ranging from flats (i.e., any residence in which a floor or ceiling borders on another dwelling) through single-family row houses to freestanding homes (cf. Meloen and Veenman, 1990:161). This distinction is coarse - it fails to differentiate between a hovel and a manor - but a greater dilemma evolves around the issue of ownership. The difference between tenants and owners does not only complicate comparisons in housing costs; the fact that tenants have no home to exchange on the market affects their prospects for market mobility.

I am about to reach the central dilemma bound to housing market positions. First the distribution of Haarlem respondents in four housing categories is presented. They are differentiated according to the type of housing in which they reside and by their status of tenant or owner. One may note in table 4.10 a familiar rank-order by comparing the percentages per ethnic category that reside as tenants in flats (first row) with those for owners of single family homes (fourth row). A large majority of Moroccans and Turks find themselves in the former position, while more indigenous Dutch find themselves in the latter. With a few nuances - to account for spatial, cost and quality variations - the contours of a housing market spectrum could be perceived, upon which immigrants improve their position by acquiring a home (cf. Rohe and Basolo, 1997).

Table 4.10 Variations in housing market positions

Housing market position	Moroc-cans	Turks	Surinamese Antilleans	'Other' immigrants	Indigenous Dutch
tenant in flat	73%	70%	43%	40%	27%
tenant in single family home	20%	10%	20%	20%	14%
owner of flat	6%	7%	8%	5%	15%
owner of single family home	1%	14%	29%	35%	44%
n (=100%)	86	153	76	95	170

The problem with this perspective concerns *social housing*. In Haarlem, approximately 58% of the housing market consists of rentals, while 37% is either government-owned or cooperative housing in which allocation and rental prices are state-regulated (Gemeente Haarlem, 1996:54). This latter percentage is comparable to national averages, but less than in the four largest cities (van Kempen, 1997:168) where an inordinate proportion of immigrants reside. The allocation and price policies differ per municipality, but precedence is generally given to large, low-income households with prolonged local residence duration (van Kempen, 1997:172). In principle, and in contrast to free market processes, individuals' prospects to rent a residence on this market increase when their financial position worsens. Succinctly stated, social housing *interventions* have 'de-commodified' a most tangible market good (cf. Blanc, 1992; Burgers, 1995:139; van Amersfoort and Cortie, 1996:685).

What are the implications for the measurement of immigrant integration? Individuals essentially have two positions, one within the social housing market and one within the free market. These positions are interrelated and, considered from divergent normative viewpoints, often at odds. Recent arrivals find themselves either dependent upon landlords or forced to purchase a home (cf. Tesser et al., 1996:137). The prospects for a home owner on the social housing market are limited, although such rentals may be the better deal as for comfort and expense. Mobility between the markets is further affected by tenants who choose to remain in social housing flats rather than use their accumulated wealth for acquisitions on the free market.

The relation between the two markets, and the attributes that specify individuals' market positions, clearly vary from city to city. In Haarlem we could not adequately analyze the relation, if only because we refrained from asking tenants to whom they pay the rent. The positional distinctions presented in table 4.10 do correspond with respondents' scores along the local index. For indigenous Dutch and immigrants overall the analysis shows that homeowners are more integrated (η=.40). When focusing upon specific minority categories however, the correspondence is neither significant nor linear. The small numbers of minorities who own their homes help clarify the statistical insignificance. However, those few minority respondents who are homeowners, particularly among Moroccans and Turks, do not score higher upon (components of) the local index. Perhaps these more *engaged* immigrants have missed the opportunity for social housing, and find themselves disproportionately dependent upon bank mortgages and the insecurities of the free market. Or perhaps they find themselves in the 'less auspicious' neighborhoods.

Neighbors: Aggregates and Agents

Moving then to the surrounding neighborhood, two qualities distinguish it from the more imminent housing market. First, as a spatial entity, the boundaries of neighborhoods vary from one resident to the next (Lee and Campbell, 1997). In subjective terms, every resident inhabits the center of his or her neighborhood, and the neighborhood's size may be affected by subjective factors. In Haarlem we observed that Moroccans, and to a lesser extent Turks, convey a spatially smaller notion of the neighborhood (*buurt*) than the other three ethnic categories. For administrative purposes, the city is commonly divided into 40 neighborhoods, ranging in population from 686 to 9572 residents, and in area from 13 to 226 hectares (Gemeente

Haarlem, 1996:W3-4). Such boundaries may seem more arbitrary than the social and visual criteria that outsiders use, but for the analysis they provide a spatial context in which samples and populations are compared.

This alludes to a second quality: the collective nature of neighborhoods. The issue here is *not* individuals' position within neighborhoods, which is not to deny that individuals - even those detached from other public domains - may occupy crucial positions (e.g., as mediators or providers) within the neighborhood environment (cf. Hortulanus, 1995:51ff). Random survey sampling techniques however are not conducive for measuring such positional distinctions, at least not before nominally exclusive distinctions in individuals' neighborhood positions are acknowledged and corroborated by respondents. The focus here is instead upon the notion of *neighborhoods'* position within cities, and how such qualifications may correspond with their residents' degree of integration. Where the image of a *vagabond* signifies the detachment of the homeless individual, the image of the *ghetto* signifies the marginalization of entire neighborhoods. One crucial difference is that the vagabond can be surveyed. The *neighborhood* however is a reification and at best an aggregate that the researcher derives from interviews with its residents. Inferring from the perspective of the individual neighborhood resident, the neighborhood offers prestige and social opportunities that are subject to change and exchange.

How does this issue tie into the positional dilemma between deprivation and dependency? Individuals strive to acquire homes in neighborhoods that signify their social success,that moreover provide the social services and opportunities needed to optimize participation in - or isolation from - the broader locality (cf. Warren, 1977). In their goal to protect or improve their (neighborhood's) position, residents are dependent upon the cooperation of other actors.

What are then the neighborhood attributes that affect individuals' integration? These obviously have normative and theoretical determinants, which vary per city in time. One source of criteria pertains to processes of immigrant concentration and segregation. Such attributes will be considered more explicitly in chapter six. Here several criteria are combined to classify neighborhoods' rank-position. The classification, derived by Haarlem's municipal research bureau, combines a variety of social-economic, social-cultural and environmental characteristics. These include statistics on: welfare beneficiaries, unemployment, minority concentrations [sic], active voters, library cardholders, annual migration balances, housing costs, pollution levels and criminality (Gemeente

Haarlem, 1991). The product ranks the 40 neighborhoods on a five-point scale ranging from 'very inauspicious' (*ongunstig*) to 'very auspicious'.

Rather than inducing a rank-order of Haarlem neighborhoods via aggregation of survey respondents' qualifications (cf. Ginsberg, 1985), we used the city's classification as measure of neighborhoods' status. In table 4.11 an overview is presented of how the five ethnic categories are distributed over these five positions.[9] The large majority of Moroccan and Turkish respondents are seen to reside in so-called 'inauspicious' neighborhoods, as opposed to a minority of 'Other' immigrants and indigenous Dutch. This result is not surprising, and not only because by definition a surplus of immigrant minorities negatively affects a neighborhood's status. More interesting is the comparison of the rank order with the evaluations we elicited from respondents concerning their neighborhoods. Among the 'Other' immigrants and indigenous Dutch the 'objective' rank-order corresponds significantly with respondents' evaluations, i.e., the more auspicious the neighborhood the more respondents positively evaluate their neighborhood environment (cf. Rigby and Vreugdenhill, 1987). However, for none of the three minority categories could the evaluations be seen to reflect the objective rank-order.[10] This would suggest that the problems immigrant minorities perceive in their neighborhood differ from those experienced by more indigenous residents. This issue of neighborhood appreciation will be examined more in depth in chapter five.

Table 4.11   Status of neighborhoods in which respondents reside

Neighborhood's status	Moroccans	Turks	Surinamese Antilleans	'Other' immigrants	Indigenous Dutch
very inauspicious (--)	32%	39%	21%	19%	13%
inauspicious (-)	45%	44%	40%	25%	27%
typical	19%	13%	27%	27%	33%
auspicious (+)	3%	3%	10%	20%	21%
very auspicious (++)	1%	1%	2%	9%	6%
n (=100%)	65	94	62	64	134

The extent in which the rank-order in five neighborhood positions reflects respondents' degree of integration is summarized in appendix I. The relation is significant for immigrants overall ($\eta=.24$) and for the indigenous

Dutch (η=.27), but not within specific immigrant categories. The weakness or lack of a statistical relation is noteworthy, first because a purely spatial distinction in twelve local districts has been seen to clarify a greater portion of index variance. Once we know the district in which respondents reside, a distinction in their neighborhoods' status does not improve estimates of their index scores.[11] It is moreover noteworthy because several criteria used to rank neighborhoods are comparable to components within the local index: namely aggregate measures for *welfare independence, local satisfaction* and *cultural participation* are all conceptually related to criteria for neighborhood status.[12] In other words, a relation between neighborhoods' status and individuals' integration could be expected by statistical design.

These findings raise doubts as to the validity of the rank-order in Haarlem neighborhoods. Considering the geographic scope however, the more pertinent question is the representability of the Haarlem case study. When the wide variation in affluence and opportunity observable in European neighborhoods is taken into account, then the Haarlem rank-order in five neighborhood positions presumably denotes but a small section of a much broader social spectrum. Within this greater context, I find it far-fetched to allocate any Dutch neighborhood the *ghetto* status. The theoretical challenge is then to derive comparative standards for neighborhood status that show when neighborhood attributes vitally affect - instead of reflect - their residents' integration.

I began this section by noting the potential offered by the neighborhood environment domain to provide reliable indicators of immigrants' integration. The potential is rooted in the domain's tangible and spatial character, which offers possibilities to measure individual wealth and social mobility. It is also rooted in the broad use of images such as *vagabonds* and *ghettos* to suggest detachment. Neither vagabonds nor ghettos however are readily accessible for survey interviews while several market factors render measurements in this domain quite ambiguous. A central obstacle is the intervention characteristic of housing and neighborhood markets. Social housing does not so much limit individuals in their prospects upon these markets; ideally they indeed function to optimize (or equalize) market opportunity. Distinct variations are observed between Haarlem immigrants and indigenous Dutch in their housing and neighborhood's position, but these variations do not consistently correspond (within minority categories) with individuals' degree of integration. These results reveal on the one hand inadequacies in the housing and neighborhood measurements that are too coarse to reveal market differences. On the other they suggest that the 'truly disadvantaged' (Wilson, 1987) are not automatically accommodated with the allocation of a flat in a more auspicious neighborhood.

Civic Positions: Political Activists and Public Nuisances

In chapter two the domain of civic life was introduced as a metaphorical umbrella, encompassing portions of all other domains. It is, however, more than simply the sum of the separate domains, as there are facets of civic life that are not readily located within other public domains. Three of these facets were specified in chapter two, namely the possibilities to move freely throughout the city, to partake in social-cultural activities, and to engage in political decision making processes. Here I briefly consider the notion of *position* in relation to these three facets.

First, with reference to the umbrella status of the civic domain, a notion of *civic* position could be delineated. It alludes to the status-rank individuals have within the city, based upon the combination of positions they occupy within the various public domains. Although rank-orders hopefully never manifest themselves to the point that residents are fully aware of their position within a single civic spectrum, it helps heuristically to perceive *local leaders* as those residents with economic pull, cultural prestige and political power. If such leaders are presumed to be maximally engaged, what is the normative counterpart to signify the locally detached? Opposed to leaders is the image not so much of the obedient, passive follower, more the disrespectful *public nuisance*. Combining the various domains into a summary position of detachment, the public nuisance is the unsocialized, jobless vagrant entirely reliant upon social welfare, and a threat to the safety and well-being of fellow citizens. This image has heuristic value; it helps illuminate the normative nature of detachment qualifications. In its composition however the image is a caricature, more a symbol for cultural intolerance than for real individuals personally responsible for their disengaged positions (cf. Mok and Reinsch, 1996:20-21).

Individuals' engagements in political decision making processes - as *citizens* - are intrinsically associated with the idea of civic activity. The issue here is how to quantify this process as individuals' rank political engagement. Except in the hypothetical context of an absolute autocracy, political decision making implies dependence upon other individuals, and then as representatives of interest groups. One could try to devise a rank-order of local political power, ranging for instance from the inactive and ignored to the engaged 'city fathers', but most positions along this spectrum would likely designate nonexclusive group affiliations. Dutch survey respondents perceive for instance that, at a national level, government ministers and parliamentarians have the greatest influence upon important decisions, while activists and voters have the least (SCP, 1998:742). Between these *positions* however, a whole spectrum of interest *groups* (instead of *individuals*) is denoted: big business, civil services, political parties, trade unions and the media. Concerning immigrants, one observes that regulations limit their right to vote until certain conditions are met,[13] while their opportunity to participate less formally in decision making processes may be limited by their segmented or 'minorized' positions (Rath, 1991). Consequently, the significance attributed to immigrants' local political engagement, as indication of the influence associated with their position, cannot be lucidly measured and interpreted.

The second facet refers to individuals' opportunity to access the public realm. More concretely, this facet translates into urban issues of public safety and participation. The positional dilemma bound to this facet is signified on the one hand by public nuisances and more normatively sanctioned threats to personal property and propriety (e.g., motorized vehicles) that affect public access. On the other, public access is dependent upon the intervention of police and other public sentries. Possible resolutions to this dilemma correspond with divergent visions of local integration. Conceived within the *tolerant* vision, the pursuance of objectives of inclusion calls for the optimization of individuals' opportunity to meet (ethnic) strangers. Local authorities have then the task of ensuring that activities which limit the access and safety of any group are kept to a minimum. With these elementary normative presumptions, the difficulties posed in ranking individuals' position within this market remain manifold. Incarceration, physical disability and social-phobia denote for instance various attributes that limit individuals' public access. Does the antithesis of these attributes signify individuals with optimal access to the public realm: e.g., the physically fit, social exhibitionist with limited prospects of being a police suspect? In short, the access and exchange of public space may be important issues on the local agenda (cf. SCP, 1999), but no clear criteria or reliable procedures are available to measure individual immigrant's position within this market.

This brings me to the third facet directly associated with positions in the civic domain: the participation in social-cultural activities. This refers to positions in civil institutions with charitable or leisure goals. The boundaries are not entirely clear-cut between this facet, and political participation on the one hand, and the use of social welfare arrangements on the other. I view it nevertheless as a market for organizational membership, separate from consumer or communicative activities less directly related to a notion of civic status. One can recognize the so-called 'high society' or 'social elites' who are, in accordance with their positions in other domains, members of exclusive clubs and associations. At the opposite end of the normative spectrum the 'social outcasts' are found: the residents who, despite the broad range of possibilities to spend significant portions of the non working day engaged in organized activities, belong to nothing. The positional dilemma manifests itself in the *voluntary* nature of active organizational membership: while no tangible goods are acquired from such activities, they are dependent upon the voluntary support and sacrifice of individuals to maintain the services provided.

Table 4.12 Variations in organizational membership

Membership position	Moroccans	Turks	Surinamese Antilleans	'Other' immigrants	Indigenous Dutch
no memberships	58%	33%	26%	24%	12%
passive memberships only	18%	42%	17%	26%	29%
active in one organization	18%	17%	39%	30%	39%
active in more organizations	5%	8%	18%	20%	19%
n (=100%)	93	159	77	100	170

We asked respondents about their membership in seven types of organizations, broadly classified as: environmental, professional, neighborhood, religious, sport, leisure (*gezelligheid*) and other organizations. Members were furthermore asked to qualify their membership as 'active' or 'passive', and to tell whether the organization's membership is (primarily) immigrant or indigenous Dutch (this latter attribute will be considered in chapter six). In table 4.12 the percentages per ethnic category are presented that express a membership affiliation. A simple rank-order in four status categories is made, ranging from 'no memberships' whatever through 'passive memberships only', on to those 'active' in 'one' or 'more organizations' (cf. SCP, 1996:542; Huls, 1997; SCP, 1998:750).

One can see from the table that most of the Moroccan respondents (58%) have no organizational affiliation, and that three-fourths of the

Turks are passive members at best. For these two categories, the active are most likely members of religious organizations. Except via channels of (passive) religious affiliation, Moroccan women in particular are detached from the social-cultural market. Residents in the other three ethnic categories display more engaged positions: most are active in one or more organizations, sports clubs being for individuals in all three categories the most likely channel of participation.

The classification into four market positions provides an elementary indication of membership differences. Such measures can obviously be improved upon quantitatively (e.g., how much is membership dependent upon investments in time and social ties?) and qualitatively (e.g., which memberships are afforded local prestige?). The relation between these two criteria reveals several methodological obstacles: monitoring hours spent in the mosque and comparing them with hours on the soccer field is tedious, disrespectful, and theoretically ambiguous.

The potential provided by such spectra to predict immigrants' degree of integration is illustrated in appendix I. Within the three minority categories, the distinctions in membership position correspond significantly with variations in index scores. However, the correspondence among the Surinamese and Antilleans ($\eta=.35$) should not be construed as 'linear'; as the so-called 'passive members' are generally more integrated than 'active' individuals. The potential to reflect differences in integration dissipates entirely by comparisons among 'Other' immigrants and the indigenous Dutch.

Three markets have been considered within the domain of civic life and, compared to housing markets, all seem quite illusive. On the market for political participation, a distinction between leaders and (non)voters has little tenability within an integration construct. Formally, not all immigrants have voting rights, while informally the influence exerted by the politically inactive may be ultimately more effective. On the market for public space, the public nuisance was imagined in a (detached) position diametrically opposed to other market participants. The exercise illustrates the normative and theoretical difficulties of conceiving a rank-order of positions in the public realm. Finally the social-cultural market for organizational activities was surveyed. This market provides more palpable possibilities to identify individuals with detached or engaged positions. The distinction does display, among Haarlem immigrant minorities, differences in individuals' engagement that correspond modestly with individuals' degree of integration.

Assessment: Market Measurements as Normative Enterprise

Three topics will be summarized that have served as focal points through-out the previous sections. I begin with empirical matters concerning the Haarlem survey findings. In this chapter the engagement of respondents upon eight hypothetical markets has been examined. The positional patterns that emerge, the expected patterns that remain diffuse, and the potential provided by specific positions to indicate individual immigrants' integration will be reviewed. Then I consider various methodological obstacles encountered, evaluating the possibilities to hurdle these restraints with more refined survey protocols. Some obstacles however are rooted not so much in specific research methods, but waver more generally between normative interpretations of positional dilemmas. The final sub-section will deal with these interpretive issues.

Discerning the Typically Detached Immigrant

The survey data has served to illustrate immigrants' differential positions. With little exception, positions have been characterized as to their *deprivation* and *dependence*. A rank-order of ethnic categories has been observed that signifies those respondents most likely to be found in deprived or (state) dependent positions: Moroccans, Turks, Surinamese and Antilleans, 'Other' immigrants, and indigenous Dutch.

What are these positions and what are the exceptions to this rank-order? In the private domain large households with an inordinate proportion of dependents are seen as problematic; the pattern is set. By education I focused upon the level of formal schooling completed. Surinamese, Antilleans and 'Other' immigrants are less deprived in diploma terms than the indigenous Dutch. I then considered who is active on the labor market, and what percentage of these are currently seeking work. More Turks are active than Surinamese or Antilleans, but the proportion of these Turks who are actively in search of paid work are equal to that of Moroccans. On the market for material security the household income among Turks is again more than by Surinamese and Antilleans. After correcting however for differences in household size, variations in per capita income (one of the five components comprising the local index) reverts to the set order. The welfare independence criterion of the local index is based on the combinations of local welfare services individuals use. More Moroccans and Turks are found dependent upon *necessary services*. Although the local homeless were not surveyed on the housing market, the established ethnic rank-order prevails concerning the proportion of tenants dependent upon landlords. This order is neatly reversed of course when counting respondents who own single family homes. Similarly, though I find it difficult to qualify any Haarlem neighborhood as a *ghetto*, a large majority of the Turks and Moroccans do live in neighborhoods classified as *inauspicious*. Finally, in the civic domain, detachment from the social-cultural market is perceived as those *deprived* of organizational affiliations, where again the set order prevails.

Regarding this rank-order, one may be inclined to conclude that individuals' ethnic category is a most simple and direct means to identify those residents in detached positions, characterized by deprivation and dependence. Two fundamental problems are associated with this line of reasoning. First, it is based on averages within and differential proportions between the five categories. The differences within groups also deserve attention. Focusing upon one nominal criterion for deprivation - a per capita income averaging less than eleven hundred guilders per month - I note for instance that most Moroccan residents are *not* deprived. Meanwhile, 10 percent of the far more populous indigenous Dutch live in poverty according to this criterion. Secondly, the reasoning infers that positional differences reflect a 'natural' order along geo-political lines. It disregards the historical, global, local and biographical processes that help clarify why more Turks have kids, and more Antilleans have diplomas. Let us not forget the research context in which the measurements were made. The survey focus upon immigrant minorities was not based upon presumptions as to their perpetual marginalization. It was prompted instead by the premise that local minorities could best identify local factors that prolong their estrangement. Moreover, they could best suggest the remedial policies that would benefit (future) minorities and other locals.

How much then do these variations in market positions correspond with individual residents' degree of integration? Throughout the chapter statistics have been discussed that denote the variance in the local index accounted for by specific positional differences. Assuming the indicators to be (statistically) interrelated, a series of multiple regression analyses was conducted to estimate the relative and combined significance of selected market factors. This technique was used in chapter three to estimate the relative significance of demographic attributes, and will also serve at the end of the forthcoming three chapters (see appendix I for more technical details). The results for positional indicators are summarized in table 4.13.

In the bottom two rows of the table, two statistics are presented per ethnic category. The top statistic presents the proportion of index variance accounted for by all six indicators combined, the bottom one the variance accounted for by a select number of indicators (i.e., those designated by an asterisk). One may note that for three of the five ethnic categories a combination of three positional indicators accounts for anywhere from 23% to 35% of the variance in category scores. Such results are much higher than those found for the six demographic attributes. The two exceptions are provided by the Moroccans and the 'Other' immigrants. Within these categories, only one positional attribute corresponds with index scores independent of the other five: for Moroccans *civic memberships* and for 'Other' immigrants *education completed*. The combined effect of all six attributes (18% resp. 27%) also differs minimally from the 'effect' observed for (five) demographic attributes.

Table 4.13 Percent of variances in local index accounted for by positional attributes, controlling for other attributes

Positional attribute	Moro-ccans	Turks	Surinam-ese Antilleans	'Other' immi-grants	All immi-grants	Indigenous Dutch
type of household	n.s.	8%*	n.s.	n.s.	2%*	3%*
education completed	n.s.	5%*	17%*	10%*	10%*	12%*
job market position	n.s.	7%*	11%*	n.s.	3%*	7%*
housing market	n.s.	n.s.	10%*	n.s.	4%*	n.s.
neighborhood's status	n.s.	n.s.	n.s.	n.s.	1%*	n.s.
civic memberships	10%*	n.s.	n.s.	n.s.	n.s.	n.s.
combined (adj.) R²	18%	28%	43%	27%	42%	40%
* indicators R² only	9%	28%	23%	21%	42%	35%
n (listwise deletion)	91	151	71	97	411	168

* = probability F < .05, n.s.= not independently significant.

For each positional attribute, listed in the upper part of table 4.13, a statistic displays whether it clarifies (additional) index variance, after having first taken the effect of the other (5) indicators into account. One may note the diffuse pattern of indicators, per ethnic category, that contribute significantly to the regression equation (designated by an asterisk). Only the Turkish sub-sample displays the same (three) significant indicators that apply for the indigenous Dutch. For the other three categories a great discrepancy can be seen (in the bottom two rows) in variance explained by all respectively by asterisked indicators. This means that (some) non-asterisked indicators also help clarify differences in index variance, but their independent effect is minimal. Two indicators - *education completed* and *job market position* - are consistently significant, namely within three of the five ethnic categories. Two indicators - *neigborhood's status* and *civic memberships* - contribute little to the regression models.

Overall, educational background provides the best indication about who is integrated and who estranged (e.g., for all immigrants the R^2 is 0.37, the partial R^2 is 0.10). However, the observation that its explanatory potential diminishes by the two most estranged ethnic categories presents interpretive problems. Few Moroccans and Turks in Haarlem have secondary and tertiary educational degrees, but these few score far less integrated than residents in other categories with comparable educational backgrounds. Has their education lacked essential qualifications? Has their residence been too brief (as newcomers or young adults) to appreciate and benefit from their local surrounding? Or is their new local environment blind to their qualifications?

No resolution to these issues could be realized based simply upon survey measurements. Besides the statistical collinearities observed between the positional measures, the relatively invariant *estrangement* among Moroccans and Turks presents an interpretive obstacle. Indeed, this obstacle could be construed as a central policy issue. In a statistical sense, one may expect that the variance in index scores accounted for by particular measures will diminish with a decrease in index variance: the smaller the variance, the more it is clarified by random measurement errors and omissions. This reasoning however does not clarify - in a social sense - why college-educated Moroccans and Turks score no more integrated than their fellow immigrants with degrees from lower secondary schools. I will return to this interpretive issue in chapter seven.

Seeking Valid Measures of Detachment

Besides the interpretation of statistical associations, methodological obstacles have been encountered that limit the validity or comparability of positional indicators. The nature of these obstacles is such that they may be expected in all domains. Several more prominent ones will be reviewed below.

First issues are considered that refer to the contours of domains, and the markets they contain. The essential issue is the incomparability of market positions because researchers and respondents maintain divergent notions of the market expanse. The problem may be reduced in part to ambiguities regarding the market good. Is the private domain bounded by the household with its communal meals and finances, or does it pertain to a less spatial notion of family in which intimacy is exchanged with kinship and marriage bonds? Education and upbringing may be perceived as market goods exchanged indirectly on every market in and outside the public domain. In this study education refers to school activities for the acquisition of diplomas. Even with this limitation to formal education however the problems of cross-curricular and cross-cultural comparisons remain. The markets for labor and material security intermesh when labor is financially reimbursed, but both markets have much broader contours and divergent internal structures. A social welfare market was described that is so expansive it encompasses processes pertinent to all other domains. The Dutch housing market is seen to be *segmented*, one state regulated and one for more liberal engagement. Each potential resident may be seen to have a position on both. This notion of a double market however is not limited to housing. It may be discerned on any market where segments vary in their degree of accessibility and intervention. The subjective nature of neighborhood boundaries is a more perceptible issue but not necessarily less ambiguous. The notion of a civic domain, finally, may enclose all these markets within a metaphorical jigsaw puzzle. Still, problems remain designating the missing pieces (i.e., those markets not contained within other domains) and the outer boundaries (i.e., the contextual distinctions between civic, regional and national integration processes).

Upon each of these markets local practices and research traditions have been sighted to sketch market boundaries and positions. Particularly *detached* positions served as points of focus. The possibilities to develop criteria for detachment, applicable in a diversity of local environments appear to vary per domain. Nominal criteria are often associated with local market characteristics, which obviously limits their comparability. This obstacle could be observed most explicitly where individuals' use of local services is drawn upon to estimate their *welfare independence*. To devise a more comparable standard along a local welfare spectrum, only those services could serve as reference points that are universally available with comparable purpose and accessibility. This is a lot to expect of local welfare markets. In the end, the validity of the *welfare independence* spectrum revolves around normative presumptions that designate the use of *necessary services* as indicative of detachment, while the use of leisure *arrangements* supported by the state is indicative of engagement. The normative issue recurs in each domain: given a specific notion of (absolute) *detachment*, how can an opposing notion of (absolute) *engagement* be identified that not only enables inter-local comparisons (by projecting the market along an acknowledged spectrum), but remains sensitive to local distinctions?

This image of a spectrum presumes a certain rank-order of positions. Associated with this presumption is the issue of measurement level. Ideally, the higher the measurement level, the more potential can be derived from statistical techniques to calculate individual market mobility, and to monitor processes of integration. For instance for the construction of the local index some questionable presumptions were needed to inject the two positional components (*per capita income* and *welfare independence*) with interval level status. For all the positional indicators considered in this chapter, the ordinal or linear (i.e., spectral) quality of the indicator remains an issue. Even where an ordinal indicator could be perceived, for instance by *level of formal education completed*, the subsequent comparison with the local index brought the linear nature of the relation into question. Similar divergencies may be seen in other domains. As obstacles they limit comparability, in that measurements that specify rank-order differences in market position vary with the normative perspective from which differences in rank are perceived.

In what ways do divergent normative perspectives generate methodological obstacles? Various examples have been encountered, all of which can be classified according to at least one of the evaluative criteria for measurement adequacy: validity, simplicity, reliability, brevity and comparability. An individual's position on the housing market is sufficient to portray all these criteria. Drawing upon the observation that Haarlem is characterized by a double housing market, a *valid* measurement of a home-owner's housing market positions must include his or her position on the social housing market. How could we define and measure possession and opportunity upon this market? We could have respondents estimate their prospects on the social housing market but, as to questionnaire *simplicity*, it is problematic to assume that residents even know whether their homes are subject to rent control. The chance that residents will supply *reliable* information concerning their home ownership is affected by their awareness of normative issues surrounding such market positions. To specify respondents' position on these markets according to divergent normative criteria, far more information would have to be gathered about the needs and rights of residents, and the quality of their housing conditions. This affects the *brevity* of the interview. Finally, we could conceivably project the divergent market attributes upon a single ordinal spectrum. The range and units along the spectrum however are not *comparable*; they will vary, with housing markets, from one city to the next. A similar review could be presented within all other domains.

In closing this sub-section, brief references are made to two other obstacles. The first concerns problems of *reliability*. I observed in many domains that the epitome of detachment would be found by those residents least likely to participate or cooperate in survey research: those without schooling, work, well-being, homes, and social-cultural affiliations. More problems arise when one bases measures of social mobility upon survey responses. How much credence for instance can be attributed to respondents' recollections of parents' education, of previous income or personal well-being? This implies that for many market spectra, survey measurements cannot adequately capture the detached lower end, or (short of panel research) the individuals' previous market positions.

The final obstacle refers to problems of sample size. The need to measure a variety of market factors, to test their theoretical or to monitor their empirical significance, increases the survey size requirements exponentially. I considered how comparative measures of job opportunity could be estimated, but such measures require thousands of respondents to realize reliable estimates. Not only the number of market parameters affects sample requirements, also the number of (sub-sample) categories subject to comparison. Our focus upon three 'minority' categories (actually four, Surinamese and Antillean samples were too small to analyze separately) enables conclusions to be drawn about the local engagement of individuals within these groups. Any observations however pertaining for instance to the position of political refugees, residents in one of the city's twelve districts, or residents of modestly-sized cities retain a less reliable character.

Acknowledging the Normative Limitations

What have I learned from these observations, as for my search for indicators of immigrant integration? Above all, the conceptual framework may help me to envision those immigrants who are detached from local markets, but the survey measurements are far from adequate for the confirmation of my suspicions. The primary obstacles that inhibit adequate measurements and comprehensive predictions are, in brief:

- Between researchers and respondents, the lack of agreement as to the boundaries dividing markets, and the criteria distinguishing the engaged from the detached, affects measurement validity. This lack of agreement is due in part to the multidimensional character of market domains. The recognition of these dimensions, and their reduction to (unidimensional) positional spectra remains a normative enterprise.
- The normative enterprise is reflected by positional dilemmas between deprivation and dependence. Within each domain a variety of normative decisions must be made (i.e., dimensions identified) about which social goods are objects of competition and exchange, and which dependencies their acquisition imply.
- Within all domains, relevant informants (e.g., the detached) and information (e.g., the regulations and interactions that shape and segment local markets) are not easily perceived via survey techniques.

The measurements in the Haarlem locality reveal no single positional indicator of individuals' engagement capable of reliably designating the individually integrated, whatever the ethnic category. The potential to recognize and interpret the explanatory or predictive value of indicators is ultimately a theoretical enterprise. Various categories of detachment have been perceived: the minimally educated, the jobless, the tenants, etc. These categories however are not exclusive. They overlap, by some ethnic categories more than others. Statistical analyses may help dissect their significance, but to link these categories, and the social actors they represent, in a causal chain of reasoning remains a theoretical act. Educational background has been identified, for instance, as the most reliable indicator of individual integration. Theory informs me of possible sources for educational deprivation, and the dependencies that individuals require for its resolution.

5 Observing Orientations

The second dimension of immigrant integration revolves around the notion of *culture*. In chapter two culture was circumscribed as the content and patterns of values, ideas and other symbolic-meaningful systems. Here, in continuation of my observations on individuals' integration, the notion of *orientation* is used to refer to specific cultures' significance in forming individuals' identity (and their thoughts and actions).

The central conceptual issue when one sets out to observe orientations is how to distinguish one culture from the next. Whether a given individual is seen to conform ritualistically to a particular culture, or to be continually oriented toward a diversity of cultures, hinges on the boundaries observed between these imaginary entities. Is *the* one local culture characterized by many contradictions, or is the locality characterized by a diversity of contradicting cultures? The issue ties into normative objectives and end-goals of immigrant integration. Would the contradictions dissipate if individual inhabitants were to adapt similar orientations? Or do immigrants, with their divergent orientations, serve precisely to enhance local culture toward a greater (e.g., more *universal*) synthesis? These issues will not be resolved here. I note however that explanations for immigrants' estrangement, which focus upon their cultural *disorientations*, are distinguished by opposing resolutions to these issues. On the one hand objectives of cultural unity are presumed where immigrants' failure to *assimilate* into *the* local culture (due for instance to 'deficiencies' or 'deviancies' in their cultural orientations) is seen as problematic. On the other hand objectives of cultural diversity are presumed where immigrants are considered ill-adapted to the *civil liberties* and *tolerance* characteristic of dynamic cultures (due for instance to a cultural 'mismatch' or to their ritualistic conformity to their cultural origins) (cf. van den Berg and Reinsch, 1983:129; Penninx, 1988:30; Willemsen, 1993).

The notions introduced in chapter two provide elementary ways to delineate cultures, namely through distinctions in (market) domains, components and polarities. Individuals' orientations are construed as their *conformity* to groups and cultures with which they are affiliated, and their *imagery* of *other* groups and cultures. These distinctions will be elaborated upon here while an extensive - but far from comprehensive - answer is given to the following question:

What significance may be attributed to individuals' various cultural orientations as indicators of their integration within the local (Haarlem) context?

The Haarlem survey data will be ordered by - and will serve to illustrate - various conceptual distinctions. For brevity's sake, I will suppress the urge to inspect the relation *between* the various (domain) orientations discussed in the forthcoming sections. Instead the presentation will be limited primarily to the (statistical) relation particular orientations display with respondents' degree of integration. This approach implies that comprehensive cultural orientations, conceived to encompass cultural polarities across market domains, will not be observed. I must concede straightaway that the data does not facilitate such perceptions. The original Haarlem project did not lend itself for extensive operationalization and measurement of more general cultural polarities, such as 'traditional' and 'modern' or 'immigrant' and 'Dutch' orientations. The purpose of the survey limited the possibility to examine whether inhabitants' views and convictions are indicative of such polarities. Moreover, I remain highly skeptical that such generalized notions are instrumental to understanding immigrants' local integration.

The presentation will focus more upon the potential provided by the conceptual model to discern cultural (in)congruence within and between ethnic categories, and individuals' compliance with local and group objectives. I expect to encounter any number of methodological obstacles in the quest to inspect cultural orientations. These obstacles form the second line of inquiry:

What methodological obstacles, pertinent to the operationalization of individuals' cultural orientation, render the measurement of immigrant integration particularly problematic?

The first section revolves around the notion of ethnic orientation. Here ethnicity is treated as an essentially private matter whose significance (or salience) for individuals' orientations in public domains is not assumed. The presentation will be quite lengthy, as conceptual and methodological issues are considered that pertain to the measurement of orientations in other domains. The section on education and upbringing concerns language and religious orientations. In the third section measures of respondents' labor orientation will be discussed, followed by a presentation of the *perceived opportunity* criterion included in the local index. The other cultural criterion within the local index, *local satisfaction*, will then be considered, and also measures of individuals' views concerning the (ethnic) diversity of social services. In a fifth section I examine the importance of individuals' affinity with their neighborhood surroundings for their residential satisfaction and their scores upon the local index. Finally, in the civic domain, variations in political orientation are reviewed before considering rudimentary measures of respondents' views on ideal communities. These latter measures are quite fundamental within the context of this study, as they denote local integration objectives, and the congruence observed among respondents and between ethnic categories.

Ethnic Orientation: Affinity, Imagery and Endowment

In this first section, concerning the private domain, any number of cultural polarities could be considered that potentially effect individuals' orientations in more public domains. These are polarities associated with 'innate' attributes. An individual is born for instance at a given time, with a certain sex, into a specific family context. Around these attributes various polarities have been conceived, e.g., cultures aligned to temporal (cf. Jones, 1994), gender (cf. Witt, 1996) and sibling differences (cf. MacDonald, 1998). Accordingly, years of conceptual refinement and instrument validation could be invested to detect how much individuals display typical temporal, gender and sibling attributes in their orientation toward their local environment.

Rather than attempt to establish the relative significance of these various cultural attributes, the section will focus on yet another endowment commonly considered a primary source of individual orientation, namely the geo-political region of origin.[1] This attribute serves *formally* throughout this study to differentiate ethnic categories. Indeed, social research on the significance of ethnicity seldom advances beyond such ascribed categorizations (cf. Leets et al., 1996:132). Drawing upon Schermerhorn's definition of an ethnic group (1970:12), I presume here that ethnic orientation refers to a *subjective* affinity, where members harbor 'memories of a shared historical past.' It also refers to more *objective* cultural components that group members share without necessarily being aware of them, where members 'focus on one or more symbolic elements.' In the sub-sections below first the measurement of individuals' ethnic *affinity* is considered. I turn then to the conceptualization and observation of individuals' *imagery* of *other* ethnic groups. A third sub-section will briefly review research initiatives to develop so-called objective measures of ethnicity independent of individuals' expressed affinity.

Ethnic Affinity

Most Dutch empirical research on ethnicity focuses upon its significance by identity formation among adolescents. The social psychologist Verkuyten for instance has examined extensively the relationship between ethnic identification and self-esteem among immigrant youth. He pays meticulous attention to methodological issues of identity measurement, but his instruments are then dependent upon respondents' readiness to score literally dozens of items. Sociologists are generally less encumbered by contextual limitations. Saharso (1992a) and Leeman (1994) for instance, in complementary studies in secondary schools, examined the divergent educational contexts and processes in which ethnicity is articulated, for immigrant and indigenous students respectively. However, their observations on individuals' ethnic affinity, and those made in anthropological studies (e.g., Buijs, 1993; Buiks, 1983; Lindo, 1996; Sansone, 1992; Werdmölder, 1990), rarely attain numerical states.

One exception is Feddema (1991), who investigated cultural orientations among Turkish and Moroccan adolescents. He observed a prevalence of 'bicultural' and 'transcultural' orientations among his respondents, and his observations were reinforced by extensive, multidimensional, quantifications of the immigrant adolescents' 'frames of reference.' His measurements however were made within the context of action research, in which intensive contacts were maintained with respondents over a period of three years. It is highly doubtful whether the categorizations and items could be briefly and reliably applied in survey research.

Another exception is provided by van Heelsum (1997) who developed and validated a survey instrument to measure the 'ethnic-cultural position' of second generation Surinamese. Several components of this instrument are pertinent to measurements of ethnic affinity. The instrument as a whole however is only applicable by research with respondents of Surinamese origin.

In short, a concise and valid instrument, generally applicable for the measurement of ethnic affinity does not exist (Phinney, 1990:510; Phinney, 1992; Leets et al., 1996:136). Social researchers interested in capturing the essential components must compromise between highly unreliable estimations, and the use of more refined instruments that are sensitive to (and elongate) the interviewer-respondent context. In the Haarlem survey, we measured three components of respondents' possible ethnic affinity, namely: their expressed *identification* with an ethnic group; the extent in which they sense they *belong* to the group identified; and their (positive or negative) *affection* associated with group membership (cf. Phinney, 1990:501ff). These components will be discussed sequentially.

Self-identification During the interview respondents were informed that they had been selected on the basis of their (parents') land of birth. They were then asked whether the categorization corresponded with how they viewed themselves and, if not, to which ethnic group if any they reckoned themselves.

Table 5.1   Variations in ethnic self-identification

Ethnic qualification	Moroccans	Turks	Surinamese Antilleans	'Other' immigrants	Indigenous Dutch
Land of origin	29%	80%	23%	32%	91%
Specific group within land	37%	3%	17%	8%	8%
'Hyphenated Dutch'	32%	15%	34%	7%	-
'Dutch' or 'Hollander'	1%	-	23%	50%	-
Disavows ethnic affiliation	-	1%	3%	3%	1%
n (=100%)	93	156	77	92	170

Table 5.1 presents an overview of the divergent answer patterns. One sees that only among indigenous Dutch and Turks a (large) majority of the respondents agree with the categorization 'Dutch' respectively 'Turk' (91% resp. 80%). Eight percent of the Dutch qualify themselves more specifically (e.g., as 'Limburger'); three percent of the Turks qualify themselves as 'Kurds.' Among the Moroccans only 29% categorize themselves as 'Moroccan,' 37% more specifically as 'Arab' or 'Berber.' In contrast to the Moroccans and Turks, more than half the Surinamese, Antilleans and 'Other' immigrants identify themselves as '(hyphenated) Dutch.' The hyphenated qualification refers to duel identifications, with the Netherlands and the geo-political origins, e.g., 'Indonesian-Dutch' or 'Dutch-German.'

These findings raise various issues, three of which will be signaled briefly here. One must wonder, to begin with, how reliable these percentages are. How would they have varied had respondents for instance been asked to choose from a preordained list of ethnic categories?[2] Secondly, the relatively high percentages of Moroccans and Surinamese/Antilleans with more specific ethnic affinities may suggest less ethnic *cohesion* within these groups; in my view they illustrate the historically complex relation between ethnicity, colonialism and nationalism (cf. Smith, 1981). Thirdly, that practically all respondents in the indigenous category acknowledge their 'Dutchness' cannot be readily corroborated with research findings elsewhere, as research is rare in which the ethnic self-identification of (dominant) indigenous groups is explicitly measured (Phinney, 1990:500; Pryor et al., 1992). Interesting is how, even in this category, practically no one disavows an ethnic identity. One could surmise that Haarlem is highly 'ethnicized.'

With a spectrum between 'ethnic' and '(hyphenated) Dutch' immigrants, a gradual distinction in self-identification is suggested. Ultimately this component of ethnic affinity refers to nominal characteristics: a respondent may identify him or herself as Hindu, or as something else. Nor do we know whether Haarlem respondents consider gender, age, occupational or recreational affiliations more central to their social identities.[3] Let us see whether other components of ethnic affinity offer more ordinal opportunities to comprehend ethnic orientation.

A sense of belonging While self-identification may signify little more than a cognitive acknowledgment that others associate the individual in question with a certain group, the affective awareness that the individual embodies 'ethnic' qualities is seldom measured (Phinney, 1990:504; Leets et al., 1996:130; cf. Nekuee and Verkuyten, 1999). We measured this 'sense' with a single question, which was posed to those respondents who had acknowledged ethnic affiliations: 'When someone says something negative about the (respondent's self-identified ethnic) group, do you have the feeling that there is something negative being said about you?' Five categories registered the frequency in which respondents feel personally affronted. This item offers an ordinal ranking of affinity. However, a more adequate measure would require more items, including questions on how individuals feel about positive group imagery (cf. Luthanen and Crocker, 1992), and how ethnic affiliation ranks with other forms of categorical affiliation. The response to the question suggests important distinctions between ethnic categories: most Turkish and Moroccan respondents say they (almost) always feel personally addressed (71% resp. 57%), while for the other three categories such frequencies apply for only one-sixth of the respondents. The reaction is rare among those respondents who identify themselves as 'Dutch' - particularly immigrants - that a negative reference to the Dutch is taken personally.

Ethnic affection Important for a notion of ethnic affinity is that individuals vary not only in the intensity with which they sense ethnic affiliations, they also vary in the affective qualities the affiliation brings forth (cf. Phinney, 1990:504ff). For example, we asked respondents: 'Are you generally proud to be a member of the (respondent's self-identified) ethnic group?' Again five answer categories registered the negative or positive scope of respondents' sentiments. The answer patterns suggest that a majority of each category is '(almost) always proud', ranging from 61% of the 'Other' immigrants to more than 85% of the Turks and Moroccans. The greatest amount of ambivalence ('sometimes I am, sometimes I am not') is encountered among the indigenous Dutch (27%). Negative sentiments (i.e., 'never proud') are more prevalent among the 'Other' immigrants (22%), particularly those of German origin who identify themselves as Dutch.

Ethnic affinity and individual integration What do these components of ethnic orientation reveal about respondents' integration? A continued affinity with one's geo-political origins is often regarded as a primary indicator, or source, of immigrant estrangement. Within particular normative and theoretical perspectives, it even serves as the central attribute in need of clarification (i.e., the dependent variable). For example in Esser's theory of immigrant integration (1980), the end-goal is signified by a shift in immigrants' affinity from their geo-political origins to the indigenous group. Such perspectives rely on presumptions concerning the salience of ethnic (or national) orientations and the *centripetality* of the integration process. Here the question concerns whether and how ethnic affinity corresponds with respondents' degree of integration according to the local index.

The statistical correspondence for the three affinity items is summarized in appendix I. The *self-identification* indicator is significant among Moroccan and Turkish residents (η=.45 resp. .22). Closer scrutiny shows that respondents in these two categories who identify with their land of origin, or a specific group within it, are more likely estranged. The *sense of belonging* indicator is significant only among Turks (η=.37). Yet one should not conclude that greater 'sensitivity' corresponds with more estrangement because the relation is not linear. The *ethnic affection* indicator is significant again for Turks, and for 'Other' immigrants and indigenous Dutch. However only within the latter category do positive ethnic affections clearly correspond with greater estrangement (i.e., the relation is linear, R =.18). When generalizing for all immigrants, those respondents who consider themselves '(hyphenated) Dutch' are likely to be more integrated (η=.20), while those that express a sense of belonging to an ethnic group are more estranged (η=.25).

These initial analysis results do not permit simple interpretations. The eta statistic does not adequately reflect the ordinal significance attributed the items, while the variance in the local index explained by the items (i.e., η^2) is quite moderate. Moreover, the responses upon the latter two items (sense of belonging and ethnic affection) pertain not to respondents' ethnic category but to their self-identified affinities. Rather than report my vain attempts to derive interpretable and statistically significant integration indicators with scaling techniques, I conclude this sub-section with a couple theoretical observations.

These rudimentary measurements do not confute the premise that affinities with geo-political origins are prohibitive for immigrants' integration. However, such affinities could well be considered more the consequence than the cause of individuals' estrangement. Identification with other 'Moroccans' for instance may not concern a shared history in Morocco, signifying instead the collective experience of local exclusion. Near the opposite end of a hypothetical affinity spectrum the German-Dutch are observed with their negative ethnic sentiments.

Could their minimal affinity clarify their high degree of local integration, or does it simply reflect the (ambivalent) historical relations between Germany and the Netherlands? In what ways do ethnic affinities and imagery interact?[4] In my view ethnic affinity is neither a necessary aid nor an impediment for immigrants' integration. Its immediate significance resides in its possible effect upon individuals' orientation toward 'opposing' cultures. Ultimately its significance must be sought in its potential to symbolize - or mystify - local interactions as conformity conflicts. Does the individual immigrant find him or herself 'caught between two cultures', drawn to one and repulsed by the other, or harmoniously allied to both (cf. Phinney, 1990:501; Feddema, 1991:12ff; van Heelsum, 1997:109)?

Ethnic Imagery

The conceptual complement to affinity is offered by *imagery*. It concerns individuals' awareness of and affection toward *other* groups. In everyday terms, images begin where *we* end and *they* are visualized. How can variant degrees of orientation toward divergent *others* be discerned? I briefly consider the possibilities and problems for survey measurement.

Academic research in this area has revolved primarily around the concept of *prejudice* that, in Allport's classic study, is defined as '. . . an antipathy based upon a faulty and inflexible generalization' (1958:10). The research tradition, with all the insights realized, has focused too much upon prejudice as an emotional affliction (rooted, e.g., in the 'authoritarian personality'). It has also focused too much upon the status of the generalizations (or 'stereotypes') as essentially - or eventually - 'true'. Moreover, prejudicial attitudes have been found an unreliable predictor of (discriminatory) behavior (Elich and Maso, 1984). As a conceptual alternative, here the orientation toward *others* consists of three components complementary to affinity, namely: (non) identification, a sense of (not) belonging, and (positive or negative) affections.

Like the term suggests, images may be likened to a screen upon which individuals project their representation of the *other*. What makes this image so interesting is the reflection it provides of *projectors*, with their controls for focus, contrast and brightness. *Focus* represents the extent in which the individual projector is aware of, and consequently has the possibility (not) to identify with the *other*. An affinity with Turkish origins for instance might correspond with an absolute lack of awareness that other ethnicities exist. Alternatively, the Turkish affinity may correspond with a focus upon 'Kurds' and 'Dutch' while the projector remains oblivious of other *others*. *Contrast* literally signifies a sense of not belonging. An ethnic Turk's image of 'the Kurd' is likely to accentuate certain elements opposed to 'the Turkish' identity, while the image of 'the Dutch' will contain other contrasting elements. *Brightness* finally can be linked metaphorically to affective illumination, i.e., the extent in which the projector is open and receptive to the *other*.

How these images may be indicative of individuals' degree of integration depends in part upon their *(in)congruence* with others' images given local integration objectives. The ethnic Turk oblivious of *others* may conform adequately to *pillarized* community objectives. However, when for instance *assimilation* prevails as community vision, the ethnic Turk's failure to focus upon *others* signifies disorientation. Another hypothetical example is the ethnic Kurd who finds him or herself at odds with Turkish imagery, while the locality as a whole prescribes end-goals of interethnic *tolerance*. The interpretative problems are symptomatic of the conformity-personality dilemma: when is imagery congruent with (the objectives of) an entire locality, or a specific (ethnic) group within it, and when is it so unique in its incongruence that it signifies disorientation?

The primary contention here is that ethnic orientation should not be conceptually reduced to a dichotomous affinity. Presuming the presence of more than two distinct ethnic cultures within a locality, individuals' conformity to local integration objectives is mediated by - and reproduces - their images of divergent *others*. In my attempts to conceive and perceive a *tolerant* community characterized by objectives of cultural diversity, the imagery approaches maximal complexity. The integrated individual focuses upon, perceives differences with, and is illuminated by, a plurality of *other* residents.

In the forthcoming sections, various examples are presented of polarities in the orientations of individuals and ethnic categories. However, we know little of their *imagery* of ethnic *others*.[5] We could observe that respondents not only express affinities with a diversity of groups (e.g., with Kurds, Turks and indigenous Dutch). They also project images concerning a diversity of *other* ethnic groups. Admittedly, this notion of multiple imagery leads to a complex matrix of orientations. It serves as contrast to the current state of Dutch survey research. With few exceptions (e.g., Shadid, 1979; Intomart, 1995; Verkuyten and Masson, 1995) images of the ethnic *other* have only been solicited among indigenous Dutch,[6] while in even the largest surveys (Hagendoorn and Hraba, 1989; Kleinpenning and Hagendoorn, 1991) no more than half a dozen groups were *re-imagined*. The obstacle is in large part methodological. Survey instruments that solicit images on a variety of ethnic groups are confronted with the law of diminishing return: due to duration and complexity, the reliability and ultimately the validity of measures yields to respondents' aggravation.

A search for more valid means to measure ethnic imagery leads to social distance methods. Social distance can be generally construed as the relative detachment from social categories that individuals perceive or prefer. Relevant for our purposes is the concept's operationalization as a behavioral *intention* (i.e., an expressed affection), specifically the intention to maintain or alter distances to specific ethnic groups (Bogardus, 1967; Fishbein and Ajzen, 1975). Characteristically, respondents are asked to convey their (dis)pleasure were they to be confronted with (more) individuals from (specific) groups, e.g., at (children's) school, at work, in the neighborhood, among friends or through marriage (cf. Shadid, 1979; Hagendoorn and Hraba, 1987). The use of such item-sets is central to Hagendoorn and his associates' research on racial stereotypes and ethnic hierarchies. They observe a consistent pattern among indigenous Dutch, who prefer the retention of more distance (i.e., encounters only in less intimate public domains) from *other* groups lower in the ethnic hierarchy (see, e.g., Kleinpenning, 1993; Hagendoorn, 1995).

The use of social distance items would not resolve all the problems associated with the measurement of imagery concerning a plurality of ethnic *others*. I conclude this sub-section with three remarks on some remaining obstacles:

- Theoretically social distance measures may adequately capture differences in *affection*. Other items however are needed to encompass notions of *identification* and *belonging*. The observation that individuals *intend* to diminish social distances with ethnic *others* reveals little about their awareness of the *other*, nor about their sense that specific cultural elements are shared.
- Secondly, the interpretation of *obliviousness* (i.e., a lack of *focus*) remains problematic. Many Haarlem responses to ethnic imagery items are cloaked in uncertainty, i.e., respondents cannot or will not differentiate along ethnic lines. Presumably such respondents, when confronted with social distance items, would consistently allocate equal distances to all *other* groups. This only serves to bury the issue: should such scores be located in the middle of a social distance scale to signify *ambivalence*? Or should they be removed from the spectrum entirely to signify individuals' lack of awareness (cf. Meertens and Pettigrew, 1995; Hondius, 1999:10)?
- Finally one is again confronted with the law of diminishing return. For the Haarlem survey, a minimum of nine items would have been necessary to construct a social distance scale (i.e., three groups times three domains), while the conceptual model dictates two dozen (four groups times six domains) as more adequate. This would require (ambivalent) respondents to cooperate with several batteries of repetitive (and even insulting) questions (cf. Hamid, 1996).

Ethnicity Objectified

The previous two sub-sections have considered ethnicity as a subjective reality, a banner upon which individuals project their affinities and aversions to others. I have noted that its measurement is dependent upon respondents' awareness, and is impeded by their (feigned) ambivalence.

Regardless of whether immigrants identify with their geo-political origins, how can elements of their cultural orientation be discerned that they share with others of similar origin, and that differentiates them from individuals originating from other regions? Without lending credence to primordialist perspectives, in which ethnicity is seen to represent innate qualities (cf. Leets et al., 1996:120), the possibilities to characterize entire categories by their (stereo)typical cultural orientations are the object of extensive psychological research. Such patterns, in their relative stability, could be seen to hasten or inhibit immigrants' integration in their new cultural environment. My purpose here is to sketch briefly research developments geared toward the development, validation and application of instruments that detect geo-political cultural patterns.

As point of departure, I focus upon Hofstede's study of international differences in work-related values (1980). Hofstede had access to nearly 120,000 survey questionnaires completed by IBM employees in 66 countries (Hofstede, 1991). Through theoretical reasoning and statistical analysis he derived four essentially distinct dimensions of culture along which response variations could be adequately described.[7] For 40 countries aggregate scores along the four dimensions were then derived. As the survey had been conducted twice (in 1968 and 1972), he could observe global shifts in value orientations that did not lead to convergences in country scores. Moreover, through comparisons with other survey sources, the universality of the conceptual structure was further validated.

Hofstede's study is exemplary in that a variety of techniques and tests are applied to derive objectified scores from a broad survey data base. The scores subsequently enable comparisons within cultures (e.g., the extent in which individuals' scores deviate from the country norm) and across cultures (e.g., the extent in which two country's mean scores diverge along the four dimensions). Ultimately one could designate which immigrants maintain work-value orientations typical of their geo-political origins, and which express orientations more characteristic of other regions. Nevertheless, the measures display obvious limitations: they are historically dated, focused upon work orientations, expressed only by employees, of a high-tech multinational corporation. Rather than delve into less conspicuous limitations, I turn instead to recent research initiatives that attempt to overcome these inadequacies. The initiatives are broadly distinguished as to their focus upon *values* or *personality traits*. The former is more closely aligned with the *moral* component of culture, the latter with the *expressive*.[8] Initiatives that focus upon *cognitive* components of culture (e.g., the designation of aggregate intelligence quotients along national or ethnic lines) are ignored here, as they are either primordialist or they will be briefly considered in the separate (public) domains.

A model for a universal structure of values, with a range of applicability beyond the domain of work, has been developed and subject to validation in at least 40 countries (Schwartz, 1992; Schwartz and Sagiv, 1995; Church and Lonner, 1998). The model specifies ten motivationally distinct value types, while theoretical postulates on their (in)congruence are also introduced. The value types are organized along two dimensions: 1) 'openness to change' (e.g., stimulation, self direction) versus 'conservation' (e.g., security, conformity, tradition) and 2) 'self enhancement' (achievement, power) versus 'self transcendence' (universalism, benevolence). A set of 56 values has been operationalized to represent the value types, 44 of which appear to have comparable meanings across cultures (Church and Lonner, 1998:42). The model's sheer complexity inhibits the validation process, as the cross-cultural interpretation and modification of each value and structural component are at issue. Should a consensus ever be reached on the model's structural validity, its applicability and durability remain at issue. Not only is it questionable whether entire ethnic categories can be reliably characterized according to their scores along the various value types, more concise instruments would subsequently be needed to estimate individual survey respondents' conformity to categorical norms.

The study of personality traits has been more successful in that research in many countries or, more precisely, in many languages has consistently reduced the dimensions of personality to a five-factor model (FFM). This so-called 'Big Five' (Goldberg, 1981) is derived by having respondents use common descriptors (i.e., linguistic adjectives) to characterize individuals (Cattell, 1943; Raad et al., 1998). Descriptors that appear synonymous are then bundled into 'traits', and these apparently resolve into structures along five dimensions: 'neuroticism,' 'extroversion,' 'openness,' 'agreeableness,' and 'conscientiousness.' The premise that the FFM presents a universal structure, in which differences in personality are observed, has thus far survived every attempt at falsification (McCrae et.al., 1998:180). Should it retain construct validity, the FFM will unquestionably simplify cross-cultural comparisons,[9] and provide standards for personality measurement (e.g., Costa and McCrae, 1992; Hoekstra et al., 1996). The FFM however is no more than a model. It may ultimately lead to more comprehensive understanding of variations in personality, but personalities remain by definition dynamic and substantively diverse. Perhaps it will eventually enable the reliable designation of 'modal personalities' (Inkeles and Levinson, 1969) per ethnic category, and show how rare such personalities are. To close with a positivistic observation, it may eventually help designate the personality traits that within specific local contexts insure - or result from - a sufficient degree of individual integration.

In this section I have sketched the contours of ethnic orientation by focusing on the distinction between *subjective* (the respondent observes) and *objective* (the respondent observed) measures. Subjective measures concern individuals' expressed affinity with an ethnic group, here differentiated in geopolitical terms.[10] I have noted that such measures are sensitive to contextual characteristics that limit reliability and comparability. Historical and societal contexts delimit which polarizations (e.g., color, religion, language) if any are at issue. For the individual *subject* these are mediated by the situational contexts (e.g., work, school, family) in which they experience ethnicity as personally relevant. The survey then offers a variety of communicative contexts in which the affinities can be expressed or denied.

These shifting and interacting contexts infuse subjective measures with a high degree of ambiguity. When do *we* end and *the others* begin? Are distinctions between *us* and *them* the source or the consequence of individuals' estrangement? In our survey ethnic affinities correspond only sporadically and moderately with integration differences within ethnic categories. More affinity aspects are in need of more adequate measurement before conclusions could be drawn within the local context.

The realization of objective measures, in which ethnic categorizations correspond with characteristic cultural polarities, would help clarify these theoretical ambiguities. However instruments developed for this purpose are (forever) subject to the complexities of cross-cultural validation, and are generally more cumbersome than subjective instruments. Moreover, imagine a consensus was to be reached on the relatively stable cultural characteristics of ethnic categories (a development that I regard - with a distinct sense of dread - as more indicative of the historical context than of the quality of scientific instruments used within it). Then conjecture would continue concerning the frequency, range and direction that individuals diverge from categorical norms.

The formal distinctions focused upon in this section - between subjective and objective, between identification, belonging and affection, between *us* and *the others* - are pertinent to all the orientational polarities considered in the coming sections. Having presented these issues here, they will not be repeated for the orientations yet to come. Let them serve more as an implicit matrix that reflects the orientational aspects we failed to measure in Haarlem. With fewer words, I will then concentrate more on what we did observe.

Language, Religion and (Intercultural) Education

Through the next five sections, various aspects of individuals' orientations will be considered that in theory or practice distinguish the integrated from the estranged. In this section several measures of cultural components are reviewed that span the private domain of family relations and the more public domain of education and upbringing. The tension is most manifest in these domains between orientations that characterize individuals' (own childhood) past, and the orientations that currently typify their relations to family and schools. With the Haarlem survey we did not resolve this tension, as we made only a few inquiries into respondents' views on family and education, and none on their childhood memories. These inquiries will be considered shortly but first a more general - cognitive - indicator will be appraised.

Language Skills

The ability to speak, write and understand Dutch is widely regarded as a prerequisite for integration into Dutch society. Language courses have become mandatory for newly arrived immigrants (van der Zwan and Entzinger, 1994; Tweede Kamer, 1996); Dutch language skills are, with mathematical aptitudes, the central criteria used to monitor educational deprivation (Tesser et al., 1995:266ff). This deprivation is considered so serious that teachers even propose the prohibition of *other* languages in schoolyards and households (van Tiggele, 1997). In a country whose global market position has relied for centuries upon multilingual merchants, the key to Dutch culture is tied policy-wise to the Dutch language (cf. Bot, 1994; Woldring, 1995). To reside among the Dutch, immigrants are expected to speak Dutch. Are those who don't necessarily estranged?

We did not subject respondents to language examinations; interviewers simply appraised their oral comprehension. The evaluations are summarized in table 5.2, where one can note that most Moroccans and Turks have at best satisfactory Dutch language skills while a large majority of the other three categories speak at least reasonable Dutch. A comparison of these evaluations with respondents' scores upon the local integration index reveals that only among Moroccans do 'deficient' Dutch language skills correspond with greater estrangement (η=.46, see appendix 1). Among Moroccans, and to a lesser extent among Turks, (only) two components within the local index appear sensitive to variations in oral Dutch skills, namely individuals' *perceived opportunity* and *cultural participation*. When considering the variations in index scores for all immigrant categories combined, observed differences in oral Dutch skills account for 11% of the variance, much less for instance than various positional indicators considered in the previous chapter.

Table 5.2   Respondents' oral Dutch language skills

Evaluation	Moroccans	Turks	Surinamese Antilleans	'Other' immigrants	Indigenous Dutch
deficient	32%	25%	7%	8%	1%
satisfactory	33%	27%	17%	11%	7%
reasonable/good	35%	49%	76%	81%	92%
n (=100%)	84	101	70	99	165

Methodologically these results are inconclusive, as we did not establish objective criteria beforehand with which interviewers could reliably categorize language skills (cf. Chiswick and Miller, 1998). More common survey practice is to solicit evaluations from respondents concerning their language capabilities (e.g., use of written and broadcasted media, languages spoken with significant others, cf. Martens and Roelandt, 1993:76; Martens, 1999:85). The more central theoretical issue concerns why an inability to converse in the prevalent language should reflect so little upon immigrants' degree of local integration. Reasoning within the formal model, clarification is found in the choice of (five) criteria used to designate individuals' location upon the local index. Within the local context, greater integration according to these criteria is not contingent upon particular communicative skills. Had criteria been used that are more in accordance with *assimilative* local objectives (see §2.6.4), such as affinity or ties with the indigenous Dutch, then other results could have been expected. The findings are nevertheless surprising since they suggest that command of Dutch has no influence upon Moroccans' and Turks' *positional engagement*, measured with *per capita income* and *welfare independence*. Apparently local networks within these categories adequately mediate for those with little command of the Dutch language.

Religious Convictions

The Netherlands is arguably the most religiously diverse country in Western Europe (Harding and Phillips, 1986:36; Eisinga et al. , 1992). Besides a balanced representation of Roman Catholic and Protestant Christian denominations, around 50% of adult Dutch expresses no affiliations to religious institutions. With a history of religious accommodation, I find it hard to believe that religious convictions could nowadays impede individuals' local integration. The Islam however presents a prominent ideological exception. Since the inception of a notion of 'Europe', the *Islam* has served to symbolize much of what *Europe* is not (Saïd, 1978; Miles, 1989), and this image of cultural incongruence has been transmitted in Dutch education and other domains up to the present (Reinsch, 1987; Rath et al., 1996).

This image provides a simple explanation for Muslim immigrants' estranged positions, but does the image signify more than Dutch intolerance? Various studies, when focusing upon the perspectives of Muslim immigrants, reveal no *subjective* contradictions between Islamic convictions and the desire or capacity to adapt *Dutch* cultural orientations (Shadid, 1979; Latuheru et al., 1994; Prins, 1996). Kemper for instance held in-depth interviews with (54) first generation Moroccan men, most of whom were either physically disabled after years of 'guest work', or they taught (Arabic) language and culture in Dutch schools. He observed that they were oriented more toward the Islam than toward Morocco as a basis to their identity. Particularly for the disabled workers, the mosque served as a source for social contact and increased personal well-being. The mosque however could hardly be regarded as a den of fundamentalist revolt (1996:225).

Table 5.3   Religious beliefs passed on to children*

Religion	Moroccans	Turks	Surinamese Antilleans	'Other' immigrants	Indigenous Dutch
None	4% (0%)	6% (0%)	30% (5%)	53% (0%)	60% (2%)
Roman Catholic	-	-	24% (29%)	24% (14%)	23% (22%)
Protestant	-	-	13% (33%)	14% (25%)	12% (33%)
Islam	95% (64%)	94% (39%)	7% (60%)	1% (100%)	-
Other	1% (100%)	1% (100%)	26% (22%)	9% (57%)	5% (44%)
n (=100%)	93	158	70	93	167

* The percentages in parentheses denote those respondents that considers religion central to their lives.

We asked respondents according to which religious doctrines or precepts they (would) rear their (eventual) children. We also looked into the importance religion has in their own lives (ranging from 'absent' to 'central' positions). The response patterns are summarized in table 5.3. If the indigenous Dutch set the (assimilative) norm, secularization is the trend: the proportion without religious affinities (i.e., upbringing intentions) range from 4% to 30% among the three minority categories, applies to 53% of the 'Other' immigrants, and to 60% of the indigenous Dutch. Nearly 95% of the Moroccans and Turks assert that their (eventual) children are raised according to Islamic precepts. Particularly Moroccans perceive religion as central to their lives, while in general Muslims are more devout than other respondents.

As indicators of individual integration these measures display sporadic significance. Variations in the index scores that correspond with affiliation were observed among the Surinamese/Antilleans and 'Other' categories (η=.40 for both). In the former category Hindus in particular score low on *welfare independence* and *perceived opportunity*; in the latter category Protestants and those without affiliation score high on *per capita income* and *perceived opportunity*. As scarcely a dozen Moroccan and Turkish respondents denied Muslim affinities, statistically significant relations with the local index need not be expected within these categories. The more devout Moroccans are generally more estranged (η=.31), specifically as to *per capita income*.

Regarding these results, the relative *conformity* in religious affiliation encountered among Moroccans and Turks is noteworthy, but this might be due to the perfunctory nature of the Haarlem measurements. Kemper for instance operationalizes six dimensions of religious orientation (1996:81ff), while the study reported by Harding and Phillips used 80 items to monitor 'European' variations in religious values (1986:248ff). In the literature, various instruments are encountered that conceive religious orientation in polar terms of intrinsic-extrinsic (Allport and Ross, 1967; Kirkpatrick, 1993), means-end-quest (Batson and Ventis, 1982), immature-mature (Dudley and Cruise, 1990), and conservative-liberal-radical (Dreger and Adkins, 1991). Even had we been more thorough, we could not have distinguished between immigrants who are poor because they are devout, and those who are devout because of their poor prospects (cf. Stark and Bainbridge, 1996).

Educational Ideals

We posed several questions to respondents that gave them the opportunity to express their (dis)satisfaction with local educational practices. Asked whether the government should subsidize separate schools for those ethnic groups that want them, the percentage positive responses range from 5% among the indigenous Dutch to (only) 20% of the Moroccans. Confronted with the open question, 'which skills should children be taught to get by in Haarlem,' a consistent 40% of each ethnic category emphasizes 'Dutch language skills'. Only a few Moroccans and Turks (also) refer to lessons in their 'own' language and culture. The various skills respondents express enabled the construction of non-parametric principal component scales that differentiate between those who emphasize *general* or more *specific* skills, and those who emphasize *social* or more *exact* curricula (cf. Reinsch et al., 1995; Naylor and Kidd, 1991). None of these indicators displayed statistical relations with respondents' index scores.

To complement these *subjective* queries, we could have estimated respondents' educational orientations according to more 'objective' measures. Polarities between 'learning' and 'grades' or between 'intrinsic' and 'extrinsic' academic goals are encountered in the literature (e.g., Alexitch, 1997; Chen, 1997; Wong and Csikszentmihalyi, 1991). Usually they serve to monitor the behavior of teachers and (adolescent) students. Except perhaps in localities where such polarities are central issues of cultural incongruence and conflict, imagining how such orientational differences would suggest (immigrant) parents' degree of integration is difficult. The significance parents' cultural orientations have upon their children's future degree of integration is, of course, the topic of endless conjecture.

Competence, Ambition and Perceived Opportunity

A particular premise in debates on integration sees the clarification for immigrants' deprivation in their limited competence and adaptability. According to this so-called 'deficit' thesis, specific ethnicities lack the necessary qualifications and ambition to undertake the social obligations bound to paid work (cf. Veenman and Martens, 1995:42). Here the notion of *competence* is briefly assessed before elaborating upon measurements of 'ambition' among respondents Subsequently the *perceived opportunity* component within the local index is presented.

Competence

The knowledge component of labor orientation alludes to what individuals (need to) *know* for successful engagement on labor and material security markets. On a general level this refers to job search and solicitation skills, laborers' rights and entrepreneurial restrictions, and the capacity to acquire financial security. More specifically it refers to qualifications that denote individuals' suitability for certain jobs and not for others. Such factors do not simply correspond with degrees of formal education. The opportunities for a Moroccan born graduate in Sahara mining technology to realize material security, satisfaction and Dutch ties on the job market are less than those for an American born clown with a knack for juggling concepts. This premise is illustrative of a *cultural mismatch* thesis: immigrants have the capacity, based on their *ethnic* expertise, to prevail in particular market segments (cf. Sowell,

1981a; Portes and Manning, 1986), but such specialized knowledge may eventually lead into a *mobility trap* (cf. Lutz, 1991; Dagevos and Veenman, 1992). The experience of so many thousand immigrants in previous decades who went from unskilled 'guest-workers' to unemployed 'welfare dependents' (Castles, 1984) is testimony to a more general axiom of supply and demand: the diversity and dynamics of job markets inhibit the identification of specific labor qualifications that will designate - from one city or one era to the next - the competent and the engaged.

(Un)willing to Work

That particular (immigrant) groups may lack the personal motivation to expand and exploit their expertise provides an ideologically dense explanation for labor market *disengagement* and local estrangement. A heterogeneous tradition of social research focuses upon those cultural mechanisms that, as an antithesis of *ambition*, serve to solidify and spread a *working class* or *underclass* culture within specific environments or groups (e.g., Harrington, 1962; Willis, 1977; Engbersen et al., 1993).

In the Haarlem survey a series of items pertained to labor orientation: respondents' views on why they have (no) work, on job opportunities, on satisfaction with the current job, and the type of (volunteer) work respondents would prefer to do. Three (sets of) items in particular provide indications of individuals' willingness to work. Asked whether they are willing to do voluntary work when assured of sufficient time and income, 43% of the Moroccan and 60% of the Turkish respondents answer affirmatively; the percentage in the other three ethnic categories hovers around 70%. Offered the choice between paid work and more financially lucrative welfare benefits, the percentage respondents that opt for the benefits ranges from 8% of the Surinamese and Antilleans to 27% the Moroccans. The percentage that prefers steady employment, even when equivalent sums could be earned with entrepreneurial activities, revolves around 50% for all categories except the Turks, only 18% of whom consistently choose employment. In corroboration with other Dutch research (Veraart, 1996:90), a much larger proportion of the Turks are found to prefer the autonomy and risks of their own business. Respondents were also asked more directly how important they perceive paid work for their *sense of belonging* ('*ergens bijhoren*'). A large majority within all ethnic categories found paid work to be '(very) important'. Interestingly, here the ethnic rank-order runs contrary to that observed by the more hypothetical labor items; identification with work is namely most prevalent among the Moroccans (93%) and Turks (87%) and least among 'Other' immigrants and the indigenous Dutch (66%).

Table 5.4   Quartile distribution along labor ambition spectrum

Quartile	Moroccans	Turks	Surinamese Antilleans	'Other' immigrants	Indigenous Dutch
unambitious (lowest 25%)	32%	23%	22%	27%	24%
rather unambitious	24%	36%	22%	26%	27%
rather ambitious	9%	14%	16%	24%	22%
ambitious (highest 25%)	36%	27%	40%	23%	28%
mean	-0.16	-0.06	0.14	-0.12	0.02
standard deviation	1.06	1.06	0.97	1.19	0.97
n (=100%)	93	159	77	100	168

These items taken separately - the willingness to partake in volunteer work, the preference for either welfare, employment or one's own business, and the importance attributed work - correspond only incidentally and moderately with respondents' scores on the local index. I have reduced them to one component that provides a simple index for *labor ambition*.[11] In table 5.4 the quartile distribution along this hypothetical spectrum (after correcting for differences due to sampling stratification) is presented per ethnic category. The largest deviations from local norms are observed by Moroccans and Surinamese/Antilleans, 36% respectively 40% of whom fall within the most ambitious quartile.[12] It is only within these two ethnic categories that significant relations are observed between more 'ambition' and a greater degree of local integration (η = .31 respectively .37).[13]

These results hardly support images of the indolent immigrant, whose estrangement is rooted in a reluctance to work. The *ambition* measure remains however far too crude to draw conclusions concerning characteristic labor orientations among immigrants. The hypothetical nature of the questions posed fails to distinguish for instance between a lack of *ambition* and a lack of *imagination*, rooted for instance in an inability to perceive paid work as a realistic option (cf. Bobo et al., 1995; Dunifon and Duncan, 1998). Nor did we delve into the divergent *intrinsic* and *extrinsic* reasons why individuals aspire to work (e.g., Harding and Phillips, 1986:153ff; Halman et al., 1987:170ff; Loscocco, 1989; de Vaus and McAllister, 1991; Reed, 1997). We observe in all categories a *subjective* affinity toward work (cf. Feddema, 1991:220ff) but more *objective* measures of work values (e.g., Hofstede, 1980; Furnham and Reilly, 1991) and personality traits (Rust, 1997) would presumably lead to a far more diffuse image of respondents' labor orientations.

Chances Compared to the Average Resident

At three moments during the interviews the visual metaphor of a weighting balance was presented, upon which local residents were arranged according to their chances for respectively housing, education and paid work. Informed that residents with a 'average prospects' are found at the middle (i.e., the fulcrum) of the seven-point (Likert) scale, respondents were asked to locate themselves upon the balance.

Table 5.5   Estimated prospects for housing, education and paid work compared to the 'average resident'

Market		Moroccans	Turks	Surinamese Antilleans	'Other' immigrants	Indigenous Dutch
Housing:	less	35%	43%	35%	32%	35%
	equal	28%	21%	36%	38%	30%
	more	37%	35%	29%	31%	36%
Education:	less	37%	33%	7%	11%	16%
	equal	18%	20%	18%	17%	18%
	more	46%	47%	76%	72%	67%
Paid work:	less	43%	40%	20%	33%	22%
	equal	31%	26%	46%	32%	27%
	more	26%	34%	35%	35%	51%
n (=100%)		81/74/81	136/150/140	72/74/69	95/97/93	162/169/157

In table 5.5 the respondents' assessments of their prospects are summarized. The estimated prospects upon the housing market do not vary significantly per ethnic category. This could be interpreted as testimony that social housing policies adequately compensate for the limited access immigrants may experience to 'free market' segments. Nearly half the Moroccans and Turks find their chances to acquire education are above the local average. Nevertheless it is upon this market that these two ethnic categories diverge most significantly from the other three (η=.34), as most Surinamese and Antilleans, 'Other' immigrants and indigenous Dutch perceive more than average educational opportunity. By the interpretation of these percentile variations upon the educational opportunity scale, one must take into account the divergent locations and eras in which respondents could acquire primary education.[14] Finally, upon the market for *paid work*, most of the indigenous Dutch find they have more than average opportunity; nearly half the Surinamese and Antilleans (46%) estimated theirs equal to the average resident, while nearly half the Moroccan and Turkish respondents (43% resp. 40%) saw for themselves less than average opportunity.

Much can be questioned and little can be verified about the reliability of these measures. They are based for instance: on presumptions concerning the similarity of respondents' focus upon and knowledge of local markets, on respondents' agreement with imagery of local opportunity being (symmetrically) distributed around a midpoint, and on respondents' capacity to assess their own distance from that point. Moreover, the derivation of a *perceived opportunity* spectrum by means of principal component analysis presumes that respondents' estimates along the three spectra are manifestations of a one-dimensional personality trait that could be coined a 'sense of opportunity'.

The derivation of this component, and its inclusion as one of five criteria that comprise the local integration index, is ultimately motivated by theoretical considerations. These are succinctly reflected in observations made by Emile Durkheim a century ago (cited by Runcimen, 1966:25):

> What is needed if social order is to reign is that the mass of men be content with their lot. But what is needed for them to be content, is not that they have more or less but that they be convinced that they have no right to more.

With similar reasoning I regard a situation, in which variations in perceived opportunity no longer diverge according to ethnic categorical distinctions, a (*tolerant*) objective of local integration processes: immigrants may have less material wealth than indigenous residents, however immigrant integration remains a legitimacy issue (only) if such collectivities experience divergent prospects for engagement on local markets. This postulate obviously pertains more to the process of *group* integration rather than that of *individuals*. That the perceived opportunity measures are included within the local index has implications for the distinction between the integrated and the estranged within a given ethnic category. It signifies that between two individuals, similar according to all other index criteria, the one who is *convinced* he or she has more prospects will score more integrated. In this sense the criterion *rewards* those immigrants ignorant of eventual discriminatory practices, and *penalizes* those conscious of their *victimized* positions.

In table 5.6 I present the quartile distribution of respondents' scores upon the *perceived opportunity* component, after correcting for differences due to stratified sampling. One may note that most (51%) of the Moroccans and Turks have scores within the lowest local quartile, while the scores of respondents in other ethnic categories fluctuate more symmetrically around the 'average resident'. In contrast with Surinamese and Antilleans, who score on average even higher than the indigenous Dutch, residents within these two minority categories find they are being short-chanced.

Table 5.6   Quartile distribution upon perceived opportunity spectrum

Quartile	Moroccans	Turks	Surinamese Antilleans	'Other' immigrants	Indigenous Dutch
inopportune (lowest 25%)	51%	51%	20%	24%	24%
rather inopportune	28%	23%	26%	31%	24%
rather opportune	11%	17%	39%	23%	26%
opportune (highest 25%)	11%	10%	16%	22%	26%
standardized mean	-0.69	-0.51	0.16	-0.019	0.1
standard deviation	1.02	0.98	0.86	0.95	1
n (=100%)	93	159	77	100	170

These theoretical notions and survey instruments invite further refinement. The concept of *relative deprivation* is central to sociological studies of urban poverty (Rowntree, 1901; Runcimen, 1966; Townsend, 1979; Hutton, 1991). A more adequate means to measure opportunity as *subjective* deprivation was not found among these studies (cf. Uys, 1991; Lobao and Thomas, 1992; van Niekerk, 1993). Measurements of *perceived opportunity* have served in (social) psychological studies to clarify individuals' political orientations (Plutzer, 1987), criminal behavior (Burton et.al. 1994) and satisfaction in life (Tillich, 1952; Reker, et al., 1987; Harlow and Newcomb, 1990). However, here again no 'average residents' are encountered whom respondents are asked to use as points of reference. In short, I note plenty of opportunity for further research.

Separate Services and Local Satisfaction

Moving on to the domain of health and welfare, this section focuses upon two aspects of cultural orientation. The first is primarily a moral issue pertinent to this domain, namely the question whether individuals condone or condemn immigrants' rights to their *own* social services. Seen from a *tolerant vision* of local integration, one would hope that residents condone such rights. The second aspect concerns *local satisfaction,* one of the five criteria that comprise the *local index.* The various items used to construct this criterion are presented, and reflections on more adequate measurements are made.

Allow me first to reflect briefly on possible *cognitive* indicators. What do immigrants (need to) know about personal health and welfare that advance their local integration? Many facets of urban life could jeopardize the health and welfare and ultimately the integration of ignorant immigrants, ranging from the impurities of tap water to the torment of poverty and racism. Where such dangers lead to individuals' dependency upon health and welfare services, they are reflected by individuals' *positions* on this market. The issue consequently pertains to those who occupy *detached* positions: are they in need and unaware of available services, or are the necessary services unavailable or inaccessible? In the Haarlem survey we encountered few references to this issue.

Opting for Separate Social Services

The past few years, there has been much discussion about social services for different groups of people. Some contend that the government should finance separate services for different groups; others contend that everyone should use the same services.

These two sentences served during the interviews to introduce a list of ten social services. Respondents were asked for each service whether they consider it appropriate that the local government provides immigrants with their *own* service.[15] An overview of the percentages per ethnic category who acknowledge this right is presented in table 5.7.

Before considering the variant answer patterns provided by the respondents, I must consider the ambiguous nature of the questions posed. We were probing respondents' convictions on issues of cultural diversity: do immigrants have divergent welfare needs, and should this difference be encouraged? Stripped of ideology, convictions are neither right nor wrong. However, the opinions were being elicited at the request of the local government; respondents were informed that their (anonymous) views would help mold multi-cultural policies. In this context, respondents may know that the local government can and does subsidize particular services for immigrants; they are being offered the opportunity to convey their personal priorities. In short, table 5.7 may reflect respondents' variant views about: cultural diversity, their immediate needs, local budgetary priorities, or the limits to government intervention.

Table 5.7   Approval of specific local services for immigrants

Type of social service	Moroccans	Turks	Surinamese Antilleans	'Other' immigrants	Indigenous Dutch
Meeting localities	29%	26%	31%	31%	53%
Library departments	23%	37%	17%	44%	53%
Women's activities	39%	36%	39%	34%	42%
Retirement homes	13%	35%	25%	15%	21%
Neighborhood activities	30%	27%	12%	12%	24%
Job mediation	20%	19%	36%	26%	33%
Sport facilities	16%	16%	3%	4%	4%
Day-care facilities	15%	14%	4%	7%	10%
Health care services	17%	20%	14%	10%	17%
Schools	20%	15%	8%	11%	5%
Mean # types condoned	2.5	2.5	1.9	2.0	2.6
n (=100%)	89	155	73	97	169

I would not dwell on the ambiguity of this set of survey questions, had I not been confounded by the answers received. The moderation exhibited by immigrant respondents - less than half acknowledged the government's right to subsidize more than two services - contrasts sharply with the number of separate services offered to immigrants in the city. Under the minority policy motto 'particular (*categoriale*) services when necessary, communal (*algemene*) services if possible,' all but two of the ten services had been subjected to some form of differentiation by local authorities. Within this context, I do not interpret the moderate legitimacy appropriated separate services to signify respondents' appreciation of cultural diversity. It reflects more their views about which services are absolutely necessary.

One sees in table 5.7 a broad divergency in the particular services found appropriate. Only among the indigenous Dutch do most approve the provision of two separate services for immigrants, namely library and meeting localities. The premise was also examined that respondents who in fact use the specific service may be more outspoken in their views; the percentages for these respondents are shown in parentheses. Only for seven of the fifty comparisons are the approval percentages significantly larger for those who use the service.

What do these opinions reveal about local and individual integration?

Some consensus is observed that certain *leisure arrangements* may retain an exclusive character, i.e., immigrant categories (particularly the female half) should be free to meet, read in their native tongue, and even retire together from active social life. The lack of approval concerning immigrants' rights to separate schools, sports and day-care (and to a lesser extent health care and job mediation) suggests more fundamental convictions, namely that such *socializing services* should promote cultural reorientation and ethnic inclusion at an early age. The analysis however does not reveal that those who deviate from this conviction are more estranged. It does reveal that, among the indigenous Dutch, the more types of particular services individuals condone the greater their index scores are likely to be (R=.23, see appendix 1). A polar trend is observed among Moroccans and Turks, i.e., the more estranged the more types of particular services are found appropriate (R=-.21 resp. -.19).

Dissatisfied Residents

At four moments during the interviews, respondents were asked to evaluate their local situation by rating it on a scale from one to ten, six signifying 'satisfactory' (*voldoende*) in accordance with Dutch educational customs.[16] The four ratings referred to respondents' home, their neighborhood, their personal life in Haarlem, and their evaluation of the city in general. Except by the personal life item, respondents were told a satisfactory grade suggests a situation sufficiently livable (*leefbaar*) that the respondent wishes to remain.

Table 5.8   Mean appraisals of home, neighborhood, local life and locality*

Object of evaluation	Moroccans	Turks	Surinamese Antilleans	'Other' immigrants	Indigenous Dutch
Domicile	5.7 (38%)	6.1 (22%)	6.6 (25%)	7.0 (12%)	7.5 (6%)
Neighborhood	6.3 (25%)	6.2 (20%)	6.9 (4%)	7.0 (9%)	7.0 (11%)
Personal local life	6.4 (19%)	6.3 (16%)	7.1 (11%)	7.3 (4%)	7.3 (5%)
Haarlem's livability	6.5 (11%)	6.8 (3%)	7.0 (3%)	7.2 (5%)	7.1 (4%)
n (=100%)	89-92	157-159	73-76	97-100	167-168

* The percentages in parentheses denote the respondents with 'unsatisfactory' appraisals (less than 6).

The evaluations of these four domains are summarized in table 5.8, where the mean scores per item are presented. In parentheses the percentage who consider their situation to be unsatisfactory (i.e., ratings less than six) is also displayed. With only modest variations, one may note that with respect to all four domains the mean scores increase and the percentage dissatisfied decrease as the categories are scanned from left to right. Moroccans and Turks are much less satisfied with these four aspects of their local lives than the indigenous Dutch. The discrepancies are greatest as for respondents' housing: the average Moroccan finds the homes less than satisfactory. Within all ethnic categories respondents concur most in their rating of Haarlem as a viable locality.

On the presumption that these four survey items represent the affection individuals harbor with respect to their social and spatial surroundings, they have been combined via principal component analysis to devise a *local satisfaction* criterion (cf. Veenhoven, 1996:11; Marshall and Firth, 1999).[17] The limited scope of this criterion prohibits its designation as a measure of individuals' personal *well-being* (cf. Diener, 1984; Horley and Lavery, 1991; Strack et al., 1991). Its inclusion as one of the five criteria that comprise the local integration index is based on (moral) reasoning comparable to that followed for the *perceived opportunity* criterion: immigrants may categorically deviate from indigenous residents as to their personal well-being; immigrant integration remains however a local issue (at least) as long as immigrants and indigenes categorically diverge in their appreciation of their local environment.

Table 5.9   Quartile distribution upon local satisfaction spectrum

Quartile	Moroc-cans	Turks	Surinamese Antilleans	'Other' immigrants	Indigenous Dutch
dissatisfied (lowest 25%)	61%	61%	40%	26%	23%
rather dissatisfied	15%	13%	27%	28%	28%
rather satisfied	17%	15%	18%	24%	22%
satisfied (highest 25%)	7%	11%	14%	22%	27%
standardized mean	-0.95	-0.87	-0.21	0.04	0.12
standard deviation	1.28	1.42	1.08	1.09	0.95
n (=100%)	93	159	77	100	170

Table 5.9 displays the quartile distributions of respondents' *local satisfaction* score compared to the *average resident*. Most of the Moroccans and Turks (61%) are in the most 'dissatisfied' quartile of this hypothetical spectrum. An inordinate percentage (40%) of the Surinamese and Antilleans

also score in Haarlem's most 'dissatisfied' quartile, while 'Other' immigrants vary minimally from the indigenous Dutch.

These measurements do not invite simple comparisons with other research on local or life satisfaction (e.g., Moller and Schlemmer, 1989; Tran and Nguyen, 1994; Neto, 1995; Scherpenzeel, 1996). Simply the decision to use a ten-step scale has its consequences for comparability, as the use of fewer steps is far more common (Veenhoven, 1993:171ff). The validity of the measures would be enhanced had a broader range of local domains been subject to respondents' ratings, e.g., labor, education, welfare and leisure markets. More central to its status of immigrant integration end-goal criterion, the component also lacks items that explicitly represent individuals' satisfaction with local interethnic relations. Its concurrent validity would be more secure were it to correlate more with the other four index criteria (see appendix II). This could be construed as testimony to the component's unreliability. In my view it attests more to the significance of the local satisfaction criterion independent of, and as supplement to, other integration criteria.

Residential Satisfaction and Neighborhood Affinity

Within the domain of housing and neighborhood environment, I find it difficult to identify cultural polarities that serve as reference points for individuals' orientations. Not that there is a dearth of cultural issues concerning immigrant integration in this domain. For instance, one of the first and more factious images concerning Muslim 'guest-workers' was their use of urban residential balconies to ritually slaughter sheep. The idea that immigrants foster divergent beliefs and customs concerning their homes and neighborhoods has been the focus of a modest Dutch research tradition (see, e.g., van Amersfoort, 1992; van Dugteren, 1993:55ff; van Kempen et al., 1994; Huls, 1996). Beyond generalizations that immigrants reside in less fashionable homes and neighborhoods, and evaluate this environment accordingly, little evidence suggests that housing and neighborhood *orientations* form a significant obstacle or indication of immigrants' local integration. Lucid testimony cannot be derived from our own survey data, if only because residential and neighborhood satisfaction (as constituents of the *local satisfaction* criterion), correlate by research design with individuals' degree of integration. With little basis to elaborate upon the notion of orientation within this domain, the presentation will remain concise. First respondents' evaluations of their homes are reviewed, seeking factors that account for differences in residential satisfaction. Then several survey items concerning respondents' neighborhood evaluations are considered, providing a measure for neighborhood *affinity*.

Home as a Neighborhood Threshold

When comparing the four appraisals respondents made of their local environment, immigrants are found particularly dissatisfied with their Haarlem homes. Residential (dis)satisfaction could reflect cultural orientations that individuals sustain irrespective of the neighborhood in which they reside (cf. Phillips, 1996; Bruin and Cook, 1997). It is perceived here more generally as the (dis)parity between individuals' housing aspirations and their current environment (cf. Priemus, 1986). Is the residential dissatisfaction we observed among immigrants a consequence of their failure to adapt their large households to cramped quarters? Or is the source of their discontent more environmental, exemplified by the view that the ('right') home is in the 'wrong' neighborhood? Although a comprehensive analyses cannot be presented in support of the environmental explanation, my purpose here is to refute the notion that immigrants' residential satisfaction registers merely 'private' (or 'cultural') differences in (dis)content. The exercise will lend credence to the premise that the local satisfaction do not simply reflect an *innate* estrangement among certain immigrant minorities. They represent instead the progress made by individuals and groups in an intrinsically *social* process.

If residential satisfaction primarily depends on immigrants' (in)capacity to reorient themselves to altered housing conditions, then significant correlations could be expected with attributes of either the household or the domicile. Dissatisfaction is then a consequence of local homes not meeting the needs and expectations of immigrant households. The homes could be considered too expensive, or the prospects of purchasing a home too low. One could postulate that the dissatisfaction simply reflects individuals' unhappiness with their personal life, and that it would be more evident among new residents. To investigate whether the residential satisfaction measure pertains primarily to individuals' immediate home situation, its statistical association with various survey items was examined, namely:

- respondents' age, sex, type of household, ethnic affinity, religious devotion, and
- residential duration, perceived housing opportunity and satisfaction with personal local life.
- Furthermore the housing types, monthly housing costs, and rooms per resident, were compared.

For the first five factors no statistically significant relations are observed within any ethnic category. The remaining six factors were entered together in a multiple regression analysis; the variance in the residential satisfaction score clarified by the six factors *combined* is displayed in the first row of table 5.10. One can observe that these 'home' factors account for 20% of the variance among Turks, and less than that within all other categories. With these results, the premise cannot be dismissed that immigrants' 'innate' orientations effect their appreciation of their domiciles. The results however hardly qualify immigrants' residential (dis)satisfaction as a purely private affair.

Table 5.10 Clarifications for variance in residential satisfaction*

Variables entered in the model	Moroccans	Turks	Surinamese Antilleans	'Other' immigrants	All immigrants	Indigenous Dutch
Home factors	16%	20%	16%	14%	17%	16%
Area factors	31%	18%	24%	22%	25%	12%
Both factors	35%	35%	27%	28%	32%	21%
n	93	159	77	100	427	170

* According to multiple regression analysis via forced entry method, sign. F < .01 for all models.

To examine an alternative explanation - that residential (dis)satisfaction primarily depends upon the neighborhood environment surrounding the home - three measures were considered: the 'objective' *status* the neighborhood has compared with other Haarlem neighborhoods (see table 4.11), respondents' subjective *neighborhood satisfaction*, and their *neighborhood affinity*, i.e., their 'sense of belonging' in the neighborhood. The variance in residential satisfaction accounted for by these three 'area' factors *combined* is displayed in the second row of table 5.10. Except for the Turkish and indigenous Dutch categories, the three factors account for approximately 25% of the variance, more than the six 'home' factors combined. That these 'area' factors correlate with residential satisfaction largely independent of the 'home' factors is shown in the third row of the table. One sees there that the variance accounted for when *all* (nine) factors are entered in the model is - excepting the indigenous Dutch - nearly twice the variance accounted for by the 'home' factors alone.

Having accounted for only one-fifth to one-third of the variance in *residential satisfaction* observed, these findings do not provide convincing evidence for either the *private* or the *environmental* postulate. Considering their proportionate effect, the findings do suggest that immigrants' residential satisfaction reflect more an appreciation of the surrounding neighborhood than the home itself. In other words, the home is appraised more for its value as a public threshold, than as a private sanctuary.

Feeling at Home in the Neighborhood

Comparable to the notion of ethnic orientation, individuals' *affection* toward their more immediate local surroundings is but one aspect of their neighborhood orientation. Individuals may also consciously identify with, or express values characteristic of, a particular neighborhood (group). In the survey explicit neighborhood identifications were not solicited from respondents. Several items however referred more generally to respondents' *sense of belonging* in their neighborhood. In table 5.11 the response categories are presented that correspond with a minimal affinity for each of these items, along with the percentages per ethnic category who offer this response. The bottom row of the table presents the percentage that, based upon a non-parametric principal component ('princal') derived from the first three items, score in the lowest quartile of Haarlem residents along a hypothetical *neighborhood affinity* spectrum.[18] One may note that for all items, and the component score, the percentage respondents who express minimal affinity with their neighborhood is greater for practically all immigrant categories than for the indigenous Dutch.

Do these expressed differences in neighborhood affinity correspond with individuals' degree of integration? Excepting the Turks, respondents within all immigrant categories who convey little neighborhood affinity are likely to score lower upon the local integration index (see appendix I). This finding is not surprising, as differences in neighborhood affinity correspond with *neighborhood* and with *local satisfaction* within all immigrant categories (e.g., R = .44 resp. .33 for all immigrants).[19] More noteworthy is that *only* among the indigenous Dutch neighborhood affinity has no relation to respondents' satisfaction and index scores.

Table 5.11 Respondents who express little affinity for their neighborhood

Indicator	Moroc-cans	Turks	Surinamese Antilleans	'Other' immigrants	Indigenous Dutch
'here means nothing for me'	17%	16%	20%	16%	16%
'(certainly) not at home here'	26%	17%	5%	17%	11%
'absolutely no friends here'	36%	25%	39%	39%	23%
'prefer return to native land'	11%	7%	14%	6%	1%
lowest 25% pc affinity score	37%	33%	29%	30%	24%
n (=100%)	89-93	153-159	72-77	96-100	166-170

The statistical relationships observed between neighborhood affinity and neighborhood satisfaction supplement those concerning residential satisfaction: a *sense of belonging* appears important for immigrants' residential and their neighborhood satisfaction, while the satisfaction expressed by indigenous Dutch seems less dependent upon such sensitivities. These observations are ambiguous testimony for the notion that immigrants diverge in their *orientations* from the indigenous Dutch. In my opinion, it is not that immigrants diverge 'innately' in their needs and aspirations. They have simply less opportunity *structurally* to reside in those more auspicious neighborhoods where neighbors are free to talk to the trees (van Lippe-Biesterfeld, 1995) without disturbing the peace (cf. Huls, 1996:62).

The fourth survey item summarized in table 5.11 - the preferred place of residence - differs in its nature from the other three items; the respondents' neighborhoods are not necessarily the objects of appraisal. A comparison of responses across ethnic categories does reveal several interesting differences. Whereas a small minority within each category opts for the current residence, around half the Moroccans and Turks would simply prefer to live 'elsewhere in Haarlem'. In contrast, more than half the 'Other' immigrants and indigenous Dutch opt for residence either 'elsewhere in the Netherlands' or 'elsewhere in the world'. These findings suggest that most immigrant minorities intend to remain in Haarlem, only their desire is to reside in other neighborhoods. This commitment to remain has been identified theoretically as crucial to immigrants' integration (cf. Collett, 1996:475; Hondius, 1999:41). The correspondence however between responses to this item and respondents' degree of integration is significant only among the 'Other' immigrants (η=.34). Only within this immigrant category are those individuals who express a preference to return to their land of origins likely to score more estranged.

Political Orientations and Local Visions

Civic life encompasses several facets that serve as focus of cultural orientations: artistic and leisure interests, political convictions and affiliations, and more generally the appreciation of public space and local objectives. To review the various cultural components systematically - cognitive, moral and affective - for all these facets would go beyond the illustrative potential of the Haarlem survey. Two response sets in the data are focused upon in this section. The first concerns respondents' affinity with political organizations. The second, respondents' views on livable localities, concerns more centrally the objectives that serve to delineate - and legitimate - processes of local integration.

Neither of these themes concerns cognitive aspects, as we did not attempt to measure respondents' knowledge of local affairs. This is not to deny its central relevance for immigrants' integration. Knowledge of public transport, police deportment, the opening hours of popular pubs, the success of local soccer teams, or the locations of concerts and charity, not only reflect individuals' integration, it undoubtedly fosters the process. The problem in part is the stipulation and selection of relevant items. Consider for example issues of citizenship. Debates on liberal, republican or communitarian models of citizenship revolve around divergent conceptions of the citizens' rights and duties, each model with its own abstract package of necessary skills (Choenni, 1992; Kymlicka, 1995; Archard, 1996; Fermin, 1999). Should the researcher succeed in developing reliable methods to measure individuals' knowledge according to one or all models, survey criteria of brevity, simplicity and comparability then present more methodological obstacles.

Local Party and Ethnic Politics

In many Dutch cities 'minority' interest groups maintain channels of negotiation and debate with local governments parallel to, but separate from, those used by established political parties. The existence and use of these channels reveal much about immigrants' position in the local political domain (Rath, 1991; de Haan, 1995; Bousetta, 1997). Correspondingly, the affinities expressed by individual immigrants for organizations within one channel or the other may reflect different degrees of integration. The only explicit reference to political affinities in the Haarlem survey concerned respondents' party preference in the most recent local elections. That an immigrant uses voting rights in local elections has been seen to correspond with various integration indicators, e.g., residential duration, language skills, and ties with indigenous Dutch (Gilsing, 1991:53ff). A distinction in respondents between those who do not use their voting rights and those who do accounts for significant differences in *local index* scores only among the Turks and indigenous Dutch (η=.26 resp. .16).

In table 5.12 the percentile distribution of electoral preferences is displayed per ethnic category. The parties are ranked according to a generally recognized national political spectrum from left to right. A distinct trend in electoral preference can be discerned from (radical) left among Moroccans to conservative right among indigenous Dutch.[20]

To infer political orientations from an incidental tick of the ballot signifies a disregard for criteria of measurement validity and reliability. There are validated (multidimensional) survey instruments to measure political orientation (e.g., Middendorp, 1978), and a substantial body of research that monitors anti-immigrant political initiatives (cf. van Donselaar, 1991; Elbers and Fennema, 1993; Scheepers et al., 1994). Considering the parallel between the left-right distribution along the political spectrum, and the distribution of ethnic categorys' scores along the integration index, one could expect leftist leanings to correspond with more estrangement. This however is not observed within any of the five ethnic categories. Brief and simple measurements along a left-right political spectrum provide little insight into (Haarlem) immigrants' individual integration.

Table 5.12 Political party choice by local elections of 2 March 1994

Electoral preference	Moroc-cans	Turks	Surinamese Antilleans	'Other' immigrants	Indigenous Dutch
Radical left (*Groen Links/SP*)	58%	29%	6%	15%	21%
Labor Party (*PvdA*)	40%	26%	52%	15%	20%
Liberal center (*D'66*)	-	12%	13%	48%	15%
Christian Democrats (*CDA*)	2%	28%	13%	7%	15%
Right (*VVD/klein rechts*)	-	6%	17%	16%	29%
n (=100%)	43	86	54	62	120

As for more specific political debates over the legitimacy of minority organizations (*zelf-organisaties*), we also solicited respondents' views on immigrant organizations. The percentage that expresses disapproval hovers around 5% within the minority categories and applies to 12% of the 'Other' immigrants and indigenous Dutch. The response patterns correspond significantly with individuals' integration scores among the Moroccans, Turks and indigenous Dutch (η=.41, .38 and .26 respectively). However, the 'direction' of the correspondence calls for divergent interpretations. Moroccans and indigenous Dutch who approve of such organizations score more integrated, approving Turks on the other hand are more estranged. Civic orientations obviously diverge within the separate ethnic categories, but it is unclear whether disagreement concerns the actual activities of immigrant organizations, or pertains more generally to local objectives of cultural unity or diversity.

Some illumination is provided by (open) responses about why such organizations are (not) needed. Most of the positive responses could be qualified in one of two ways: some emphasize that immigrants have specific problems and interests requiring particular attention and expertise, others see such organizations as *interpreters* that serve to *guide* immigrants into local culture. These responses provide not so much an indication of individual integration, but shed light upon local integration objectives of cultural unity or diversity: immigrant interest groups can be perceived as a self-evident characteristic of culturally diverse - and *tolerant* - localities, they can also be evaluated for their *assimilative* role in pursuing objectives of cultural unity (cf. Mullard et al., 1990:58ff). The observation that a specific group of (relatively integrated) Turks disapprove of Turkish organizations could be interpreted within the context of these *incongruent* objectives.

Imagining the Ideal City

Cultural (in)congruence was circumscribed in chapter two as a (lack of) consensus between indigenous and immigrant groups concerning local integration *objectives*. Do Haarlem residents differ in their conceptions of an integrated locality? Several queries in the survey addressed this issue. In three separate items, respondents were asked to choose between two (polar) attributes of an ideal city: *freedom* or *equality, unity* or *diversity,* and *privacy* or *sociability*. One may recognize in these six ideals the central objectives of local integration delineated in table 2.1.[21]

Table 5.13 Preferences for (polar) attributes of an ideal city

Attribute	Moroc-cans	Turks	Surinamese Antilleans	'Other' immigrants	All immigrants	Indigenous Dutch
Freedom	19%	46%	55%	68%	61%	57%
Equality	81%	54%	45%	32%	39%	43%
Unity	43%	61%	20%	23%	29%	20%
Diversity	57%	39%	80%	77%	71%	80%
Privacy	31%	13%	39%	45%	39%	62%
Sociability	69%	87%	61%	55%	61%	38%
n (=100%)	84-86	137-146	67-69	92-98	389-407	162-168

The patterns of respondents' preferences are summarized in table 5.13. Although the trend is not 'linear', respondents in more estranged immigrant categories do opt more for a combination of 'equality, unity and sociability,' while indigenous Dutch generally opt for 'freedom, diversity and privacy'. While the indigenous majority of residents apparently underwrite principles of individual freedom and the right to privacy, many if not most immigrant minorities express their support of more egalitarian and sociable ideals. Taken at face value, this disparity alludes to fundamental issues that surround the immigrant integration process: Should immigrants expect the same opportunities and privileges as indigenous residents? Can the provision of such opportunities and privileges be legitimately withheld by democratic consensus? How much local social opportunity should be provided immigrant individuals and entire groups, before they are expected to comply with and pursue local integration objectives? When does the lack of consensus concerning local integration objectives signify a process of local disintegration?

The primary dimension of incongruence between indigent and immigrant objectives resides in the (interactive) polarity between *privacy* (endorsed by 62% of the indigenous Dutch) and *sociability* (endorsed by 61% of all immigrants). More consensus is observed concerning ideals of *freedom* and *cultural diversity*, although most of the Moroccan and Turks are technically *disoriented* considering their preference for opposing ideals. Succinctly stated, immigrants in their ideal sketch are more likely to endorse a *tolerant* local vision, whereas proportionally more indigenous Dutch sketch the contours of a *pillarized* vision. A rigorous and schematic interpretation of these results, according to Schermerhorns' distinction in patterns of social process (see Figure 1.1) would lead to the conclusion that Haarlem immigrants - instead of being integrated - are confronted with a process of 'forced segregation'. This conclusion however would rely upon the normative premise that 33% of the indigenous Dutch and 19% of the immigrant respondents (namely those individuals who explicitly opt for a *pillarized* respectively *tolerant* combination of local ideals) designate the integration objectives for their respective groups.

Considering the inadequacy of these measures, they have little legitimacy as signifiers of local integration objectives. Blanket characterizations in three abstract notions as to the ideal direction of local processes would be, if used as the basis for local policies, an affront to social science and local citizenry. These items are in need of validation and, considering their abstract nature, should above all be complemented by extensive series of items per local domain (cf. Phalet et al., 1999:53ff). Such abstract ideals are moreover ambiguous across linguistic lines and interview contexts. In the final chapter I will return to this issue, qualifying the development of instruments that more adequately measure individuals' compliance with local integration objectives as an important research initiative.

The development of such instruments would conceivably result in the designation of integration criteria more normatively attuned to divergent objectives than those five contained in the *local index*. The extent in which respondents' endorsements of civic ideals correspond with their degree of integration is in any event insubstantial. Among the indigenous Dutch, those who endorse ideals of cultural *diversity* and *freedom* are generally more locally integrated ($\eta = .32$ resp. .25). As for the immigrant categories, only among the Turks does a preference for *equality* correspond with higher integration scores ($\eta=.20$). An elaboration upon these observed relations would require an entire framework of theoretical and normative presumptions concerning the nature and dynamics of individuals' influence upon, and sensitivity to, local processes. It seems more expedient to summarize the various manifestations of diversity and incongruence encountered in this chapter.

Assessment: The Elusiveness of Congruous Orientations

In the previous sections, observations on the relation between culture and immigrant integration have lead to an eclectic review of Haarlem circumstance, measurement problems and theoretical issues. Perhaps the most important conclusion that can be drawn from the excursion is that the conceptualization of a lucid theory, which explicates the relation between cultural orientations and integration end-goals, deserves central priority. Arbitrary analyses of differences in individuals' orientations has led me to observe numerous spurious, insignificant and ambiguous relations to their integration scores. As a brief summary I consider here the various problems encountered in this chapter that confuse perceptions and measurements of cultural orientations. With an overview of cultural divergencies observed among survey respondents, I first examine their potential to clarify variations in integration scores. Then the methodological obstacles encountered during this chapter are considered. A third sub-section will deal with more central theoretical issues that guide my attempts to comprehend who is integrated, and who disoriented.

Searching for Disoriented Immigrants

In the survey conducted among 600 Haarlem residents, did we observe distinct cultural differences within and between the ethnic categories? Do these correspond with variant degrees of integration? Because the survey's primary purpose was to monitor residents' views regarding local issues, and not to realize comprehensive measurements of their (dis)orientations, a distinct degree of uncertainty and inadequacy qualify any answer to these queries.

A variety of tendencies have been observed in this chapter that could provide support for the postulate that certain ethnic categories are less locally integrated because they diverge more in their cultural orientations. Particularly Moroccans and Turks express more affinity with their respective regions of origin than with their country of residence. More individuals within these categories speak either poor or no Dutch, not only identify with but express more devotion to non-Christian religious persuasions, convey aberrant labor market ambitions of welfare reliance or self-employment, and harbor leftist political preferences. However, when these tendencies are subjected to more detailed analysis, by which orientational differences *within* ethnic categories are compared with individuals' integration scores, the basis for the postulate dissipates. Those Moroccans do score generally more integrated who identify themselves as '(hyphenated) Dutch', speak proficient Dutch, express less religious devotion or more labor ambition. Yet the statistical relations are not always 'linear', while the variance in the integration index scores accounted for by any single indicator rarely exceeds 10% percent. Within the other ethnic categories the correspondence between these cultural divergencies and degree of integration are even less consistent, and less significant.

Table 5.14 Percent of variances in local index accounted for by orientational measures, controlling for other components

Orientational component	Moroc- cans	Turks	Surinam- ese Antilleans	'Other' immi- grants	All immi- grants	Indige- nous Dutch
ethnic self-identity	7%*	2%*	n.s.	4%*	1%*	n.s.
oral Dutch skills	n.s.	n.s.	n.s.	n.s.	1%*	n.s.
religious devotion	n.s.	n.s.	n.s.	n.s.	10%*	n.s.
labor ambition	n.s.	n.s.	6%*	n.s.	n.s.	n.s.
approval separate social services	n.s.	2%*	n.s.	n.s.	n.s.	n.s.
neighborhood affinity	6%*	n.s.	n.s.	9%*	4%*	n.s.
approval ethnic organi- zations	n.s.	8%*	n.s.	n.s.	n.s.	n.s.
combined (adj.) R^2	34%	15%	12%	15%	22%	10%
* indicators R^2 only	24%	14%	11%	13%	22%	-
n (listwise deletion)	92	157	77	97	418	165

* = probability F < .05, n.s.= not independently significant).

These findings are summarized in table 5.14 where, like tables 3.4 and 4.13, the total variance in the local index accounted for by selected orientational measures is displayed. Of the various orientational measures discussed in this chapter, seven measures are shown that: 1) represent all six local domains, 2) correspond significantly with integration scores within one or more immigrant categories, and 3) are least ambiguous in their interpretation. The first four measures listed in the table refer to more general cultural polarities often considered sources of immigrant estrangement, namely: ethnicity, language, religion, and ambition. Three complementary measures represent more specific indicators of respondents' local convictions and affections, namely: their views on immigrant groups' rights to their *own* social services, their *sense of belonging* in their respective neighborhoods, and the extent in which they condone local civic organizations along ethnic lines. I draw three conclusions from the results presented in the table:

- When compared with the significance of positional indicators, these seven indicators display little explanatory potential. Among Moroccans the index variance accounted for by all measures combined is a respectable 34%, but within the other four ethnic categories the percentages range between 10% and 15% (see the table's next-to-bottom row). Such results fail to substantiate the premise that immigrants' integration is primarily dependent upon their own reorientation.
- No orientational indicator can be identified that consistently correlates with index scores independent of other indicators. The measure that contributes most substantively differs for each ethnic category: for Moroccans variations in 'ethnic self identity,' for Turks divergent views on 'ethnic organizations,' for Surinamese and Antilleans variant 'labor ambitions,' and for 'Other' immigrants fluctuations in 'neighborhood affinity.' For all immigrants together, differences in 'religious devotion' accounts for nearly 10% of the index variance apart from the variance clarified by the other six measures. Another orientational indicator that occupies a central role in debates on immigrant integration, 'Dutch language skills,' displays little to no explanatory potential separate from other attributes. Such results fail to substantiate blanket assertions that a specific cultural attribute is crucial for immigrants' integration.
- Particularly among the indigenous Dutch, the observed variations in these orientational measures clarify little as to individuals' integration scores. For two of the seven indicators, 'ethnic self-identification' and 'oral Dutch skills,' the insignificance can be attributed to the lack of variation observed among respondents. That none of the other five measures clearly differentiates between the integrated and the estranged provide little insight into those cultural attributes that characterize the suitably oriented. Besides the simplistic suggestion to 'feel Dutch' and 'speak Dutch,' I am

at a loss to identify cultural attributes, based on these findings, to which immigrants should conform.

These observations provide little reason for optimism regarding the possibilities to develop survey instruments that reveal cultural components relevant for immigrants' individual integration. Although we have encountered several indicators that clarify statistically significant proportions of the variances in integration scores, the indicators themselves have three recurring weaknesses:

- fragmentary (i.e., invalid) and unreliable measurements,
- an interpretation that is reliant in part upon knowledge of the local survey context, and
- in part upon normative presumptions concerning local integration objectives.

The modest predictive potential that may be attributed to ideologically prominent factors such as ethnic orientation, religious convictions, language skills, and labor aspirations would be more noteworthy, if the measurements were more adequate. Immigrants' *local satisfaction* is seen to correspond consistently with their *neighborhood affinity*. When compared with the capacity among the indigenous Dutch to appreciate local life without expressing affinities to their neighborhood environment, this is one finding that authorities in other cities should take to heart.

Projecting Orientations into a Mathematical Realm

The notion of orientation is deceptively simple. It alludes to spatial circumstance in which an elementary instrument, the compass, shows where one is and the direction one is facing. When used to represent individuals' cognitive, moral and affective relations to reifications known as cultures, the image becomes visibly strained. The individual or, less tangibly, the *mind* is at once awash in a multidimensional storm. An ongoing collision between external stimuli and bodily sensors informs the mind where it is and how it feels. The mind on its part demands to know what it is, and where it is going. What is the direction? Dependent upon the number of metaphysical and social domains, moral standards and worldly distractions, the mind may imagine literally every which way at once. The researchers' challenge is to conceive, perceive, measure and compare these mental odysseys. It is not that simple, but if visual images and music can be digitalized, what prohibits the digitalization of orientations?

To begin with, the mind in its individual manifestations, contains more interactive potential. Individuals reflect upon and react to their environment, gradually altering themselves and their physical surroundings in the process. This point has already been emphasized in chapter three. It is repeated here concerning the tension encountered between *affinity* and *image* that reflects the relation between 'subject' and 'object'. A greater ethnic affinity is observed among Moroccans and Turks. How much do individuals in these two categories *naturally* identify with their geo-political origins, and how much is their affinity cultivated by encounters with *others* that *remind* them of their origins? This interactive tension plays a role in all sub-domains of orientation. To *be* a Muslim for instance can be experienced as self-evident; however it is the image of the Islam projected by others that leads Muslims to reappraise their affinity consciously and continually. Indigenous Dutch residents seem to appraise dispassionately their neighborhood environment for its capacity to fulfill various functions. Are the neighborhood views conveyed by immigrants more fervent because the legitimacy of their presence forms a primary object of dispute? The issue is how this tension can be unraveled. How can individuals' expression of whom they are, what they believe and how they feel be separated from their reflections upon the image *others* project?

If survey instruments are able to dissect the relation between affinity and image, another issue (re)presents itself. Contrary to musical notes or visual images, much less agreement exists as to the components that comprise orientations. An immigrant from the Rif region is categorized as a 'Moroccan', while the person in question not only may lack affinity with 'Moroccans', he or she may be entirely unaware (before emigration from the region) that 'Moroccans' exist. This issue was touched upon by the interpretation of responses in which residents appear unaware of other ethnic categories. A complementary problem was encountered where the category 'Islam' was presumably too broad to denote essential differences in religious orientation. The issue returns in every domain and within all components of cultural orientation. Which languages need to be learned? Are distinctions between paid employment and entrepreneurship relevant for an elderly disabled immigrant? Is there a moral distinction between separate social services for immigrants, women, the elderly, or combinations of the three? How can neighborhood affinities be compared, when the neighborhood expanse differs from one person to the next? When is an organization exclusively 'immigrant', and when is it 'political'? All these queries ultimately refer to the identification of cultural polarities that in the given social context present possible sources of incongruence. The identification of such polarities is a theoretical and normative issue focused upon in the final sub-section.

The premise that individuals' orientations are more than a bipolar vacillation between 'immigrant' and 'indigenous' culture, indeed that they vacillate between many cultures characteristic of local domains, magnifies the measurement problems. The problem in part is one of sheer numbers. This chapter is permeated with apologies for the inadequacies in the survey data. Few components are constructed from two items or more. Such concessions to survey brevity limit (the possibilities to test for) the measures' reliability, and their construct validity. Given a bipolar orientation, a strict allegiance to the strictures of the formal conceptual model would call for multiple items on at least six components, namely to monitor knowledge, beliefs and affective aspects of both affinity and imagery. For orientations considered more plural in their polarities - for instance by ethnicity, language, religion, labor, neighborhoods and politics - these numbers expand with each additional pole.

A recurring problem is subsequently one of measurement level. When a cultural component is operationalized over a dozen items, each with five or seven-point ordinal response categories, researchers generally will not hesitate to assume the combined scale to be sufficiently interval for parametric analysis. Confronted with only two or three items of this nature, the mathematical distortions are more apparent. The derivation of non-parametric 'princal' components in this chapter reflects the assumption that such constructs have a heuristic value exceeding that of their separate items. One possible consequence of this assumption is that such components are endowed with explanatory potential. Nevertheless they remain mathematical projections of *mental programs*, and must be treated accordingly.

Permit me to assume for just one paragraph, that the measurements are made in sufficient and parametric numbers. Consequently a mass of data is available that enables the location of respondents' orientations within any number of multidimensional mathematical spectra. The ultimate purpose in collecting and comparing all these numbers is to recognize frequencies, correlations and clusters that will help identify those respondents who are disoriented and estranged. The fundamental obstacle then becomes the sheer complexity of the data. Mathematical relations with increasing levels of abstraction are observed between items, components, polarities, domains and cultures. Moreover, these levels are connected according to mathematical relations. The relations are not obvious. They are derived from mathematical, theoretical and normative presumptions, beginning for instance with the issue: should item scores be averaged or weighted? They culminate with the normative issue: what signifies consensus concerning local objectives? The opportunities to follow spurious relations, to draw illogical inferences, to misinterpret magnitudes, are endless. A mathematical representation of multifarious cultural orientations is conceivable. Yet without the theoretical focus to seek, examine and interpret the significance of particular relations, the numbers remain an incongruous mass.

Integrating Cultural Diversification

Considering the orientational differences observed within and across ethnic categories, how can the individually disoriented be identified? When a locality displays and extols a wide range of personalities, which cultural components deserve immigrants' conformity? Such normative issues are tied to a theoretical concern that has motivated this study, namely the question whether the concept of integration can adequately represent local processes of cultural diversification. In search of resolutions to these issues, I have dismissed bipolar distinctions between *immigrant* and *Dutch* or *traditional* and *modern* orientations as too simplistic. Conceptualizations of more multifarious orientations however are quite complex. What then are essential orientations that warrant conceptualization and measurement? In (research) practice, this ultimately depends on the designation of specific integration objectives, and the criteria used to monitor them.

Drawing upon Schermerhorn's notion of centrifugal social trends, several community visions have been distinguished - *organic, pillarized, socialized* and *tolerant* - characterized by objectives of cultural diversity (see table 2.1). Such visions, and the empirical processes they idealize, are construed as local integration when immigrants and indigenous groups endorse and pursue cultural diversity (among other objectives). Has this consensus been observed among the Haarlem respondents? We did explicitly ask respondents whether unity or diversity would characterize their ideal locality. Excepting the Moroccans and Turks, a large majority in each category opt for the latter. This response pattern could be construed to represent, in Schermerhorn's terminology, a process of 'forced segregation:' the centripetal preference for cultural unity by many Moroccans and most Turks is at odds with the centrifugal preference expressed by most other residents. Several other orientations observed in the previous sections lend credence to this interpretation, e.g., the disapproval expressed by particular Moroccans and Turks of ethnic political organizations and of separate social services for immigrant groups. I surmise that these minorities have little faith in objectives of cultural diversity when they find their detachment and exclusion intolerable, and they sense their cultural orientations are met with intolerance. However, little effort has been made to substantiate this interpretation by identifying distinct clusters of (disoriented) 'centripetalists' among the Moroccan and Turkish respondents. More valid classifications could presumably be derived had we subjected more respondents to more extensive queries concerning their affinity with integration objectives and minority policies, and their imagery of those who harbor divergent orientations.

The notion of *consensus* concerning integration objectives is on its part afflicted with normative ambiguity. Should individuals and entire groups consciously comply? What individual end-goals does this imply? The two orientational components within the local integration index, *perceived opportunity* and *local satisfaction*, provide potential nuance and clarity. They not only present nuances between the integrated and the estranged; they eventually suggest those domains and integration issues in which a lack of consensus corresponds with residents' disaffection. Here again, a necessary complement to these two criteria would concern individuals' appraisal of local interethnic relations.

In short, integrating cultural diversification entails an increasing consensus within and across ethnic categories that the locality could and should be characterized by individuals divergent in their knowledge, beliefs and affections. *Disorientation* refers then to those individuals who in their affinities and imagery fail to uphold these ideals. The notion of *congruence* within this context pertains to those particular cultural components that are seen to foster mutual understanding, toleration and affection between individuals and groups. The problem however, for the individual resident and for the social researcher, is to distinguish between those cultural components whose polarities are congruous, and those that foster disaffection and conflict in their incongruity.

As an alternative to research designed to observe and identify cultural 'deficits' and 'mismatches' between individuals and groups, how can survey research monitor processes of cultural diversification and retain a semblance of theoretical and methodological parsimony? The research should be less concerned with the comprehensive observation and measurement of cultural differences. Instead it should focus upon the domains and components of cultural congruence. I have suggested that positive imagery of *others* - toleration - is an essential component. Essential would be to know when, and understand why, toleration dissipates and people want to bash in each other's heads.

6 Calculating Contacts

The third dimension within the construct of immigrant integration revolves around the concept of *interaction*. It refers in this study to exchanges between actors representing different ethnic categories. Here I am concerned with interaction for its potential to account for differences in integration. At the micro level, manifestations of interaction are reflected by a concept of *(inter-ethnic) contacts*: exchanges between individuals (with divergent geo-political regions of origin).

The concept of interaction occupies a key location in the literature on ethnic relations. At least since the early decades of the 20th century, with the research of Robert Park and his colleagues in the Chicago School, the alleviation of ethnic and racial prejudice has been considered not only the cause but also the consequence of more spatial proximity and interaction between racial and ethnic categories (Park and Burgess, 1925). This *contact thesis* has served to legitimate government policies in various countries and domains. School desegregation and busing programs, affirmative and positive action on the labor market, and housing allocation programs are all based upon the presumption that social inequalities and intolerance will be mitigated through the regulation of interethnic contacts. The *direction* of this causal relation illustrates the dynamics of integration theory and practice: much of the social sciences is concerned with the clarification of behavior through the interplay of structural and cultural factors; in the contact thesis behavior is construed as a catalyst for structural and cultural change.

The contact thesis is but one theoretical perspective that focuses upon the parameter of interaction by immigrant integration. It underwrites the importance of *interethnic exchange* whereas alternative perspectives, which I order under the conceptual banner of *ethnic seclusion*, focus more upon the development of ethnic networks as a necessary if not permanent phase of immigrant integration. I use this distinction between interethnic (or inclusive) and seclusive (or exclusive) interactions was used to delineate community *visions* (see table 2.1). The distinction for instance between *tolerant* and *pillarized* *vision*s of integrated communities is rooted in the interactive dimension. While the tolerant vision focuses upon, and appreciates, the interactions *across* ethnic boundaries, the pillarized vision focuses upon the interactions *within* ethnic boundaries.

In my attempts to conceive and measure immigrants' integration into localities characterized by cultural diversity, my perceptions are shaped by the tolerant vision. Regarding European reality with this vision in mind, I am lead to articulate two premises, one on the nature, the second concerning the objectives of local interactions. First, urban environments offer individuals a variety of opportunities for contacts in which one's geo-political origins are ideally, if not in actuality, irrelevant. Secondly, the pursuance of local objectives of cultural and interactive diversity implies that exchanges are made across a diversity of ethnic boundaries. This second premise implies for instance that an individual Moroccan's integration is not only reflected by the contacts with the indigenous Dutch (the focus of an *assimilated* vision), and by the contacts with other Moroccans (the focus of a *pillarized* vision). It is also reflected by the contacts with locals from other ethnic backgrounds. In chapter two such eclectic contacts were denoted, for lack of an adequate concept encountered in the literature, with the notion of *eclusion*. The notion of eclusive behavior complements those of seclusive and inclusive in characterizing the types of contacts individual immigrants initiate to resolve (initial) states of local isolation and estrangement. In table 6.1 the four types are schematically located.

Table 6.1   Four types of contactual behavior for immigrants

Contacts with other immigrants	Contacts with indigenous residents	
	no	yes
no	isolated	inclusive
yes	seclusive	eclusive

These distinctions in contactual behavior allude to, and correspond to a certain extent with, prevailing distinctions in ethnic orientation encountered in the (social-psychological) literature (cf. Berry et al., 1986; Phinney, 1990:502; Oudenhoven et al., 1996:469). The *isolated* immigrant alludes to the notion of the ethnically 'marginalized' who lack affinities with either the immigrant or indigenous group. *Seclusion* alludes to the 'separated' individual oriented primarily to the group with his or her ethnic origins. *Inclusion* corresponds with the 'assimilated' individual oriented primarily toward the indigenous group. The notion of *eclusion* however alludes to the possibility that individuals have ties with *other* immigrants besides those with similar ethnic origins. This notion therefore fails to correspond with notions of 'acculturated' or 'bicultural,' which pertain more commonly to individuals oriented toward *both* their 'own' ethnic origins and indigenous cultures.

In this chapter the explanatory potential of these four complementary notions is examined. I also examine their measurability within the six domains of local integration. To this end a selection of empirical studies is considered that have been conducted in the Netherlands, focusing again upon the Haarlem survey. Succinctly stated, I seek an answer to the following query:

What significance may be attributed to individuals' (interethnic) contacts as indicators of their integration within the local (Haarlem) context?

Besides distinctions in the interethnic nature of contacts, I have delineated various concepts in chapter two that pertain to the quality of these contacts. Contacts can be characterized by their *functionality* and *intimacy*; they are experienced by one or both actors along moral parameters of *(in)dignity*; and qualified - by actors and less active observers - along a spectrum ranging from *congeniality* to *hostility*. As introduction to this chapter, I divulge that measurement of the latter two parameters will receive little attention in the forthcoming pages. Only in the past two decades has research on ethnic conflict focused upon its manifestations in individual contacts (Stanfield, 1995:370). Dutch researchers (e.g., van Dijk, 1987, 1993; Essed, 1984, 1991) have had a prominent role in developing this approach, but survey research methods have as yet been inadequate in measuring concepts of *everyday racism* or *ethnic hostility*. Such obstacles to the qualification - and quantification - of interethnic contacts form the second line of inquiry:

What methodological obstacles, pertinent to the operationalization of individuals' (interethnic) contacts, render the measurement of immigrant integration particularly problematic?

I commence with the private domain, focusing upon the significance of (ethnic) partners for individuals' local integration. The consideration of contacts in the domain of education and upbringing will be brief, as no relevant measurements were made in the Haarlem survey. Nevertheless, some problems bound to the perception of social networks in schools will be reviewed. The labor market, and more concretely the work floor, as a domain of networks and cliques will then be examined. This is followed by analyses of survey responses concerning residents' friends: the frequency, and the local and ethnic nature of these contacts. Turning to the neighborhood environment, Haarlem statistics on immigrant concentration and segregation are focused upon for their potential to illuminate contactual differences. Finally, in the domain of civic life, individuals' participation in social-cultural activities and (ethnic) organizations will be examined. Particularly the cultural participation measure, one criterion that helps comprise the *local integration index*, will be considered. In the closing section an answer is formulated to the two queries above.

Parents and Partners: Perforating Ethnic Barriers

Immigration is for most individuals a family affair. For most of the first generation immigrants surveyed, the primary motive for moving to the Netherlands was to form and raise a family, or to reunite with family members. The importance of family networks - and more generally processes of chain migration - for the integration of individual immigrants is commonly presumed and difficult to verify (cf. Esveldt et al., 1995; Staring et al., 1998). For instance, I note that for Turks differences in household composition account for nearly 10% of the variance in their integration scores. Particularly those Turks residing in multiple-adult households score higher, which suggests the possible benefits of immigrant family networks. However, the data does not allow me to discern which Turks live in fact with extended families in the household or vicinity, nor are similarly significant relations between household types and integration scores observed within other immigrant categories. In this section the focus is on interethnic distinctions within families, as I first consider whether variations in integration scores are related to the (inter)ethnic nature of partner relationships. Then parental distinctions are viewed, to examine whether respondents with ethnically mixed parentage diverge significantly in their degree of integration.

Sleeping with Others

Are immigrants with indigenous partners more integrated? Any answer to this question is conditional upon the social-cultural context in which the partnership is perceived and pursued. Just before World War II for instance, 'interracial' marriages were still outlawed in 30 of the 48 United States (Merton, 1976:225). In various Southern states a 'black' man risked lynching (i.e., terminal estrangement) should he be suspected of sexual relations with a 'white' woman (cf. Hondius, 1999:33ff). As domain of interaction between divergent ethnic groups, partnerships are commonly considered the last and most personal barriers on the integration path (Blumer, 1965; Hagendoorn, 1993). By the endeavor to conceive local integration from a *tolerant* vision, those immigrants who have hurdled this barrier provide, in their numbers and their experience, a simple barometer of local integration objectives (cf. Bagley et al., 1997).

Research on interethnic partnerships in the Netherlands is primarily focused upon two general themes: estimates of their proportional *occurrence*, and of their *acceptance* among the general public. Harmsen (1998) reports that of the approximate 435,000 married couples with at least one partner born elsewhere, roughly 60% concern so-called mixed partners born in two different lands. This percentage varies widely when calculated according to the land of origin of one partner. For more than 80% of the married immigrants born in the (former) Dutch East Indies, the Dutch Antilles or other countries of the European Union, the partner is not born in the same land; most have partners born in the Netherlands. For immigrants from Suriname the percentage drops to forty, while only 10% of the married Turkish and Moroccan immigrants have partners born outside Turkey respectively Morocco.

As for *acceptance*, according to the 1988 Eurobarometer 50% of the Dutch interviewed expressed no qualms should their child or sibling marry a Turk, while 65% saw no problem with a Surinamese in-law (Dekker and van Praag, 1990). These percentages are comparable to those observed among Turks (54%) and Moroccans (60%) when asked (in 1994) whether they would accept a Dutch partner for their child (Martens, 1995:100). Hondius, in the one comprehensive Dutch study on (religiously or ethnically) mixed partnerships, observes a growing acceptance since the 1960's (1999:179). Through in-depth interviews with 88 mixed couples on their relations with family and friends, she concludes that these ('successful') partnerships are characterized not so much by an enthusiastic acceptance of cultural difference (cf. Walzer, 1993), but more by the avoidance (*ontwijking*) of confrontations through the negation of difference (1999:315ff).

In the Haarlem survey, respondents residing with partners were asked to identify their partners' ethnic background. In two immigrant categories - the Surinamese/Antilleans and the 'Other' immigrants - several immigrants are encountered with 'Dutch' partners; this contrasts with only one Moroccan and no Turk (see table 6.2). Many respondents in all five ethnic categories classify their partners neither as 'Dutch,' nor within the same ethnic group as them-selves. Most of these classifications refer presumably to the same geo-political category as the respondent (e.g., an Arab-Moroccan with a 'Moroccan-Dutch' partner, a Surinamese-Creole with a 'Hindu,' a Hollander with a 'Brabander'). These response patterns allude to two demographic principles by processes of (ethnic) partner selection: 1) the less the ethnic category is represented in the vicinity, the fewer prospects for seclusive partnerships, and 2) the longer the time span since immigration the less inclination toward seclusion (cf. Lieberson and Waters, 1988:204ff).[1] However, a refusal to answer the survey query, or the assertion that one's partner 'belongs to no ethnic group', character-ize roughly half the responses given by Surinamese/Antillean and 'Other' respondents with partners. This item non response may be considered indicative for the avoidance dispositions signaled by Hondius. It might also denote that the question was found highly personal and inappropriate for the survey context (cf. Meloen and Veenman, 1988).

Table 6.2 Partner's ethnicity according to respondents

Ethnic qualification	Moroc-cans	Turks	Surinamese Antilleans	'Other' immigrants	Indigenous Dutch
No partner	32%	15%	32%	17%	20%
Same as respondent	32%	76%	14%	27%	72%
Different but not Dutch	16%	5%	9%	5%	1%
Dutch or 'Hollander'	1%	-	11%	10%	-
'None' or unknown affiliation	20%	3%	35%	41%	8%
n (=100%)	92	148	66	78	133

One may note that the categories in table 6.2 neatly correspond with the conceptual distinction between *isolated* (i.e., 'no partner'), *seclusive* ('the same as respondent'), *eclusive* ('different but not Dutch') and *inclusive* ('Dutch or Hollander'). Do these patterns of interethnic partnership reflect differences in respondents' integration scores? Comparisons within ethnic categories reveal only among Moroccans a greater degree of integration by the less seclusive respondents (η=.37). In the other immigrant categories a mean tendency toward higher index scores is perceived by those with *other* partners (i.e., eclusive or inclusive ties). This tendency however is too diffuse, and the number of respondents too small, to withstand tests for statistical significance. In short, the evidence does not warrant the conclusion that mixed partnership advances immigrants' integration. When considered at the level of local integration, the observation that these immigrants with *other* partners are also no more *estranged*, is modest testimony to the *acceptance* of mixed marriages.

Being Raised by Others

Besides the ethnic orientation of eventual partners, the data contains references to the countries in which respondents' parents were born.[2] Similar to the influence ascribed to partner choice, the premise I consider here is that immigrants, whose parents diverge in their land of origin, are themselves more positively disposed toward *others*. This disposition might be reflected, for instance, by less seclusive friendships and marriages (cf. Hechter, 1978; Nauck et al., 1990; van Heelsum, 1997:143). Only within two ethnic categories could this *mixed parentage* be observed. Among the Surinamese and Antilleans, 23% has mixed parentage including 10% with one parent born in the Netherlands. By the 'Other' immigrants 68% has parents with divergent countries of birth including 52% with one parent born in the Netherlands. Those with mixed parentage, and particularly with one parent born in the Netherlands, do convey more *eclusive* behavior, at least in the proportion of their contacts with friends from *other* categories. They also generally score more integrated than immigrants with *seclusive* parentage ($\eta=.29$); when the comparison however is limited to individuals within the same ethnic category no significant differences are discerned.

Measuring Mixed Households

These observations on the significance of mixed marriages and parentage raise several methodological issues. Three will be interwoven here: the categorical distinctions made, the number of observations, and the reliability of response. The analysis results for mixed partnerships illustrate the risks when generalizing across immigrant categories. Immigrants who see their partners as ethnically divergent score more integrated ($\eta=.38$). The generalization however primarily reflects the fact that few mixed partnerships were observed in the more estranged Moroccan and Turkish categories. I would surmise that the observed statistical relations between partnership and immigrant's integration are largely spurious. Still, the possibility cannot be dispelled that Moroccans and Turks are estranged precisely because they are more seclusive in their partnerships. The focus here (and throughout this study) on statistical relations *within* categories serves to elucidate the causal or spurious nature of such relations: only among Haarlem Moroccans does mixed partnership appear to encourage individuals' integration.

Besides the respondents' own ethnic backgrounds, other categorical distinctions help clarify whether mixed partnership affects integration. Is the respondent married to a Dutch man or woman? Has the couple been married more than seven years?[3] Such factors could not be considered within the survey context. The possibilities to calculate the relation between (mixed) partnership and immigrant integration are limited when only fifty respondents recognize their partner as ethnically different. A survey of 600 respondents is then quite inadequate when considering the interaction of ethnicity and gender factors across time (cf. Lieberson and Waters, 1988, who use US census data). Partner and parental relations can be categorized according to a variety of criteria: e.g., spatial, legal, biological, economic, and emotional. For purposes of reliability and comparison, researchers and respondents must agree on the specific perspective. We only asked about *partners* in a spatial sense, as adults with whom respondents share a household. How much would the response patterns vary had we asked respondents to identify - and designate the location of - their legal spouse? To examine the effect of mixed parentage, we should have confronted respondents with our knowledge of their registered ethnic parentage, and ask them to characterize their parental ties. How many points on an integration index do immigrants earn who are hesitant to share their private affairs with government researchers?[4] Considering these obstacles to brevity, comparability and reliability, I surmise that the functional and intimate parameters of immigrants' private behavior are not adequately measured with survey techniques.

Classmates: (Re)counting Schoolyard Ties

In the latter half of the 1980's, the percentage school children of foreign origin was not only on the increase within Dutch cities, the percentage per primary school also began to fluctuate markedly (Dors et al., 1991). In the four largest cities, the segregation of immigrants across schools and school districts rose steadily through the early 1990's, while comparable indices for immigrant populations across residential districts suggested a stabilization or even decline of segregation processes (Tesser et al., 1995:245). The formation of so-called 'black' schools, with high concentrations of immigrant children, is commonly attributed to the actions of indigenous parents who choose to (re)place their children in schools elsewhere in the city. A complementary, though much more modest, tendency could be observed within specific immigrant groups to establish their *own* (e.g., Islamic or Hindu) schools.

In this section I first reflect upon the methodological obstacles that inhibit efforts to discern the relation between the ethnic composition of classrooms and schools on the one hand, and individuals' integration on the other. Then the research methods are considered that have been used to measure patterns of interethnic contact within schools. In closing, the possibilities to survey interethnic contacts in the domain of education and upbringing are discussed more generally.

Childhood Seclusion and Adult Integration

The proportion of immigrant children within classes and schools *is* a Dutch local issue, but what is the consequence for children's future degree of integration as adults? The methodological obstacles that prohibit a lucid answer to this query are virtually insurmountable. One would have to account for instance for: differences in group, class and school contexts; variations in immigrant concentrations from primary school through to the end of pupils' school careers; distinctions in the quality and the quantity of interethnic contacts; and above all the isolation of, and control for, other factors. In acknowledging the enormity of these obstacles, there remain at least three reasons to focus upon processes of interethnic exclusion or inclusion in the domain of education and upbringing:

- Most individuals' educational careers continue into adulthood (Martens, 1995:50).
- The methods used for the study of educational contacts may be of use in other social domains.
- These processes are presumably affected if not directed by adults - parents and teachers - with their variant interethnic behavior.

These three themes are touched upon sequentially in the next three subsections.

Students' Integration

Twelve percent of the Haarlem immigrants (aged 18 and older) are currently enrolled in school, as opposed to an approximate 5% of the indigenous Dutch. This percentile difference is clarified by the relative youth of immigrants, and by their divergent positions on the labor market.[5] Being enrolled in school corresponds significantly with a greater degree of integration (only) among Moroccans and Turks (η=.44 resp. .20). Beyond general inquiries as to the (curricular) types of schooling in which they participate, respondents were not asked to quantify or qualify the (interethnic) characteristics of their educational activities. Turkish students are seen to have more eclusive ties within their circle of friends than other Turks (η=.30), but this relation between the student status and more eclusive ties is not observed within other ethnic categories.

Observing Classroom Friendships and Hostilities

I am unaware of recent Dutch research in which the interethnic nature of educational contacts is analyzed among adults (cf. van der Zee, 1989; Saharso, 1992b:368). The two most comprehensive Dutch studies on inter ethnic contacts in education focus upon relations in primary schools (see Dors, 1987; Teunissen, 1988).[6] Both adapted sociometric techniques to monitor contactual differences. Such techniques are comparable to social distance measures in that they are also used to monitor individuals' imagery of *others* in a variety of contexts. Sociometric procedures however are more general where they measure not only respondents' intentions but also their expressed behavior; they are more concrete in that they elicit information on respondents' behavior toward real individuals instead of a hypothetical - and stereotypical - *other* (cf. Kidder and Judd, 1986:240ff). With the data produced, individuals' relative location within a social network can be specified: i.e., the differential patterns of inclusion and exclusion according to individual and circumstantial character-istics. The technique applied by Dors and Teunissen relies upon the assumption that respondents - and researchers - are acquainted with and have access to all network participants. For random samples of urban populations the presump-tion is untenable.

Survey Measurement of Educational Contacts

A more applicable technique by the measurement of contacts in random survey samples is the so-called 'egocentric' form of network analysis (Knoke and Kuklinski, 1982). Egocentric techniques characteristically focus upon individu-als as centers of their own social network. In interview protocols the network is generally surveyed by having respondents first generate a list of persons with whom they have or had contact. Subsequently respondents are asked to characterize each person and qualify their relation according to pertinent research parameters: e.g., ethnicity, locality, domains of exchange, functional-ity and intimacy. With the technique a wealth of contactual data can be gathered within a brief interval. It has however various limitations, e.g.:

- The number of persons named by respondents affects the brevity of the interview and the validity of the data.
- Individuals' are generally unable to identify indirect or hostile contacts.
- The subjective nature of respondents' views of personal and contactual qualities present various reliability problems (Marsden, 1990).

In the forthcoming sections several studies will be cited in which network analysis techniques were used. Specific to issues of (family) upbringing, a survey conducted among Turkish immigrants in Germany (Nauck et al., 1997) merits reference here. With use of egocentric techniques, the social networks are compared of parent-children dyads. The ethnic composition of these networks is seen to correlate significantly between generations; they are also seen (within a nine factor causal model) to mediate the influence of parents' education and ethnic orientation upon that of their children.[7] The study illustrates the possibility to derive comparable measures of exclusion and inclusion within the private and educational domains. It also exemplifies the complexities and ambiguities when interpreting the (indirect or intermediate) importance of interethnic contacts for individuals' integration.

Colleagues and Clients: Working on Networks

This section addresses the issue how immigrants' activities on the labor market can be conceived as isolation or sociability, and whether such distinctions provide adequate indicators of immigrant integration. Three topics will serve as particular focus of attention:

- the actions taken by immigrants to find work,
- the work floor as an arena of (interethnic) contacts, and
- the possible consequences of having paid work for immigrants' contacts in other domains.

The link between these three topics is provided by the notion of *social capital*. It refers to individuals' potential to know and impress the right people. Social capital is often called upon in theoretical perspectives as clarification for labor market mobility (cf. Coleman, 1988; Bourdieu, 1992; Roelandt, 1994:140ff; Veenman and Martens, 1995:43), and to elucidate the relevance of labor market contacts for individuals' activities upon other markets. These topics will not be considered in-depth; my purpose is again to review several conceptual and measurement problems when examining the relevance of labor market contacts for individuals' integration.

Connecting Supply with Demand

The first topic - the actions taken by individuals to find work - does not refer to their educational background, which within the conceptual framework is denoted by one's positional and orientational qualifications. It refers more specifically to the social channels used by individuals to convey their labor needs and qualifications upon the market. Moroccans and Turks in search of paid work have been seen to rely greatly upon *informal channels* accessible for a limited group, for instance job openings advertised through word-of-mouth. Indigenous Dutch, and to a lesser extent Surinamese and Antilleans, use more the formal channels accessible for all, for instance government labor exchanges (WRR, 1989:115; Hooghiemstra et al., 1990:52ff). Informal channels may provide access to enclaves of seclusive labor opportunity (cf. Portes and Manning, 1986; Kloosterman et al., 1997) where formal networks are restricted by the exclusionary proclivities of indigenous employers (van Beek, 1993). For an impression of how Haarlem residents with paid work succeeded in finding their jobs, respondents were asked to identify their primary intermediary. The answers are summarized in table 6.3.

Table 6.3 Channels used by respondents to acquire (current) job

Channel	Moroccans	Turks	Surinamese Antilleans	'Other' immigrants	Indigenous Dutch
self initiative	35%	21%	45%	27%	39%
informal channel	18%	47%	10%	18%	28%
formal channel	38%	31%	38%	45%	22%
other channels	9%	1%	8%	10%	11%
n (=100%)	34	78	40	60	116

The table displays only modest differences between the ethnic categories. Perhaps the most prominent distinction is that nearly half the working Turks (47%) use *informal channels* - contacts were made via family or friends - as opposed to less than 20% in other immigrant categories. By the greater majority of these Turks (84%) the intermediary are *immigrant* family or friends, a result comparable with percentages found in other Dutch studies (Martens, 1995:68, Veraart, 1996:61, Martens, 1999:54). Surinamese and Antilleans (45%), and to a lesser extent indigenous Dutch, refer more often to one of three general categories of *self initiative*: individuals either found work by temporary employment bureaus, by uninvited applications to employers, or (primarily among indigenous Dutch) by establishing their own business. The Moroccans and 'Other' immigrants with paid jobs refer more often to *formal* labor channels: the regional labor exchange or newspaper advertisements.

Where one might expect those who use *formal channels* to be more estranged, a significant relation between the channel used and integration scores is not observed within any ethnic category. Such results are not necessarily surprising. Much depends on the local context in which the various market channels exist. For instance, a town with several major employers who hire primarily through formal channels differs from one with many small entrepreneurs who seek employees within their personal network. Ultimately the distinctions may say more about individuals' engagement within their ethnic category, for instance status differences within the Turkish 'enclave'. They also reflect the group's marginalization within the locality; as the Moroccans' greater reliance upon state-controlled networks might exemplify. Before drawing such conclusions, more research would be necessary concerning the structure of local networks.

A Working (Floor) Mix

When I consider the historical background of much European immigration, rooted in the demand for unskilled laborers to do menial work that indigenous Europeans, were unwilling to do, an image arises of oppressed immigrants populating factory production lines occasionally interspersed with an indigenous overseer. This notion of *secluded* immigrant laborers can be contrasted with less pejorative images of ethnic enterprises or entire market segments where convergences of immigrants capitalize upon their specific qualifications (Jiobu, 1988:220ff; Waldinger, 1995). *Inclusive* or *eclusive* notions however correspond more closely with prevailing Dutch integration objectives: the equal representation of immigrants within all sectors and levels of government and big business (WRR, 1989:32ff).

Without reference to such images, we asked those respondents with paid work whether they usually collaborate with indigenous Dutch, immigrants from their land of origin, or an ethnic mix of primarily *others* ('van alles'). Their responses, summarized in table 6.4, show that excepting Moroccans and Turks, a large majority work mainly with indigenous Dutch colleagues.

Upon comparing the percentile distributions in table 6.4 across ethnic categories, one could conclude that immigrants are gradually occupying labor positions that bring them in more frequent contact with indigenous Dutch.[8] This premise however cannot be verified. No local statistics are available from the 'guest-worker era' of the 1960s and 1970s that would corroborate the image of more secluded laborers in the past (cf. Shadid, 1979:177). Consequently we have no simple way to discern whether seclusive work floors are being transformed into more inclusive ones, or alternatively that seclusive enterprises have generally disappeared while their workers have joined the labor reserve (cf. Veenman and Martens, 1996:40). Furthermore, we did not measure whether immigrants who work primarily with indigenous Dutch have more contact with their Dutch colleagues than those who work more seclusively.

Table 6.4 Ethnic background of respondent's colleagues

Colleagues' ethnicity	Moroc-cans	Turks	Surinamese Antilleans	'Other' immigrants	Indigenous Dutch
works alone (isolated)	3%	1%	3%	3%	8%
mainly immigrants (seclusive)	9%	33%	3%	5%	1%
ethnic mix (eclusive)	32%	20%	18%	20%	13%
mainly indigenous Dutch	56%	45%	78%	72%	79%
n (=100%)	34	75	40	61	117

This last observation alludes to more general measurement problems concerned with the functionality and intimacy of labor contacts. Variations in job contexts are virtually infinite. The relevance of situations in which laborers interact with each other - with supervisors, employers, clients and the general public, to exchange various goods, within formal and informal hierarchical structures - cannot be adequately captured with standardized questions soliciting for instance the ethnicity of colleagues with whom respondents prefer to work. A more extensive array of survey questions could however provide more insight as to laborers' opportunities to communicate informally with each other, and whether labor activities are experienced as exclusionary processes (cf. Boxman, 1992; de Vries, 1992; Veraart, 1996). The distinction in four categories of labor contacts presented in table 6.4 - operationalizations of isolated, seclusive, eclusive and inclusive laborers - does not in any event reflect differences in respondents' integration scores.

Work as Impetus for Social Contacts

Those immigrant respondents who collaborate more with indigenous Dutch are not found to score more integrated. The fact however that a person is (inter)active upon the labor market may affect his or her (interethnic) activities in other domains. This premise, that paid work draws immigrants out of their isolation (cf. WRR, 1989:16), serves as a cornerstone upon which immigrant integration policy has developed. The premise has been questioned in theory (Lutz, 1992). Among indigenous Dutch the relation between labor market position and, for instance, cultural participation has been found quite weak (van Beek and Knulst, 1991:48). Yet little is known about the relation among immigrants (Campbell et al., 1994:app5).

To examine the relation, a distinction was made between respondents in three labor market positions: those with paid work, those in search of paid work, and those inactive upon the market. These three groups were compared, per ethnic category, for differences in their social contacts. The five indicators used to represent social contacts, and the extent in which their variations might be clarified by respondents' variant labor market positions, are as follows:

- The *mean frequency of contacts* with close friends varies significantly *only* among Turks. Turkish workers generally see their closest friends *less* often than the Turks with other labor market positions.
- The *proportion of these contacts* that are *eclusive*, i.e., concerning close friends with another ethnic origin, *is not* clarified by differences in labor market position within any of the five ethnic categories.
- The *number of civic organizations* in which respondents are active members *does not* correspond with differences in labor market position for any of the five categories.
- The ethnic composition of these organizations, ranging from exclusively immigrant to exclusively Dutch, varies *only* among the indigenous Dutch. Those Dutch active on the labor market participate more often in less exclusively Dutch organizations ($\eta=.23$).
- The *cultural participation* criterion of the local index, i.e., the frequency in which social-cultural activities are undertaken, corresponds with differences in labor market activity for *all* ethnic categories *except* the Turks. Those inactive upon the market are generally less active culturally; those actively seeking work are less easily characterized.

For those with paid jobs, the relation between these five contactual indicators and the ethnic composition of respondents' work environment was examined, to discern whether those in more inclusive or eclusive work environments are more publicly active. Only the first indicator reviewed, the mean frequency of contacts with close friends, varies significantly and only among Turks and 'Other' immigrants. These two categories diverge however as to the nature of this relation. Turks in *inclusive* work environments generally see their close friends more often, while by the 'Other' immigrants those in seclusive environments have more frequent contacts.

These findings are neither clear nor consistent. They suggest that a (weak) relation between labor market activity and immigrants' contacts in other domains does exist, and that for Turks this relation varies essentially from that of other categories. The indicators themselves however remain questionable in their adequacy. To draw less ambiguous conclusions, more extensive measures of immigrants' positions and contacts upon the labor market are necessary.

This brings me to more general observations on contacts within the domain of work and material security. The measurements made in the survey provide little evidence that adequate indicators for interethnic interactions are at hand. This need not be construed as a particular shortcoming of the survey data; in the country's most comprehensive and representative survey on immigrants' work situation, only one item pertains to respondents' (ordinal estimate of) labor contacts (Martens, 1995:125). Considering the diversity of work environments, this minimal measurement is not surprising. The notion of the *isolated* worker for instance, with a paucity of contacts, is a virtual anomaly in urban settings. A lone clerk in a store may have no colleagues, but a continuous flow of customers (or creditors). A lone craftsperson in a shop may have few customers, but a continuous flow of radio waves. The notion could be reserved for those inactive upon the labor market. Then conceptual tensions must be resolved concerning distinctions between paid and unpaid labor, and between formal and informal work.

The issues multiply when distinctions between *seclusive, inclusive* and *eclusive* workers are considered. Desk bureaucrats and cleaning personnel may work in the same eclusive office. How often do such contacts evolve into ties? To develop more valid distinctions, network analysis techniques could be used to explore the significance of contacts in the work environment for immigrants' integration (cf. Wellman and Berkowitz, 1988). Such measurements however cannot be lucidly interpreted without being complemented by other (non survey) observations that clarify when and why specific work environments are characteristically inclusive or exclusive (cf. Waldinger, 1995; Staring et al., 1998). With network analysis we might verify for instance that Turks more than other immigrant respondents work in seclusive environments. Only with a combination of participant observation, in-depth interviews and (macro) market analysis could the rise and demise of such *enclaves* be understood for their integrative significance (cf. Burgers and Engbersen, 1999).

Friends: Locals and *Others*

Interactions in the domain of health and welfare could be conceived as individuals' various encounters with medical professionals and welfare workers. Again a broader conception of this domain is used, one in which personal well-being is presumably dependent upon individuals' potential to call upon friends and family when in need of attention, advice, care or cash. Immigrants may not only possess limited means to attain schooling and work. When they lack an adequate social network to whom they can turn, their dependence upon social services becomes manifest. *The immigrant* may be viewed in this sense as symbolic for all the detached and disoriented individuals residing in urban environments (cf. Hall, 1991). A contrasting image focuses upon the (presumed) solidarity within immigrant communities, which offers an alternative for the expense and bureaucracy of the disintegrating welfare state (cf. Zijderveld, 1993).

A wealth of Dutch research exists on social networks and their importance for individuals' well-being (cf. Jansen and van den Wittenboer, 1992). Few studies focus upon such networks among immigrants (cf. Uniken Venema and van Wersch, 1992) and those that do rely heavily upon methods of participant observation (e.g., Sansone, 1992; Lindo, 1996). The survey items used to monitor immigrants' social network are usually brief and trite. Respondents are asked either to quantify their contacts with fellow immigrants and indigenous Dutch via ordinal adjectives (Martens, 1995:125; Intomart, 1995:23), or they are asked to estimate the frequency of particular contacts in a given period (CBS, 1985 and 1986). Such data provide at best a rough indication of the density and ethnic composition of immigrants' social networks.

The data in the Haarlem survey is hardly more refined. Respondents were asked to think of five friends or family members with whom they have frequent contact but who do not reside in the respondent's household. They were subsequently asked to convey for each the land of origin, whether the person resides or had resided in Haarlem, and the frequency of their contact. A contact was described as a visit, telephone call, exchange of letters, or similar act of communication. The survey context inhibited us from confronting respondents with more personal questions concerning the functionality and intimacy of these contacts. Nevertheless, the fifteen bits of information do provide elementary indicators of the four types of interethnic contacts considered in this chapter. These will be presented in sequence, after which the possibilities to collect more adequate survey data will be discussed.

A Paucity of Local Ties

That specific respondents are *isolated* as to their social contacts could be observed in three ways: a person has few ties; a person has few ties in the vicinity; or a person has infrequent contacts with ties. Concerning the first measure, nearly all the Haarlem respondents were willing and able to convey information on at least one friend, while approximately 10% within most ethnic categories failed to describe the requested five. As a group the Moroccans form the exception here, in that only 55% described all five. Focusing on the second measure, when current Haarlem residents are perceived as ties 'in the vicinity', then within all five ethnic categories variations in isolation are evenly distributed along the six points from 'zero' to 'all five' ties in the vicinity. For instance, the percentage with no local ties hovers around 15%, ranging from 9% of the indigenous Dutch to 22% of the Surinamese and Antilleans. Regarding the third, a measure for contact frequency was derived by averaging respondents' estimations for all (five) ties. These means are aggregated, per ethnic category as to contacts per year, just below the dashed line in table 6.5. One sees that the mean for four of the five categories is around 100 times a year, i.e., about twice a week. Moroccans as a category are again the exception with a mean of 76 times a year, while the standard deviation around the mean is greatest among Turks.

Table 6.5 Characteristics of respondents' contacts with close friends

Contactual characteristic	Moroc- cans	Turks	Surinam- ese Antilleans	'Other' immi- grants	Indige- nous Dutch
isolated (no locals or # ties < 4)	41%	16%	27%	19%	12%
seclusive (all *own* category)	61%	53%	18%	7%	78%
inclusive (all indigenous Dutch)	3%	3%	18%	46%	-
eclusive (not only *own* and Dutch)	23%	16%	34%	37%	22%
mean contacts per year (standard deviation)	76 (58)	104 (89)	98 (61)	102 (79)	94 (73)
% contacts with *others*	25%	21%	59%	89%	7%
n^9 (= 100%)	91	158	74	97	169

To designate the *isolated* respondent a variety of criteria can be derived from these measures. The first row in table 6.5 summarizes a combination of two criteria: the lack of local ties (i.e., no locals named among five friends), or the inability (or unwillingness) to name more than three friends. The percentage of respondents that meet either of these two criteria is seen to range from 12% of the indigenous Dutch to 41% of the Moroccans. In none of the five ethnic categories does this nominal distinction correspond significantly with respondents' degree of local integration.[10] Two more continuous criteria were also devised. The *mean frequency of contact*, summarized in table 6.5, corresponds with differences in integration scores among the 'Other' immigrants and the indigenous Dutch (R=.21 resp.-.18). A second indicator allowed for variations in vicinity *and* frequency.[11] According to this criterion, the more isolated Turks and 'Other' immigrants are likely to be more estranged (R=-.16 resp. -.38).

These findings do not provide clear testimony that local and frequent social ties are conducive for individuals' integration. That various indicators identify Moroccans as isolated testifies to the indicators' mutual consistency. Still, as predictors of integration scores they fail to provide congruous results. This can be attributed in part to the primitive distinctions in network size and vicinity. The spatial distinction between locals and non locals requires more refinement, a conclusion that could also be drawn for the (lack of) distinctions in contact medium. On a more theoretical level, the ambiguous results are also due to the divergent end-goals that combine to form individuals' integration score. Greater isolation generally correlates with *less* perceived opportunity, local satisfaction and cultural participation. However, particularly within the more estranged ethnic categories, it also correlates with *more* per capita income and welfare independence. These latter two findings lead again to ambiguous interpretations. With more (work and) wealth immigrants are less dependent upon a local social network for contact and support. One could also conclude that the absence of a local network, combined with limited access to social services, forces immigrants to find more lucrative (and perhaps less legal) work. With more refined theories and instruments, such ambiguities are transformed into nuances.

A Profusion of Seclusive Ties

Two measures for seclusion were derived from the items that concern the lands of origin respondents associate with their friends. These items are characterized by considerable non response, signifying respondents' ambivalence - or obliviousness - regarding such qualifications. Nevertheless, in three of the five ethnic categories most of the respondents referred only to ties within their *own* ethnic category (see second row of table 6.5), namely the Moroccans (61%), the Turks (53%) and the indigenous Dutch (78%). Within the category of 'Other' immigrants, an opposing pattern is observed, in that a large majority of the respondents (72%) identified *none* of their ties as sharing their land of origin. Among the Surinamese and Antilleans the group of *seclusive* respondents is comparable in size to the (eclusive) group who says *none* of their ties has Surinamese respectively Antillean origins (namely 18% resp. 26%).

One must take into account when interpreting these percentages that the statistical probability of an arbitrary immigrant encountering a resident from their land of origin is much less than the chance that two indigenous Dutch residents make 'contact'. This concerns demographic variations: 82% of the adult population is indigenous Dutch, while the largest immigrant group (the Dutch Indonesians) comprises less than 4% of the local population. If respondents only had ties with local residents, the statistical probability (i.e., independent of all social-historical bases) that all five ties are indigenous Dutch is approximately 38% (that is $.825^5$). The probability that all five contacts originate from another geo-political region is, for most regions, less than one in ten billion ($.01^5$).

In the next section the variation in these probabilities per local district will be considered. The question here is whether these differences correspond with respondents' degree of integration. This depends of course upon the specific criterion for *seclusion*. A nominal distinction, between those respondents who only name friends from the same region of origin and those who name *other* friends, displays significant differences within all four immigrant categories: the secluded are generally more estranged.[12] This measure can be transformed into a more continuous criterion in various ways. One is summarized in the bottom row of table 6.5. This statistic represents respondents' estimated number of (annual) contacts with *other* friends as a percentage of their sum-total amount of contacts.[13] The statistic is the binomial inverse of respondents' proportional contacts with friends having the same origin, e.g., where Moroccans' contact with *others* averages to 25%, this implies that their proportional contact with Moroccans averages to (100% - 25% =) 75%. The variations in these percentages correlate significantly with differences in integration scores within all four immigrant categories (see appendix I).

These findings underwrite the relevance of the seclusion notion. Immigrants who maintain contacts primarily with friends from their land of origin are generally more estranged than immigrants with a greater ethnic diversity of friends. Nevertheless, the findings must be treated with caution. For one, the variant statistical probabilities that a given immigrant contacts an *other* renders comparisons across ethnic categories rather senseless. The Moroccan and Turkish samples display degrees of seclusion similar to the indigenous Dutch, but the statistic for the latter group can hardly be regarded as indicative of similarly seclusive networks. Discretion is therefore necessary when interpreting correlations with integration criteria where various immigrant groups are combined, as with Surinamese and Antilleans, with the category 'Other' immigrants, and with the weighted correlations for all local immigrants.

Other reasons for caution are more theoretical in nature. The relations observed with immigrants' integration scores may be considered entirely spurious. For instance, with a simple control for individual differences in educational level, the correlations diminish markedly in the Surinamese and

Antillean category (from .50 to .27). They are no longer significant in either the Turkish or 'Other' immigrant categories. Seclusion is, in other words, not necessarily an obstacle to immigrants' integration; it may be in itself a consequence of more fundamental obstacles. Reasoning from a pillarized vision, I could surmise that the Haarlem findings do not invalidate notions of ethnic *incorporation* (Portes and Manning, 1986) as an alternative integration path. The finding that the weakest correlations between seclusive ties and integration scores are observed among Turks, the ethnic category that in various domains displays cohesive attributes, attests to the necessity to interpret results within spatial and temporal contexts.

A Prevalence of Dutch Ties

Moving on to the notion of *inclusive* ties, it refers here to the number (and the role) of indigenous Dutch in immigrants' social networks. In our survey, this notion pertains particularly to those immigrants whose list of friends contains only indigenous Dutch. The percentage of these respondents per ethnic category ranges from 3% among Moroccans and Turks, through 18% among Surinamese and Antilleans, to 46% of the 'Other' immigrants. A complementary criterion for the indigenous Dutch - those who referred only to immigrants as their close friends - is met by two respondents. The integration scores of those with only inclusive ties do not differ from those with fewer Dutch ties.

A more continuous indicator derived from the data displays more significant correlations with the local index. It reflects not so much the *number* of Dutch friends respondents name, but the *mean frequency of contacts* with these friends. Immigrants' contact frequencies with Dutch ties are (much) lower than with ties from their region of origin. Those who maintain more frequent contacts have generally higher degrees of integration.

These results must again be viewed with the necessary caution. They do fail to corroborate the premise that having an abundance of indigenous ties is indicative for immigrants' integration. More important is the intimacy with which these ties are maintained (cf. Granovetter, 1973).

An Ethnic Diversity of Ties

The notion of *eclusive* residents, who have an ethnic diversity of ties, was operationalized as those respondents who include in their list of ties at least one person of foreign descent divergent from their own. Respondents who meet this criterion are represented in the fourth row of table 6.5. The range across ethnic categories goes from 16% of the Turks to 37% of the 'Other' immigrants.

Among the indigenous Dutch, 22% identified at least one friend of foreign descent.

In contrast to the inclusive, the eclusive in all immigrant categories are consistently more integrated than those with less diversity in their ties. The difference however is only statistically significant among Moroccans and Turks (η=.28 resp. .22). The percentage of respondents' contacts maintained with *others* is a more continuous criterion that, as already mentioned above by the sub-section on seclusion, correlates significantly with integration scores by all four immigrant categories.

These results illustrate how survey designs can depart from strict dichotomies between seclusive and inclusive contacts. Indeed, that the eclusive distinction clarifies differences in integration (only) among 'minority' categories can be interpreted quite succinctly. *Eclusive* ties are primarily observed among *young* immigrants who have developed such friendships, and other integration opportunities, in local schools. The numbers are too small to substantiate this interpretation, and problems of multi-collinearity inhibit more general comparisons with inclusive immigrants. Nevertheless, it would be short-sighted in the face of demographic developments - when viewed from a tolerant vision - to consider eclusive ties a 'rest' category.

Producing More Adequate Measures

The excursion along the four contactual types illustrates the variant perceptibility and relevance of immigrants' social network. The question remains how the contacts could be measured to provide more adequate insights into the functionality and intimacy of individuals' social networks. By simply having respondents estimate their contacts with frequent ties, we rely upon several questionable presumptions, namely that:

- When asked to consider friends and family frequently contacted, individuals will identify those intimates essential for their well-being.
- Individuals and ethnic categories deviate minimally in the number (i.e., five) of family and friends that represents their core circle of intimates.
- Estimates as to the frequency, 'ethnicity' and locality of such contacts are unaffected by the interview context.

Compared with the (interactive) technique used in the survey, two other techniques of egocentric network analysis have more potential to measure the functionality and intimacy of individuals' networks: the *role relation*, and *exchange* techniques (van Tilburg, 1985; van der Poel, 1993).

With the list of five friends and family that respondents generated, no information was conveyed as to the intimacy associated with these ties, nor the position they occupy in respondents' social network. The role relation method characteristically focuses upon this issue, for instance by tallying the frequency of contacts respondents maintain with friends in a spectrum of social domains. Van Heelsum (1997:94ff) used this method where she solicited the number of 'significant others' that Surinamese respondents have within the household, among further family, in school or work domains, and in the clubs or organizations in which they participate. The method has three distinct advantages compared with the interactive technique.

- By systematically traversing domains the chance that respondents overlook specific contacts is diminished.
- The distinction in roles or domains provides more insight into where respondents' networks are characterized by isolation or seclusion, e.g., van Heelsum's respondents named on average less than two significant others associated with school or work.
- The general contours of the network become more visible. Van Heelsum's respondents for instance identified an average of twelve 'significant others'.

Besides these advantages, the method is distinctly more time-consuming. Moreover, it provides little insight as to the adequacy of the social network for the respondents' personal well-being.

The *exchange* technique addresses this last problem, where it tallies the number of names respondents' convey in response to everyday queries, such as 'who do you turn to when you want to discuss personal problems' or 'who would you ask if you needed to borrow $f500$?' With a select number of queries, that section of social networks can be chartered that fulfill specific personal needs (cf. Kunst et al., 1996:22ff; Adriaanse, et al.; 1997:83ff). This technique combines various qualities of the other techniques. For instance, the affective range of an individual's network can be reliably drawn (cf. Fischer, 1982; van der Poel, 1993). When combined with the name-generating technique it provides an estimate as to the *density* of the network, i.e., the extent in which specific friends are relied upon to fulfill a multiplicity of personal needs. It also reveals the disadvantages of these techniques: besides being time-consuming, the nature of the questions asked and the information requested is quite personal. The survey contexts in which the technique is applicable are therefore limited.

However, when regarding the paucity of Dutch survey research in which issues of immigrants' social networks are addressed, and the potential empirical and theoretical relevance encased in such research, I surmise more survey opportunities could be cultivated.

Neighbors: Residing Next to Potential Ties

Comparable to the issue of 'black' and 'white' schools, the concentration of 'minority' immigrants in specific areas of the Netherlands' larger cities has been an ongoing topic of research and policy debates. That immigrants settle more in some areas than others has been considered a source of: neighborhood tension (Bovenkerk et al., 1985), ethnic tolerance and communal action (de Jong, 1987), cultural deprivation (van Amersfoort, 1987) and cultural capital (Teule and van Kempen, 1991), social isolation (Entzinger, 1991), criminality (Bovenkerk, 1994) and educational deprivation (Tesser et al., 1996). Research and policy debates diverge where they focus upon immigrant concentration *or* segregation as issues. Literally speaking, a focus on *concentration* problematizes immigrants as producers of a 'ghetto' culture whereas a focus on *segregation* perceives immigrants more as victims of marginalization and exclusion (cf. Mullard et al., 1990:62ff). These divergent views are not necessarily antithetic. Here however they are associated with divergent community visions of *assimilation* respectively *tolerance*.

My purpose in this section has a more limited scope. Having access to population data on the ethnic distribution of Haarlem adults across twelve city districts, the utility of measures for concentration and segregation are considered as indicators of the four types of (interethnic) contact. Because the district in which respondents reside reveals much about their integration scores, the question arises how these districts vary in their potential for respondents of divergent ethnic origin to meet each other.

This sub-section will be brief and technical, instead of presenting more in-depth the survey possibilities to monitor ethnic interactions in neighborhoods. The choice is mainly motivated by a lack of exemplary empirical data. It is based moreover on the belief that such interactions in are quite benign. One of the first Dutch studies on interethnic contacts in 'concentrated' neighborhoods was conducted in a Haarlem flat complex (van Niekerk et al., 1989). The researchers held a series of in-depth interviews with residents of divergent ethnic origin, guided by notions rooted in the ecological perspective of the *contact thesis*, and were prepared to monitor signs of interethnic hostility and intolerance. The study produced a wealth of citations and observations on the city's high-rise low-rent flat life. Overall, residents were seen to keep to themselves while interethnic contacts are sparse and unspectacular. Our 1994 survey, even where we focused upon the more 'concentrated' neighborhood clusters, led to similar conclusions (Reinsch et al., 1995:106ff).

Social and Spatial Isolation

Where the previous sections have focused upon domains bounded primarily by *social* institutions - the family, school, work and friendships - the neighborhood environment is more clearly a *spatial* context. This offers distinct measurement possibilities but it also increases the conceptual confusion. Take for instance the notion of the *isolated* immigrant. Is a person isolated when contacts within the neighborhood are limited, *or* when contacts are limited to the neighborhood instead of the greater city? The focus is here upon individuals' potential contacts within the *neighborhood* context. Within this context, individuals are perceived as *socially isolated* when they have no ties within the neighborhood, and *spatially isolated* when they reside in (secluded) homes or in sparsely populated neighborhoods where prospects for contact are few. This conception of spatial isolation, one may note, emanates a normative ambiguity. In urban environments, secluded homes and neighborhoods are commonly associated with commodities of privacy and wealth. Haarlem has for instance several sparsely populated neighborhoods whose homes are in high demand. Haarlem also has sparsely populated industrial areas where, according to our informants, newcomers and particularly immigrants are met with hostility by the indigenous residents. Whereas in other domains the notion of (social) isolation denotes - and problematizes - immigrants' lack of contacts, here the interpretation of spatial isolation is more problematic.

A measure of *spatial* isolation is based upon variant district population densities. In Haarlem these range from 24 to 102 residents per hectare, with a mean of 47 (Gemeente Haarlem, 1995:W4). A measure of *social* isolation could be derived from a query as to the number of friends respondents have in the neighborhood, those without friends being considered socially isolated. Neither measure corresponds significantly with individuals' degree of integration. The premise was also considered that the type of home in which individuals reside also affects their isolation within the neighborhood. For instance, residents in flats with portal entries may differ in their integration from those residing in gallery flats, on the one hand, and single family homes, on the other. Any significant statistical relations observed within ethnic categories - they were lacking entirely for Moroccans and Turks - disappear under control for the district in which one resides.

Concentration and Seclusive Contacts

How could distinctions between social and spatial seclusion be perceived and measured in the neighborhood domain? For the social facet one could consider the functionality and intimacy of contacts that individuals maintain with neighbors from their region of origin. The spatial facet is construed as the demographic chance of meeting such neighbors, independent of social-historical circumstance. This probability is clearly tied to the notion of concentration: the more an ethnic category is concentrated in particular areas of the city, the greater the statistical chance that its members encounter each other. In the previous section I observed for instance that with proportional representations of 1%, the chance of a seclusive contact is one in a hundred. The proportion of Haarlem's adult population represented by the five ethnic categories is presented in the first row of table 6.6. One may note that the three minority categories together account for only 5.2% of adult residents; at district level this percentage ranges from 0.8% (in *Duinwijk*) to 14.0% (in *Boerhaavewijk*). When compared to mean percentages of 31% in Amsterdam and 29% in Rotterdam for 'minorities' (Tesser et al., 1995:56), such concentrations seem quite diluted.

Table 6.6 Isolation and segregation indices at district levels*

Index	Moro-ccans	Turks	Surinamese Antilleans	'Other' immigrants	Indigenous Dutch
Category's population	1605	3061	1727	15329	101066
% of Haarlem adult population	1.3%	2.5%	1.4%	12.5%	82.3%
chance to meet *own* category	2.2%	3.5%	1.9%	13.1%	82.5%
chance to meet *(other)* immigrants	18.1%	15.8%	17.8%	5.3%	17.4%
chance to meet indigenous Dutch	79.6%	80.8%	80.2%	81.7%	82.5%
segregation index	30.2	27.1	24.4	10.6	12.4

* For resident eighteen years and older as of 15 March 1994.

If minorities were equally distributed over all Haarlem districts, then the chance of having a neighbor from a minority category would be in all districts 5.2%. How much greater are the chances due to minority concentrations in specific districts? A statistic that embodies such proportional differences is the so-called isolation index P*.[14] This index also considers variations in district populations to yield a summary statistic for meeting probabilities. Various index scores for probabilities within and across Haarlem ethnic categories are displayed in table 6.6. In row two the scores are displayed for *spatial seclusion*: the mean chance of meeting district residents from the same ethnic category. A comparison of these percentages suggests that individuals within 'minority' categories have little chance of meeting each other, but the chances are greater than suggested by their proportional share in the local population.

Segregation and Inclusive Contacts

The isolation index P* is a summary measure (i.e., at local level across districts) that denotes the meeting chances between any two population categories. This provides the possibility to compare a given immigrant's chance of meeting individuals from other immigrant categories with his or her chance of meeting indigenous Dutch. The former helps comprise a measure of *spatial eclusion* while the latter represents *spatial inclusion*. The indices for these probabilities are also displayed in table 6.6. Except the particular category of indigenous Dutch, the three chance percentages have an asymmetrical relation; the greater the one the smaller the others while together they add to 100% (disregarding roundoff differences). Comparing the immigrant categories, the Moroccans are seen to have the best chance of meeting *other* immigrants (18.1%) while 'Other' immigrants have the best chance of meeting indigenous Dutch (81.7%).[15]

These indices provide local insight about how meeting chances vary the more immigrants are separated from each other and from indigenous Dutch. A comparison with other localities is however cumbersome, since the P* scores are sensitive to local variations in proportional representation. 'Other' immigrants' chance for (eclusive) contacts with residents from minority categories is for instance 5.3%. This percentage compares favorably with the 5.2% were immigrants proportionately distributed over all Haarlem districts. Still, a comparison with the chance to meet 'minorities' in The Hague (13.1%) or Rotterdam (23.2%) says initially little about minority segregation in the three cities (cf. Tesser et al., 1996:81ff).

A widely used measure for spatial segregation, the dissimilarity index, considers variations in proportional representation to deliver a summary statistic representing the spatial distance between two categories.[16] When one category's representation is compared with the rest of the area's population, the index is known as the segregation index. An example of this index is displayed in the bottom row of table 6.6, where for each of the five ethnic categories a segregation statistic is presented. The indices represent the percentage of the category that would need to move across district boundaries to realize proportional representation (i.e., zero segregation); it ranges from 10.6 among 'Other' immigrants to 30.2 for Moroccans. An index for the three 'minority' categories combined amounts to 24.3. This compares with minority segregation in the city of Utrecht (24.2), is half that of Rotterdam (46.1) and The Hague (51.0) and one third of the indices reflecting Afro-Americans' segregation in various U.S. cities (Tesser et al., 1995:64).[17]

Immigrant Concentrations and Individual Integration

The fact that more immigrants reside in some local areas than in others is, as pointed out in opening this section, the focus of continuous research and debate. Indeed, the origins of the contact thesis in the studies of the Chicago school concern *spatial* processes of integration. Few observations can be made here that allude to this tradition. Empirically the survey data offer little insight into immigrants' actual neighborhood contacts, while the proportional distribution of immigrants over local districts is not characterized by exceptional variations. With only survey data to rely upon, the risks of drawing conclusions based on spurious relations are manifest. With these limitations in mind, the relation has been examined between respondents' meeting chances at district level - to make seclusive, inclusive and eclusive contacts - and their integration scores.

Within the Moroccan and Turkish categories none of these measures for potential contact are seen to correlate significantly with respondents' degree of integration. Such results are in themselves not surprising, as the integration scores among these immigrants vary insignificantly across local districts. Still, this renders the findings (discussed in chapter three) even more noteworthy. Despite their widely variant prospects to have neighbors with *other* geopolitical origins, Turks and Moroccans do not differ in their integration from one local district to the next. For the other three ethnic categories, district variations in potential contacts do display significant correlations with individuals' integration scores. Particularly the greater chance to meet 'minorities' in a district correlates negatively with integration, and particularly among the Surinamese and Antilleans (R=-.40, see appendix I). These findings conform to those observed in the four larger Dutch cities: district minority concentrations account minimally for specific integration differences among Turks and Moroccan, and significantly among Surinamese and indigenous Dutch (Tesser et al., 1995:218ff). For none of the ethnic categories do the variant prospects to have *other* neighbors fully account for the variance observed across districts in integration scores. These findings provide modest support for the premise that immigrants' residence in more *segregated* districts is simply *indicative* of their estrangement. They better serve to refute the premise that immigrants are estranged *because* they reside in districts characterized by immigrant concentrations.

In this section the means to conceive and measure *spatial* notions of isolation, seclusion, inclusion and eclusion have been examined. During this excursion several obstacles have been encountered. The notion of spatial isolation is found ambiguous where it refers to end-goals of privacy and home ownership, and to a paucity of potential contacts. The distinction between the other three notions is little more than categorical. Their (asymmetrical) correlation to each other implies that measures of spatial seclusion are largely superfluous; they clarify in Haarlem little more nor less than measures for spatial inclusion. More in general, these indices for potential contacts, when calculated at district level, are presumably too coarse to characterize the inter-ethnic relations within neighborhoods (cf. Tesser et al., 1996:69).

Public People: Meeting Total Strangers

Many interactive themes remain that can be reckoned to the domain of civic life. These are classified within three general facets. First the Haarlem measure for *participation in social-cultural activities* is presented, a component of the local index. Then the *freedom of movement* and *public communication* facets are briefly considered.

Seeking Cultural (Inter)Action

A primary facet of civic life concerns social-cultural participation. What a person does - outside eventual educational, upbringing and labor activities - has in this study helped to differentiate between the integrated and the estranged. That participation is considered crucial for individuals' relation to their surrounding environment is based on an intrinsically sociological presumption. When individuals are detached as to their material security and self-reliance, and disenchanted as to their perceived opportunity and the appreciation of their urban surroundings, then their absolute estrangement is signified by a withdrawal from public life. Here I presume that the individual who frequents public areas to seek contact with fellow residents displays at least a remnant of *sociability*, and embodies the promise of renewed opportunity and engagement. Moreover, the presumption pertains not only to the (nearly) estranged: the more individuals combine cultural activities with their local positions and orientations, the more they form an integral part of the local community (cf. Bourdieu, 1992).

As a complement to two *positional* criteria and two *orientational* criteria, only this one *behavioral* criterion helps form the integration index.[18] This criterion is itself an (unrotated) principal component factor reduced from eight survey response items. Each item registers the estimated frequency that respondents visit localities (such as cafés or museums) or events (such as markets or festivals, see table 6.7). The component can be interpreted to represent - in one normally distributed factor revolving around the 'average' adult resident - the relative frequency that respondents traverse public areas and are liable to meet total strangers.

Table 6.7   Respondents' mean annual participation in cultural activities*

Locality or activity	Moroccans	Turks	Surinamese Antilleans	'Other' immigrants	Indigenous Dutch
weekly market	62 (100)	54 (30)	48 (30)	30 (12)	28 (12)
sports match	11 (0)	7 (0)	9 (0)	8 (0)	8 (0)
party outside home	6 (2)	14 (6)	11 (6)	9 (6)	8 (6)
café	13 (0)	29 (1)	17 (0)	25 (6)	18 (0)
dancing/disco	4 (0)	6 (0)	10 (0)	1 (0)	2 (0)
music/ballet/drama	1 (0)	1 (0)	6 (0)	6 (2)	6 (2)
museum/exhibition	1 (0)	1 (0)	2 (0)	3 (2)	4 (2)
event/fair/festival	1 (0)	1 (0)	2 (1)	2 (1)	2 (2)
n =	89-92	156-157	74-76	97-99	169-170

* The figures denote mean (and median) frequency estimates for the previous year.[19]

The eight response-items contained within the cultural participation component differ in various ways: some represent receptive and others active cultural manifestations (e.g., museums/exhibitions resp. dancing/discos); some are freely accessible for all and others may be seclusive (e.g., weekly markets resp. parties); some are frequented daily and others are annual events (e.g., cafés resp. fairs/festivals); and some may be considered outings of 'popular' as opposed to 'high' culture (e.g., sports matches resp. music/ballet/drama performances). The items were selected for their comparability with other Dutch surveys on cultural participation (e.g., Knulst, 1989; Intomart, 1989; Campbell et al., 1994; Huls, 1997) and represent only a rough fraction of individuals' leisure time in which strangers might be met.

For each of the eight response-items, mean (and median) frequency of participation are displayed in table 6.7. One can infer that on average residents undertake only two of the eight activities more than once a month, namely visits to markets and cafés. The median frequencies reveal that, with few exceptions, most residents in minority categories never attend any of these local activities besides weekly markets and parties. This has distinct consequences for their participation scores. The principal component was reduced from the response patterns after correcting for sample stratification, which yielded a participation spectrum with the *average resident* in the middle. As the two majority categories therefore set the component norm, those respondents have high scores who frequently attend a variety of activities. The participation in three activities has little effect upon respondents' scores (i.e., their 'loadings' on the component are less than .50, see appendix II), namely visits to sports matches, markets, and dancings or discotheques. This operational bias implies that immigrants have to do more than sport, shop and dance to be counted an active local participant. In table 6.8, which displays the quartile distributions along the participation spectrum, one can observe that most of the Moroccans and Turks have scores in the lowest local quartile. An inordinate proportion of the Surinamese and Antilleans (35%) also have lowest quartile scores, but the average category score diverges minimally from the local mean.

Table 6.8 Quartile distribution upon cultural participation spectrum

Quartile	Moroc-cans	Turks	Surinamese Antilleans	'Other' immigrants	Indigenous Dutch
non-participant (lowest 25%)	61%	52%	35%	25%	24%
relatively inactive	17%	27%	25%	23%	26%
relatively active	11%	13%	18%	26%	25%
active participant (highest 25%)	11%	9%	22%	26%	25%
standardized mean	-0.62	-0.5	-0.07	0.02	0.02
standard deviation	0.87	0.85	1.19	1.01	1
n (=100%)	93	159	77	100	169

The cultural participation criterion serves within this study as an estimate of residents' *potential* to meet other locals in their leisure time. Obviously more adequate instruments could be applied. For instance more reliable means have been developed that monitor the proportion of time individuals spend outside the confines of neighborhoods, jobs and schools traversing the city's streets (see, e.g., Ujimoto, 1982; Intomart Qualitatief, 1989), although they are short on brevity. Combined with network analysis techniques, such instruments could help to focus upon *actual* instead of potential contacts. However, with reference to the premise that motivates the measurement of cultural participation as integration end-goal, the issue remains civic and (inter) ethnic isolation. Who rarely leaves the household? What keeps them off the streets? Where do they dare to go? Viewed from a tolerant vision, the ultimate concern is not so much the cultural activities in which individuals participate, but that they are willing and able to participate at all.

Assuming that the notion of *isolation* is embodied in the cultural nonparticipant, let me briefly consider more sociable types of (inter)cultural behavior. We asked those respondents who are active members of a local club or civic organization to qualify its ethnic composition. The answers were noted upon a five-point scale ranging from 'exclusively Dutch' ('*autochtoon*') to 'exclusively immigrant ('*allochtoon*'). The response patterns, when reduced to a princal factor, could be interpreted to reflect the seclusive, inclusive or eclusive nature of the organizations in which active respondents' participate. Only among Moroccans does the factor correlate significantly with respondents' index score (R=.42). It mainly distinguishes between (18) Moroccans who participate in mosque activities, and (17) more integrated Moroccans active in less seclusive organizations. Such measurements of interethnic cultural participation remain rare in Dutch survey research (cf. Campbell et al., 1994; Rath and Kloosterman, 1996).

No-go Areas and In-crowds

The second civic facet - the *freedom of movement* throughout the city - encompasses themes of crime, public safety and discrimination. These are construed as factors that limit individuals' spatial access, leading to social and spatial *isolation*. Examples abound: civil agencies or commercial enterprises where immigrants are greeted with hostility, particular areas where street gangs intimidate, or simply inordinate police surveillance. Conceivably notions of *seclusion, inclusion* and *eclusion* encompass individuals' strategies for dealing with these barriers: seeking 'safety in numbers', do immigrants move with their *own* crowd, an indigenous one, or as eclectics in an ethnic mix? These notions may be pertinent for interactions within particular localities or social circles. Their measurement entails two basic shortcomings, one methodological the other theoretical. Methodologically, individuals' *orientations* (i.e., views and convictions) on crime and public safety are regularly surveyed. However no brief, simple and reliable survey protocols are available to measure individuals' *experiences* with interethnic crime and discrimination (cf. Bouw and Nelissen, 1988; Bol and Wiersma, 1997; Rodrigues, 1997). Theoretically, it is questionable which insights such notions and their measurements can provide about immigrants' integration. A notion of *isolation* may help identify those individuals confined to their secluded neighborhoods (cf. Entzinger, 1991). However, when a person's access to public areas is affected by (interethnic) hostility this reflects less directly upon his or her individual integration; it signifies more the absence of local integration.

Local Media

The third and final facet - processes of *public communication and debate* - is differentiated into three realms of activity: electoral activity, involvement in political organizations and civic debates, and participation in protests against prevailing political practices (cf. Gilsing, 1991). The realm of electoral activity was already discussed in chapter five, where respondents' political party preferences were found to have little correspondence with their degrees of integration. In that section the second realm was also briefly considered, namely respondents' views on ethnic political organizations. Activities in the first and third realms are surveyed readily around elections. Here local media is briefly viewed as a channel of civic involvement.

Communications research in the USA has shown the consumption of local media to correspond with specific phases in individuals' integration process (McLeod et al., 1996; Stamm et al., 1997). In the Netherlands, the desirability and availability of local media programs and periodicals directed especially toward immigrants have been ongoing political issues (Schakenbos and Marsman, 1988; Brants et al., 1998). This implies that immigrants' *potential* access to information on civic affairs varies from one locality to the next. More specifically it varies in the extent that *seclusive* (i.e., programs and periodicals in immigrants' native languages) and *inclusive* media channels are available at the local level. Methodological issues here concern the distinction between *isolated* and more *sociable* local media consumers. Are the isolated those bereft of access to local media, or those bereft of all media? Should a distinction be made between individuals' access to information on local political issues and, for instance, their access to the local cultural agenda? Among those with access to local media, the distinction between seclusive, inclusive and eclusive consumption leads to more measurement problems. In Haarlem for instance, with a daily newspaper and regional radio stations, we only asked respondents how often they listened to the (weekly) radio programs with information for various 'minorities.' Without more comprehensive measurements of respondents' media consumption - including an analysis of the content of such 'seclusive' broadcasts - there is limited means to discern the functionality of local media for respondents' political involvement. In any event, only among Moroccans are listening habits indicative of respondents' integration (η=.33). The results are moreover ambiguous: those Moroccans who 'never' or 'always' listen are generally less estranged than the occasional listeners.

Assessment: Isolating Contactual Processes

The observations in this chapter have been interwoven through three themes. Noting the paucity of survey research on immigrants' social contacts, I have assessed methodological obstacles that serve to sustain this state of affairs. Upon a more conceptual level, the adequacy of a notion of isolation, and alternative notions of (interethnic) sociability, has been considered in various domains. Finally the survey data has been examined to discern the possible relations between individuals' contacts and their degree of integration. These three lines of inquiry will be reviewed in the paragraphs below.

The Meaning of Contacts

When considering the measurement and interpretation of *exchanges* between individuals, various obstacles have been encountered in this chapter. With reference to the *contact thesis*, such exchanges are not simply presumed to vary with the separate individuals' positions and orientations. In their dynamic they potentially alter these positions and orientations. To monitor this process, the use of survey techniques is a crucial means to elicit information from individuals concerning their (interethnic) contacts. Particularly egocentric techniques of network analysis offer a veritable means to survey the range, functionality and intimacy of individuals' social contacts. I surmise that a more extensive use of network analysis techniques in Dutch research is needed to better comprehend the dynamics of interethnic relations. However, many methodological obstacles remain when examining the tensions between processes of inclusion and exclusion on the one hand, and the avoidance of interethnic hostilities on the other. These obstacles will be reviewed while referring to the five criteria used in this study to delineate adequate measurements.

A reliance upon survey techniques raises first issues of *reliability*. Most of the behavioral data in the survey concerned respondents' estimates of the frequency in which people are encountered or locations used. The accuracy of such estimates is clearly less than attainable for instance from self-report diary techniques. More fundamental are the inaccuracies that arise from individuals' propensity to provide socially acceptable answers. This severely limits the possibility to analyze exclusionary behavior - the avoidance of contact - motivated by racial imagery. In the Netherlands ('real-life') experimental techniques have displayed more potential to unveil exclusionary behavior (Bovenkerk, 1978; van Beek, 1993; Gras et al., 1996).

These limitations concern the personal nature of the interviewer-respondent relation. For the measurement of behavioral intimacies, the survey context is moreover insufficiently personal. Dutch researchers have used minimally-structured, in-depth interview techniques to monitor immigrants' experiences with, e.g., ethnically mixed partnership (Hondius, 1999), racial discrimination (Essed, 1991) and work floor relations (Lutz, 1991). To confront survey respondents with prestructured queries concerning such themes breaches standards of interview *simplicity*. A personable survey ambience can be created in which respondents are willing to relate intimate feelings of loneliness and isolation (Tilburg, 1985; Knipscheer et al., 1995; Adriaanse et al., 1997). They place however distinct demands upon the respondent, the interviewer and the survey's eventual purpose. The purpose of the Haarlem survey for instance, to register individuals' views and experiences concerning local policy issues, could not be easily rhymed with personal and intimate inquiries.

Simplicity alludes to the affective limits of survey intrusions upon personal privacy. The *brevity* criterion alludes to temporal limits. To survey individuals' contactual experience in domains central to immigrant integration policy - namely education, work and social-cultural activities - lengthy and complex questionnaire protocols are needed to capture the variety of possible experience in these domains.

This variety of contacts that individuals experience in public domains raises methodological issues of *comparability*. How can measurements be realized that enable comparisons between ethnic categories, domains and localities? In the previous two chapters this criterion has been referred to regularly when considering measurement categories or intervals perceived in integration indicators. The focus upon *potential* contacts in local districts pertains explicitly to problems of comparability. Before one concludes for instance that Haarlem minorities are less segregated than those residing in larger Dutch cities, presumptions have to be made concerning the comparability of 'minority' and 'local district' categorizations. Moreover, the conclusion reveals little about Haarlem minorities' potential contacts with *other* residents, when compared for instance to the potential contacts of minority residents in Rotterdam. With individuals' (incomparable) difference in opportunity to meet *others* in essentially all public domains, their actual contacts with others are even more difficult to compare.

Finally, two methodological obstacles have been encountered that in their centrality concern issues of measurement *validity*. Concerning notions of functionality, intimacy and hostility, the first obstacle is the reliance upon individuals' subjective perspective. When measurements of these notions are limited to survey response, for instance via network analysis techniques, literally half the contactual process remains unobserved. The tension, which evolves when the functionality and intimacy of ties are not mutually appreciated, is not perceived. Nor are the hostilities perceived that are perpetrated through contacts only indirectly or unconsciously associated with the social network. This obstacle clearly calls for the complementary use of other measurement techniques.

The second obstacle pertains to conceptual distinctions between positional, orientational and behavioral dimensions of integration. The distinction is based upon the premise that social contacts are observable and measurable entities, that affect and are affected by the positions and orientations of actors involved in the contact. However, these entities remain infused with positional and orientational qualities. Measurements of potential contact refer to positional attributes of opportunity; measurements of actual contacts are, without reference to orientational attributes of affection, socially meaningless. This conceptual web leads to the conclusion that the adequate measurement of contactual processes requires a clear distinction between the perspective and experience of actors involved in the contact, and the structural and cultural contexts in which the contact occurs. Moreover, an adequate measurement of contactual processes cannot be realized without taking into account the significance attributed the processes by the various actors involved.

Denoting the Isolated Immigrant

The second line of analysis followed in this chapter revolves around the notion of *contact*, specifically the premise that individuals can be distinguished according to the (interethnic) nature of their contacts. A distinction in four types of behavior has been examined for its potential to characterize respondents in each of the six local domains.

The notion of the isolated individual - diametrically opposed to the other three behavioral types - denotes a person with a relative paucity of contacts. Three dimensions or spectra have been identified upon which the paucity or profusion of contacts are counted. The *spatial* dimension refers to the location of contacts, e.g., those who only maintain written or electronic instead of physical ties are isolated in a spatial sense. The *temporal* dimension refers to the length of contacts, e.g., those who see ties briefly or infrequently are isolated in a temporal sense. The *social* dimension refers to a variety of attributes that infuse a contact with meaning, e.g., those whose contacts lack the functionality and intimacy of ties can be considered socially isolated.

Within each of these dimensions the notion of *potentiality* refers to the possible or probable limits to actual contact. These clearly vary per dimension and domain, and are sensitive to measurement conventions. In a spatial sense potential educational contacts vary from zero (for students in a correspondence school) to the number of fellow students, e.g., in the classroom, the schoolyard or the school career. In a temporal sense, potential contacts with colleagues at work could be limited for instance by the time spent at work, in the presence of colleagues, or during coffee breaks and other informal moments. In a social sense potentiality refers to the chance to realize a particular tie, e.g., the chance to marry a Moroccan is limited by the number of accessible, unmarried Moroccans that meet gender preferences.

These distinctions help to perceive and measure contacts as entities, but what do they signify? Or more concretely, what is problematic about a paucity of contacts? This is obviously a matter of perspective. Policy makers at a local level have their reasons to encourage the detached and disoriented immigrant to seek contacts via social-cultural activities. Such perspectives are manifested here in that *cultural participation* is used as criterion to help comprise the integration index. This perspective is conceptually distinct from the subjective perspective of (isolated) individuals: the person may or may not perceive the paucity of contacts as a problem (cf. Adriaanse et al., 1997:98ff). That the problematic character of social isolation is dependent upon perspective and context has been noted in several sections. The partnerless respondent is no more estranged within any of the ethnic categories; among Moroccans they are even less estranged. Only among 'Other' immigrants are those who seldom see their friends more estranged; among indigenous Dutch these 'temporally' isolated are generally more integrated. One could even expect that those residents of urban districts characterized by spatial isolation (i.e., more square meters per resident) are wealthier in a material sense, although in Haarlem they are not necessarily more integrated.

Three (interethnic) behavioral alternatives to isolation have been distinguished and discerned in various domains. Two of these, *seclusive* and *inclusive* types, pertain to contacts or ties with the immigrants' *own* respectively with the indigenous group. The third, for which I initiate the notion of *eclusion*, refers specifically to contacts with *other* immigrant groups. Perceived from a *tolerant* community vision, the eclusive contact is presumably as meaningful as the inclusive one. With the survey data, possibilities and problems by the perception and operationalization of these distinctions has been examined in all six domains. Two problems have been noted that undermine the adequacy of the distinction. First, where research subjects are relied upon to qualify their own behavior in (inter)ethnic terms, problems of reliability, comparability and simplicity (reflected by inordinate non response) prevail. Secondly, seclusive, inclusive and eclusive contacts are intrinsically related, in that they combine to form the whole of an individual's contacts. However, the (statistical) potential to realize these variant contacts varies per domain and per ethnic category. This raises technical problems (e.g., of comparability and collinearity) when clarifying the significance that positional and orientational factors have upon individuals' interethnic behavior.

Interethnic Contacts and Individual Integration

The various items contained in the survey that pertain to residents' (interethnic) contacts have served to illustrate conceptual and measurement issues in this chapter. The items are far from comprehensive: in the domain of *education and upbringing*, and in *housing and neighborhood environment*, no items explicitly concerned the interethnic nature of respondents' contacts. In the domain of *work and material security*, our inquiries as to the channels used to obtain work, and concerning the contacts with colleagues, revealed that Moroccans and particularly Turks labor more seclusively. Those who do are not more estranged. In the *private domain* the potential effect of interethnic parentage and partnerships upon individuals' integration was examined. A significant relation was only observed among Moroccans: those who convey that their partner has the 'same' ethnicity are more estranged than those with eclusive partnerships. The most extensive measurements were reported in the fourth section on *health and welfare*, concerning the frequency, proximity and interethnic nature of the friendships respondents maintain outside the household. The indicators that account for the most index variances are:

- a measure that reflects the frequency and proximity of contacts with ties (specifically among Turks and 'Other' immigrants),
- a nominal distinction in respondents with only seclusive ties (particularly among Moroccans and 'Other' immigrants), and
- a measure asymmetric to seclusion representing the proportion of respondents' contacts with *other* ethnic categories (particularly significant among Surinamese and Antilleans).

Only one other behavioral item corresponds with immigrants' integration and then only among Moroccans, namely that those active in seclusive organizations are more estranged than Moroccans active in more eclusive organizations.

Comparable to presentations in the previous three chapters, the results of multiple regression analyses are summarized in table 6.9. Six behavioral indicators have been selected that correspond significantly with respondents' degree of integration within at least one immigrant category.[20] Five of these are described in the paragraph directly above. A sixth indicator - the percentage adult minority residents in respondents' local district - is not derived from the survey sample but from population data..

One may note (in the next-to-last row of table 6.9) that the variance in index scores clarified by the six indicators combined ranges from a modest 6% among the Turks to 31% among Surinamese and Antilleans. Per ethnic category, only one or two indicators (denoted by an asterisk) account for index variance independent from the other five indicators. However, comparable to the findings in previous chapters, the ethnic categories differ as to the specific indicators that account for integration differences.

Table 6.9 Percent of variances in local index accounted for by behavioral components, controlling for other components

Behavioral component	Moro-ccans	Turks	Surinam-ese Antilleans	'Other' immi-grants	All immi-grants	Indigenous Dutch
partner's ethnicity	n.s	n.s.	n.s.	n.s.	3%*	n.s.
frequency/proximity of contacts with ties	n.s.	4%	n.s.	9%*	9%*	n.s.
secluded (all friends in ethnic category)	6%*	n.s.	n.s.	n.s.	-	n.s.
proportion contacts with other categories	n.s.	n.s.	8%*	n.s.	-	n.s.
% minorities in local district	n.s.	n.s.	8%*	5%*	6%*	7%*
ethnic mix of active organizations	4%*	n.s.	n.s.	n.s.	3%*	n.s.
combined (adj.) R^2	16%	6%	31%	28%	29%	7%
* indicators (adj.) R^2		3%	33%	20%	29%	7%
n (listwise deletion)	91	158	74	97	427	161

* = probability F < .05, n.s.= not independently significant.

The analyses showed the following results:

- No behavioral indicator independently clarifies variances in integration scores within all four immigrant categories.

- Characteristic of the more integrated Turks and particularly 'Other' immigrants is the frequency of their contacts with friends, and the relative proximity of these friends.
- Characteristic of the more estranged Moroccans and particularly Surinamese and Antilleans is the absence of friends from other ethnic categories.

These results suggest that those immigrants who reside in less segregated districts, and have realized non seclusive friendships, are generally more integrated. However, considering the variant parameters of interethnic behavior, these measurements provide at best a cursory glimpse of the contacts respondents maintain in their everyday lives. Before the Haarlem context could serve to substantiate the 'contact thesis,' more comprehensive research techniques should be applied, and more comprehensive measurements must be made.

7 Evaluating Integration

What has structured interviews among immigrant and indigenous residents of a Dutch city revealed about their degree of integration? In the previous four chapters a detailed answer has been presented to this question. After so much nuance, a more succinct overview is provided in the sections below. My efforts to order and evaluate the survey data began with the presentation of a formal model of immigrant integration. First various normative, theoretical and methodological issues, encountered during the previous chapters, are summarized. Given these variant contexts and considerations, summary findings of the analysis are presented. Specifically, those measures will be evaluated that consistently serve to clarify differences in residents' integration. Moreover, I will focus upon the many differences observed *between* 'minority' groups as to possible integration directions and barriers.

Normative Necessities

The original project in which the survey was conducted is in a certain sense characteristic of Dutch empirical research on immigrant integration. Immigrants' (and indigenous') views and experiences are solicited concerning a variety of issues presumably pertinent to the integration process. The responses are ordered and summarized to display individual attributes and convictions indicative of differences between immigrant and indigenous groups. To clarify these differences - or to test social theories - the statistical relations between various indicators are then examined. The common conclusion is that certain immigrant groups are not (yet) integrated, as exemplified by their (continued) poor social positions, aberrant affinities and problematic contacts. Succinctly stated, integration is treated as a series of *barriers*, and social research serves to describe and eventually clarify the nature of these barriers. However, the designation of integration end-goals beyond these barriers, and whether they can be reached either by dismantling or bypassing the barriers, are issues more common to political than academic debate. Immigrants' inordinate joblessness for instance is widely regarded and monitored as an impediment to their integration. Yet what employment specifically precipitates, and which alternative activities conceivably serve a similar purpose, are factors rarely made explicit in survey research designs.

The *objectives* and *end-goals* delineated in chapter two concern these paragon directions the integration process purportedly takes. With reference to Schermerhorn's notion of centripetal and centrifugal trends, diametrically opposed directives within each of the three central integration dimensions have been identified. At the local integration level these have been consistently called *objectives*. Assuming local objectives prescribe normative criteria for the evaluation of individuals' integration, these latter criteria have been denoted as *end-goals*. For the derivation of the index upon which residents are ranked as to their degree of integration, end-goal measurements were selected that reflect a combination of objectives characteristic for what I call the *tolerant vision*.

The perception and interpretation of Haarlem integration processes from a tolerant vision are based upon explicitly normative considerations. National policies on immigrant integration have for the past two decades underscored the principle that immigrant groups have intrinsic rights to participate in Dutch society according to their divergent customs and convictions. However, to encourage processes of cultural diversification as objective of immigrant integration raises distinct social and conceptual tensions. A primary motive for this study therefore was to consider how the conceptual tensions could be resolved. Schermerhorn's work provides an important basis with the qualification that *integration* refers to any process in which immigrants *comply* with the activities and objectives of indigenous residents. Within the conceptual framework, the tolerant vision represents in short a particular combination of (policy) objectives. Only with the compliance of both immigrants and indigenous residents do these objectives signify the (legitimate) contours of local integration. In the next three paragraphs I shall briefly review how these objectives have been operationalized.

In the structural dimension, these objectives concern the distribution of social goods: the optimization of *civil liberties* to produce, exchange and possess is presumably opposed to objectives of *social equality*. At the individual level civil liberty is reflected by end-goals of *self-reliance*, which on its part is opposed to *selflessness* (i.e., a compliance with communal norms of possession). With reference to (centrifugal) civil liberty objectives characteristic of the tolerant vision, two operational criteria for self-reliance were selected from the survey data. One, *welfare independence, is* a spectrum upon which respondents are ranked according to their use of social services. The other, *per capita income,* is a function of monthly household income and the number of household members.

Within the cultural dimension an opposition is perceived between (centripetal) objectives of *cultural unity* and *cultural diversity*. The former signifies the compatibility of cognitive, moral and expressive symbolic systems within public domains. The latter can be conceived (and reified) as a continuous dynamic between polar cultures to attract the affinity of individual subjects. At the micro level of individual orientations, these objectives correspond with end-goals of *conformity* respectively *personality*. End-goals of conformity imply normative criteria about what individuals should know and believe, while end-goals of personality evolve more loosely around rights to life, liberty and the pursuit of happiness. The two orientational criteria included in the integration index, namely *perceived opportunity* (estimates of relative prospects for education, housing and work) and *local satisfaction* (with personal life, the home, neighborhood and locality) are more closely aligned with objectives of cultural diversity. Beyond their validity as measures of individuals' appreciation of their local lives and liberties, they are concurrently indicative of integration processes at a local level. I presume here that prerequisite for the realization of a tolerant community is that immigrants - as groups - are comparable to indigenous residents as to their (variant) appreciation of local circumstance.

Within the interactive dimension the focus is directed upon interactions between immigrant and indigenous groups. (Centripetal) objectives of *inclusion* characteristic of the tolerant vision signify an optimal - and harmonious - dissolution of group boundaries. Contrarily, objectives of *seclusion* signify minimal - and harmonious - interactions across boundaries, to preserve for instance the cultural cohesion of the separate groups. These objectives are reflected at the micro-level of individual behavior by end-goals of *sociability* or *privacy*. As end-goal criterion for sociability a measure of *cultural participation* was selected, in the presumption that the individual who frequents local activities and localities has more prospects of meeting strangers - whatever their ethnic origin. Perceived from a tolerant vision, this measure of (potential) sociability could be complemented within the integration index by measures for the (ethnic nature of) contacts individuals maintain. However, due to various reasons recounted below, this behavioral criterion was not included in the index.

This review illustrates the possibilities provided by the conceptual model to allow for divergent integration criteria. Should one for instance regard immigrant integration more as conformity to indigenous culture and inclusion in indigenous networks, then this would lead to the selection of more stringent empirical criteria. The five 'tolerant' criteria applied in this study represent in this sense a less cohesive integration perspective that can be associated with liberal political ideologies: immigrant residents should be self-reliant, satisfied with their lot, and social-culturally active; however with whom they socialize and whether they have any affinity with local culture is their own business.

Various tensions characterize the relation between the normative objectives combined within the tolerant vision, and the measures selected from the
survey to denote individuals' success at complying with these objectives.

- First, the presumption that local objectives are reflected directly by, and
  realized through, individuals' pursuance of particular end-goals grossly
  simplifies the relation between local and individual integration. The
  problems with this presumption will be reviewed in chapter eight.
- The Haarlem survey-questionnaire was not originally designed to measure
  individual residents' integration. However, in my attempts to make sense
  of survey measures, the framework does not merely represent residents'
  responses in more abstract terms. It serves more comprehensively to
  identify relevant integration components in need of (more adequate)
  measurement.
- According to the formal notion of integration derived from Schermerhorn,
  the compliance with tolerant objectives signifies individuals' integration
  only when immigrants *and* indigents agree upon these objectives. Various
  items served in the survey to elicit respondents' visions of ideal communities. Besides the more methodological issue concerning these items'
  adequacy to designate local objectives, a normative issue concerns the
  degree of consensus. The measures suggest a lack of consensus as to all
  three tolerant objectives: most Moroccans and Turks envision a more
  egalitarian community, most Turks a more culturally unified one, and most
  indigenous Dutch underwrite privacy end-goals. A strict application of
  Schermerhorn's notions could lead me to conclude that the city exemplifies
  more a process of 'forced segregation' than any of the eight visions of 'local
  integration' delineated in table 2.1.
- Even if most of the immigrant and indigenous residents were to agree upon
  local objectives, a tension remains between individuals' expressed end-
  goals and their current circumstance. For instance, the pursuance of
  inclusion objectives implies the realization of interethnic contacts.
  Whereas most Haarlem immigrants underwrite these objectives, and
  generally emphasize the importance they attribute to friendships with
  indigenous Dutch, they differ per category and local district as to their
  potential to meet such locals. On their part, the indigenous majority has
  far less potential to meet local immigrants, while those who express having
  such ties are not seen to score more integrated. Such discrepancies would
  render the meaning of residents' degree of integration rather opaque, had
  this sociability criterion been combined with the other criteria within the
  local index.

The local integration index was derived from a principal component analysis of the five criteria. The index distributes respondents in a bell curve around the zero score of the 'average resident.' With this ranking, integration is alluded to as an individual attribute that can be observed in the mathematical realm shared by the five criterion components.

This assumption has its problems, one being the difficulty to describe the index in terms more concrete than 'factor loadings' and 'standard deviations.' It has however distinct advantages. For instance, the ranking may suggest integration to be an individual attribute, still it is based on a local mean and not, as often happens, on the presumed deviations from an archetypical native. Moreover, rather than a nominal distinction between the integrated and the estranged, the ranking is continuous. If I were specifically interested in targeting particular groups, e.g., those living under the poverty level who are socially isolated, then nominal classifications would suffice. The continuous index provides more statistical potential to examine the significance of other factors - the metaphorical integration barriers - upon individuals' rankings.

This brings me to a final consideration. With only one exception, a recurring rank order of ethnic categories is observed, according to mean values upon the five criterion components: the Moroccans score lowest, followed by Turks, Surinamese and Antilleans, 'Other immigrants,' then indigenous Dutch.[1] This does not imply that individuals score either consistently low or high upon all components, according to their geo-political origin. The fusion of five criteria into one index is sensitive to this nuance: a person's presumed estrangement according to one criterion is eventually compensated by higher scores according to other criteria.

With the integration index, as operational monitor of a tolerant vision, an explicitly normative criterion occupies a central location in the study. I consider this inherent to the analysis of immigrant integration. With the stipulation of this criterion as the (dependent) factor in need of clarification, it is tempting to think that the further analysis coud be conducted purely through the application of scientific logic. The research process is however, like any social process, beset by moments where one must choose between disparate norms.

Theoretical Exploration and Refutation

The conceptual framework is presented explicitly as a model *of* a theory. A distinction in parameters, and dimensions within parameters, renders material with which theories are built. The material are concepts, stored in separate parts of the model, that can be mixed in various ways to illuminate the integration process. The model presumes a relation between the concepts; theory explicates what the relation is.

With the model exploratory steps have been taken toward theoretical formulations. Five attributes of immigrant and indigenous residents are together denoted as *individual integration* and used to allocate each respondent a relative score. Per dimension, per domain and per ethnic category survey measures of concepts have been systematically sought, in which respondents are ranked similar to their index score. The result, summarized in Appendix I, is a diffuse and puzzling pattern of numbers, signifying differences in index rank apparently accounted for by specific indicators. At first sight the results are promising - a combination of indicators accounts for nearly two-thirds of the variance in integration observed among Haarlem immigrants. Sufficient material is unveiled to formulate some audacious postulates: e.g., 'only among indigenous residents are women more estranged than their male counterparts;' and 'the residential district in which individual immigrants reside reveals more about their integration than the geo-political region from which they originate.' Theory however is more than a set of hypotheses inferred from statistical contingencies. It is an ongoing reconsideration and delineation of concepts, their reciprocal relationships, their operationalization and measurement, in variant social contexts. Throughout the study I have withstood the temptation to dissect the theoretical relation between specific (sets of) indicators, nor have I sufficiently sought to diminish the ambiguity by testing disparate hypotheses. Instead I have chosen to focus upon issues of measurement.

This is not to suggest that this study has a purely exploratory character. It is imbedded in a theoretical tradition in which the immigrant integration process has been perceived, conceptualized and monitored from countless vantage points. The framework could be considered a derivation of those devised by Schermerhorn (1970) on the one hand and Engbersen/Gabriëls (1995) on the other (and the theoretical groundwork upon which their models are based). In every section of the previous four chapters references are made to the wide variety of empirical research in which the particular area of the framework is examined. In each section I find myself in the footsteps of others, examining to what extent integration barriers identified elsewhere are perceptible in Haarlem.

The formal model is an (inter)subjective rearrangement of conceptual material; the statistical analysis of the relations between indicators and index is a rudimentary step in theory formulation and refutation; and the survey data provides a broad range of comparative measures in one European city. In their combination little has been confirmed and only peremptory propositions have been repudiated. We are far from a comprehensive understanding of immigrant integration but - comparable to the concept itself - the process is what counts.

Measurement Compromises and Comparability

Assuming that without adequate measurements, theoretical inquiries remain in the realm of speculation, measurement obstacles by structured interviews have been regularly confronted in the previous chapters. These obstacles were not only observed with respect to the Haarlem data. More generally, they denote the (im)possibility to devise a comprehensive survey instrument to monitor immigrants' integration. In chapter three, five measurement criteria were introduced; *adequacy* refers in this study to the extent in which these criteria are met. While the criteria are intertwined in myriad ways, they are here sequentially reviewed to identify primary obstacles. These obstacles can be summarily qualified as an ongoing tension between the theoretical practice of conceptual relations and the empirical practice of interviewer-respondent communications.

Validity is commonly construed as the most general criterion to which the other four are subordinate. It refers to the lucidity and comprehensiveness of operationalizations and measurements in their empirical representation of concepts. Concretely stated: do the survey-items measure in practice the concept as theoretically intended? This penultimate criterion presupposes a conceptual clarity foreign to the integration construct. The abstract character of the parameters within the construct inhibits clear distinctions. This has been observed for instance where the behavioral dimension is intrinsically bound, and often conceptually linked, to positional and orientational dimensions. Should a consensus be realized as to the conceptual structure of the integration construct, the empirical practice has complementary ambiguities. Problems of validity are then readily apparent when interviews are conducted in a variety of (immigrant) languages.

Reliability refers to the consistency of results should measurement procedures be repeated. In theoretical practice, where reliability concerns the certainty attributed to general inferences drawn from population samples, a recurring obstacle is the number of sample cases needed to examine the complex conceptual patterns inherent to the integration construct. At an empirical level, throughout the study obstacles have been encountered that compromise reliability, for instance the reliance upon respondents' memory to monitor their integration through time.

Particularly with reference to individuals' orientations, controls for reliability require survey protocols characterized by multiple and repetitive items. This entails compromises with the criterion of *brevity*. Concessions to brevity severely limited orientational and behavioral measurements in Haarlem interviews, with their average duration of 80 minutes. In theoretical practice, the brevity criterion is mirrored by objectives of conceptual parsimony. Again with reference to orientations, I observe the dilemma that bipolar conceptions, e.g., between 'immigrant' and 'indigenous' affinities, lack the necessary nuance while multipolar conceptions are at once complex.

The fourth criterion, for which in this study the term *simplicity* has been applied, refers empirically to the requisition that respondents' dignity should not be affronted, for instance through intricate or insulting inquisitions as to their cognitive or moral capacities. This criterion yields obstacles in all three dimensions: inquiries concerning respondents' eventually detached positions, the measurement of their knowledge in most domains, and the registration of their behavior by (interethnic) contacts. These obstacles are refracted by practices of theoretical simplicity, i.e., reductionist interpretations in which for instance the culture of specific ethnic categories are construed as a peremptory integration barrier.

Comparability as final criterion concerns the application of standards to evaluate the relative significance of measurements, and of concepts. The criterion plays a role in every step of the measurement process, from the delineation of concepts to the use of techniques to analyze interview responses. Comparability presumes points of reference, and it is the choice between disparate points of reference that renders measurement as much a normative as a rational process. In the Haarlem survey the selection and formulation of items allowed for references to research elsewhere. Yet more important, a single standardized questionnaire was designed for interviews within all immigrant and indigent sub-samples, to enable comparisons between their respective populations. The results of this process are then unique within the Dutch research tradition on immigrant integration: a systematic comparison of a broad range of attributes, measured among representative samples of immigrant and indigenous residents in one city, for their (statistical) potential to clarify individual differences in integration.

In short, the measurement of individuals' integration through structured interviews is a continuous practice of compromise between the disparate criteria that endow the measurements with meaning. Particularly measurements of individuals' orientations entail considerable concessions to brevity, simplicity and reliability. This also applies to a lesser extent for measurements of individuals' behavior toward ethnic 'others.' Having culminated this process, some meaningful measurements are due for review.

Divergent Origins, Inordinate Barriers

Throughout the past four chapters many survey measures have been presented, in search of clarification for differences in residents' degree of integration. Each chapter culminated with a brief overview of indicators that accounted for significant portions of index variance under control for other indicators. In this way an impression has been given as to the explanatory potential of respectively demographic, positional, orientational and behavioral indicators. Moreover, the similarities and differences between ethnic categories as to the most illuminating indicators could be discerned. To conclude this statistical excursion, several findings will be considered when the analysis is no longer limited to measures within a specific dimension of individual integration. With so many indicators, distributed across conceptual dimensions, what is their relative and combined potential to clarify differences in residents' integration?

Explanatory Apparitions and Actual Barriers

This final excursion begins with a selection of five measures indicative of individual attributes that are commonly construed as barriers to integration. The selection is based on three criteria:

- The indicator has accounted in this study for significant differences in integration scores within at least two of the four immigrant categories.
- The indicator can be *adequately* measured - relatively speaking of course - according to the five criteria discussed in the previous section.
- The indicator serves as a focal point in Dutch policy or public debates.

The five measures that meet these three criteria are:

- the *level* of formal *education* completed, differentiated in four categories;
- the *position* on the *labor market*, differentiated in five categories;
- the *language(s)* in which the interview was conducted, differentiated in three categories;[2]
- the *religious faith* respondents would pass on to eventual offspring, differentiated in five categories; and
- the *percentage* adults residing in the respondent's local district, who are classified within one of the three so-called *'minority'* categories).

To what extent do these five indicators serve to explain differences between the integrated and the estranged? In the first row of table 7.1 I display the percentage variance in integration scores that is accounted for when these five indicators are entered in a single multiple regression equation. Comparing the more estranged ethnic categories on the left, to those with higher mean index scores on the right, an ascending explanatory potential is perceived: among Moroccans only 19% and Turks 24% of the index variance, compared with 35% for 'Other' immigrants and a respectable 48% when the analysis is conducted upon the combined (and reweighed) sample of *all* immigrants.

These results suggest that most differences in individuals' integration would remain, even when barriers of limited education, joblessness, divergent linguistic skills, 'aberrant' religious convictions, and residential concentrations are removed. They also illustrate an expository risk. Analysis results for all immigrants combined suggest that literally one-third of the index variance could be ascribed to three attributes particularly characteristic of the two more estranged 'minority' categories: namely their 'preference' to speak another language, to raise Muslim children, and to reside in 'immigrant enclaves.'

Table 7.1 Variance in integration scores clarified by selected indicators

Indicators	Moro-ccans	Turks	Surinam-ese Antilleans	'Other' immi-grants	All immi-grants	Indige-nous Dutch
education, labor position, language, religion, and minority concentrations	19%	24%	29%	35%	48%	31%
optimal selection of indicators per ethnic category*	42%	39%	44%	54%	64%	35%

* The selection of indicators are underlined in appendix I.

Many factors help clarify why residents of Turkish or Moroccan origin are generally less integrated than other immigrants. These factors are enveloped to a certain extent by the 'region of origin' indicator, which has been seen to clarify 15% of the index variance for *all* immigrants. Because this indicator is not entered in the analysis here, its correlation with index scores is channeled indirectly through these three attributes. The index variance clarified by these five indicators when generalizing for all local immigrants is, in other words, partly spurious. It could lead to the similarly spurious inference that personal attributes characteristic of individuals with particular origins are not indicative of, but are in themselves barriers to, immigrants' integration. To diminish the risk of spurious inferences, the focus in this study has been upon comparisons *within* the five ethnic categories from which representative samples were drawn. In technical terms, this means that the factor 'region of origin' has been kept (mostly) constant.[3]

The search for survey indicators that optimally clarify index variances results in a diffuse selection of five to seven indicators per ethnic category.

In appendix I the various indicators are designated by a line under the appropriate statistic; the variances in index scores that they clarify are presented in the bottom row of table 7.1. One may observe that the indicators account for anywhere between 35% and 54% of the index differences within the five ethnic categories. In the sub-sections below these findings provide two topics of discussion: the measures that consistently distinguish between the integrated and the estranged; and the apparent barriers to integration specific to each minority category.

The Variant Significance of Individuals' Social Positions

In the search for factors that clarify differences in integration, four indicators are consistently significant within all five ethnic categories. All four can be construed as indicative of individuals' position on central markets for social goods, namely the position on educational, labor, housing and neighborhood markets. Considering the continued focus upon these factors in theories and policies on immigrant integration, their importance for individuals' integration within the Haarlem context comes as little surprise. Without delving again into the nuance needed to qualify the relation between these four indicators and residents' integration scores, two issues deserve summary consideration. The first concerns the divergent theoretical significance that can be attributed to these four indicators. The second concerns the variant statistical significance these indicators have in clarifying integration within the five ethnic categories compared in this study. In considering these two issues, variant phases in the integration process reflected by these measures, between the acquisition of primary needs, and the realization of personal goals, will be emphasized.

Theoretical vagaries Considering their potential to clarify differences in index scores, none of these indicators can be construed as representing a barrier whose removal is essential for individuals' successful integration. Of the four however, the reduction of educational differences between individuals and entire ethnic categories has the least ambiguous role as a catalyst to immigrant integration. The observation that two-thirds of the Moroccans and Turks have completed no more than primary education implies that these residents lack essential knowledge and skills to compete for positions upon other markets. The importance of education seems irrefutable, provided immigrant groups are also part and partial to local principles of meritocracy.

Education has a temporal quality; it refers to adults' activities in the past and it prepares the youth and entire societies for the future. The significance of immigrants' current position on the labor market is more ambiguous. Whereas knowledge is rarely lost, jobs are lost all the time. Had we interviewed

Moroccan and Turkish residents twenty years ago, we would presumably have observed less disaffection. Particularly among those 'guest workers' who primarily migrated for labor motives, more would be encountered whose personal goals were related to work and self-reliance. How many Turks and Moroccans now collecting disability - and who collectively comprise a most estranged group of residents[4] - were brimming with optimism and local satisfaction twenty years ago? Employment provides a source of material wealth and welfare independence, but among the more estranged immigrant categories the employees hardly earn more than their cohorts on welfare. For those individuals who derive little security or satisfaction from their work, the dilemma then becomes quite manifest: why waste life and limbs when time could be more profitably and pleasantly invested in schooling and fooling around?

The importance attributed to individuals' positions on the housing market is similarly sensitive to the vagaries of market processes. Comparable to the perennial dilemma associated with work - a necessary evil *and* a source of personal fulfillment - the possession of a roof above one's head is both a primary necessity *and* a symbol of social status. The segmented housing market characteristic of most Dutch localities reflects this ambiguity: on the one hand the social housing market for those needy tenants who have acquired specific rights, and on the other hand the free market subject to minimal state intervention. I have argued that individuals have divergent positions on these markets, and that particularly among Turks homeowners are encountered who would conceivably be more content as tenants in less expensive social housing.

The significance of the neighborhood or local district in which individuals reside can also be described with comparable dilemmas. An immigrant may depend upon the (limited) opportunities provided by an 'ethnic enclave,' but may also long for the status and self-reliance embodied by residence in more auspicious neighborhoods. In this vein the ecological nature of neighborhoods as social and spatial entities require multilevel analysis methods to detect whether they form either an impediment to individuals' integration, or an end-goal more tangible than personal income or welfare independence. The measurements presented in this study to qualify Haarlem neighborhoods and districts are clearly inadequate for this purpose. I have used them nevertheless to argue that the inauspicious neighborhoods in which Turks and Moroccans primarily reside are rarely a reflection of personal 'choice;' most of these immigrants have their sights set on other local neighborhoods or districts where they hope to find more reason to 'feel at home.'

Methodological mismatches These observations on the ambiguous significance of social positions help to clarify the second issue deserving a summary focus:

why do differences in social positions observed among the more estranged minority categories account for so little variance in their integration scores? The extent in which measures of these four positions[5] account for index variance displays a curious pattern: from 14% among Moroccans and 20% among Turks, through 27% among Surinamese/Antilleans and 32% for indigenous Dutch, to 40% among 'Other' immigrants (and 46% for all immigrants). One answer is tautologically simple: whereas the social mobility realized by 'Other' immigrants and indigenous Dutch bring them more clearly along the metaphorical integration path (or up the status ladder), the social mobility achieved by individuals within more estranged minority categories is (as yet) less indicative of individuals' realization of personal end-goals.

This ambiguity pertains in theory to the dilemmas alluded to above. It is also by design a tendency to which the integration index - with its derivation from five divergent criteria - is sensitive. Let me briefly run through the three domains to illustrate my point, it being that particularly Turks and Moroccans in their competition for social goods generally expend an inordinate amount of time and dignity. In education I have noted that the progress booked by the more educated Turks apparently costs them inordinate amounts of disaffection. Among Moroccans I am inclined to conclude that the more highly educated are simply too young to have profited appreciably from their (Dutch) schooling. With respect to the domain of work and material security I have noted that Moroccans and Turks do not earn appreciably more with their paid jobs than their cohorts on welfare. From various measures of labor orientation it can be inferred that the nature of the work they do is less a source of pride than of disaffection. Upon the housing market the effect of mobility among Moroccans is insignificant, if only because a mere handful of Moroccans is encountered who own their own homes, while the ambivalent position occupied by some Turkish homeowners has already been emphasized. Finally, why the district in which individuals reside is less indicative of integration among Moroccans and Turks than among other residents concerns, in part, a lack of measurement refinement. Surinamese and Antilleans, and particularly 'Other' immigrants, reside more often in the (very) auspicious neighborhoods that typify the better districts and the realization of personal goals, a process reflected by their index scores. Some Turks and Moroccans also reside in the better districts, but they are concentrated in the inauspicious neighborhoods that these districts also have. These findings reflect comparability problems. We observe that Moroccans and Turks benefit less from their local engagement. The problem in part is that the calibration of the integration index and indicators limits our perception of these benefits, as they are eclipsed by the benefits other residents derive from their formal education and paid jobs.

Beyond these issues of measurement, index design, and market conceptions, more substantive theoretical explanations are available for the observation that the more estranged minority categories appear inert in their social mobility. These may be sought in various disciplines and levels of analysis: e.g., cultural or genetic attributes of individuals, the consequences of market dynamics for the underclass, the successive phases of interethnic contact. My inclination is to seek clarification in the exclusion-inclusion dynamic of ethnic interactions. Turks and Moroccans are more susceptible, and eventually more sensitive, to the exclusive and even discriminatory behavior of other locals (cf. Vermeulen and Penninx, 2000:222ff). Such behavior is not prevalent, but the tendency is evident. The tendency helps clarify why the improvement of educational, labor and housing positions does not lead to the same degree of self-reliance and local satisfaction observed among other respondents. Those minorities actively engaged in public domains are confronted with this exclusive behavior and even consciously sense it. In facing these exclusionary tendencies they may moreover sense a metaphorical 'pull from behind:' the ethnic group that provides compassion and solicits affinity. How individuals react within these interactions varies from person to person, and from one ethnic category to the next. In the next sub-section I sketch a brief profile of the more integrated members of the three minority categories examined in Haarlem.

Disparate Processes of Exclusion and Seclusion

Having focused upon four measures of social positions, each of which accounts for significant differences in integration within most ethnic categories, let us now briefly consider the disparities. Why do specific indicators serve to clarify integration only within particular immigrant categories? Rather than review the broad selection of measures that optimize the clarification of differences within the separate ethnic categories, a more abbreviated source is used. For each category four indicators are sought - a demographic, positional, orientational and a behavioral - that in their combination optimally clarify differences in integration. The results are presented in table 7.2.

The percentages displayed in the first column show that within all categories a combination has been found that accounts for 30% or more of the index variance. Even more noteworthy is the diversification. A focus upon the three minority categories for instance reveals that no indicator helps optimize explained variance in more than one category. This pattern of diversity, supplemented by results discussed in the previous chapters and summarized in appendix I, suggest differential patterns and phases of individual integration.

Moroccans make up literally the most estranged ethnic category; five out of six have a degree of integration that classifies them within the lowest quartile of Haarlem residents. Most lack paid work; a large majority has completed no more than primary education; and three-fourths are inactive in civic organizations. As for their local and informal ties, Moroccans are generally more isolated than individuals in other immigrant groups. The problem in part is a lack of seclusive alternatives to counteract exclusionary processes. Besides the mosque, ethnic networks of informal or formal support are not discernable. The contours of two groups can be perceived, not entirely distinct of course, who are less estranged. A group with (menial) paid jobs is ambivalent in the appreciation of its lot. A larger group of younger, more recent immigrants, is more optimistic in its local prospects, consciously cultivating a Moroccan-Dutch identity and actively participating in (ethnically mixed) social-cultural activities. This second group cannot be considered more self-reliant but, regarding its orientation and behavior, it intends to be.

Table 7.2   Indicators that optimally account for index variance

Ethnic category ($\sum$ adj. R^2)	Demographic	Positional	Orientational	Behavioral
Moroccans (39%)	age	civic memberships	ethnic self-identification	ethnic composition of organizations
Turks (30%)	residential district	labor market position	approval ethnic organizations	frequency/vicinity of contacts with ties
Surinamese Antilleans (41%)	district minority concentrations	educational level completed	labor ambition	percentage contacts with 'other' ties
'Other' immigrants (45%)	residential district	educational level completed	neighborhood affinity	frequency/vicinity of contacts with ties
All immigrants (52%)	residential district	educational level completed	religious faith	frequency/vicinity of contacts with ties
Indigenous Dutch (30%)	gender	educational level completed	preference for cultural diversity	-

Turks as a category are less estranged than Moroccans; three quarters however have integration scores within Haarlem's lowest quartile. Turks are more active than other local minorities upon the labor market, while they also display a greater ethnic cohesion and sociability. Networks of informal and formal contacts are discernable - in neighborhoods, on the labor market, in welfare and social-cultural organizations. These networks provide various (seclusive) alternatives to compensate for the exclusionary practices of which the Haarlem Turks are particularly sensitive.[6] The existence of these networks renders the qualification of more integrated Turks ambiguous. On the one hand many of those with poor prospects for mobility on education and labor markets are active in - and appear satisfied with - their participation in seclusive networks. On the other, those who occupy more lucrative educational and labor positions are more consciously oriented toward indigenous culture and activities. The latter group also tend to be more critical of Turkish cohesion and are susceptible to the disaffection and isolation that accompanies such views. The distinction between these two groups can be imagined as a 'fracture' *along* the index. On the one side are detached Turks with affinities toward their cultural origins; those who appreciate the Turkish networks and organizations are generally more satisfied and consequently score more integrated. On the other side are generally younger, more self-reliant Turks, whose integration scores are tempered by their dissatisfaction with local (interethnic) processes.

Surinamese and Antilleans are scattered further along the integration index. Only 40% has integration scores in the city's lowest quartile, while nearly a third score higher than the 'average resident.' Less impeded by Dutch linguistic barriers, and more often educated in Dutch schools, many of these residents have reaped the benefits of higher forms of secondary education while harboring outspoken ambitions on the labor market. A diffuse sub-category has encountered more impediments, particularly those who migrated to the Netherlands as adults and have therefore had less opportunity to attend Dutch schools and to cultivate the (interethnic) ties that education offers. The contours of informal and seclusive networks are perceived mainly among the disaffected and welfare dependents, residing in the social housing flats of a couple 'concentrated' city districts.

Minority means These generalizations, in qualifying variations between minority categories, overlook the much greater nuance perceived within ethnic categories. They illustrate how immigrants' (centrifugal) orientation toward, and (seclusive) contacts with, local residents from their region of origin are not necessarily impediments to their social mobility. Instead I see it particularly among Turks as a means to cope with continued social deprivation. Differences in social position generally account for variations in individual integration *across* minority categories; differences in cultural orientation clarify more specifically *within* minority categories how individuals deal with their estrangement.

Considering the temporal limitations of the survey, residents being monitored only once, these observations on the primacy of structural processes retain a speculative nature. They rely heavily upon the premise that individuals' *perceived opportunity* is emblematic for their potential to participate in local activities, and to comply with local objectives. Among resident minorities I have focused upon divergent sources from which individuals derive their sense of opportunity. Young Moroccans experience with their Dutch affinities and social-cultural activities more local prospects than older more seclusive compatriots. More Turks derive hope, and security, from their involvement in Turkish networks that apparently enable labor market access. Among the Surinamese and Antilleans those who have completed higher education are generally more optimistic about their local prospects than similarly educated indigenous Dutch. These divergent channels of perceived opportunity could be aligned with various phases in the integration process that immigrants pursue. Before concluding that such phases are necessary, sequential, or teleological, more presumptions and observations must be made.

I will not continue this cognitively dissonant activity - stereotyping patterns of differentiation - for the more populous and therefore more diversified categories of 'Other' immigrants and indigenous Dutch. Instead I will conclude with more general observations on the significance of the empirical analysis.

Diversity in a Dutch City

The structured interviews among Haarlem residents reveal the endless variations in their integration process. With all the epistemological limitations bound to a single survey, the simple observation that 600 residents of the same locality provide such diffuse response patterns to the same hundred questions illustrates the need to perceive immigrant integration in differential terms. To round off this evaluation of the survey findings, I briefly consider their significance along methodological, theoretical and local policy lines.

Never before have representative samples of immigrant and indigenous residents within the same Dutch city been subjected to the same, comprehensive set of questions concerning local integration processes. The standardized survey represents in itself a concession to the diversity of social issues deemed pertinent for any particular group. A primary advantage is that systematic comparisons can be made to a statistical construct of 'the average resident,' and to (members of) other local groups. With measurements in all dimensions and domains of individual integration, concessions have been made to measurement adequacy. The comprehensiveness more adequately reflects the dynamic character of the integration process, while revealing the relative significance of divergent factors.

The comparison also sheds light upon theoretical issues. Assuming the generality of the local context and the integration criteria, it provides testimony for the primary importance of structural processes, particularly in domains of education and labor. Nevertheless, the acquisition of higher education and paid work is seen to be neither a necessary step nor a sufficient guarantee for individuals' integration. Although the results raise doubts as to the efficacy of a survey focus upon measures of cultural orientation, they do provide insights as to how immigrants differ in the way they perceive their own estrangement. Explanations for Turks' and Moroccans' lack of integration could be primarily seen in structural terms. Differences in cultural orientation and social behavior help clarify why within these minority categories some individuals are more optimistic about their local prospects than others. The Haarlem measures are significant not only for respondents' various perceptions of their own integration, but also for respondents' divergent perceptions of local integration. When integration is presumed to be a consensus as to the centripetal or centrifugal direction of local process, then research must focus more upon the relation between respondents' views, and their own social processes.

Finally the findings imply distinct - though not new - directions for local integration policy. These can be inferred from the conclusions above. Interventions in educational and labor domains should serve as focal points to enable individuals' equal access and optimal use. That such objectives imply a focus upon immigrant youth seems self-evident, but this is a moral issue. The findings reveal namely that a greater estrangement is found among an older generation of immigrants - jobless, minimally educated, disaffected and socially isolated. To rekindle these immigrants' prospects for education and work may exceed the capacity of local authority, but it can provide the social-cultural facilities to welcome these estranged migrant laborers back into the community. The survey exemplifies in short how research can differentiate, within the geo-political categorizations of minority policy, between the integrated and the estranged. It is ultimately a policy prerogative either to neglect or accommodate these groups, either to stigmatize or appreciate them.

8 Appreciating Immigrants

In the previous five chapters survey measurements made in one city have served as an empirical frame of reference. While ordering these measurements within a conceptual model their adequacy, and more generally that of empirical research on immigrant integration, has been reviewed. Many obstacles have been encountered that inhibit lucid clarifications for individuals' integration into urban environments. The review is a testimony to the limitations of social research, and its possibilities.

The emphasis in these final pages is upon the possibilities. More specifically, I address the issue how social research can contribute to the realization of localities in which cultural diversity is not construed as an impediment to local integration, but as an objective. The immigrant integration concept is widely associated with notions of assimilation or the melting pot, with their allusions to cultural absorption and dissolution. A primary motive behind this study has been to examine how it can be allied with notions of immigrant cultures as worthy of preservation and cultivation. With references to a *tolerant vision*, this motive has been professed whenever the normative character of integration criteria is considered.

By summarily reflecting upon these efforts to conceptualize and measure immigrants' integration, the potential for social research to monitor their integration into tolerant communities will be outlined. First the conceptual model will be used to elucidate the notion of integrated diversity. The idea of ranking residents as to their degree of integration will then be examined for the possibility of designating integrated inhabitants of tolerant communities. These conceptual and normative hermeneutics concern social processes that form the empirical object of social research. In a third section the functions of surveys, as complement to other techniques for discerning tolerant communities and their inhabitants, will be assessed. The contours of a research program will be briefly sketched, inasmuch as salient imbalances have been encountered in this study. As these reflections assume that the social sciences fulfill an auxiliary function for social policy and society, a final section addresses the purpose and practice of policy on immigrant integration.

Conceptual Contours of a Tolerant Vision

A formal model of immigrant integration provides the conceptual foundation for this study. The model is largely inspired by the framework Schermerhorn (1970) proposed for the study of ethnic relations within nation-states. His work is particularly germane in that he sees integration not only in processes in which culturally divergent groups are literally fused into a single culture, but also in social processes that lead to increasing cultural diffusion. Emblematic for integration is that subordinate groups agree upon and pursue the communal *objectives* set forth by superordinate groups. Schermerhorn distinguishes integration then from processes of 'forced assimilation' or 'forced segregation.' These distinctions help specify the notion of integrated diversity as denoting processes in which local residents agree upon and comply with objectives of cultural diversity.

Diversity pertains here to *cultural* processes, one of three central *dimensions* of local integration distinguished in the formal model. The tolerant vision is outlined further by communal objectives concerning the other two dimensions. Within the *structural* dimension it refers to objectives of civil liberty (i.e., a minimum of state intervention), which are conceptually opposed to objectives of social equality characteristic for more egalitarian visions. Within the *interactive* dimension it refers to objectives of (interethnic) inclusion, which are opposed to objectives of (interethnic) exclusion more exemplary for so-called pillarized visions. Social interactions within and between groups are widely conceived as a manifestation of either structure or culture. The merits of a conceptual distinction in a third - interactive - dimension can be discerned where a tolerant vision is literally enhanced by interethnic exchanges.

Six *domains* of local integration have been differentiated in the model. All domains could be characterized by the cultural polarities espoused in a tolerant vision. Limitations are needed however, as a complete lack of consensus concerning what individuals should know, believe and need reflects more a vison of anomie and anarchy than of toleration. The acceptable range of diversification within and across local domains is clearly a substantive issue, the continuous focus of political and academic debate. Rex (1996:14ff) argues for instance that objectives of cultural diversity are viable only within the private domain and, to a certain extent, in the domain of education and upbringing. In other domains it might legitimate state and civil practices of differential treatment that would conflict with the inclusive objectives of the tolerant vision.

The tension between the toleration of cultural diversity and exclusionary practices alludes to *temporal* issues. Are there conceivable phases by the realization of tolerant communities, in which differential treatment effectuates a more equitable end? The Dutch experience with cultural minority policies is characterized for instance by state interventions to establish and to support separate educational, welfare, labor and social-cultural facilities for specific immigrant groups. These are widely construed as temporary in nature, instrumental for the preservation of minority cultures, but only until minorities have acquired access to - or are no longer excluded from - communal facilities. For the realization of tolerant objectives the issue is not *whether* cultural diversity should be facilitated by state interventions, but *when*. Provided the cultural practice of minorities is not in conflict with communal objectives, when should the state intervene to curb their forced assimilation? Such questions represent ongoing issues; any consensus on the toleration of cultural and interactive practices - and the legitimacy of state encroachments on civil liberties - is temporary.

This study has focused upon relations between non-Europeans and more indigenous residents of a Dutch locality. The notion of cultural diversity however is not limited to eventual differences between immigrant and indigenous cultures. Cultural polarities characterize all local domains, and these have no intrinsic conjunction with immigrant-indigenous distinctions. This depends upon the *perspective(s)* taken to appraise the integration process. The issue being raised here is the designation of minority groups and their spokespersons, as the legitimation of local integration hinges upon their compliance with the activities and objectives of a local 'majority.' For instance, I can identify no formal reason that a group of indigenous residents, whose unique neighborhood culture is about to be destroyed by urban renewal projects, embody any less a minority perspective. Reasoning less formally, I observe Europeans to be culturally diverse; their variant perspectives on immigrant integration signify their appreciation of *perpetual* diversification.

This brings me to a final distinction, which concerns the *level* upon which integration is conceived and perceived. The tolerant vision is formulated here as a perception of integration directives at the local level of an urban setting. To conceive such processes without allusions to a national or European level is admittedly quite taxing, as localities evolve within more extensive state and civil contexts. References to immigrant, minority or ethnic groups, and their variant cultural cohesions, allude to integration processes at a group level. This study has focused primarily upon processes between *individuals*, but then individuals who reside in the same urban setting. To appraise the integration of individual residents, a correspondence had to be presumed between personal criteria and local objectives. What criteria could possibly be applied to identify the integrated residents of a tolerant community? This explicitly normative issue is addressed in the next section.

Appraising Residents of the Tolerant Community

No localities exist, at least in European societies, that exemplify the objectives of the tolerant vision. A portrayal of its inhabitants is then largely the product of speculation. Problematic presumptions must be made, particularly concerning two of the integration parameters. The first has just been mentioned, namely the relation between processes at individual and at local *level*. Here a one-on-one correspondence is presumed: individuals are a reflection of their local surroundings, which on its part is the sum of its separate inhabitants. Sociologists since Durkheim have taken issue with these premises, as we perceive individuals not as witless cogs in social machines, nor do these individuals have the machine under control. More specifically, a tolerant community cannot compel its residents to underwrite objectives of cultural diversity. Should all residents endorse such objectives, this does not necessarily yield a diversified community. Nevertheless, the normative supposition is made here that compliance with community objectives signifies the more integrated inhabitant.

The second presumption concerns integration's *temporal* character, namely that the realization of a tolerant community proceeds via the gradual accretion of integrated residents. Besides its obvious relation with the first presumption, the key word here is *gradual*. A case could be made for the dialectical premise that local integration evolves more through cataclysmic phases. For instance, before major portions of the populace learn to appreciate tolerant objectives, perhaps they can better first experience totalitarian apartheid regimes. However, to keep this treatise lucid and consistent, the supposition is made here that the integrated resident meets end-goal criteria, and not the eventually conflicting criteria of an intermediate phase.

The criteria themselves are delineated in the formal model. They are a combination of *end-goals* associated with the three primary dimensions of individual integration. In the forthcoming paragraphs the criteria, and more operational measures, are summarized sequentially.

The individual counterparts for structural objectives of civil liberty are presumed to be positional end-goals of *self-reliance*. More specifically, the integrated inhabitant of the tolerant community is not dependent upon state interventions for the acquisition of social goods in the various local domains. This criterion relies upon two assumptions: that the state only intervenes to provide necessary social services for those inhabitants who are otherwise condemned to socially marginalized roles, and that these services are accessible for all who need them. In this study a combination of measures for personal income and the use of local social services represent residents' integration according to the self-reliance criterion.

Individual counterparts for cultural objectives of diversity are orientational end-goals of *personality*. This criterion should not be confused with the personality concept used in psychology, which refers formally to the mental and behavioral attributes characteristic of any individual. It is used here to signify diversification from the orientational conformity of cultural clones: the personality goal is a pattern of knowledge, beliefs and affections that is optimally unique. In operational terms this end-goal presents paradoxical measurement problems because in a locality that prides itself on the lack of cultural clones there are, by definition, no norms to rank diversifications in personality. The key word is *optimal*. Rather than focusing upon the infinite means in which orientations diverge, the issue is the designation of orientational aspects that individuals should minimally share for the pursuance of tolerant objectives. These are in my view quite minimal, as individuals should not be condemned for the way they think, only for their social behavior. Measures of individuals' convictions concerning tolerant objectives of civil liberty, cultural diversity, and social inclusion may suffice. However for the integration criteria applied in this study such measures were not used, in part because they revealed little consensus between immigrants and indigenous residents regarding tolerant objectives. Instead the index contained measures for individuals' perceived opportunity and satisfaction with their local situation. These criteria refer to prerequisites at group level for the realization of a tolerant vision, namely that immigrant groups compare favorably with indigenous groups as to their (variant) appreciation of local processes. Formulated more concretely, as long as particular groups are less optimistic about their local prospects, then state interventions are needed to secure a more equitable intercultural exchange.

Tolerant objectives of *inclusion* are reflected by individuals' (congenial) exchanges with divergent 'others.' In operational terms this criterion emulates proportional differences in representation. When for instance 20% of the residents of a tolerant community are immigrants, then 20% of any individual's local contacts should be with immigrants. The austerity of such a criterion is presumably a boon for statisticians and proponents of positive action. Its application however raises theoretical and policy issues that have been the subject of countless studies, including this one. The theoretical issues concern the task of unraveling clarifications about why the criterion is not met. By social policy, issues of legitimacy arise when promoting inclusive behavior. Assuming processes of stigmatization and discrimination to be entirely social in their nature, no inherent reason remains in my view why a criterion of proportional contacts could not be applied in all civic domains. It was not however applied in this study. As behavioral criterion a measure for participation in local social-cultural activities was used. This criterion is presumed to measure *sociability* - behavior that increases one's prospects of encountering divergent locals.

In short, the integrated resident of the tolerant community endorses local objectives, is self-reliant and, while complying with minimum norms of social conduct, participates in culturally diverse networks of local exchange. An index of Haarlem residents' relative success in meeting these criteria has fulfilled a central role in this study. Its use required the explication of methodological, theoretical and normative presumptions, while it serves primarily to simplify the complex relation between divergent criteria. In exchange for these presumptions and reductions, the index represents in one measure the multidimensional, multilevel nature of the local integration process. It has served to identify and compare impediments to integration encountered by new residents. Moreover, the index has helped reveal aspects of integration that need more research attention, particularly concerning the development of survey instruments. The more compelling revelations are considered in the next section.

Measuring Immigrant Integration

How can survey research contribute to the realization of tolerant communities? First, the survey provides a means to qualify the popular support for tolerant objectives. The stipulation of this normative range - across local domains and across 'majority' and 'minority' groups - is crucial to the delineation of tolerant communities and their integrated residents. The survey addressed this issue and revealed fundamental differences between and within immigrant and indigenous groups. However, before surveys serve as a legitimate means to monitor inhabitants' convictions concerning the desired direction of local integration processes, more adequate instruments must be developed.

No matter how community objectives are ordained - preferably via democratic electoral processes - surveys can help identify the more and less integrated residents. Conceivably the same instruments that require further development to detect the desired direction of local integration processes can be used to monitor individuals' endorsement of tolerant objectives. For end-goal criteria of self-reliance I have illustrated the possibilities to rank individuals according to their positions in other domains besides *work and material security*. The reliability and validity of such measures can be readily improved upon, although the development of standardized instruments that enable interlocal comparisons is impeded by local variations in social welfare facilities, and by the differential access these services have. Instruments to measure end-goal criteria of inclusive social behavior are, at least in the Netherlands, rarely encountered in empirical research. Network analysis provides definite prospects for further survey refinement. In short, the possibilities are clearly available to develop more adequate local indices that rank residents according to their compliance with tolerant objectives.

Beyond a survey practice, in which normative criteria are applied to distinguish between the integrated and the estranged, lies the theoretical practice in which explanations are sought for the distinctions discerned. Here is where the possibilities never end. A primary motive behind the presentation of the formal model was the need for a conceptual framework with which clarifications for immigrants' local integration could be compared and evaluated. The literature offers a wealth of theoretical models concerning immigrant integration (e.g., Goldlust and Richmond, 1973; Shadid, 1979; Esser, 1980; Mullard et al., 1990; Engbersen and Gabriëls, 1995b; McLeod et al., 1996; Swyngedouw et al., 1999; Vermeulen and Penninx, 2000). However, none of the models encountered provides the survey researcher with a framework of parameters that reveal whether measurements are comprehensive, and where alternative clarifications for differences in integration could be sought.

Having used the model to order and evaluate survey data, I find a comprehensive instrument to be clearly infeasible, assuming that an arbitrary respondent is unwilling to undergo an entire day of interrogation. The analysis presented in the previous four chapters does suggest that, in comparison with measures of orientation and social behavior, measures of individuals' variant positions are more expediently surveyed. Moreover, the positional measures are consistently more significant, in statistical terms, when seeking clarification for differences in individuals' integration scores. This could be construed as testimony for the primacy of structural processes by immigrant integration. However, when clarifying differences *within* (Moroccan and Turkish) minority groups, orientational and behavioral measures are seen to be comparably explanatory. Succinctly stated, I surmise that when entire groups are structurally marginalized, the more compliant derive their prospects from specific cultural affinities and social activities. The model provides a framework for theories on immigrants' integration, but before such theories clarify the complex relation between dimensions and domains of local integration more adequate and comprehensive measures must be made. Meanwhile, more longitudinal surveys must be conducted to monitor the integration dynamic through time.

This study has focused upon the possibilities provided by survey methods to measure individuals' integration within a local context. That other methods of empirical observation are necessary to support, complement and confute such measures has been noted throughout the study. Already the formal distinction in levels of integration alludes to processes at national and global level whose significance for the realization of civil liberty, cultural diversity and social inclusion are more than everything the local schools could ever provide. Indeed, a primary reason I have refrained from reformulating the survey findings into a causal theory is that the observations remain short-sighted, particularly concerning processes at local level and higher. Within the local context, the use of complementary research methods is essential to understanding structural and interactive processes, as many now classic studies have testified (e.g., Elias and Scotson, 1965; Rex and Tomlinson, 1979; Wilson, 1987). To perceive the local markets where social goods are produced and exchanged, the researcher needs to combine a diversity of perspectives. Otherwise, there is literally no basis to interpret survey measures of individual opportunity, self-reliance, and expressed behavior. Particularly concerning the observation of behavior, complementary perspectives are needed that discern more than the potential for inclusive contacts within a given domain. Why do individuals fail to capitalize on the possibilities for intercultural contact? When is exclusive behavior motivated by a conscious avoidance of cultural differ-ence, and when by a sensory incapacity to recognize diversity? Such issues, and many more like them, require insights from various (interdisciplinary) viewpoints before survey instruments can be relied upon to monitor individuals' compliance with tolerant objectives of interethnic inclusion.

Succinctly stated, surveys can stipulate the objectives of a tolerant community, identify residents who comply with community norms, and help clarify how local objectives and individual end-goals are met. However, like any research method surveys lack objectivity while they alter reality. They should be integrated within a program of research that, in its diversity and dynamics, reflects the process it purportedly perceives and explicates.

Social Policy and Immigrant Integration

A vision is outlined here of a community in which immigrant and indigenous residents exchange their social goods in a process of continuous diversification, subject to a minimum on control and revision by state authority. The vision would be naive if one inferred that it could be realized with a minimum on state interventions. On the contrary, it is based on the presumption that the state occupies a central role in directing the integration process.

The state referred to here is an entity as continuous as the migration occurring at its borders. Despite the focus in this study upon the local context, the perspective is taken from the vantage point of a European community, in which the political, economic and cultural barriers that divide nations have gradually disappeared. The globalization process, clearly if not consistently advancing across the European continent, has its implications for all levels of state authority. At the local level it implies that immigrants can no longer be treated as temporary residents, such as migrant laborers and colonial compatriots were so often viewed in the past. The continuous migration of individuals and groups into and throughout Europe confronts the local authority with the task of mediating the integration process between indigenous and immigrant groups.

Applying Schermerhorn's distinction between centripetal and centrifugal trends, coupled with the distinction in three dimensions, I have identified eight hypothetical visions of immigrant integration. A centripetal alternative to the tolerant vision, calling for the pursuance of cultural unity instead of cultural diversity, has been denoted the *assimilative* vision. Considering the continuously prominent role the notion of assimilation occupies in European policies on immigrant integration it represents a serious response to globalization processes. Reasoning within the conceptual framework, I need to emphasize two conditions bound to the pursuance of an assimilative vision. First, it calls for the compliance of *both* indigenous *and* immigrant inhabitants. Like any local objective, policy prerogatives of cultural unity without compliance are - per definition - non integrative. Second, the assimilative vision signifies the evolution of a new, communal culture, a literal melting pot infused with indigenous and immigrant cultural elements. This condition is rooted in the premise that interactions between culturally diverse groups alter the culture of both groups. To consider integration as a one-way process of immigrant adaptation is no longer assimilative. It denotes instead a *racialized* vision, in which an exclusive bastion is built to protect the illusion of a local culture from global influences. The tolerant vision is less reactionary, as it appreciates the continuous cultural impulse of immigration (cf. Walzer, 1997:48ff).

What are then the implications of the tolerant vision for local policy? Simply stated, the endorsement and pursuance of tolerant objectives. With reference to the terminology that has symbolized local policy directives the past decennia, this does not imply a choice for either 'multi-cultural,' 'minority' or 'participation' policies. Dependent upon the prosperity, diversity and harmony of local circumstance, integration policies are a combination of all three. Objectives of multi-culturalism - the preference here is for the less static and stigmatic notion of *diversification* - are embodied by the encouragement of cultural innovation, be it the innovation of immigrant expression, or the improvisation upon more indigenous symbols. Cultural policies however are not limited to the promotion of post-modern folklore; they more generally concern the embracement of difference within the moral framework of the global community. Objectives of civil liberty are pursued not so much by principles of state laissez-faire, more by the provision of educational opportunity for all, and welfare services for the needy. When the needy are concentrated in particular groups, this may require the implementation of so-called *minority* policies. Finally, objectives of inclusion are pursued through policies that dismantle potentially discriminatory barriers to immigrants' local interaction and *participation*.

These principles, simultaneously speculative and personal, are in need of further specification within local domains. They are presented here as divergence to the notion of local political administrations, in liberal democracies, as an intermediary between national interests and citizens' volition. A tolerant community is not served by intimations to seek its own civil course while the local administration languishes in the role of technocratic manager. Authority implies the dissemination of a vision in which the prerequisites for local integration are specified, and the civic responsibilities are shared.

Notes

Chapter One

1   Schermerhorn formulated a more precise definition: '... integration is not an end-state but a process whereby units or elements of a society are brought into an active and coordinated compliance with the ongoing activities and objectives of the dominant group in that society' (1970:14).

2   This issue of divergent policy objectives became explicit when, again with Utrecht University colleagues, we advised the city of Utrecht to merge minority policies into more general policies focused upon the alleviation of social deprivation (Burgers et al., 1996). How should Utrecht officials delineate and locate the socially deprived? Had we alternatively targeted the 'socially isolated' or 'intolerant resident' what criteria and instruments could be implemented to identify those residents who should benefit directly from such policies?

Chapter Two

1   Immigrant categorizations that focus only upon differences in nationality (i.e. citizenship) exclude those residents with origins in the colonial Dutch West or East Indies. The exclusion of third generation or more implies that a number of inhabitants who are targeted by minority policy, including caravan-dwellers and Moluccan youth, are categorized as indigenous Dutch. Like most local Dutch registry offices, Haarlem's does not register foreign descent past the second generation.

2   Complementing the definition of immigrant, the indigenous Dutch are those individuals born in the Netherlands, whose parents were both born in the Netherlands.

3   Schermerhorn asserted that a specific relation exists between the three variables highlighted here: 'the first two deal with the former relationship (between subordinates and dominant groups) and are correlative with each other; the third variable operationalizes the latter relation (between subordinates and the society as a whole)' (1970:16).

4   For the identification and formulation of these three issues, I was initially inspired by theoretical distinctions made by Thurlings (1977:127-242). Despite the influence of his work for Dutch research (cf. Musschenga, 1986; Choenni, 1992; Reinsch et al, 1995; Fermin, 1997), the distinctions made here display more parallels with Schermerhorn's framework.

5   The formulation of dimensional issues in terms of dilemmas is based upon Thurlings (1977). The perception of social structures and social inequality as the competition of

individuals and groups upon various commodity markets is inspired by - though not strictly derived from - Banton (1983).

6   Another implication is that socalled 'black' or 'informal' market segments, where state regulations and interventions are minimal, are not construed as separate or unregulated sectors. Such segments are perhaps subject to alternative patterns of regulation, but they do not constitute an autonomous or 'bastard' domain (cf. Peters, 1993:175ff; Engbersen and Gabriëls, 1995b:30ff; Rath, 1995) upon which alternative goods are exchanged.

7   Pressing the metaphor that launched this section, let me reformulate the issue as follows. At a macro level a profusion of markets is perceived; at a micro level one sees a mass of individuals frantically maneuvering to improve their prospects, trading simultaneously on all these markets. These individuals can be likened to the hyperactive brokers on the floor of a stock exchange. What about those with paid work on the labor market: do they represent islands of relative tranquility in this volatile chaos, able to maneuver with ease and efficiency?

8   Besides the use of *other* when referring to an individual's relation to individuals or entire categories with a divergent geo-political origin, I will extensively use the term 'Other' (i.e. with a capital 'O') in the forthcoming chapters when referring to (Haarlem) immigrants who are not included in one of the three minority categories.

9   That, within the formal conceptual model, individual behavior is not a micro complement to local interactions reflects the conceptual tensions between contacts and behavior. The difference for instance between actual and potential contacts is quantifiable, while 'behaviors' are more difficult to perceive and count. On the other hand, the behavioral nature of any direct contact between individuals indicates how problematic quantification may be. The problem partially resides in the unit of analysis, as any communication, intimacy, object, service, etc. that an individual exchanges with another individual can be broken down into a continuous number of contacts. This methodological issue, bound to the distinction between contacts and ties, will be considered in chapter six.

10   A definition of discrimination influential in Dutch ethnic studies is 'the unequal treatment of individuals or groups due to attributes that in the context of interaction are irrelevant' (Elich and Maso, 1984:10ff). With this definition, discrimination is a particular form of exclusion in which 1) ethnic descent (for example) serves as conscious reason for the differential treatment, and 2) this ethnic disparity is not considered a legitimate reason for differential treatment.

11   Characteristic for Dutch local policies has been the establishment of separate channels of negotiation and political debate in which 'minority representatives' communicate directly with civic officials. The potential this process harbors to marginalize immigrant categories in local politics has been demonstrated by Rath (1991).

12   Based on research in Rotterdam' neighborhoods, Anderiessen and Reijndorp (1991) observed that indigenous Dutch and Surinamese, particularly single mothers on welfare, more often sustain family networks so that a significant portion of their everyday lives take place in a limited area of the city. Immigrants originating from Mediterranean lands maintain contacts with family and friends who are spread much more throughout the city, and continent.

13   The practice of positive action policies reflect the fundamental dilemmas contained within egalitarian visions that focus upon ethnically stratified manifestaions of social inequality. On the one hand, they propagate the preferential treatment of individuals from socially deprived categories, and are consequently (overly) sensitive to 'color'. On the other hand the preferential treatment is based on the presumption that these individuals possess qualifications articulated within dominant cultures. The treatment is consequently 'blind' to the eventual qualifications articulated within subordinate (e.g. 'immigrant') cultures.

14   The 'tolerant' qualification in its everyday connotation ('able to withstand extremes') is misleading in that it alludes to (behavioral) discomfort and (cultural) arrogance. I find more appropriate everyday terms such as 'open-minded' or 'permissive' rather awkward. The term utilized here corresponds with Walzer's higher degrees of toleration cited above in the sub-section on cultural orientation (1993:5): '3) openness to others, curiosity, respect, a willingness to listen and learn; and 4) the enthusiastic endorsement of difference'.

Chapter Three

1   The percentages are based upon data supplied by the Haarlem registry office pertaining to all registered inhabitants born prior to 15 March 1976 (n = 122,842 as of 15 March 1994). Among immigrant Haarlemmers, an estimated 10% are (second generation and) native to the city.

2   For discriminant analysis for instance, a minimum of 20 subjects per variable is advised (Stevens, 1996:288). A MANOVA analysis examining the effect of six variables within six distinct groups requires anywhere from 21 to 170 subjects per group, dependent upon the expected effect (Stevens, 1996:229). The larger the sample however, the more likely correlations between two variables meet criteria of statistical significance.

3   These two groups are necessarily combined as their local populations are too small to warrant multi-variate analysis techniques. The decision refers in part to the two (neighboring) regions historical-cultural antecedents as Dutch colonies. 24 of the 77 respondents in this category are of Dutch Antillean origin.

4   For the analyses in the forthcoming chapters, the 'Other' immigrants (note the capital 'O') have been classified into one of four regions of origin, namely: Western Europe (50 respondents, including 27 of German origin and one each from Australia, South Africa and the USA), Indonesia (a former Dutch colony, 29 respondents), Eastern Europe (11, including 5 from former Yugoslavia), and a rest category of 11 from the 'poor world' (6 from the continent of Africa and 5 from southern Asia). We failed to ascertain whether any of these respondents are - as political refugees - also targeted by Dutch minority policies.

5   The percentage of the total Haarlem population (149,788) comprised by these five categories is: Turks 3.1%, Moroccans 1.6%, Surinamese/Antilleans 1.6%, Other immigrants 11.3% and indigenous Dutch 82.5%. These figures are based upon an internal report from Haarlem's research and statistics bureau, and refer to the situation as of 1 January 1992 (see Reinsch et al., 1995:39). The estimated national percentages on that date were, respectively: 1.6%, 1.3%, 2.3%, 10.4% and 84.4% (Martens et al., 1994:16).

6   In the Haarlem survey for instance, five duration factors were measured: 1) age, 2) years since immigration, 3) duration of residence in Haarlem, 4) in the neighborhood and 5) in the present residence. Pearson correlations between these factors for all first generation immigrants (weighted n=215) range between .57 and .85. The entry of all five factors in multiple regression analyses - the technique applied in the coming chapters to estimate the relative significance of integration indicators - leads to unacceptable tolerance levels, i.e. the effect of one factor cannot be discerned while controlling for the effect of the other four (see e.g. Martens and Veenman, 1997).

7   The Haarlem stratified samples were representative for the five sub-populations, according to X^2 tests for age and sex distributions. Residential duration and district concentrations deviated from population distributions for several ethnic categories (see Reinsch et.al., 1995:259 ff). For all analysis results presented here, these deviations were corrected with weighting factors. One deviation was not corrected: only one interview was realized among adult Surinamese/Antilleans in Haarlem-East, where seven interviews should have been held.

8   Table 3.3 would become more complex were all the relevant totals presented upon which percentages are drawn. Most of these can be derived via interpolation, for instance the fact that 75 Turkish women were eventually interviewed with an actual participation of 80% implies that contact was originally realized with a total of (75(100÷80)=) 94 Turkish women. The item non-response percentages are mean scores per category, percentuated from 100 possible missings. The interview durations are also mean scores per category, presented in minutes.

9   The actual response percentages for Moroccan and Turkish women interviewed by men (100% resp. 76%) are misleading in that many of these interviews were arranged via the mediation of third parties (e.g. fieldwork coordinators).

10   According to interviewers, the proportion affected by others present ranged from 10% of all the Surinamese and Antilleans to 18% of the Moroccan respondents. Particularly partners tend to take issue, but also many school-aged children reacted openly to the opinions expressed by their parents.

11   It also fails to take into account that individuals may be far more 'sociable' in neighboring localities, where they for instance find more opportunity to cultivate either inclusive or seclusive ties.

12   For instance, immigrants' proportional contact with local ties (as opposed to their non-local ties) could be construed as a measure of their local affinity and sociability. However, this potential index component does not correlate sufficiently with the other five components for *all* residents, due to the weak correlations within the largest ethnic category: the indigenous Dutch. Whereas Haarlem immigrants indeed tend to score more integrated who have a surplus of local ties, this does not apply for the 'typical' resident (see further chapter six, section four).

13   Actually, first the item-non responses were recoded on the two components with a significant percentge of missings (namely per capita income and perceived opportunity, ± 10%) to the mean value per ethnic category. For the remaining missing values, the principal component analysis was conducted with substitution to the local mean.

14 In the search for a single index, an auxiliary criteria by the analysis was a variation upon the socalled scree test, the maximum difference between the variances accounted for by the first and second component extracted (see Stevens, 1996:366). The second component in this solution accounted for 20.2% of the components' variance. According to Stevens, components are reliable derivations when at least four of the contributing items have loadings of .60 or more. The component fails to meet this criteria, but the limited number of contributing items serves as an extenuating circumstance.

15 The fact that the standard deviation within each ethnic category is just less than 1.0 signifies that an alternative observation - the percentage within a category who is more integrated than the average resident - is slightly less. For instance, the estimated percentage 'better than average integration' is among the Moroccans not 7% but 5%. Within the other four ethnic categories, the estimated percentage residents less integrated than the average respondent are (reading from left to right in table 3.4): 11% for Turks, 35%, 46% respectively 53% for indigenous Dutch. Based on the standard deviation, the 'estimates' for respondents more integrated than the average resident are respectively: 10%, 34%, 45% and 53%. The 'actual' percentage of respondents within the sub-samples with positive integration scores is respectively: 4%, 9%, 35%, 50% and 58%.

16 The effect of interviewers' gender (η=.19) can be attributed largely to the fact that several multi-lingual women were employed for the interviews with those 'Other' immigrants who presumably (based on their 'poor world' geo-political origin and residential duration) would have difficulty with questions posed in Dutch.

17 In order to arrive at this and all other measures for 'All immigrants', the data set was reweighed to correct for the stratified nature of the four sub-samples. After correction, 37% of all Haarlem immigrants could be considered 'minorities' according to national policies (including 'Other' immigrants from Portugal, Italy and former Yugoslavia), 31% to be 'Western European' (including Australians, South Africans and Americans), 21% 'Dutch Indonesian', while 11% orginated from 'other' (i.e. Eastern European, African and Asian) regions.

18 A combination of generation and age factors was also examined, distinguishing between 'pioniers' (arriving before 1974), 'first' generation (arriving between 1974 and 1984), 'newcomers' (arriving after 1984) and 'second'generation (born in the Netherlands, or arriving after 1984 younger than 13) (cf. Swyngedouw et al., 1999:73). The categorization indicates that the 'second generation' are more integrated in all four immigrant categories; their mean degree of integration being equal to the 'average' resident. The differences in index scores clarified by this categorization are significant only among Moroccans and Turks (η=.38 resp..25).

19 For instance, the four districts with the highest mean scores (*Duinwijk, Spoorbaan Leiden, Oude Stad* and *Molenwijk*) house 27% of all adult residents but only 16% of the Turks and 12% of the Moroccans. 30% of the adult population resides in the four districts (*Haarlem-Oost* and the three *Schalkwijk* districts) with the lowest mean index scores, where 52% of the Turks and 60% of the Moroccans reside.

Chapter Four

1   This not only suggests immigrants' faith in meritocratic principles. Educational opportunity *is* one of the three items within the *perceived opportunity* component (see chapter five). That individuals' perceived educational opportunity correlates with the actual level of education completed seems self evident (cf. Reinsch et al., 1995:140).

2   The 'subjective' nature of this categorization should be noted. No effort was made to check the reliability of respondents' answers, nor were they questioned concerning the formal status of their position. We consequently do not know, for instance: the nature of the jobs held, who is legally employed, the eventual salary received, the search behavior of the jobless or whether they are registered at the regional labor exchange. The categories deviate in other ways from CBS distinctions between an active and a potential labor force (cf. Schiepers et al., 1993:9): part-time workers include all respondents who work on averge 1 to 32 hours/week (27% of these work less than 12); the disabled/retired category contains all respondents who explain their inactive position as primarily a physical disability, and all jobless respondents older than 65. 28 of the respondents said they were self-employed: 15% of the indigenous Dutch, 4% of the Surinamese/Antilleans, and 2% of the 'Other' immigrants.

3   A comparison with percentages obtained from national surveys (Martens, 1995:119) suggests that Haarlem Morrocans, Turks and indigenous Dutch are generally more active upon the labor market (with nationally the active labor force comprising respectively 37%, 43% and 63% of the potential labor force). The percentage jobless of the active labor force appears for all minority categories to be less than national percentages.

4   Respondents simply had to locate their net income in one of nine categories, ranging from 'less than $f1100$' to 'more than $f3900$' (cf. Martens and Veenman, 1996:126). Household income aggregates were then based upon the midpoint of each category, with $f900$ and $f4100$ serving as midpoint for the lowest resp. highest categories.

5   The statistic is namely the household income estimate divided by a budgetary equivalence factor. The latter is based on the number of adults and children within the household (a single adult = 1.00, each additional adult adds $\pm$ 0.4 and each child $\pm$ 0.25 to the factor, see CBS, 1996:102).

6   All nine categories are characterized as *social services* in the theorerical sense that they support processes of social reproduction, and in the practical sense that they are state financed institutions. Such non-commercial services can be differentiated from *producer services* that support industrial production, and from *personal services* that are privately run enterprises directed towards individual consumption and leisure (see Esping-Andersen, 1990:196).

7   The divergent percentages require some explication. Many services may not be used directly by respondents themselves, but by children in their household (e.g. day-care, schools, activity centers). This may help explain why indigenous Dutch (most of whose households are characterized by a lack of young children) make relatively little use of such services. Why relatively few Moroccans make use of youth services and sport facilities, though a large majority reside in households with young children, begs further explanation. Few respondents gave credence to the premise that exclusionary practices

limit their access to local social services (see Reinsch et al., 1995:128ff).

8   The statistical order was calculated with a homogeneity analysis technique (see van de Geer, 1993). The two dimensional solution provided respondent scores for the number of social services utilized along the first dimension. The second dimension reflected the spectrum presented here: the relative possibility that a respondent is engaged in a particular area of the social service market. The location of each service type along this mathematical spectrum was subsequently used to calculate respondents' market position. The divergent weights, presented here in accordance with their rank-order in table 4.8, are -.299, -.217, -.200, -.096, .000, .016, .036, .165 and .261. By applying the respective weight to each service utilized, respondents' cumulative scores ranged from -.81('dire straits') to .48 ('easy straits'). The mean, before standardization, was -.11 with a standard deviation of .29. The standardized scores summarized in table 4.9 are re-weighed to correct for sampling stratification.

9   The Haarlem sample contained ten neighborhood clusters in which immigrants were 'concentrated' and which together constituted one-third (197/600) of the total survey. These respondents, although they had more than random chance to be selected, have been included in analyses as they did not affect the total survey representativity in terms of age, gender or local district. They have been excluded from the overview presented in table 4.11 however, as they are inordinately residents of 'inauspicious' neighborhoods.

10   The statistic is sensitive to the fact that relatively few minorities reside in '(very) auspicious' neighborhoods, all of whom evaluated their neighborhood positively. It is the gradation between 'very inauspicious' and 'typical' that elicited relatively invariant evaluations from 'minority' residents.

11   Beyond the qualifications presented in the previous note, the (lack of) explanatory potential is due in part to the fact that the four districts of *Schalkwijk* are not differentiated into smaller neighborhoods with variant status

12   When the data analysis includes all Haarlem immigrants (weighted to correct for survey stratification) it is indeed variances in these three components within the local index that are significantly accounted for by variations in neighborhood status.

13   In the Netherlands immigrants must legally reside five years in a city before acquiring the right to participate (actively and passively) in local elections. They must be Dutch citizens to participate in national elections.

Chapter Five

1   With this singular focus upon ethnicity as primary cultural polarity, I forego the possibility to examine cultural differences aligned with social class. While I personally harbor the conviction that more explanatory value can be derived from monitoring the social class in which individuals are born and raised, the Haarlem survey data provides little opportunity to distinguish between class orientations (cf. Miles, 1982; Feddema, 1991; Hof and Dronkers, 1993; Roelandt, 1994).

2   Van Heelsum's instrument included identification with pre-ordained categiories. The

percentages she observes among second generation Surinamese do compare remarkably with our Haarlem findings for Surinamese and Antilleans (1997:88). In her study however, the percentage 'hyphenated' among the 'Dutch' Surinamese is significantly lower: one quarter of the 57%. In Haarlem they comprised three fifths of the 57%.

3   To this end, a method initially developed by Kuhn and McPartland (1954) has often been applied (Verkuyten, 1992:135). Respondents are asked to enter any number of categorizations and dispositions to complete 'I am ...' statements. The order and proportion of references to ethnic categories may then indicate the salience of ethnicity within respondent's self-identification. Van Heelsum (1997:82ff) applied the method in her study, and observed that a majority of second generation Surinamese refrained from any ethnic reference whatsoever.

4   In Penninx' conceptual model for 'ethnic-cultural position' (1988), the allocation of ethnic attributes by the host culture is a central component. Van Heelsum's survey instrument (1997) also monitors how second generation Surinamese perceive this allocation process..

5   Only two sets of survey questions solicited ethnic imagery. In one we asked respondents to designate which of six ethnic groups had adapted itself most (and least) to make Haarlem a 'viable' city. That 'Hollanders' (i.e. indigenous Dutch) generally ranked high according to all ethnic categories would suggest that 'forced assimilation' (see figure 1.1) is not a local issue. That 'Moroccan-Dutch' generally ranked least adapted, even according to Moroccans, would indicate that their integration - irrespective of the community vision - *is* a local issue. In the second imagery question, respondents were asked their preference for a next-door neighbor in terms of ethnic origin. A majority within all ethnic categories expressed 'no preference'.

6   This generalization requires qualification. There has been research concerning immigrants' images of the Dutch (most notably Willems and Cottaar, 1989; Willems, 1998), and survey research concerning specific images, particularly the Dutch as racist/intolerant and discriminatory (e.g. Rişvanoğlu-Bilgin et al., 1986; Veraart, 1996; van Heelsum, 1997). But no systematic survey measurements concerning the diversity and prevalence of ethnic imagery.

7   The four dimensions along which respondents' so-called 'mental programs' could be characterized were labeled 'power distance,' 'individualism,' 'masculinity,' and 'uncertainty avoidance.' In terms of immigrants' central integration dilemmas presented here, power distance pertains mainly to issues of dependence or deprivation, individualism and masculinity to conformity or personality, and uncertainty avoidance to exclusion or solitude

8   Hofstede differentiates between values concerning 'the desirable' and 'the desired' (1980:20ff). 'The desirable' refers to what *ought* to be desired by people in general. Such values express direction; the corresponding norm has an absolute or ideological nature while terms commonly used to measure individuals' orientation are 'good,' 'right,' 'agree' and 'should.' The 'desired' refers to what individuals (i.e. survey respondents) actually desire for themselves. Such values expres intensity; the corresponding norm has more a phenomenological or pragmatic nature while terms commonly used to measure individuals' orientation are 'important,' 'successful,' 'attractive' and 'preferred.' Throughout this chapter, the distinction made between individuals'beliefs and their affections closely

correspond with the distinction between the desired and the desirable.

9   See for instance the special issue of the Journal of Cross Cultural Psychology (January 1998, volume 29, number 1) devoted to developments in international research on the FFM.

10   The Harvard Encyclopedia of American Ethnic Groups (Thernstrom, 1980) lists a total of 14 criteria empirically applied to characterize ethnic groups: 1) geo-political origin, 2) migratory status, 3) race, 4) language or dialect, 5) religious faith, 6) ties that transcend kinship, neighborhood and local boundaries, 7) shared traditions, values and symbols, 8) literature, folklore and music, 9) food preferences, 10) settlement and employment patterns, 11) special political interests, 12) institutions that secure and maintain the group, 13) an internal sense of distinction, and 14) an external sense of distinction (cited in Leets et.al., 1996:116).

11   With due respect for the - nominal and ordinal - measurement levels, a principal component analysis by alternating least squares (henceforth abbreviated by 'princals') was conducted (see e.g., de Leeuw and van Rijckevorsel, 1988; van de Geer, 1993). The ambition factor has an 'eigen value' of .33, which suggests at best a weak correspondence between the four items and the ambition princal.

12   An analysis of variance revealed that among Moroccans differences in ambition correspond significantly with differences in gender, generation, age and labor market engagement (i.e. middle-aged first-generation Moroccan women inactive on the labor market tend to be less 'ambitious'), but not with levels of formal education. More noteworthy is that such qualifications cannot be made for any other ethnic category.

13   By multiple regression analyses of various integration indicators, the labor ambition measure accounts for no significant integratin index variance independent of indicators for educational level and labor market position.

14   For instance 26% of the first generation immigrants state they had no opportunity to attend school in their land of origin, with significant differences between Moroccans (35%) and Surinamese/Antilleans (10%).

15   The (10) questions were literally: 'Do you find it appropriate that the city provides (immigrant category) with their own (service type).' The exact formulation depended upon the sub-sample: those of Moroccan, Turkish, Surinamese or Antillean origin heard their own ethnic category posed; 'Other' immigrants and indigenous Dutch heard 'immigrants' (allochtonen) posed as more general category.

16   The designation of this 'satisfactory' point was formulated explicitly in the question. Nevertheless the reliability of the measurements are sensitive to the fact that respondents vary in their experience with such (Likert) scales. In Turkish schools for instance, a ten point scale with five denoting 'satisfactory' is more customary.

17   The analysis was conducted after correcting for differences due to sampling stratification, with the extracted component accounting for 49% of the variance in the four items. All items 'loaded' adequately upon the component (domicile - .50, neighborhood - .78, personal life - .72 and locality - .76), although particularly among the indigenous Dutch

the domicile-item displayed low correlations with the other three items. See appendix II for the correlations of the four separate satisfaction items with individuals' scores upon the local integration index.

18   The four queries were: 'what do you consider your neighborhood,' 'do you feel at home in this neighborhood,' 'do many of your friends live in the neighborhood,' and 'if you were free to choose, where would you prefer to reside?' The neighborhood affinity princal had an eigen value of .478 for the first three tems, with 'loadings' (i.e. multiple fit) of .75, .71 and .61 respectively. These correspond among Haarlem immigrants with an Rs of .45, .50 and .48 respectively.

19   The Turks form an exception. The correlation between neighborhood affinity (according to the princal score) and local satisfaction is less pronounced (R=.26) while a negative correlation is observed with two other components of the local index, namely *per capita income* and *welfare independence* (R=-.24 resp. -.21). These statistical interactions are due in my view to the situation in several inauspicious Haarlem neighborhoods (namely *Rozenprieel, Frans Hals and Leidsebuurt*) where relatively large concentrations of Turks reside in (more publicly accessible) low-rise homes and have established in their positional detachment modestly ethnic 'enclaves'.

20   Six indigenous Dutch respondents (5%) voted for the *Centrum Democrats*, a party that openly propagates racial policies of immigrant exclusion. This party is not included in the spectrum presented in table 5.12. Its inclusion on the right end of the spectrum would not yield a significant relation between party choice and integration score.

21   The freedom-equality polarity (Rokeach, 1973:165ff) has been posed often in surveys on value orientations. Harding and Phillips for example in a survey on European values observed that the majority (56%, n=1221) of the Dutch sub-sample opted for 'freedom' (1986:86ff).

Chapter Six

1   Lieberson and Waters denote these two factors as opportunity and disposition to in-marry. They identify two other general factors: disposition to out-marry with specific groups, and social-economic factors, particularly differences in educational background.

2   The information was not obtained directly from respondents, but via the local registry office, and was used initially to ascertain the ethnic category in which individuals are classified. We did not verify the information with respondents, and for 97 of them (16%) - all first generation immigrants - the land of origin of at least one parent remained unknown. The percentages in the text refer to the 70 Surinamese/Antilleans and 89 'Other' immigrants whose parents' land of birth were both registered.

3   Aliens who are married to Dutch nationals for three years or longer have residence rights by an eventual divorce. Particularly among immigrant men there is an inordinate statistical chance of divorce between three and seven years of marriage to a Dutch national (Harmsen, 1998:47).

4   Within all immigrant categories except the Surinamese and Antilleans, respondents who

refused to qualify their partner's ethnicity scored on average 0.30 or higher on the (standardized) index scale.

5　　Within the ethnic categories, students represent 20% to 25% of the 'part-time workers,' the 'jobless seeking work,' and the 'inactive with job potential.' Immigrants are over-represented in these labor positions, while it remains a theoretical issue whether they attend school because they are job-less or are job-less because they attend school. The percentage students among the 'full-time workers' and 'retired/disabled' is consistently under the 10%.

6　　'Comprehensive' in the sense that large samples were 'surveyed': 68 classrooms with a total of 1549 pupils in the Dors study; 36 classrooms and 689 pupils in Teunissen's study. Characteristic for the data gathered is pupils' rating of classroom 'friends' as well as 'foes' (adapted from Bartel, et al., 1973 resp. Newcomb and Bukowski, 1983).

7　　Other factors measured in the model are childrens' 'linguistic skills', and the awareness of discrimination perceived within the two generations.

8　　The one prominent exception, the (33% minority) group of secluded Turks, is composed largely of those laborers who found their jobs via informal networks of family or friends.

9　　The column percentages do not sum to 100% as the separate row categories are neither mutually exclusive (the isolated category does not rule out the remaining three) nor comprehensive (the last three categories exclude those who name a combination of ties only from their 'own' and the indigenous Dutch category).

10　Nor do the separate criteria provide significant indicators. Differences in proportion of local friends fails to discriminate for any of the five categories. Differences in absolute number of friends named is only significant among the indigenous Dutch: those who named less than five ties are generally less integrated (η=.24).

11　The indicator was constructed via a non-linear canonical correlation analysis ('overals'). In this technique variables in the analysis are treated as sets, i.e. each 'friend' is characterized by the set of contact frequency and vicinity data. The rank order (object) scores, when reweighed and standardized for the entire Haarlem population, suggest that Moroccans and Turks display the greatest isolation: e.g. the scores for 54% of the Turks and 47% of the Moroccans are in the 'most isolated' local quartile.

12　Those respondents who made no mention of indigenous Dutch (for Dutch respondents: 'immigrants') in their list of five, were subsequently asked whether they had any at all in their circle of friends. The ordinal variations, ranging from 'no, certainly not' (a majority in all five ethnic categories) to 'yes certainly', did not correspond significantly with integration scores. These results attest to the adequacy of noting only five friends.

13　Per respondent, the statistic is: ((number of friends from *other* regions) x (mean contact frequency with friends from other regions)) ÷ ((mean contact frequency with all friends named) x (number of friends named)).

14　The formula for the isolation index is $_xP^*_y = \sum_i (x_i \div X) \times (y_i \div T_i) \times 100$ where X is the total population of a category residing in a given area, x_i is the number of category members residing in sub-area i, T_i is the total population of sub-area i, and y_i represents the population of the reference category residing in i (Lieberson, 1982:67; Tesser et al.; 1996:82). When calculating the meeting chance within a category x = y.

15 For clarity's sake: the indices for '(*other*) immigrants' presented in row three is based on a P* combining the other three immigrant categories as the reference category y (except for the P* for indigenous Dutch). The heterogeneous group of 'Other' immigrants is treated in short as a single category because the available population data did not enable the differentiation of these residents into their various geo-political regions of origin.

16 The formula for the index is $D = \frac{1}{2} \sum_i abs [((x_i \times 100) \div X) - ((y_i \times 100) \div Y)]$ where X is the area population of the focus category and x_i its population in sub-area i, while Y respectively y_i are that of a reference group (Lieberson, 1982:62; Tesser et al.; 1996:63). The index ranges from 0 (two groups display proportionally equivalent distributions in all areas) to 100 (two groups are entirely segregated from one another, i.e. in no area are individuals from both groups in residence).

17 See Stearns and Logan (1986) for a more detailed comparison of the P*, the dissimilarity index, and a third index - the correlation ration or eta² - and their (combined) potential to represent concentration and segregation processes.

18 Most of the behavioral measures considered in this chapter are either inapplicable for many respondents (e.g. contacts with colleagues) or are normatively biased towards either seclusive or inclusive ties. Two measures are applicable for all respondents and (in my view) normatively congruent with a tolerant vision, namely the proportion of eclusive ties and the proportion of ties with local residents. However because these criteria correlate minimally with the five criteria that comprise the index - particularly among the indigenous Dutch - their inclusion would reduce the reliability and heuristic value of the resulting index.

19 For this overview, and for the component extraction, the coded estimates of participation frequency were transformed from ordinal to interval level. The following transformations were implemented: 'less than once per year' = 1, 'once or twice per year' = 2, '3 to 11 times per year' = 6, 'once per month' = 12, '2 to 3 times per month' = 30, 'once per week or more' = 100, 'daily' = 350. This coding scheme helps clarify how e.g. within the Moroccan and Turkish categories the 'weekly market' is visited on average more than 52 times the previous year.

20 Due to the incomparability between categories as to individuals' ties with *other* locals (i.e., the potential to maintain seclusivie ties is much less among Surinamese, Antilleans and Other'immigrants), the analyses for 'All immigrants' were conducted without the two indicators that refer to these interethnic local ties.

Chapter Seven

1 The one exception is the perceived opportunity criterion, according to which the Surinamese and Antilleans outrank even the indigenous Dutch.

2 The three categories are 'Dutch,' 'Dutch and another,' and 'Arabic, Turkish or English.' This

simple distinction in oral Dutch skills reflects variations in three immigrant categories (the percentage 'mixed' resp. 'non-Dutch' interviews): Morrocans (16%, 57%), Turks (13%, 75%) and 'Other' immigrants (1%, 5%). The distribution for all Haarlem immigrants, reweighed to correct for sample stratification, is 4% resp. 18%.

3   The three presumed barriers - language, religion and 'enclave' residence - are then seen to clarify considerably less than one-third of the index variance, namely 18% among Surinamese and Antilleans, 13% among Moroccans and 12% among Turks.

4   The (standardized) score of the (32) Moroccan and Turkish respondents who had immigrated prior to 1980 and conveyed a 'disabled' labor market position averages to - 1.99, i.e. a mean rank more estranged than 97.7% of the adult Haarlem population.

5   For clarity's sake: besides the measures for educational and labor market position described by the analysis presented in table 7.1, the other two measures referred to here concern a four-category indication of housing market position and a twelve-category differentiation in local districts.

6   Asked for instance how authorities could encourage local integration, 28% of the Turks cited equitable treatment ('*gelijke behandeling*') in their answers, compared to 10% of the Surinamese/Antilleans and less than 5% of the respondents in the other three categories.

Bibliography

Abram, I. (1995), *Identiteit en Imago: Tussen conflict en dialoog*, Algemeen Pedagogisch Studiecentrum, Utrecht.

ACOM (Advies Commissie Onderzoek Minderheden) (1991), *Allochtone vrouwen in Nederland*, Ministerie van Binnenlandse Zaken, Den Haag.

Adler, S. (1977), 'Maslow's Need Hierarchy and the Adjustment of Immigrants', *International Migration Review*, vol. 11(4), Winter, pp. 444-451.

Adriaanse, K., van de Wardt. J.W. and Hortulanus, R.P. (1997), *Sociale Integratie en Segregatie in Amsterda: Een onderzoek naar zelfredzaamheid, maatschap-pelijke participatie en sociale cohesie*, Universiteit Utrecht-ASW, Utrecht.

AFS (Anne Frank Foundation) (1993), *Feiten tegen Vooroordelen*, AFS-NBLC-SDU, Amsterdam-The Hague.

Alexitch, L.R. (1997), 'Students' Educational Orientation and Preferences for Advising from University Professors', *Journal of College Student Development*, vol. 38(4), pp. 333-343.

Allee, J.G. (ed.) (1977), *Webster's Dictionary for Everyday Use*, Barnes and Nobles, New York.

Allport, G. (1958), *The Nature of Prejudice*, Doubleday Anchor Books, Garden City New York.

Allport, G.W. and Ross, J.M. (1967), 'Personal Religious Orientation and Prejudice', *Journal of Personality and Social Psychology*, vol. 5, pp. 432-442.

Amersfoort, J.M.M. van (1974), *Immigratie en Minderheidsvorming: Een analyse van de Nederlandse situatie, 1945-1973*, Samsom, Alphen aan den Rijn (English publication, 1982, Cambridge University Press).

Amersfoort, J.M.M. van (1987), *Etnische woonpatronen, vier benaderingen van woonsegregatie toegepast op Amsterdam*, Universiteit van Amsterdam - Sociaal Geografie, Amsterdam.

Amersfoort, H. van (1992), 'Ethnic Residential Patterns in a Welfare State: Lessons from Amsterdam', *New Community*, vol. 18, pp. 439-456.

Amersfoort, H. and Cortie, C. (1996), 'Social Polarisation in a Welfare State? Immigrants in the Amsterdam Region', *New Community*, vol. 22(4) pp. 671-687.

Anderiessen, G. and Reijndorp, A. (1991), 'Op zoek naar de Onderklasse: Hetero-geniteit en Sociaal Isolement in Stadsvernieuwingswijken', *Migrantenstudies*, vol. 6(3), pp. 49-63.

Angell, R.C. (1968), 'Social Integration', in D.L. Sills (ed.), *International Encyclopedia of the Social Sciences*, Collier MacMillan, London, pp. 380-386.

Apthorpe, R. (1985), 'Integration', in A. Kuper and J. Kuper (eds), *The Social Science Encyclopedia*, Routledge & Kegan Paul, London, pp. 401.

Archard, D. (1996), 'Political and Social Philosophy', in N. Bunnin and E.P. Tsui-James (eds), *The Blackwell Companion to Philosophy*, Blackwell Publishers, Oxford.

Asante, M.K. and Gudykunst, W.B. (eds) (1989), *Handbook of International and Intercultural Communication*, Sage, Newbury Park.

Baker, V.J. (1983), 'Honkbal op klompen: Een theoretisch model van socio-culturele integratie', *Mens en Maatschappij*, vol. 58(4), pp. 383-398.

Bagley, C. (1973), *The Dutch Plural Society*, Oxford University Press, London.

Bagley, C., Huizen, A. van Huizen and Young, L. (1997), 'Multi-ethnic Marriage and Inter-culturalism in Britain and the Netherlands', in D. Woodrow et al. (eds), *Intercultural Education: Theories, Policies and Practices*, Ashgate, Aldershot, Hampshire, pp. 317-326.

Bakker, B.F.M. (1994), 'De CBS Standaard Beroepenclassificatie 1992', *Tijdschrift voor Arbeidsvraagstukken*, vol. 10(4), pp. 322-335.

Banton, M. (1983), *Racial and Ethnic Competition*, Cambridge University Press, Cambridge.

Bartel, H.W., Bartel, N.R. and Grill, J.J. (1973), 'A Sociometric View of some Integrated Open Classrooms', *Journal of Social Issues*, vol. 29(4), pp. 451-465.

Barth, F. (1969), *Ethnic Groups and Boundaries: The Social Organization of Ethnic Differences*, George Allen & Unwin, London.

Batson, C.D. and Ventis, W.L. (1982), *The Religious Experience: A Social Psychological Perspective*, Oxford University Press, New York/London.

Bauböck, R. (ed.) (1994), *From Aliens to Citizens: Redefining the Status of Immigrants in Europe*, Avebury, Aldershot.

Beek, K.W.H. van (1993), *To be Hired or Not to be Hired, the Employer Decides: Relative Chances of Unemployed Job-seekers on the Dutch Labor Market*, University of Amsterdam Dissertation, Amsterdam.

Beek, P. van and Knulst, W. (1991), *De Kunstzinnige Burger*, Sociaal Cultureel Planbureau, Rijswijk.

Bell, W. (1954), 'A Probability Model for the Measurement of Ecological Segregation', *Social Forces*, vol. 32, pp. 357-364.

Berg, H. van den and Reinsch, P.Q. (1982), *Racisme in Schoolboeken: Het Gladde Ijs van het Westerse Gelijk*, SUA, Amsterdam.

Berger, P.L. and Berger, B. (1972), *Sociology: A Biographical Approach*, Basic Books, New York/London.

Berry, J. (1989), 'Imposed Etics-Emics, Derived Etics-Emics: The Operationalization of a Compelling Idea', *International Journal of Psychology*, vol. 24, pp. 721-735.

Berry, J., Trimble, J. and Olmedo, E. (1986), 'Assessment of Acculturation', in W. Lonner and J. Berry (eds), *Field Methods in Cross-Cultural Research*, Sage, Newbury Park CA, pp. 291-324.

Blanc, M. (1992), 'From Substandard Housing to Devalorized Social Housing: Ethnic Minorities in France, Germany and the UK', *European Journal of Intercultural Studies*, vol. 3(1), pp. 7-25.

Blumer, H. (1965), 'The Future of the Color Line', in J. McKinney and E. Thompson (eds), *The South in Continuity and Change*, Seeman, Durham.

Bobo, L., Zubrinsky, C.L., Johnson, J.H. Jr. and Oliver, M.T. (1995), 'Work Orientation, Job Discrimination, and Ethnicity: A Focus Group Perspective', *Research in the Sociology of Work*, vol. 5, pp. 45-85.

Bol, M.W. and Wiersma, E.G. (1997), *Racistisch Geweld in Nederland: Aard en Omvang, Strafrechtellijke Afdoening, Dadertypen*, Gouda Quint, Deventer.

Bollini, P. and Siem, H. (1995), 'No Real Progress towards Equity: Health of Migrants and Ethnic Minorities on the Eve of the Year 2000', *Social Science and Medicine*, vol. 41(6), September, pp. 819-828.

Bonacich, E. (1972), 'A Theory of Ethnic Antagonism: The Split Labor Market', *American Sociological Review*, vol. 37, pp. 547-559.

Bot, K. de (1994), 'Comment', *International Journal of the Sociology of Language*, no. 110, pp. 193-201.

Bourdieu, P. (1992), 'Economisch Kapitaal, Cultureel Kapitaal, Sociaal Kapitaal', in D. Pels (ed.), *Opstellen over Smaak, Habitus en het Veldbegrip*, Van Gennep, Amsterdam, pp. 120-141 (English publication: 'The Forms of Capital', in J. G. Richardson (ed.), *Handbook of Theory and Research for the Sociology of Education*, Greenwood Press, New York, 1986).

Bourdieu, P. (1997), 'Cultural Reproduction and Social Reproduction', in J. Karabel and A.H. Halsey (eds), *Power and Ideology in Education*, Oxford University Press, New York, pp. 487-511.

Bousetta, H. (1997), 'Citizenship and Political Participation in France and the Netherlands: Reflections on Two Local Cases', *New Community*, vol. 23(2), April, pp. 215-231.

Bouw, C. and Nelissen, C. (1988), *Gevoelige Kwesties*, Universiteit Leiden - COMT, Leiden.

Bovenkerk, F. (1978), *Omdat Zij Anders Zijn: Patronen van Rasdiscriminatie in Nederland*, Boom, Meppel.

Bovenkerk, F. (1986), *Een Eerlijke Kans: Over de Toepasbaarheid van Buitenlandse Ervaringen met Positieve Actie voor Etnische Minderheden op de Arbeidsmarkt in Nederland*, Ministerie van Binnenlandse Zaken en Ministerie van Sociale Zaken en Werkgelegenheid, Den Haag.

Bovenkerk, F. (1994), 'A Delinquent Second Generation? Explanations for the Extent, Nature and Causes of Juvenile Crime in Various Migrant Groups', *Research Notes from the Netherlands*, vol. 3(2), pp. 2-10.

Bovenkerk, F. (1994a), 'Over de oorzaken van de criminaliteit van allochtone jongeren', in Commissie Montfrans, Met de neus op de feiten: Advies aanpak jeugdcriminaliteit, Den Haag, Ministerie van Justitie.

Bovenkerk, F., Bruin, K., Brunt, L. and Wouters, H. (1985), *Vreemd Volk, Gemengde Gevoelens: Etnische Verhoudingen in een Grote Stad*, Boom, Amsterdam/Meppel.

Boxman, E.A.W. (1992), *Contacten en Carrière: Een Empirisch-Theoretisch Onderzoek naar de Relatie tussen Sociale Netwerken en Arbeidsmarktposities*, Thesis, Amsterdam.

Brands, J., Egas, G., Karsten, S. and Wendrich, E. (1977), *Andere Wijs over Onderwijs: Naar een Materialistische Onderwijssociologie*, LINK, Nijmegen.

Brants, K., Crone, L. and Leurdijk, A. (1998), *Media en Migranten: Inventarisatie van Onderzoek in Nederland*, Universiteit van Amsterdam-Communicatie Wetenschap/Werkgroep Migranten en Media van de NVJ, Amsterdam.

Brief, A.P, Brett, J.F., Raskas, D. and Stein, E. (1997), 'Feeling Economically Dependent on One's Job: Its Origins and Functions with Regard to Worker Well-being', *Journal of Applied Social Psychology*, vol. 27(15), pp. 1303-1315.

Brink, B. van den (1994), 'De Civil Society als 'Kloppend Hart' van de Maatschappij: Drie Filosofische Visies', in P. Dekker (ed.), *Civil Society: Verkenningen van een Perspectief op Vrijwilligerswerk*, SCP/VUGA (Serie Civil Society en Vrijwilligerswerk, Deel I), Rijswijk/Den Haag, pp. 49-66.

Brislin, R.W., Lonner, W.J. and Thorndike, R.M. (1973), *Cross-Cultural Research Methods*, Wiley & Sons, New York.

Brouwers, Y.C.J., Deurloo, M.C., Klerk, L. de (1987), *Selectieve Verhuisbewegingen en Segregatie: De Invloed van de Etnische Samenstelling van de Woonomgeving op Verhuisgedrag*, Universiteit van Amsterdam - Instituut voor Sociale Geografie, Nederlandse Geografische Studies 40, Amsterdam.

Brown, M.E. (ed.) (1993), *Ethnic Conflict and International Security*, Princeton University Press, Princeton.

Brown, M.E. (1997), 'Causes and Implications of Ethnic Conflict', in M. Guibernau and J. Rex (eds), *The Ethnicity Reader: Nationalism, Multiculturalism and Migration*, Polity Press, Cambridge UK, pp. 80-100.

Bruin, M.J. and Cook, C.C. (1997), 'Understanding Constraints and Residential Satisfaction among Low-income Single-parent Families', *Environment and Behavior*, vol. 29(4), July, pp. 532-553.

Bryant, C.G.A. (1997), 'Citizenship, National Identity and the Accommodation of Difference: Reflections on the German, French, Dutch and British Cases', *New Community*, vol. 23(2), April, pp. 157-172.

Buijs, F. (1993), *Leven in een Nieuw Land: Marokkaanse Jongemannen in Nederland*, Jan van Arkel, Utrecht.

Buiks, P.E.J. (1983), *Surinaamse Jongeren op de Kruiskade: Overleven in een Etnische Randgroep*, Van Loghum Slaterus, Deventer.

Burgers, J. (1995), 'Inpassen en Aanpassen: De Huisvesting van Allochtonen', in G. Engbersen and R. Gabriëls (eds), *Sferen van Integratie: Naar een Gedifferentieerd Allochtonenbeleid*, Boom, Amsterdam/Meppel, pp. 137-156.

Burgers, J. (1996), 'Natte Vingers en Vuile Handen, Over het Schatten van het Aantal Illegale Vreemdelingen: Een Reactie op Böcker en Groenendijk', *Migranten-studies*, vol. 12(1), pp. 14-26.

Burgers, J. and Engbersen, G. (eds) (1999), *De Ongekende Stad*, Boom, Amsterdam.

Burgers, J., Reinsch, P., Snel, E. and Tak, H. (1996), *Burgers als Ieder Ander: Een Advies Inzake Lokaal Beleid en Minderheden*, Utrecht University-AWSB, Utrecht.

Burgess, E.W. (1925), 'The Growth of the City: An Introduction to a Research Project', in R.E. Park, E.W. Burgess and R.D. Mackenzie (eds), *The City*, University of Chicago Press, Chicago.

Burton, V.S. Jr., Cullen, F.T., Evans, T.D. and Dunaway, R.G. (1994), 'Reconsidering Strain Theory: Operationalization, Rival Theories, and Adult Criminality', *Journal of Quantitative Criminology*, vol. 10(3), pp. 213-239.

Campbell, H.W., Reinsch, P.Q. and Driessen, P.G.P. (1994), *Etniciteit en Cultuurparticipatie: Een Onderzoek naar de Deelname van Leden van Etnische Groepen aan Cultuuruitingen in Nederland*, Stichting Studia Interetnica, Maarssen.

Campfens, H. (1979), *The Integration of Ethno-Cultural Minorities: A Pluralist Approach*, Ministry of Cultural Affairs, Recreation and Social Welfare, The Hague.

Castles, S. (1984), *Here for Good: Western Europe's New Ethnic Minorities*, Pluto Press, London.

Castles, S. (1995), 'How Nation-States Respond to Immigration and Ethnic Diversity', *New Community*, vol. 21(3), July, pp. 293-308.

Castles, S. and Kosack, C. (1973), *Immigrant Workers and Class Structure in Western Europe*, IRR/Oxford University Press, London.

Cattell, R.B. (1943), 'The Description of Personality: Basic Traits Resolved into Clusters', *Journal of Abnormal and Social Psychology*, vol. 38, pp. 476-507.

CBS (Centraal Bureau voor de Statistiek) (1985), *De Leefsituatie van Turken en Marokkanen in Nederland, 1984*, Staatsuitgeverij/CBS Publikaties, Den Haag.

CBS (1986), *De Leefsituatie van Surinamers en Antillianen in Nederland, 1985*, Staatsuitgeverij/CBS Publikaties, Den Haag.

CBS (1993), 'De Overgang van Enquête Slachtoffers Misdrijven naar Enquête Rechtsbescherming en Veiligheid', *Recht en Statistiek*, no. 16, Voorburg/Heerlen.

CBS (1994), *Statistiek der Verkiezingen, 1994, Gemeenteraden, 2 maart*, Voorburg/Heerlen.

CBS (1996), *Regionale Inkomensverdeling, 1994, Kerncijfers*, Voorburg/Heerlen.

Chen, A., Liu, Z. and Ennis, C.D. (1997), 'Universality and Uniqueness of Teacher Educational Value Orientations: A Cross-Cultural Comparison between USA and China', *Journal of Research and Development in Education*, vol. 30(3), Spring, pp. 135-143.

Cherribi, O. (ed.) (1994), *Islam en de Democratie: Een Ontmoeting, Frits Bolke-stein: Mohammed Arkoun*, Contact, Amsterdam.

Chiswick, B.R. and Miller, P.W. (1998), 'Language Skill Definition: A Study of Legalized Aliens', *International Migration Review*, vol. 32(4), pp. 877-900.

Choenni, A.O. (1997), *Veelsoortig Assortiment: Allochtone Ondernemerschap in Amsterdam als Incorporatietraject 1965-1995*, Universiteit van Amsterdam dissertation, Amsterdam.

Choenni, C.E.S. (1992), 'Allochtonen en Burgerschap', in WRR, *Burgerschap in Praktijken, Deel 1*, SDU, Den Haag, pp. 57-97.

Church, A.T. and Lonner, W.J. (1998), 'The Cross-Cultural Perspective in the Study of Personality: Rationale and Current Research', *Journal of Cross Cultural Psychology*, vol. 29(1), January, pp. 32-62.

Cohen, J. and Arato, A. (1992), *Civil Society and Political Theory*, MIT Press, Cambridge, MA.

Coleman, J. (1988), 'Social Capital in the Creation of Human Capital', *American Journal of Sociology*, vol. 94, supplement, pp. s95-120.

Collet, B. (1996), *Citoyennetés et Mariage Mixte en France et en Allemagne*, EHESS, Paris.

Costa, P.T. Jr. and McCrae, R.R. (1992), *Revised NEO Personality Inventory (NEO-PI-R) and NEO Five-Factor Inventory (NEO-FFI) Professional Manual*, Psychological Assessment Resources, Odessa, FL.

Cross, M. and Waldinger, R. (1997), 'Economic Integration and Labour Market Change', in M. Cross and R. Waldinger (eds), *Key Issues for Research and Policy on Migrants in Cities*, Utrecht University-ERCOMER (discussion papers prepared for the Second International Metropolis Conference), Utrecht.

CTHOA (Commissie Toekomstscenario's Herverdeling Onbetaalde Arbeid) (1995), *Onbetaalde Zorg Gelijk Verdeeld*, Ministerie van Sociale Zaken en Werkgelegenheid/VUGA, Den Haag.

Dagevos, J. (1998), *Begrensde Mobiliteit: Over Allochtone Werkenden in Nederland*, Van Gorcum, Assen.

Dagevos, J. and Veenman, J. (1992), *Succesvolle Allochtonen*, Uitgeverij Boom, Meppel/Amsterdam.

Dagevos, J.M., Martens, E.P. and Veenman, J. (1996), *Scheef Verdeeld: Minderheden en hun Maatschappelijke Positie*, Van Gorcum, Assen.

Dekker, P. and Praag, C.S. van (1990), *Opvattingen over Allochtonen in Landen van de Europese Gemeenschap*, Sociaal Cultureel Planbureau, document no. 8, Rijswijk.

Diener, E. (1984), 'Subjective Well-being', *Psychological Bulletin*, vol. 95, pp. 542-575.

Dijk, T.A. van (1987), *Communicating Racism*, Sage Publications, Newbury Park, CA.

Dijk, T.A. van (1993), *Elite Discourse and Racism*, Sage Publications, Newbury Park, CA.

Dirken, J.M. (1969), *Arbeid en Stress: Het Vaststellen van Aanpassingsproblemen in Werksituaties,* Wolters-Nordhoff, Groningen.

Donselaar, J.G. van (1991), *Fout na de Oorlog: Fascist and Racist Organisations in the Netherlands, 1950-1990*, Bakker, Amsterdam.

Dors, H.G. (1987), *Vriendschap en Sociale Relaties in Multi-etnisch Samengestelde Schoolklassen*, Studio AWP (dissertation), Amsterdam.

Dors, H.G., Karsten, S., Ledoux, G., Steen, A.H.M. and Meijer, P.G. (1991), *Etnische Segregatie in het Onderwijs: Beleidsaspecten*, Universiteit van Amsterdam - SCO, Amsterdam.

Dreger, R.M. and Adkins, S.A. (1991), 'A Restandardization of a Brief Scale of Religious Orthodoxy, Religious Humanism, and Religious Radicalism', *International Journal for the Psychology of Religion*, vol. 1(3), pp. 173-181.

Driessen, G.W.J.M. (1990), *De Onderwijspositie van Allochtone Jongeren: De rol van Sociaal-economische en Etnisch-culturele Factoren, met Speciale Aandacht voor het Onderwijs in Eigen Taal en Cultuur*, Universiteit Nijmegen - ITS (dissertation), Nijmegen.

Dronkers, J. and Ultee, W. (eds) (1995), Verschuivende Ongelijkheid in Nederland: Sociale Gelaagdheid en Mobiliteit, Van Gorcum, Assen.

Dudley, R.L. and Cruise, R.J. (1990), 'Measuring Religious Maturity: A Proposed Scale', Review of Religious Research, vol. 32(2), December, pp. 97-109.

Dugteren, F. van (1993), Woonsituatie Minderheden: Achtergronden en Ontwikkeling 1982-1990 en Vooruitzichten voor de Jaren Negentig, Sociaal en Cultureel Planbureau/VUGA, Rijswijk/Den Haag.

Dunifon, R. and Duncan, G.J. (1998), 'Long-run Effects of Motivation on Labor-market Success', Social Psychology Quarterly, vol. 61(1), pp. 33-48.

Durkheim, E. (1970), Suicide: A Study in Sociology, Free Press, New York (originally published 1893).

EECom (Commissie van de Europese Gemeenschappen) (1990), Immigratiebeleid en Sociale Integratie van Immigranten in de Europese Gemeenschap, Brussel, sec(90) 1813 def./2, 12 October.

Eekert, P. van and Gelderloos, E. (1990), Vroeger was de Wereld Groter: Reacties op Langdurige Werkloosheid bij Turken, Marokkanen en Surinamers, Jan van Arkel, Utrecht.

Eisinga, R., Felling, A., Peters, J., Scheepers, P. and Schreuder, O. (1992), Religion in Dutch Society: Documentation of a National Survey on Religious and Secular Attitudes in 1985, Steinmetz Archief, Amsterdam.

Elbers, F. and Fennema, M. (1993), Racistische Partijen in West-Europa: Tussen Nationale Tradities en Europese Samenwerking, Stichting Burgerschapskunde/Nederlands Centrum voor Politieke Vorming, Leiden.

Elias, N. (1970), Wat is Sociologie?, Het Spectrum, Utrecht/Antwerpen.

Elias, N. and Scotson, J.L. (1965), The Established and the Outsiders, Frank Cass & Co., London.

Elich, J.H. and Maso, B. (1985), Discriminatie, Vooroordeel en Racisme in Nederland, Ministerie van Binnenlandse Zaken/Adviescommissie Onderzoek Minderheden, Den Haag/Leiden.

Ellemers, J.E. (1995), 'Immigratieproblemen: Een Sociologische en Sociaal-psychologische Benadering', in J.E. Ellemers, Modernisering, Macht, Migratie: Opstellen over Maatschappij en Beleid, Boom, Amsterdam/Meppel, pp. 250-275.

Engbersen, G. (1990), Publieke Bijstandsgeheimen: Het Ontstaan van een Onderklasse in Nederland, Stenfert Kroese, Leiden.

Engbersen, G. and Gabriëls, R. (eds) (1995a), Sferen van Integratie: Naar een Gedifferentieerd Allochtonenbeleid, Boom, Amsterdam/Meppel.

Engbersen, G. and Gabriëls, R. (1995b), 'Voorbij Segregatie en Assimilatie', in G. Engbersen en R. Gabriëls (eds), Sferen van Integratie: Naar een Gedifferentieerd Allochtonenbeleid, Boom, Amsterdam/Meppel, pp. 15-47.

Engbersen, G., Schuyt, K., Timmer, J. and Waarden, F. van (1993), Cultures of Unemployment, Westview Press, Boulder.

Engbersen, G., Vroman, J.C. and Snel, E. (eds) (1996), Arm Nederland: Het Eerste Jaarrapport Armoede en Sociale Uitsluiting, VUGA uitgeverij, Den Haag.

Engbersen, G., Vroman, J.C. and Snel, E. (eds) (1997), *De Kwetsbaren: Het Tweede Jaarrapport Armoede en Sociale Uitsluiting*, Amsterdam University Press, Amsterdam.

Entzinger, H. (1984), *Het Minderhedenbeleid*, Boom, Amsterdam/Meppel.

Entzinger, H. (1985), 'The Netherlands', in Hammar, T. (ed.), *European Immigration Policy: A Comparative Study*, Cambridge University Press, Cambridge.

Entzinger, H.B. (1991), 'Etnische Minderheden, Stedelijke Armoede, Gettovorming', *Sociologische Gids*, vol. 38(1), pp. 37-47.

Entzinger, H. (1994), 'Changing Policy Approaches and Scenarios for the Future', in H. Entzinger et al. (eds), *Immigrant Ethnic Minorities in the Dutch Labour Market*, Thesis, Amsterdam, pp. 149-165.

Entzinger, H., Siegers, J. and Tazelaar, F. (eds) (1994), *Immigrant Ethnic Minorities in the Dutch Labour Market: Analyses and Policies*, Thesis, Amsterdam.

Eppink, A. (1981), *Cultuurverschillen en Communicatie*, Samsom, Alphen a/d Rijn.

Eppink, A. (ed.) (1983), *Kind Zijn in Twee Culturen: Jonge Marokkaanse en Turkse Kinderen in Nederland*, van Loghum Slaterus, Deventer.

Esping-Andersen, G. (1990), *The Three Worlds of Welfare Capitalism*, Polity Press Cambridge.

Essed, Ph. (1984), *Alledaags Racisme*, Feministische Uitgeverij Sara, Amsterdam.

Essed, Ph. (1991), *Understanding Everyday Racism*, Sage Publications, Newbury Park, CA.

Essed, Ph. (1994), *Diversiteit, Vrouwen, Kleur en Cultuur*, Ambo, Baarn.

Essed, Ph. and Reinsch, P. (1991), *Interculturalisering: Over Oude en Nieuwe Routes bij het GVB*, Universiteit Amsterdam - CRES, Amsterdam.

Esser, H. (1980), *Aspekte der Wanderungssoziologie: Assimilation und Integration von Wanderen, Ethnischen Gruppen und Minderheiten*, Luchterhand Verlag, Darmstadt/Neuwied.

Esveldt, I., Kulu-Glasgow, I., Schoorl, J. and Solinge, H. van (1995), *Migratie-motieven, Migratienetwerken en Partnerkeuze van Turken en Marokkanen in Nederland*, NIDI, Den Haag.

Eurostat (1998), 'EU has nearly 5 million people from Med 12', *memo 4/98*, Eurostat Press Office, Luxemburg.

Everts, H., Golhof, A., Stassen, P. and Teunissen, J. (1986), *De Kultureel-etnische Situatie op OVB-scholen*, Universiteit Utrecht, Utrecht.

Fanon, F. (1971), *Zwarte Huid, Blanke Maskers*, A.C. Bruna & Zoon, Utrecht/Amsterdam.

Fase, W. (1994), *Ethnic Divisions in Western European Education*, Waxmann, Münster/New York, 1994.

Feddema, R. (1991), *Op Weg Tussen Hoop en Vrees: De Levensoriëntatie van Jonge Turken en Marokkanen in Nederland*, Van Arkel, Utrecht.

Fermin, A. (1997), *Nederlandse Politieke Partijen over Minderhedenbeleid, 1977-1995*, Universiteit Utrecht-ISOR, Utrecht.

Fermin, A. (1999), 'Inburgeringsbeleid en Burgerschap', *Migrantenstudies*, vol. 15(2), pp. 96-112.

Fischer, C. (1982), *To Dwell among Friends: Personal Networks in Town and City*, University of Chicago Press, Chicago.

Friedberg, R.M. (1993), *Immigration and the Labor Market*, Massachusetts Institute of Technology Dissertation, Boston.

Furer, J.W., König-Zahn, C. and Tax, B. (1995), *Het Meten van de Gezondheidstoestand: Psychische Gezondheid*, Van Gorcum, Assen.

Furnham, A. and Reilly, M. (1991), 'A Cross-cultural Comparison of British and Japanese Protestant Work Ethic and Just World Beliefs', *Psychologia: An International Journal of Psychology in the Orient*, vol. 34(1), March, pp. 1-14.

Furnivall, J.S. (1948), *Colonial Policy and Practice*, Cambridge University Press, Cambridge.

Ganzeboom, H. (1989), *Cultuurdeelname in Nederland: Een Empirisch-Theoretisch Onderzoek naar Determinanten van Deelname aan Culturele Activiteiten*, Van Gorcum, Assen.

Geer, J.P. van de (1993), *Multivariate Analysis of Categorical Data: Theory (vol. II) and Application (vol. III)*, Sage Publications (Advanced Quantitative Techniques in the Social Sciences Series), London.

Geertz, C. (1973), *The Interpretation of Cultures*, Basic Books, New York.

Gemeente Haarlem (1991), *Haarlemse Buurten Vergeleken: Een Onderzoek naar de Kwaliteit van het Woon- en Leefmilieu*, Gemeente Haarlem Sector BWE, Onderzoek & Statistiek, Haarlem

Gemeente Haarlem (1995), *Jaarstatistiek 1994*, Bureau Onderzoek en Statistiek, Haarlem.

Gemeente Haarlem (1996), *Jaarstatistiek 1995*, Gemeente Haarlem Sector BWE, Onderzoek & Statistiek, Haarlem.

Gemert, F. van (1998), *Ieder Voor Zich: Kansen, Cultuur en Criminaliteit van Marokkaanse Jongens*, Het Spinhuis, Amsterdam.

Giddens, A. (1994), *Beyond Left and Right: The Future of Radical Politics*, Polity Press, Cambridge.

Gilmore, S. (1992), 'Culture', in Borgatta & Borgatta (eds), *Encyclopedia of Sociology*, MacMillan, New York, vol. 1, pp. 404-411.

Gilsing, R. (1991), *De Politieke Participatie van Migranten in Nederland*, Katholieke Universiteit Nijmegen - De Wetenschapswinkel, Nijmegen.

Ginsberg, Y. (1985), 'Dimensions of Neighborhood Prestige Perceptions: Findings from Tel Aviv', *Social Science Quarterly*, vol. 66(3), September, pp. 724-732.

Goldberg, L.R. (1981), 'Language and Individual Differences: The Search for Universals in Personality Lexicons', in L. Wheeler (ed.), *Review of Personality and Social Psychology (Volume 2)*, Sage Publications, Beverly Hills, CA, pp. 141-165.

Goldlust, J. and Richmond, A.H. (1973), 'A Multivariate Model of Immigrant Adaptation', *International Migration Review*, pp. 193-225.

Gordon, M.M. (1963), *Assimilation in American Life*, Oxford University Press, New York.

Gould, S.J. (1996), *Full House: The Spread of Excellence from Plato to Darwin*, Three Rivers Press, New York.

Gowricharn, R.S. (ed.) (1993a), *Binnen de Grenzen: Immigratie, Etniciteit en Integratie in Nederland*, De Tijdstroom, Utrecht.

Gowricharn, R.S. (1993b), 'Integratie als Normatief Proces', in R.S. Gowricharn (ed.), *Binnen de Grenzen: Immigratie, Etniciteit en Integratie in Nederland*, De Tijdstroom, Utrecht, pp.173-184.

Gowricharn, R. (1995), 'Integratie in een Verbeelde Werkelijkheid', in G. Engbersen and R. Gabriëls (eds), *Sferen van Integratie: Naar een Gedifferentieerd Allochtonenbeleid*, Boom, Amsterdam/Meppel, pp. 204-222.

Granovetter, M. (1973), 'The Strength of Weak Ties', *American Journal of Sociology*, vol. 78, pp. 1360-1380.

Gras, M., Bovenkerk, F., Gorter, K., Kruiswijk, P. and Ramsoedh, D. (1996), *Een Schijn van Kans: Twee Empirische Onderzoekingen naar Discriminatie op Grond van Handicap en Etnische Afkomst*, Gouda Quint, Deventer.

Gudykunst, W.B. (1994), *Bridging Differences: Effective Intergroup Communication*, Sage Publications, Beverly Hills, CA.

Guest, A.M. and Stamm, K.R. (1993), 'Paths of Community Integration', *Sociological-Quarterly*, vol. 34(4), November, pp. 581-595.

Haan, I. de (1995), 'Over de Grenzen van de Politiek: De Integratie van Allochtonen in de Sfeer van de Politiek', in G. Engbersen and R. Gabriëls (eds), *Sferen van Integratie: Naar een Gedifferentieerd Allochtonenbeleid*, Boom, Amsterdam/Meppel, pp. 157-180.

Haan, W. de (1997), 'Minorities, Crime and Criminal Justice in the Netherlands', in I.H. Marshall (ed.), *Minorities, Migrants and Crime: Diversity and Similarity across Europe and the United States*, Sage Publications, London.

Haan, W. de and Bovenkerk, F. (1995), 'Sociale Integratie en Criminaliteit', in G. Engbersen and R. Gabriëls (eds), *Sferen van Integratie: Naar een Gedifferentieerd Allochtonenbeleid*, Boom, Amsterdam/Meppel, pp. 223-248.

Habermas, J. (1988), 'Individuierung durch Vergesellschaftung', in J. Habermas, *Nachmetafysisches Denken*, Suhrkamp, Frankfurt am Main.

Hagendoorn, L. (1993), 'Ethnic Categorization and Outgroup Exclusion: Cultural Values and Social Stereotypes in the Construction of Ethnic Hierarchies', *Ethnic and Racial Studies*, vol. 16(1), pp. 26-51.

Hagendoorn, L. (1995), 'Intergroup Biases in Multiple Group Systems: the Perception of Ethnic Hierarchies', *European Review of Social Psychology*, vol. 6, pp. 199-228.

Hagendoorn, L. and Hraba, J. (1989), 'Foreign, Different, Deviant, Seclusive and Working Class: Anchors to an Ethnic Hierarchy in the Netherlands', *Ethnic and Racial Studies*, vol. 12, pp. 441-467.

Hall, S. (1991), 'Het Minimale Zelf', in *Het Minimale Zelf en Andere Opstellen*, SUA, Amsterdam, pp. 195-200 (originally published in *ICA-Documents 6*. 'Identity: The real me', London, 1988, pp. 44-46).

Hall, S. et al. (1978), *Policing the Crisis: Mugging, the State, and Law and Order*, MacMillan Education, London.

Halman, L., Heunks, F., Moor, R. de and Zanders, H. (1987), *Traditie, Secularisatie en Individualisering: Een Studie naar de Waarden van de Nederlanders in een Europese Context*, Tilburg University Press, Tilburg.

Hamid, P.N. (1996), 'The Validity of an Unobtrusive Measure of Social Identity', *Social Behavior and Personality*, vol. 24(2), pp. 157-168.

Hammar, T. (ed.) (1985), *European Immigration Policy: A Comparative Study*, Cambridge University Press, Cambridge.

Harding, S. and Phillips, D. (1986), *Contrasting Values in Western Europe: Unity, Diversity and Change*, MacMillan Press, London.

Harlow, L. and Newcomb, M.D. (1990), 'Towards a General Hierarchical Model of Meaning and Satisfaction in Life', *Multivariate Behavioral Research*, vol. 25(3), July, pp. 387-405.

Harmsen, C.N. (1998), 'Naar Geboorteland Gemengde Huwelijken', *Allochtonen in Nederland*, CBS, Voorburg/Harmsen, pp. 45-49.

Harrington, M. (1962), *The Other America: Poverty in the United States*, Harmondsworth, New York.

Hartman-Eeken, M.M.J. (1992), *Over Integratie*, Ministerie van Binnenlandse Zaken, Den Haag.

Hechter, M. (1978), 'Group Formation and the Cultural Division of Labor', *American Journal of Sociology*, vol. 48(2), pp. 293-318.

Heelsum, A.J. van (1993), 'De Invloed van de Etnische Afkomst van Interviewers in een Interview Rond Etniciteit', *Migrantenstudies*, vol. 9(2), pp. 16-34.

Heelsum, A.J. van (1997), *De Etnisch-Culturele Positie van de Tweede Generatie Surinamers*, Het Spinhuis, Amsterdam.

Hoek, J. van der (1994), *Socialisatie in Migrantengezinnen: Een Basis voor Opvoedingsondersteuning*, De Tijdstroom, Utrecht.

Hoekstra, H.A., Ormel, J. and Fruyt, F. de (1996), *Handleiding NEO Persoonlijkheids Vragenlijsten NEO-PI-R en NEO-FFI*, Swets & Zeitlinger, Amsterdam.

Hof, L. van 't and Dronkers, J. (1993), 'Onderwijsachterstanden van Allochtonen: Klasse, Gezin of Ethnische Cultuur?', *Migrantenstudies*, vol. 9(1), pp. 2-26.

Hoffman, E. and Arts, W. (1994), *Interculturele Gespreksvoering*, Bohn Stafleu Van Loghum, Houten/Diegem.

Hofstede, G. (1980), *Culture's Consequences: International Differences in Work-Related Values*, Sage Publications, London.

Hofstede, G. (1991), 'Empirical Models of Cultural Differences', in N. Bleichrodt and P.J.D. Drenth (eds), *Contemporary Issues in Cross-Cultural Psychology*, Swets and Zeitlinger, Amsterdam, pp. 4-20.

Hondius, D. (1999), *Gemengde Huwelijken, Gemengde Gevoelens: Aanvaarding en Ontwijking van Ethnisch en Religieus Verschil sinds 1945*, SDU, Den Haag.

Hooghiemstra, B.T.J., Kuipers, K.W. and Muus, Ph.J. (1990), *Gelijke Kansen voor Allochtonen op een Baan? Wervings- en Selectieprocessen op de Arbeidsmarkt voor On- en Laaggeschoolden*, University of Amsterdam - Instituut voor Sociale Geografie, Amsterdam.

Hooghiemstra, B.T.J. and Niphuis-Nell, M. (1995), 'Allochtone Vrouwen', in *Sociale Atlas van de Vrouw, Deel 3*, Sociaal en Cultureel Planbureau, Rijswijk.

Horley, J. and Lavery, J.J. (1991), 'The Stability and Sensitivity of Subjective Well-Being Measures', *Social Indicators Research*, vol. 24(2), March, pp. 113-122.

Horowitiz, D.L. (1985), *Ethnic Groups in Conflict*, University of California Press, Berkeley, CA.

Horst, H. van der (1996), *The Low Sky: Understanding the Dutch*, Nuffic/Scriptum, Den Haag/Schiedam.

Hortulanus, R.P. (1995), *Stadsbuurten: Een Studie over Bewoners en Beheerders in Buurten met Uiteenlopende Reputaties*, VUGA, Den Haag.

Hortulanus, R.P., Liem, P.P.N. and Sprinkhuizen, A.M.M. (1992), *Welzijn in Dordrecht*, University Utrecht - ASW, Utrecht.

Hortulanus, R.P., Liem, P.P.N. and Sprinkhuizen, A.M.M. (1993), *Domeinen van Welzijn: Welzijnsbeleving en Welzijnsbeleid in de Jaren '90*, VUGA, Den Haag.

Huls, F.W.M. (1996), 'Allochtonen en hun Woonbeleving', in Huls, F.W.M. and P. van der Laan (eds), *Allochtonen in Nederland*, CBS, Voorburg/Heerlen, July, pp. 55-63.

Huls, F.W.M. (1997), 'Allochtonen en Maatschappelijke Participatie', *Allochtonen in Nederland*, CBS, Voorburg/Heerlen, pp. 43-50.

Hurrelmann, K. (1975), *Erziehungssystem und Gesellschaft*, Rowohlt, Hamburg.

Hutton, S. (1991), 'Measuring Living Standards Using Existing National Data Sets', *Journal of Social Policy*, vol. 20(2), April, pp. 237-257.

Inkeles, A. and Levinson, D.J. (1969), 'National Character: The Study of Modal Personality and Sociocultural Systems', in G. Lindsey and E. Aronson (eds), *The Handbook of Social Psychology (Volume 4)*, Addison-Wesley, Reading, MA, pp. 447ff.

Intomart Qualitatief (1989), *Cultuurparticipatie: Een Onderzoek naar Cultuurdeelname van de Nederlandse Bevolking*, Intomart, Rijswijk.

Intomart B.V. (1995), *Allochtonen over Nederlanders*, NCB/IKON, Utrecht /Hilversum.

ITS (Institute for Applied Sociology) (1994), *Gebiedsrapporten: Resultaten Taal- en Rekentoetsen*, Catholic University Nijmegen, Nijmegen.

James, A.D., Tucker, M.B. and Mitchell-Kernan, C. (1996), 'Marital Attitudes, Perceived Mate Availability, and Subjective Well-being among Partnered African American Men and Women', *Journal of Black Psychology*, vol. 22(1), pp. 20-36.

Jansen, W. and Wittenboer, G.L.H. van den (eds) (1992), *Sociale Netwerken en hun Invloed*, Boom, Meppel.

Jiobu, R.M. (1988), *Ethnicity and Assimilation*, SUNY Press, Albany.

Jones, J.M. (1994), 'An Exploration of Temporality in Human Behavior', in R.C. Schank and E. Langer (eds), *Beliefs, Reasoning, and Decision Making: Psycho-Logic in Honor of Bob Abelson*, Lawrence Erlbaum Associates, Hillsdale, NJ, pp. 389-411.

Jones-Correa, M. (1988), 'Different Paths: Gender, Immigration and Political Participation', *International Migration Review*, vol. 32(2), Summer, pp. 326-349.

Jong, W. de (1986), *Inter-Etnische Verhoudingen in een Oude Stadswijk*, Eburon, Delft.

Junger, M. (1990), 'Studying Ethnic Minorities in Relation to Crime and Police Discrimination', *British Journal of Criminology*, vol. 4, pp. 493-503.

Junger-Tas, J., Terlouw, G. and Klein, M. (eds) (1994), *Delinquent Behavior among Young People in the Western World: First Results of the International Self-Report Delinquency Study*, Kugler, Amsterdam.

Kaplan, A. (1964), *The Conduct of Inquiry: Methodology for Behavioral Science*, Thomas Y. Crowell, New York.

Kempen, R. van (1991), *Lage-Inkomensgroepen in de Grote Stad: Spreiding en Concentratie in Amsterdam en Rotterdam*, University Utrecht - Faculteit Ruimtelijke Wetenschappen, Utrecht.

Kempen, R. van (1997), 'Turks in the Netherlands: Housing Conditions and Segregation in a Developed Welfare State', in Ş. Özüekren and R. van Kempen (eds), *Turks in European Cities: Housing and Urban Segregation*, University-ERCOMER, Utrecht, pp. 158-190.

Kempen, R. van, Floor, H. and Dieleman, F.M. (1994), *Wonen op Maat: Een Onderzoek naar de Voorkeuren en Motieven van Wooncustomers en te Verwachten Ontwikkelingen daarin, Deel 3: Woonsituatie en Woonwensen*, University Utrecht - Faculteit Ruimtelijke Wetenschappen, Utrecht.

Kemper, F. (1996), *Religiositeit, Etniciteit en Welbevinden*, Catholic University Nijmegen (dissertation), Nijmegen.

Kemper, F. (1998), 'Gezocht: Marokkanen. Methodische Problemen bij het Werven en Interviewen van Allochtone Respondenten', *Migrantenstudies*, vol. 14(1), pp. 43-57.

Kidder, L.H. and Judd, C.M. (1986), *Research Methods in Social Relations*, CBS Publishing Japan, New York.

Kirkpatrick, L. (1993), Fundamentalism, Christian Orthodoxy, and Intrinsic Religious Orientation as Predictors of Discriminatory Attitudes', *Journal for the Scientific Study of Religion*, vol. 32(3), September, pp. 256-268.

Kleinpenning, G. (1993), *Structure and Content of Racist Beliefs: An Empirical Study of Attitudes, Stereotypes and the Ethnic Hierarchy*, University Utrecht - ISOR, Utrecht.

Kleinpenning, G. and Hagendoorn, L. (1991), 'Contextual Aspects of Ethnic Stereotypes and Interethnic Evaluations', *European Journal of Social Psychology*, vol. 21, pp. 331-348.

Kloosterman, R., Leun, J. van der and Rath, J. (1997), *Over Grenzen: Immigranten en de Informele Economie*, Het Spinhuis, Amsterdam.

Kloprogge, J., Martens, E.P., Roelandt, Th. and Veenman, J. (1994), 'Verschillen in Onderwijspositie, Gedeeltelijk Verklaard', in J. Veenman and Th. Roelandt (eds), *Onzeker Bestaan*, Boom, Amsterdam, pp. 79-108.

Knipscheer, C.P.M., Jong-Gierveld, J. de, Tilburg, T. van and Dykstra, P.A. (eds) (1995), *Living Arrangements and Social Networks of Older Adults: First Results*, Free University Press, Amsterdam..

Knoke, D. and Kuklinski, J.H. (1982), *Network Analysis*, Sage Publications, Newbury Park, CA.

Knulst, W. (1989), *Van Vaudeville tot Video: Een Empirisch-Theoretische Studie naar Verschuivingen in het Uitgaan en het Gebruik van Media sinds de Jaren Vijftig*, Sociaal Cultureel Planbureau, Rijswijk.

König-Zahn, C., Furer, J.W. and Tax, B. (1995), *Het Meten van de Gezondheidstoestand: Algemene Gezondheid*, Van Gorcum, Assen.

Korf, D. and Deben, L. (1997), *Dak- en Thuislozen in Amsterdam 1997: Tel- en Consumenten Onderzoek*, Het Spinhuis, Amsterdam.

Kornalijnslijper, N. (1988), Minderheden en Structurele Belemmeringen in de Volkshuisvesting, *Migrantenstudies*, vol. 4(1), 67-78.

Kroeber, A. and Parsons, T. (1958), 'The Concepts of Culture and Social System', *American Sociological Review*, vol. 23, pp. 582-583.

Kuhn, M.H. and McPartland, T.S. (1954), 'An Empirical Investigation of Self-Attitudes', *American Sociological Review*, vol. 19, pp. 68-76.

Kunst, M., Reinsch, P. and Hortulanus, R. (1995), 'Integratie Vraagt Visie', *Tijdschrift voor de Sociale Sector*, September, pp. 4-9.

Kunst, M., Snel, F.G. and Hortulanus, R. (1996), *Welzijn tussen Vraag en Aanbod: Een Wijkanalyse van Utrecht-Noord*, University Utrecht-ASW, Utrecht.

Kymlicka, W. (1995), *Multicultural Citizenship*, Clarendon Press, Oxford.

Landecker, W.S. (1955), 'Types of Integration and their Measurement', in P.F. Lazarsfeld and M. Rosenberg, *The Language of Social Research*, The Free Press, Glencoe, IL, pp. 19-27 (originally published in American Journal of Sociology, vol. 56, 1951, pp. 332-340).

Latuheru, E.J., Vries, E.M. de and Jong, M.J. de (1994), *Integratie Belemmerd? Een Onderzoek naar Belemmerende Factoren bij de Integratie van Turken, Koerden en Marokkanen in Nederland*, Erasmus University Rotterdam - RISBO, Rotterdam.

Lee, B.A. and Campbell, K.E. (1997), 'Common Ground? Urban Neighborhoods as Survey Respondents see Them', *Social Science Quarterly*, vol. 78(4), December, pp. 922-936.

Leeman, Y. (1994), *Samen Jong: Nederlandse Jongeren en Lessen over Inter-Ethnisch Samenleven en Discriminatie*, Van Arkel, Utrecht.

Leets, L., Giles, H. and Clement, R. (1996), 'Explicating Ethnicity in Theory and Communication Research', *Multilingua*, vol. 15(2), pp. 115-147.

Leeuw, J. de and Rijckevorsel, J.L.A. van (1988), 'Beyond Homogeneity Analysis', in J.L.A. van Rijckevorsel and J. de Leeuw (eds), *Component and Correspondence Analysis*, John Wiley, Chichester UK.

Lieberson, S. (1981), 'An Asymmetrical Approach to Segregation', in C. Peach, V. Robinson and S. Smith (eds), *Ethnic Segregation in the Cities*, Croom Helm, London.

Lieberson, S. and Waters, M.C. (1988), *From Many Strands: Ethnic and Racial Groups in Contemporary America*, Russell Sage Foundation, New York.

Liem, P. (2000), *Stapvoets Voorwaarts: Maatschappelijke Status van Surinamers in Nederland*, Thela Thesis Publishers, Amsterdam.

Lijphart, A. (1968), *The Politics of Accommodation: Pluralism and Democracy in the Netherlands*, University of California Press, Berkeley.

Lindo, F. (1996), *Maakt Cultuur Verschil?*, Het Spinhuis, Amsterdam.

Lippe-Biesterfeld, I. van (1995), *Dialoog met de Natuur: een Weg naar een Nieuw Evenwicht*, Ankh-Hermes, Deventer.

Littlewood, R. and Lipsedge, M. (1989), *Aliens and Alienists: A Study of Mental Illness among Ethnic Minorities in the UK, and the Influences on How these Illnesses are Diagnosed*, Unwin Hyman, London.

Lobao, L.M. and Thomas, P. (1992), 'Political Beliefs in an Era of Economic Decline: Farmers' Attitudes toward State Economic Intervention, Trade, and Food Security' in *Rural Sociology*, vol. 57(4) Winter, pp. 453-475.

Loscocco, K.A. (1989), 'The Instrumentally Oriented Factory Worker: Myth or Reality?', *Work and Occupations*, vol. 16(1), February, pp. 3-25.

Lucassen, J. and Penninx, R. (1997), *Nieuwkomers, Nakomelingen, Nederlanders: Immigranten in Nederland, 1550-1993*, Het Spinhuis, Amsterdam.

Luthanen, R. and Crocker, J. (1992), 'A Collective Self-Esteem Scale: Self-Evaluation of One's Social Identity', *Personality and Social Psychology Bulletin*, vol. 18(3), June, pp. 302-318.

Lutz, H. (1991), *Welten Verbinden - Türkische Sozialarbeiterinnen in den Niederlanden und der Bundesrepublik Deutschland*, IKO - Verlag für interkulturelle Kommunikation, Frankfurt am Main.

Lutz, H. (1992), 'Integreert Arbeid? Migranten, Arbeidsmarkt en Beleid in Nederland', *Migrantenstudies*, vol. 8(2), pp. 3-13.

MacDonald, K. (1998), 'Evolution, Culture, and the Five-Factor Model', *Journal of Cross Cultural Psychology*, vol. 29(1), January, pp. 119-149.

Marger, M.M. (1991), *Race and Ethnic Relations: American and Global Perspectives*, Wadsworth Publishing Co, Belmont, CA.

Marsden, P.V. (1990), 'Network Data and Measurement', *Annual Review of Sociology*, vol. 16, pp. 435-463.

Martens, E.P. (1995), *Minderheden in Beeld: Kerncijfers uit de Survey Sociale Positie en Voorzieningengebruik Allochtonen 1994* (SPVA-94), Erasmus University Rotterdam-ISEO, Rotterdam.

Martens, E.P. (1999), *Minderheden in Beeld: SPVA-98*, Erasmus University Rotterdam-ISEO, Rotterdam.

Martens, E.P. and Roelandt, Th. (1993), *Allochtone Ouderen in Nederland: Kerncijfers over de Sociaal-Economische Positie en de Sociale Participatie van Turkse, Marokkaanse, Antilliaanse en Molukse Ouderen*, Erasmus University Rotterdam-ISEO, Rotterdam.

Martens, E.P., Roijen, J.H.M. and Veenman, J. (1994), *Minderheden in Nederland. Statistisch Vademecum 1993/1994*, SDU, Den Haag.

Martens, E.P. and Veenman, J. (1996), 'De Positie van Etnische Minderheden in de Nederlandse Samenleving', in *Jaarboek Minderheden 1996*, Bohn Stafleu Van Loghum, Houten.

Martens, E. and Veenman, J. (1997), 'De Betekenis van Generieke en Etnisch-Specifieke Factoren bij de Verklaring van Achterstand van Etnische Minderheden', Paper presented at the NSV Sociology 'Market day', Utrecht 29 May.

Maslow, A.H. (1970), *Motivation and Personality*, Harper & Row, New York (originally published 1954).

McColl, M.A., Carlson, P., Johnston, J., Minnes, P., Shue, K., Davies, D. and Karlovits, T. (1998), 'The Definition of Community Integration: Perspectives of People with Brain Injuries', *Brain-Injury*, vol. 12(1), January, pp. 15-30.

McCrae, R.R., Costa, P.T., Pilar, G.H. del, Rolland, J.-P. and Parker, W.D. (1998), 'Cross-Cultural Assessment of the Five Factor Model: The Revised NEO Personality Inventory', *Journal of Cross-Cultural Psychology*, vol. 29(1), January, pp. 171-188.

McLeod, J.M., Daily, K., Guo, Z., Eveland, W.P. Jr., Bayer, J., Yang, S. and Wang, H. (1996), 'Community Integration, Local Media Use, and Democratic Processes', *Communication Research*, vol. 23(3), April, pp. 179-209.

Meertens, R.W. and Pettigrew, T.F. (1997), 'Is Subtle Prejudice Really Prejudice?', *Public Opinion Quarterly*, vol. 61, pp. 54-71.

Meloen, J.D. and Veenman, J. (1988), *Het is Maar de Vraag ... Onderzoek naar Responseffecten bij Minderhedensurveys*, Erasmus University Rotterdam-ISEO, Rotterdam.

Meloen, J.D. and Veenman, J. (1990), *Het is Maar de Vraag ... Onderzoek naar Responseffecten bij Minderhedensurveys*, Koninklijke Vermande, Lelystad.

Merton, R.K. (1976), 'Intermarriage and the Social Structure', in R.K. Merton, *Sociological Ambivalence and Other Essays*, New York, pp. 217-250 (first published in *Psychiatry: Journal of the Biology and Pathology of Interpersonal Relations*, vol. 4, August 1941, pp. 361-374).

Middendorp, C. (1978), *Progressivensss and Conservatism*, Mouton Publishers, Berlin/New York.

Miles, R. (1982), *Racism and Migrant Labour*, Routledge & Kegan Paul, London.

Miles, R. (1989), *Racism*, Routledge, London/New York.

Miles, R. (1993), 'Integrating Immigrants in Europe', in R. Miles, *Racism after 'Race Relations'*, Routledge, London/New York.

Mok, A.L. (1990), *In het Zweet uwes Aanschijns*, Stenfert Kroese, Leiden.

Mok, I. and Reinsch, P. (1993), *Op Zoek naar een Multi-etnisch Perspectief: Analyse van een Viertal Nieuwe Aardrijkskunde Methodes*, PAREL, Utrecht.

Mok, I. and Reinsch, P. (eds) (1996), *Kieskleurig: Handleiding Intercultureel Lesmateriaal*, Samsom/Parel, Alphen a/d Rijn/Utrecht (Published in English as, *A Colourful Choice: Handbook for Intercultural Teaching Materials*, European Platform for Dutch Education, 1999).

Moller, V. and Schlemmer, L. (1989), 'South African Quality of Life: A Research Note', *Social Indicators Research*, vol. 21(3) June, pp. 279-291.

Mullard, C., Nimako, K. and Willemsen, G. (1990), *De Plurale Kubus: een Vertoog over Emancipatiemodellen en Minderhedenbeleid*, Warray, Den Haag.

Mungra, G. (1990), *Hindoestaanse Gezinnen in Nederland*, University Leiden-COMT, Leiden.

Musschenga, A.W. (1986), 'De Politieke Conceptie van een Pluralistische Democratie', in A. W. Musschenga and J. Tennekes (eds), *Emancipatie en Identiteit. Over de Positie van Etnische Groepen*, VU-uitgeverij, Amsterdam.

Nauck, B., Kohlmann, A. and Diefenbach, H. (1997), 'Familiäre Netzwerke, Intergenerative Transmission und Assimilationsprozesse bei Türkischen Migrantenfamilien', *Kölner Zeitschrift für Soziologie und Sozialpsychologie*, vol. 49(3), September, pp. 477-499.

Naylor, F.D. and Kidd, G.J. (1991), 'The Predictive Validity of the Investigative Scale of the Career Assessment Inventory', *Educational and Psychological Measurement*, vol. 51(1), Spring, pp. 217-226.

Nekuee, S. (1996), *De Sociale Integratie van Vluchtelingen: Een onderzoek naar de UAF-Studenten*, University Utrecht-Sociology (doctoraal scriptie), Utrecht.

Nekuee, S. and Verkuyten, M. (1999), 'Emotionele Distantie en Integratie: Iraanse Politieke Vluchtelingen in Nederland', *Mens & Maatschappij*, vol. 74(3), pp. 218-234.

Neto, F. (1995), 'Predictors of Satisfaction with Life among Second Generation Migrants', *Social Indicators Research*, vol. 35, pp. 93-116.

Newcomb, A.F. and Bukowski, W.M. (1983), 'Social Impact and Social Preference as Determinants of Children's Peer Group Status', *Developmental Psychology*, vol. 19, pp. 856-867.

NIBUD (Nationaal Instituut voor Budgetvoorlichting) (1997), *Bestedingspatronen van Allochtone Huishoudens in de Vier Grote Steden*, NIBUD, Utrecht.

Niekerk, M. van (1993), *Kansarmoede: Reacties van Allochtonen op Achterstand*, Het Spinhuis, Amsterdam.

Niekerk, M. van and Rath, J. (eds) (1996), 'Themanummer Concentratie en Segregatie', *Migrantenstudies*, vol. 12(2).

Niekerk, M. van, Sunier, Th. and Vermeulen, H. (1989), *Bekende Vreemden: Surinamers, Turken en Nederlanders in een Naoorlogse Wijk*, Het Spinhuis, Amsterdam.

Niesing, W. (1993), *The Labour Market Position of Ethnic Minorities in the Netherlands*, Erasmus University Rotterdam (dissertation), Rotterdam.

OECD (Organisation for Economic Co-operation and Development) (1998), *Immigrants, Integration and Cities - Exploring the Links*.

Ogbu, J.U. (1978), *Minority Education and Caste: The American System in Cross-Cultural Perspective*, Academic Press, New York.

Ogbu, J. (1996), 'Essential Background Knowledge', lecture at the IMES/ASW conference *Does Culture Make a Difference?*, Amsterdam, 15 November.

Oudenhoven, J.P. van, Willemsma, G. and Prins, K. (1996), 'Integratie en Assimilatie van Marokkanen, Surinamers en Turken in Nederland', *De Psycholoog*, December, pp. 468-471.

Park, R.E. (1925), 'Suggestions for the Investigation of Human Behaviour in the Urban Environment', in R.E. Park, E.W. Burgess and R.D. Mackenzie (eds), *The City*, University of Chicago Press, Chicago.

Park, R.E., Burgess, E.W. and Mckenzie, R.D. (eds) (1976), *The City*, University of Chicago Press, Chicago (originally published in 1925).

Parsons, T. (1960), 'Durkheim's Contribution to the Theory of Integration of Social Systems', in K. Wolff (ed.), *Emile Durkheim, 1858-1917: A Collection of Essays with Translations and Bibliography*, Ohio State University Press, Columbia, OH, pp.118-153.

Pels, T. (ed.) (1994), *Opvoeding in Chinese, Marokkaanse en Surinaams-Creoolse Gezinnen*, Erasmus University Rotterdam-ISEO, Rotterdam.

Pels, T. (1998), 'Opvoeding in Marokkaanse Gezinnen en de Plaats van Onderwijs: Verandering en Continuïteit', *Migrantenstudies*, vol. 14(2), pp. 133-148.

Pels, T. and Veenman, J. (1996), 'Onderwijsachterstanden bij Allochtone Kinderen: Het Ontbrekende Onderzoek', *Sociologische Gids*, vol. 43(2), pp. 131-145.

Penninx, R. (1988), *Minderheidsvorming en Emancipatie: Balans van Kennisverwerving ten aanzien van Immigranten en Woonwagenbewoners*, Samsom, Alphen a/d Rijn.

Penninx, R. (1992), *Wie Betaalt en Wie Bepaalt*, Ministerie van Binnenlandse Zaken, Den Haag.

Peters, B. (1993), *Die Integration Moderner Gesellschaften*, Suhrkamp, Frankfurt am Main.

Petersen, W. (1975), *Population*, Macmillan, New York.

Pettigrew, T.F. (1995), 'Het Belang van Verhoudingen tussen Groepen in Nederland voor Sociaal-Wetenschappelijke Theorievorming', *Migrantenstudies*, vol. 11(1), pp. 49-57.

Phalet, K., Rycke, L. de and Swyngedouw, M. (1999), 'Culturele Waarden en Acculturatievormen bij Turken en Marokkanen in Brussel', in M. Swyngedouw, K. Phalet and K. Deschouwer (eds), *Minderheden in Brussel: Sociopolitieke Houdingen en Gedragingen*, VUB-Press, Brussel, pp. 41-73.

Phillips, G.Y. (1996), 'Stress and Residential Well-Being', in H.W. Neighbors and J.S. Jackson (eds), *Mental Health in Black America*, Sage, Thousand Oaks, CA, pp. 27-44.

Phinney, J.S. (1990), 'Ethnic Identity in Adolescents and Adults: Review of Research', *Psychological Bulletin*, vol. 108(3), pp. 499-514.

Phinney, J.S. (1992), 'The Multigroup Ethnic Identity Measure: A New Scale for use with Diverse Groups', *Journal of Adolescent Research*, vol. 7, pp. 156-176.

Plutzer, E. (1987), 'Determinants of Leftist Radical Belief in the United States: A Test of Competing Theories' in *Social Forces*, vol. 65(4), June, pp. 1002-1019.

Poel, M.G.M. van der (1993), *Personal Networks: A Rational Choice Explanation of their Size and Composition*, Swets & Zeitlinger, Lisse.

Portes, A. and Manning, R.D. (1986), 'The Immigrant Enclave: Theory and Empirical Examples', in S. Olzak and J. Nagel (eds), *Competitive Ethnic Relations*, Academic Press, Orlando.

Preiswerk, R. (1980), 'Ethnocentric Images in History Books and their Effect on Racism', in R. Preiswerk (ed.), *The Slant of the Pen: Racism in Children's Books*, World Council of Churches, Geneva, pp. 131-139.

Priemus, H. (1986), 'Housing as a Social Adaptation Process: A Conceptual Scheme', *Environment and Behavior*, vol. 18(1), January, pp. 31-52.

Prins, K.S. (1996), *Van 'Gastarbeider' tot 'Nederlander': Adaptatie van Marokkanen en Turken in Nederland*, University Groningen (dissertation), Groningen.

Pryor, E.T., Goldmann, G.J., Sheridan, M.J. and White, P.M. (1992), 'Measuring Ethnicity: Is 'Canadian' an Evolving Indigenous Category?', *Ethnic and Racial Studies*, vol. 15(2), April, pp. 214-235.

Raad, B. de, Perugini, M., Hrebíčková, M., Szarota, P. (1998), 'Lingua Franca of Personalities: Taxonomies and Structures Based on the Psycholexical Approach', *Journal of Cross-Cultural Psychology*, vol. 29(1), January, pp. 212-232.

Rath, J. (1988), 'Political Action of Immigrants in the Netherlands: Class or Ethnicity', *European Journal of Political Research*, vol. 16, pp. 623-644.

Rath, J. (1991), *Minorisering: De Sociale Constructie van 'Etnische Minderheden'*, SUA, Amsterdam.

Rath, J. (1995), 'Beunhazen van Buiten: De Informele Economie als Bastaardsfeer van Sociale Integratie', in G. Engbersen and R. Gabriëls (eds), *Sferen van Integratie: Naar een Gedifferentieerd Allochtonenbeleid*, Boom, Amsterdam/Meppel, pp. 74-109.

Rath, J. and. Kloosterman, R. (eds) (1998), *Rijp en Groen: Het Zelfstandig Ondernemerschap van Immigranten in Nederland*, Het Spinhuis, Amsterdam.

Rath, J., Penninx, R., Groenendijk, K. and Meyer, A. (1996), *Nederland en Zijn Islam: Hoe een Ontzuilende Samenleving Reageert op een 'Nieuwe' Geloofsgemeenschap*, Het Spinhuis, Amsterdam.

Reed, K. (1997), 'Orientations to Work: The Cultural Conditioning of Motivation', *Australian and New Zealand Journal of Sociology*, vol. 33(3), November, pp. 364-386.

Reinsch, P.Q. (1987), 'Kromzwaarden en Kamelen: Islamieten in Schoolboeken', in J. Dubbelman and J. Tanja (eds), *Vreemd Gespuis*, Ambo/Novib, Baarn/Den Haag.

Reinsch, P.Q. (1990), *Een Anti-Racistische Lezing van het WRR-Rapport 'Allochtonenbeleid'*, PAREL, Utrecht.

Reinsch, P.Q., Kunst, M. and Hortulanus, R. (1995), *Allemaal Haarlemmers: Contouren van een Lokaal Integratiebeleid*, Gemeente Haarlem-Sector BWE, Haarlem.

Reker, G.T., Peacock, E.J. and Wong, T.P. (1987), 'Meaning and Purpose in Life and Well-being: A Life-Span Perspective', *Journal of Gerontology*, vol. 42, pp. 44-49.

Rex, J. (1986), 'The Role of Class Analysis in the Study of Race Relations - A Weberian Perspective', in J. Rex and D. Mason (eds), *Theories of Race and Ethnic Relations*, Cambridge University Press, Cambridge, pp. 64-83.

286 Measuring Immigrant Integration

Rex, J. (1996), *Ethnic Minorities in the Modern Nation State: Working Papers in the Theory of Multiculturalism and Political Integration*, MacMillan/St. Martin's Press, London/New York.

Rex, J. and Tomlinson, S. (1979), *Colonial Immigrants in a British City: A Class Analysis*, Routledge & Kegan Paul, London.

Rigby, K. and Vreugdenhill, A. (1987), The Relationship between Generalized Community Satisfaction and Residential Social Status', *Journal of Social Psychology*, vol. 127(4), August, pp. 381-390.

Rispens, J., Hermanns, J.M.A. and Meeus, W.H.J. (eds) (1996), *Opvoeden in Nederland*, Van Gorcum, Assen.

Risvanoglu-Bilgin, S., Brouwer, L. and Priester, M. (1986), *Verschillend als de Vingers van een Hand: Een Onderzoek naar het Integratieproces van Turkse Gezinnen in Nederland*, University Leiden-COMT, Leiden.

RMO (Raad voor Maatschappelijke Ontwikkeling) (1998), *Integratie in Perspectief: Integratie van Bijzondere Groepen en van Personen uit Etnische Groeperingen in het Bijzonder*, SDU Uitgevers, Den Haag.

Rodrigues, P.R. (1997), *Anders Niets? Discriminatie naar Ras en Nationaliteit bij Consumententransacties*, Koninklijke Vermande, Lelystad.

Roelandt, Th. (1991), 'Marginalisering, Etnische Herkomst en de Onderklasse: Een Theoretische Verkenning', *Migrantenstudies*, vol. 7(3), pp. 6-20.

Roelandt, Th.J.A. (1994), *Verscheidenheid in Ongelijkheid: Een Studie naar Etnische Stratificatie en Onderklassevorming in de Nederlandse Samenleving*, Thesis Publishers, Amsterdam.

Roelandt, Th. and Veenman, J. (1987), *Beter Meten 1: Aanbevelingen bij het Rapportagesysteem Toegankelijkheid en Evenredigheid*, Erasmus University Rotterdam-ISEO, Rotterdam.

Roelandt, Th. and Veenman, J. (1989), *Beter Meten 2 Aanbevelingen bij het Rapportagesysteem Toegankelijkheid en Evenredigheid*, Erasmus University Rotterdam-ISEO, Rotterdam.

Rohe, W.M. and Basolo, V. (1997), 'Long-Term Effects of Homeownership on the Self-Perceptions and Social Interaction of Low-Income Persons', *Environment and Behavior*, vol. 29(6), November, pp. 793-819.

Rokeach, M. (1973), *The Nature of Human Values*, The Free Press, New York/London.

Rowntree, B.S. (1901), *Poverty - A Study of Town Life*, MacMillan, London.

Rublee, C.B. and Shaw, S.M. (1991), 'Constraints on the Leisure and Community Participation of Immigrant Women: Implications for Social Integration', *Loisir-et-Societe/Society-and-Leisure*, vol. 14(1) Spring, pp. 133-150.

Runciman, W.G. (1966), *Relative Deprivation and Social Justice: A Study of Attitudes to Social Inequality in 20th Century England*, University of California Press, Berkeley/Los Angeles.

Rust, J. (1998), 'The validation of the Orpheus minor scales in a working population', *Social Behavior and Personality*, vol. 26(4), pp. 399-406.

Ryan, W. (1976), *Blaming the Victim*, Vintage Books, New York.

Saharso, S. (1985), 'De Tweede Generatie: (voor Eeuwig) Verloren tussen Twee Culturen?', *Psychologie en Maatschappij*, vol. 32, pp. 371-385.

Saharso, S. (1992a), *Jan en Alleman: Etnische Jeugd over Etnische Identiteit, Discriminatie en Vriendschap*, Van Arkel, Utrecht.

Saharso, S. (1992b), 'Door Dik en Dun: Over de Mogelijkheiden en Onmogelijkheden van Interethnische Vriendschap', *Jeugd en Samenleving*, no 5/6, pp. 367-379.

Saharso, S. and Prins, B. (1999), 'Multicultureel Burgerschap: Een Introductie', *Migrantenstudies*, vol. 15(2), pp. 62-69.

Said, E.W. (1978), *Orientalism*, Routledge & Kegan Paul, London/New York.

Sampson, R.J. (1991), 'Linking the Micro- and Macrolevel Dimensions of Community Social Organization', *Social Forces*, vol. 70(1), September, pp. 43-64.

Sansone L. (1992), *Schitteren in de Schaduw: Overlevingsstrategieën, Subcultuur en Etniciteit van Creoolse Jongeren uit de Lagere Klasse in Amsterdam, 1981-1990*, Het Spinhuis, Amsterdam.

Schakenbos, E. and Marsman, G.W. (1988), *Migranten en de Media: Een Literatuurstudie naar Trends in het Mediagebruik van Etnische Minderheden in Zes West-Europese Landen*, Masua, Nijmegen.

Scheepers, P., Eisinga, R. and Felling, A. (1994), 'Het Electoraat van Extreem-Rechts: Theoretische Verklaringen, Empirische Bevindingen, Conceptualiseringen en Operationaliseringen', *Bijdrage aan de studiedag over 'Extreem-rechts' bij het CBS in Voorburg*, 11 November.

Scheffer, P. (2000), 'Het Multiculturele Drama', *NRC Handelsblad*, Saturday 29 January, p. 6.

Schermerhorn, R.A. (1970), *Comparative Ethnic Relations: A Framework for Theory and Research*, Random House, New York.

Scherpenzeel, A.C. (1996), 'Satisfaction in the Netherlands', in W.E. Saris, R. Veenhoven, A.C. Scherpenzeel and R. Brunting (eds), *A Comparative Study of Satisfaction with Life in Europe*, Etövös University Press, Budapest.

Schiepers, J.M.P., Gessel-Dabekaussen, A.A.M.W. van, Elkink, A.J. (1993), *Equivalentiefactoren Volgens de Budgetverdelingsmethode: Uitkomsten Gebaseerd op de CBS-Budgetonderzoeken 1986-1990*, VUGA, Den Haag.

Schnabel, P. (2000), *De Multiculturele Illusie: Een Pleidooi voor Aanpassing en Assimilatie - Met Replieken van Ruben Gowricharn en Ineke Mok*, Forum, Utrecht.

Schwartz, S.H. (1992), 'Universals in the Context and Structure of Values: Theoretical Advances and Empirical Tests in 20 Countries', in M. Zanna (ed.), *Advances in Experimental Social Psychology* (vol. 25), Academic Press, Orlando FL, pp. 1-65.

Schwartz, S.H. and Sagiv, L. (1995), 'Identifying Culture-Specifics in the Content and Structure of Values', *Journal of Cross-Cultural Psychology*, vol. 26(1), pp. 92-116.

SCP (Sociaal en Cultureel Planbureau), *Sociaal en Cultureel Rapport* (1996), SCP/VUGA,Rijswijk/Den Haag.

SCP (1998), *Sociaal en Cultureel Rapport*, Rijswijk/Den Haag, SCP/VUGA.

SCP (1999), *De Stad op Straat: De Openbare Ruimte in Perspectief*, SCP, Rijswijk.

Shadid, W.A. (1979), *Moroccan Workers in the Netherlands*, University Leiden, (dissertation), Leiden.

Shadid, W.A. (1998), *Grondslagen van Interculturele Communicatie: Studieveld en Werkterrein*, Bohn Stafleu Van Loghum, Houten (etc.).

Sinclair, J. (ed.) (1987), *Collins English Language Dictionary*, Collins ELT, London.

Sixma, H. and Ultee, W. (1983), 'Een Beroepsprestigeeschaal voor Nederland in de Jaren Tachtig', *Mens en Maatschappij*, vol. 59, pp. 360-382.

Smith, A. (1981), *The Ethnic Revival*, Cambridge University Press, Cambridge.

Smith, M.G. (1965), *The Plural Society in the British-West Indies*, University of California Press, Berkeley.

Smith, M.G. (1986), 'Pluralism, Race and Ethnicity in Selected African Countries', in J. Rex and D. Mason (eds), *Theories of Race and Ethnic Relations*, Cambridge University Press, Cambridge.

Sowell, Th. (1981a), *Markets and Minorities*, Basic Books, New York.

Sowell, Th. (1981b), *Ethnic America*, Basic Books, New York.

Spain, D. (1988), 'The Effect of Changing Household Composition on Neighborhood Satisfaction', *Urban Affairs Quarterly*, vol. 23(4), June, pp. 581-600.

Springers, A. (1995), 'Family Reunification Versus Family Formation Migration', *Netherlands Official Statistics*, vol. 10, Summer, pp. 31-35.

Stamm, K.R., Emig, A.G. and Hesse, M.B. (1997), 'The Contribution of Local Media to Community Involvement', *Journalism and Mass Communication Quarterly*, vol. 74(1), Spring, pp. 97-107.

Stanfield, J.H. (1995), 'Racial and Ethnic Conflict Studies: Methodological Dilemmas', in J.B. Gittler (ed.), *Research in Human Social Conflict: Racial and Ethnic Conflict, Perspectives from the Social Disciplines*, JAI Press, Greenwich, CT/London, UK, pp. 365-381.

Staring, R., Leun, J. van der, Engbersen, G. and Kehla, J. (1998), *Patronen van Incorporatie: In- en Uitsluiting van Illegale Migranten binnen Etnische Gemeenschappen*, Erasmus University Rotterdam - FSW-Sociologie, Rotterdam.

Stark, R. and Bainbridge, W.S. (1996), *A Theory of Religion*, Rutgers University Press, New Brunswick, NJ.

Stearns, L.B. and Logan, J.R. (1986), 'Measuring Trends in Segregation: Three Dimensions, Three Measures', *Urban Affairs Quarterly*, vol. 22(1), September, pp. 124-150.

Stevens, J. (1996), *Applied Multivariate Statistics for the Social Sciences*, Lawrence Erlbaum Associates, Mahwah NJ.

Strack, F., Argyle, M. and Schwarz, N. (eds) (1991), *Subjective Well-being: An Interdisciplinary Perspective*, Pergamon Press, Oxford UK.

Swaan, A. de (1988), *In Care of the State: Health Care, Education and Welfare in Europa and the USA in the Modern Era*, Oxford University Press, New York.

Swyngedouw, M., Phalet, K. and Deschouwer, K. (eds) (1999), *Minderheden in Brussel: Sociopolitieke Houdingen en Gedragingen*, VUBPress, Brussel.

Tesser, P.T.M., Dugteren, F.A. van and Merens, A. (1997), *Rapportage Minderheden 1997*, Sociaal en Cultureel Planbureau/VUGA, Rijswijk/Den Haag.

Tesser, P.J.M., Merens, J.G.F. and Praag, C.S. (1999), *Rapportage Minderheden 1999: Positie in het Onderwijs en op de Arbeidsmarkt*, Sociaal en Cultureel Planbureau, Rijswijk.

Tesser, P.T.M., Praag, C.S. van, Dugteren, F.A. van, Herweijer, L.J. and Wouden, H.C. van der (1995), *Rapportage Minderheden: Concentratie en Segregatie*, Sociaal Cultureel Planbureau, Rijswijk.

Teule, R. and Kempen, R. van (1991), 'Getto's of Concentratiegebieden: Goudkusten Versus Steenpuisten?', *European Journal of Intercultural Studies*, vol. 38(1), pp. 48-59.

Teunissen, J. (1988), *Etnische Relaties in het Basisonderwijs: 'Witte' en 'Zwarte' Scholen in de Grote Stad*, University Wageningen (dissertation), Wageningen.

Teunnissen, J. and Matthijssen, M. (1996), 'Stagnatie in Onderwijsonderzoek naar de Etnische Factor bij Allochtone Leerlingen: Een Pleidooi voor Theoretische en Methodologische Vernieuwing', *Sociologische Gids*, vol. 43(2), pp. 87-99.

Thurlings, J.M.G. (1977), *De Wetenschap der Samenleving*, Samson, Alphen a/d Rijn.

Tiggele, D. van (1997), 'Beheersing Nederlands Sleutel tot Integratie', *De Volkskrant*, 7 February.

Tilburg, T. van (1985), The Betekenis van Ondersteuning in Primaire Sociale Relaties, VU Uitgeverij, Amsterdam.

Tillich, P. (1952), *The Courage to Be*, Yale University Press, New Haven, CT.

Townsend, P. (1979), *Poverty in the United Kingdom*, Penguin, Harmondsworth.

Tran, T.V. and Nguyen, T.D. (1994), 'Gender and Satisfaction with the Host Society among Indochinese Refugees', *International Migration Review*, vol. 28(2), Summer, pp. 323-337.

Trappenburg, M.J. (1993), *Soorten van Gelijk: Medische-Ethische Discussies in Nederland*, Tjeenk-Willink, Zwolle.

Tromp, B. (1992), 'Recept: Verzuiling', in Podium, *Meningen over Medelanders Integratie of Assimilatie uit de Nederlandse en Belgische Pers*, Nederhof Produktie, Amsterdam, pp.120-23.

Turnhout, T. van (ed.) (1995), *Denkend aan Haarlem ...*, Gottmer/Schuy, Haarlem.

Tweede Kamer (1983), *Minderhedennota*, vergaderjaar 1982/1983, 16102, nrs. 2021. (Tweede Kamer, 1993/94:6), Den Haag.

Tweede Kamer (1994), *Integratiebeleid Etnische Minderheden. Contourennota*, vergaderjaar 1993/1994: 23684, nr. 1, Den Haag.

Tweede Kamer (1996), *Regels met Betrekking tot de Inburgering van Nieuwkomers in de Nederlandse Samenleving*, 25 114, nrs 1-2, Den Haag.

Tweede Kamer (1997), *Wet Inburgering Nieuwkomers*, vergaderjaar 1996/1997: 25114, Den Haag.

Tylor, E. (1924), *Primitive Culture*, Smith (originally published in 1871), Gloucester, MA.

Ujimoto, K.V. (1985), 'The Allocation of Time to Social and Leisure Activities as Social Indicators for the Integration of Aged Ethnic Minorities', *Social Indicators Research*, vol. 17, pp. 253-266.

Uniken Venema, H.P. (1989), *Toen Ik Hier Kwam was Ik Kerngezond: De Gezondheid van Turken in Nederland*, Bohn, Scheltema en Holkema, Utrecht.

Uniken Venema, H.P. (1995), 'Etnische Minderheden', in H.P. Uniken Venema and H.F.L. Garretsen (eds), *Het Meten van de Gezondheidstoestand: Gezondheidsonderzoek bij Moeilijk Bereikbare Groepen*, Van Gorcum, Assen.

Uniken Venema, H.P. and Wersch, S.F.M. van (1992), *Gezondheid van Marokkaanse Vrouwen: Gezondheidsbeleving, Ziektegedrag en Sociale Netwerken van Marokkaanse en Nederlandse Vrouwen in Rotterdam*, Gemeentelijke Gezondheidsdienst voor Rotterdam en Omstreken, Rotterdam.

Uys, T. (1991), 'The Experience of Relative Deprivation in a Black Urban Community', *South African Journal of Sociology*, vol. 22(4), December, pp. 117-124.

Vaus, D. de and McAllister, I. (1991), 'Gender and Work Orientation: Values and Satisfaction in Western Europe', in *Work and Occupations*, vol. 18(1), February, pp. 72-93.

Veenhoven, R. (1993), *Happiness in Nations: Subjective Appreciation of Life in 56 Nations, 1946-1992*, Erasmus University Rotterdam-RISBO, Rotterdam.

Veenhoven, R. (1996), *Leefbaarheid van Landen*, University Utrecht-AWSB, Utrecht.

Veenman, J. (1994), *Participatie in Perspectief: Ontwikkelingen in de Sociaal-Economische Positie van Zes Allochtone Groepen in Nederland*, Bohn Stafleu Van Loghum, Houten/Zaventem.

Veenman, J. (1995), 'Integratie en het Onderwijs', in G. Engbersen and R. Gabriëls (eds), *Sferen van Integratie: Naar een Gedifferentieerd Allochtonenbeleid*, Boom, Amsterdam/Meppel, pp. 110-136.

Veenman, J. (1997), 'Armoede onder Allochtonen', in G. Engbersen, J.C. Vrooman and E. Snel (eds), *De Kwetsbaren: Het Tweede Jaarrapport Armoede en Sociale Uitsluiting*, Amsterdam University Press, Amsterdam, pp. 211-228.

Veenman, J. (1999), *Participatie en Perspectief: Verleden en Toekomst van Etnische Minderheden in Nederland*, Bohn Stafleu van Loghum/Koninklijke Vermande, Houten/Lelystad.

Veenman, J. and Martens, E. (1995), *Op de Toekomst Gericht: Tweede Generatie Allochtonen in Nederland*, VUGA, Den Haag.

Veraart, J. (1996), *In Vaders Voetspoor: Jonge Turken op de Arbeidsmarkt*, University Utrecht-AWSB, Utrecht.

Verkuyten, M. (1988), *Zelfbeleving en Identiteit van Jongeren uit Ethnische Minderheden*, Gouda Quint, Arnhem.

Verkuyten, M. (1990), 'Self-Esteem and the Evaluation of Ethnic Identity among Turkish and Dutch Adolescents in the Netherlands', *Journal of Social Psychology*, vol. 130, pp. 285-297.

Verkuyten, M. (1992), *Zelfbeleving van Jeugdige Allochtonen: Een Socio-Psychologische Benadering*, Swets & Zeitlinger, Amsterdam/Lisse.

Verkuyten, M. (1999), *Etnische Identiteit: Theoretische en Empirische Benaderingen*, Het Spinhuis, Amsterdam.

Verkuyten, M. and Masson, K. (1995), "New Racism', Self-Esteem, and Ethnic Relations among Minority and Majority Youth in the Netherlands', *Social Behavior and Personality*, vol. 23(2), pp. 137-154.

Vermeulen, H. (1990), 'De Multi-Etnische Samenleving op Buurtniveau', in H.B. Entzinger and P.J.J. Stijnen (eds), *Etnische Minderheden in Nederland*, Open Universiteit, Heerlen.

Vermeulen, H. (1992), 'De Cultura: Een Verhandeling over het Cultuurbegrip in de Studie van Allochtone Etnische Groepen', *Migrantenstudies*, vol. 8(2), pp. 14-30.

Vermeulen, H. (ed.) (1997), *Immigrant Policy for a Multicultural Society: A Comparative Study of Integration, Language and Religious Policy in Five Western European Countries*, Migration Policy Group, Brussels.

Vermeulen, H. and Penninx, R. (eds) (1994), *Het Democratisch Ongeduld: De Emancipatie en Integratie van Zes Doelgroepen van het Minderhedenbeleid*, Het Spinhuis, Amsterdam.

Vermeulen, H. and Penninx, R. (eds) (2000), *Immigrant Integration: The Dutch Case*, Het Spinhuis, Amsterdam.

Vries, S. de (1992), *Working in Multi-Ethnic Groups: The Performance and Well-Being of Minority and Majority Workers*, Gouda Quint, Arnhem.

Waldinger, R. (1995), 'The 'Other Side' of Embeddedness: A Case-Study of the Interplay of Economy and Ethnicity', *Ethnic and Racial Studies*, vol. 18(3), July, pp. 555-580.

Walker, A. and Maltby, T. (1997), *Ageing Europe*, Open University Press, Buckingham, UK.

Wallman, S. (1982), *Living in South London*, Gowers, Aldershot.

Walzer, M. (1983), *Spheres of Justice: A Defence of Pluralism and Equality*, Martin Robertson, Oxford.

Walzer, M. (1991), 'The Idea of Civil Society', *Dissent*, Spring, pp. 293-304.

Walzer, M. (1993),'The Politics of Difference: Statehood and Toleration in a Multi-Cultural World', Key note speech at congress, '*Tolerantie en Minderheden*', Nijmegen, 28 October.

Walzer, M. (1997), *On Toleration*, Yale University Press, New Haven/London.

Warren, D.I. (1977), 'The Functional Diversity of Urban Neighborhoods', *Urban Affairs Quarterly*, vol. 13(2), December, pp.151-179.

Warren, D.I. (1978), 'Explorations in Neighborhood Differentiation', *The Sociological Quarterly*, vol. 19, Spring, pp. 310-331.

Weber, M. (1918), 'The Distribution of Power within the Political Community: Class, Status, Party', in M.Weber, *Economy and Society: An Outline of Interpretive Sociology*, University of California Press, Berkeley etc., pp. 926-938.

Wellman, B. and Berkowitz, S.D. (eds) (1988), *Social Structure: A Network Approach*, Cambridge University Press, Cambridge.

Werdmölder, H. (1990), *Een Generatie op Drift: De Geschiedenis van een Marokkaanse Randgroep*, Gouda Quint, Arnhem.

Willems, W. (1998), *Het Water van Nederland Gedronken - Stemmen van Migranten*, Meulenhoff, Amsterdam.

Willems, W. and Cottaar, A. (1989), *Het Beeld van Nederland: Hoe Zien Molukkers, Chinezen, Woonwagenbewoners en Turken de Nederlanders en Zichzelf?*, Ambo/Novib, Baarn/Den Haag.

Willemsen, G. (1993), 'Kronkelpaden van de Creoolse Cultuur', in R.S. Gowricharn, (ed.), *Binnen de Grenzen: Immigratie, Etniciteit en Integratie in Nederland*, De Tijdstroom, Utrecht, pp. 102-112.

Willis, P.E. (1977), *Learning to Labour: How Working Class Kids get Working Class Jobs*, Gower, Aldershot.

Wilson, W.J. (1987), *The Truly Disadvantaged: The Inner City, the Underclass, and Public Policy*, The University of Chicago Press, Chicago/London.

Wirth, L. (1945), 'The Problem of Minority Groups', in R. Linton (ed.), *The Science of Man in the World Crisis*, Columbia University Press, New York.

Witt, S.D. (1996), 'Traditional or Androgynous: An Analysis to Determine Gender Role Orientation of Basal Readers', *Child Study Journal*, vol. 26(4), pp. 303-318.

Woldring, H.E.S. (1995), 'Political Integration and Linguistic Plurality', *History of European Ideas*, vol. 20(1-3), January, pp. 109-114.

Wong, M.M. and Csikszentmihalyi, M. (1991), 'Motivation and Academic Achievement: The Effects of Personality Traits and the Quality of Experience', *Journal of Personality*, vol. 59(3), September, pp. 539-574.

WRR (Wetenschappelijke Raad voor het Regeringsbeleid) (1979), *Ethnic Minorities*, SDU, Den Haag.

WRR (1989), *Allochtonenbeleid*, SDU, Den Haag (the English version, *Immigrant Policy*, was published in 1990).

Yinger, J.M. (1994), *Ethnicity: Source of Strength - Source of Conflict?*, SUNY, Albany.

Zee, J.H. van der (1988), *Zwarte Studenten aan de Rijksuniversiteit Groningen: Een Verkennend Onderzoek naar Etnocentrisme en Racisme aan de Groningse Universiteit*, University Groningen-Androgogisch Inst., Groningen.

Zijderveld, A.C. (1993), *De Culturele Factor: Een Cultuursociologische Wegwijzer*, VUGA, Den Haag.

Zusman, M.E. and Olsen, A.O. (1977), 'Gathering Complete Responses from Mexican-Americans by Personal Interview', *Journal of Social Issues*, vol. 33(4), pp. 46-55.

Zwan, A. van der and Entzinger, H.B. (1994), *Beleidsopvolging Minderhedendebaat*, Ministerie van Binnenlandse Zaken, Den Haag.

Appendix I: Integration Indicators

On the following pages I present an overview of indicators that in the Haarlem survey exhibit a statistically significant (probability F < .05) association with respondents' *local integration index* score. Two measures of association are used: for indicators measured at nominal or ordinal level the eta, for interval level indicators (indicated by a # in the first column) Pearson's correlation. All analysis results here and in the text that pertain to 'all minorities', 'all immigrants' or 'all adult residents' have been reweighed to correct for differences due to sample stratification.

The indicators are listed according to the order they are discussed in the study. The first two sections (between the dashed lines) pertain to interview and demographic variables respectively (chapter 3). These are followed by sections on positional (chapter 4), orientational (chapter 5) and behavioral (chapter 6) indicators. An asterisk (*) denotes those indicators that by multivariate analysis clarify statistically significant portions of index variance under control for other indicators within the same dimension of integration. Underlined and **boldfaced** statistics also denote indicators entered in multiple regression models; the total variance in the index (i.e., the adjusted R^2) explained by these models are presented in the final rows of the table. For those indicators transformed into dummy variable-sets for multiple regression analysis, the reference categories are presented following the table, as well as specifications on the methods used.

Table I.1   Significant indicators of integration index score

Indicator # = interval level measurement	Moroc- cans	Turks	Surinamese Antilleans	'Other' immi- grants	All immi- grants	Indige- nous Dutch
gender interviewer				.28	.19	
language interview	.42	.38			.48	-
# interview duration		-.35		-.44	-.27	
interview ambience				.31	.27	
# cultural item nonresponse			-.27	-.20	-.22	-.24
clustered or aselect					.13	.21

Indicator # = interval level measurement	Moroc-cans	Turks	Surinamese Antilleans	'Other' immi-grants	All immi-grants	Indige-nous Dutch
region of origin	-	-		.36*	.39*	-
gender						.21*
# age	-.40*	-.28*			*	-.25
# age at migration	-.26	-.23	-.32			-
migration motive	.53	.24			.29	-
# migration year	.25					-
generation		.24			.29	-
residential district		*	.49*	.56*	.51*	.37*
# residence duration	-.22					-.28*
∑ R² demographic *	16%	14%	13%	26%	35%	18%
household type		.29*			.25*	.25*
household breadwinner	.33	.29				
education level	.34	.43*	.51*	.55*	.61*	.49*
Dutch education			.49	.48	.47	.46
labor market position	.46	.34*	*	.42	.39*	.41*
housing market position			.33*	.42	.40*	.40
# housing costs per room	.22			.26	.24	
neighborhood's status					.21*	.27
civic memberships	.34*	.26	.35		.21	
∑ R² positional *	9%	28%	23%	21%	42%	35%
ethnic self-identification	.45*	.22*		*	.20*	
ethnic belonging		.37			.25	
ethnic affection		.27		.34	.31	.26
oral Dutch skills	.46				.33*	
religious faith			.40	.40*	.56*	
religious devotion	.31			.31	.41*	
labor ambition	.31		.37*			

Indicator # = interval level measurement	Moroc-cans	Turks	Surinamese Antilleans	'Other' immi-grants	All immi-grants	Indige-nous Dutch
# approval separate social services	-.21	-.19*				.24
preferred place of residence				.34	.28	
neighborhood affinity	_.31*_		.33	_.30*_	_.22*_	
voting right used		.26				.16
left-right electoral vote					.34	
approval local ethnic organizations	.41	_.38*_				.26
choice for freedom → equality		.20			-.20	-.25
choice for cultural unity → diversity					.24	_.32_
choice for sociability → privacy					.13	
∑ R² orientational *	24%	14%	11%	13%	22%	-
lives with partner	-.31					
partner's ethnicity	.37				_.38*_	
work search channel						.31
# mean contact frequency with ties				.21	.18	-.18
# frequency/proximity of contacts with ties	_.16*_			_.38*_	_.35*_	
seclusive ties only	.36*	.19	.31	.36	-	
# proportion contacts with other categories	.23	.17	_.50*_	.24	-	
# mean contact frequency with Dutch ties	.21	.20		.21	.31	-.16
some eclusive ties	.28	.22			.23	
# % minorities in district			_-.40*_	-.29*	-.35*	-.26*
# category % in district			-.36		-	
# % Dutch in district			.33	.25	.19	
# % 'others'in district			-.32	-.29	-	

Indicator # = interval level measurement	Moroc- cans	Turks	Surinamese Antilleans	'Other' immi- grants	All immi- grants	Indige- nous Dutch
# ethnic composition of active organizations	*.42**				.41*	
∑ R² behavioral *	16%	3%	33%	20%	29%	7%
∑ R² all * indicators (n)	40% (93)	39% (151)	45% (74)	53% (99)	63% (398)	35% (168)
∑ R² underlined indicators (n)	42% (93)	39% (152)	44% (74)	54% (99)	64% (412)	35% (168)
∑ R² * demographic and positional indicators (n)	24% (93)	30% (151)	27% (74)	33% (100)	51% (407)	35% (168)
∑ R² 4 *boldface* indicators (n)	36% (93)	30% (155)	41% (74)	45% (100)	52% (422)	30% (168)

Reference Categories for Dummy Variables

Interview indicators: gender - female; language - Dutch; ambience - reasonable to good; sample - aselect.

Demographic indicators: region of origin - Surinamese for the category Surinamese/Antillean and Western Europe for the category 'Other' immigrants and by analyses for 'All immigrants;' gender - female; migration motive - work; generation - first; district - historic center (*Oude Stad*).

Positional indicators: household type - single person; household breadwinner - primarily respondent; educational level/Dutch education - primary school at best; labor market position - full time work; housing market position - tenant in flat; neighborhood status - very inauspicious; civic memberships - none.

Orientational indicators: ethnic self-identification - land of origin; ethnic belonging - yes always; ethnic affection - yes always; oral Dutch skills - reasonably good or better; religious faith - none; religious devotion - none; voting right used - yes; electoral vote - none; approval ethnic organizations - yes, certainly.

Behavioral indicators: lives with partner - no; partner's ethnicity - same as respondent (and respondents without partners); work search channel - formal network used; seclusive contacts only - 'other' friends named.

Multiple Regression Procedures Applied

The regression analyses were conducted with listwise deletion of missing cases, while allowing for a constant in the regression equation. All results that refer to the combined variance explained by a particular set of indicators (i.e., '$\sum R^2$') are based on analyses in which all the indicators are entered at once into the equation.

The selection of asterisked indicators was made in two phases. First, per dimension a limited number of indicators were selected (five to seven) that:
- correspond significantly with index scores in at least one immigrant category;
- in their combination encompass a maximum number of domains;
- display a minimal number of missing cases, and
- display a maximum on response variation (see tables 3.5, 4.13, 5.14 and 6.9 respectively).

Second, a stepwise regression procedure was used, all indicators but one being entered on the first step. Those indicators that, when entered on the second step, significantly increase the regression models' (adjusted) explained variance (prob $F < .05$) are designated by an asterisk.

Those indicators that are also <u>underlined</u> were selected by first entering all asterisked indicators in the regression model. Then via a so-called backward procedure, those indicators are removed that fail to significantly account for index variance independent of the other indicators in the model (prob. $F > .10$). The indicators that are not removed have been underlined.

The four *boldfaced* indicators were selected via a trial and error method, in which per ethnic category a set consisting of a demographic, positional, orientational and a behavioral indicator is sought that in their combination clarify the greatest percentage of index variance.

To consider the potential effect upon index scores 'clarified' by the interview context, a two-step regression analysis was conducted per ethnic category. In the first step all <u>underlined</u> indicators are entered into the model, in the second those interview indicators presented in the (first section of the) table above that correspond significantly with index scores. For three of the five ethnic categories the interview indicators did not significantly improve the model. Among the Turks, the 'language interview' indicator in particular raised the $\sum R^2$ from 39% to 46%. Among 'Other' immigrants 'interview duration' in particular raised the $\sum R^2$ from 54% to 63%. For all immigrants this latter indicator significantly improved the model's $\sum R^2$ from 64% to 69%.

Appendix II: Index Correlations

The set of six matrices (tables II.1-6) displays per ethnic category the correlations between the five components that form the local integration index. Two measures of association are presented: below and to the left of the diagonal Pearson's correlations (assumes interval measurement level), Spearman's rho (ordinal level) above and to the right. The asterisks within the matrices denote significant levels of 0.05 (*) respectively 0.01 (**).

Table II.7 provides an overview of Haarlem survey items' whose correlation with the index is arranged by research design in that these items help constitute one of the five index components.

Table II.1 Correlation matrix local index components for residents of Moroccan origin (n=93)*

Index Component	Integration Index	Per Capita Income	Welfare Independence	Perceived Opportunity	Local Satisfaction	Cultural Participation
Integration Index	-	.221*	.556**	.619**	.501**	.467**
Per Capita Income	.283**	-	-.167	.122	-.051	.095
Welfare Independence	.544**	-.128	-	.082	.206*	.167
Perceived Opportunity	.632**	.191	.084	-	.010	.200
Local Satisfaction	.568**	-.026	.172	.050	-	.005
Cultural Participation	.445**	.033	.203	.141	-.037	-

* Pearson's correlation (below diagonal) and Spearman's rho (above and to the right).

Table II.2 Correlation matrix local index for residents of Turkish origin (n=159)*

Index Component	Integration Index	Per Capita Income	Welfare Indepen-ence	Perceived Opportunity	Local Satisfac-tion	Cultural Participa-tion
Integration Index	-	.325**	.479**	.624**	.550**	.427**
Per Capita Income	.337**	-	.045	.036	-.027	.026
Welfare Independence	.521**	.145	-	.181*	-.023	.122
Perceived Opportunity	.628**	-.034	.191*	-	.146	.156*
Local Satisfaction	.567**	-.009	-.046	.108	-	.049
Cultural Participation	.517**	.096	.173*	.231**	.079	-

* Pearson's correlation (below diagonal) and Spearman's rho (above and to the right).

Table II.3 Correlation matrix local index components for residents of Surinamese or Antillian origin (n=77)*

Index Component	Integration Index	Per Capita Income	Welfare Indepen-dence	Perceived Oppor-unity	Local Satisfac-tion	Cultural Participa-tion
Integration Index	-	.587**	.490**	.594**	.506**	.591**
Per Capita Income	.627**	-	.084	.430**	.177	.139
Welfare Independence	.450**	.033	-	.137	-.047	.208
Perceived Opportunity	.597**	.338**	.089	-	.195	.070
Local Satisfaction	.598**	.241	.053	.217	-	.180
Cultural Participation	.546**	.188	.161	.010	.110	-

* Pearson's correlation (below diagonal) and Spearman's rho (above and to the right).

Table II.4 Correlation matrix local index components for residents of 'Other' immigrant origin (n=100)*

Index Component	Integration Index	Per Capita Income	Welfare Independence	Perceived Opportunity	Local Satisfaction	Cultural Participation
Integration Index	-	.583**	.501**	.626**	.325**	.576**
Per Capita Income	.584**	-	.188	.291**	-.076	.106
Welfare Independence	.555**	.258*	-	.089	.020	.190
Perceived Opportunity	.622**	.218*	.116	-	-.048	.259**
Local Satisfaction	.418**	-.021	.046	.003	-	.066
Cultural Participation	.514**	.094	.106	.226*	.024	-

* Pearson's correlation (below diagonal) and Spearman's rho (above and to the right).

Table II.5 Correlation matrix local index components for residents of Indigenous Dutch origin (n=170)*

Index Component	Integration Index	Per Capita Income	Welfare Independence	Perceived Opportunity	Local Satisfaction	Cultural Participation
Integration Index	-	.541**	.558**	.711**	.513**	.508**
Per Capita Income	.505**	-	.205*	.244**	.166*	.100
Welfare Independence	.539**	.186*	-	.166*	.149*	.123
Perceived Opportunity	.706**	.177*	.140	-	.253**	.237**
Local Satisfaction	.556**	.085	.133	.257**	-	.117
Cultural Participation	.505**	.010	.087	.245**	.120	-

* Pearson's correlation (below diagonal) and Spearman's rho (above and to the right).

Table II.6 Correlation matrix local index components for all Haarlem respondents (reweighed n=599)*

Index Component	Integration Index	Per Capita Income	Welfare Independence	Perceived Opportunity	Local Satisfaction	Cultural Participation
Integration Index	-	.512**	.544**	.685**	.488**	.518**
Per Capita Income	.511**	-	.225**	.197**	.099*	.107**
Welfare Independence	.563**	.212**	-	.149**	.118**	.095*
Perceived Opportunity	.693**	.185**	.157**	-	.199**	.266**
Local Satisfaction	.555**	.094*	.144**	.228**	-	.117**
Cultural Participation	.513**	.043	.113**	.247**	.120**	-

* Pearson's correlation (below diagonal) and Spearman's rho (above and to the right).

Table II.7 Pearson's correlations of index (sub)components with local index*

Component / Item-indicators	Moroccans	Turks	Surinamese Antillians	'Other' immigrants	All immigrants	Indigenous Dutch
ethnic index	.933*	.914*	.972*	.930*	.984*	.998*
per capita income	.28*	.34*	.63*	.58*	.59*	.50*
% household dependents	-.40*	-.33*	-.47*	-.25	-.37*	-.22
source household income	.34	.30		.49	.43	.42
welfare independence	.54*	.52*	.45*	.56*	.60*	.54*
job exchange/soc.security η	-.25*	-.23*	-.31*	-.38*	-.39*	-.32*
housing services η		-.21*	-.31*	-.42*	-.38*	-.40*
legal/police/fire η					-.17*	
health/nursing services η		-.21*			-.11	
day-care/nursery centers η						
neighborhood centers η	.27*				.12	
educational services η	.28*	.23*				

Component Item-indicators		Moroc-cans	Turks	Surinam-ese Antillians	'Other' immi-grants	All immigrants	Indige-nous Dutch
sport facilities	η	.49*	.27*	.23		.22*	
libraries	η	.45*	.40*		.20	.26*	.33*
perceived opportunity		.63*	.63*	.60*	.62*	.63*	.71*
educational opportunity		.66*	.40*	.49*	.55*	.58*	.53*
labor opportunity		.51*	.56*	.51*	.44*	.45*	.45*
housing opportunity			.42*		.30*	.26*	.52*
local satisfaction		.57*	.57*	.60*	.42*	.54*	.56*
evaluation of personal life		.33*	.45*	.51*	.42*	.48*	.35*
evaluation of domicile		.41*	.35*	.44*	.22	.34*	.31*
evaluation of neighborhood		.44*	.40*	.47*	.38*	.43*	.45*
evaluation of city's viability		.34*	.27*		.23	.31*	.43*
cultural participation		.44*	.52*	.55*	.51*	.55*	.50*
weekly market						-.19*	
sports match		.34*				.14*	
party outside home		.32*	.22*		.25	.19*	
café					.28*	.20*	.27*
dancing/disco		.21	.31*	.23			
music/ballet/drama		.27*	.28*		.22	.24*	.26*
museum/exhibition				.40*	.35*	.38*	.20*
event/fair/festival		.30*		.36*	.30*	.31*	.18

* For indicators measured at nominal or ordinal level, designated by an "η" in first column, the eta statistic is displayed. (* = F probability < .01).

Index